AF607852

Systemic functional perspectives of Japanese

Functional Linguistics

Series Editor: Robin Fawcett, Cardiff University

This series publishes monographs that seek to understand the nature of language by exploring one or other of various cognitive models or in terms of the communicative use of language. It concentrates on studies that are in, or on the borders of, various functional theories of language.

Recently published
Morphosyntactic Alternations in English Functional and Cognitive Perspectives
Edited by Pilar Guerrero Medina

An Introduction to the Grammar of Old English: A Systemic Functional Approach
Michael Cummings

Text Type and Texture
Edited by Gail Forey, Geoff Thompson

Reading Visual Narratives
Image Analysis of Children's Picture Books
Clare Painter, J. R. Martin and Len Unsworth

Forthcoming
Choice in Language: Applications in Text Analysis
Edited by Gerard O'Grady, Tom Bartlett and Lise Fontaine

Systemic Phonology
Recent Studies in English
Edited by: Wendy L. Bowcher, Bradley A. Smith

Contrastive Discourse Analysis
Functional and Corpus Perspectives
Edited by Maite Taboada, Susana Doval Suárez, Elsa González Álvarez

Systemic functional perspectives of Japanese

Descriptions and applications

Edited by
Elizabeth A. Thomson and William S. Armour

SHEFFIELD UK BRISTOL CT

Published by

UK: Unit S3, Kelham House, 3 Lancaster Street, Sheffield, S3 8AF

US: ISD, 70 Enterprise Drive, Bristol, CT 06010

www.equinoxpub.com

First published 2013

© Elizabeth A. Thomson, William S. Armour and contributors 2013

All rights reserved. No part of this publication may be reproduced or transmitted in any form or by any means, electronic or mechanical, including photocopying, recording or any information storage or retrieval system, without prior permission in writing from the publishers.

British Library Cataloguing-in-Publication Data
A catalogue record for this book is available from the British Library.

ISBN-13 978-1-84553-053-2 (hardback)

Library of Congress Cataloging-in-Publication Data

Systemic functional perspectives of Japanese : descriptions and applications / edited by Elizabeth A. Thomson and William S. Armour.
p. cm. -- (Functional linguistics)
Includes bibliographical references and index.
ISBN 978-1-84553-053-2 (hb)
1. Japanese language--Grammar. 2. Systemic grammar. 3. Japanese language--Data processing. I. Thomson, Elizabeth A. (Elizabeth Anne), 1961- II. Armour, William.
PL534.S97 2007
495.6’5--dc22

2006102934

Typeset by Catchline, Milton Keynes (www.catchline.com)
Printed and bound in Great Britain by Lightning Source UK Ltd., Milton Keynes and Lightning Source Inc., La Vergne, TN

Contents

List of Contributors vii

Foreword 1

1 Systemic functional theory: description and application 3
Elizabeth A. Thomson and William S. Armour

PART 1: DESCRIPTION

2 How to argue in Japanese: a systemic functional interpretation of the logico-semantic relations in Japanese exposition 23
Motoki Sano and Elizabeth A. Thomson

3 Description of MOOD in Japanese: examining Mood types in a selected set of texts 65
Nagisa Fukui

4 The system of THEME in Japanese 101
Elizabeth A. Thomson

5 Classifying natural phenomena through language: lexicogrammatical resources for constructing taxonomies in Japanese biology textbooks 137
Chie Hayakawa

6 Nominalisation and nouniness as meaning strategies in Japanese political manifestos 173
Kinuko Sato (Suto) and Christopher Barnard

PART 2: APPLICATION

7 Learning how to mean in Japanese as an additional language 210
William S. Armour and Reiko Furuya

8 Modelling writing: using the genre approach in the Japanese as a foreign language classroom 254
Yuko Ramzan & Elizabeth A. Thomson

9 A computational model of language in context and its application to the understanding of Japanese text 285
Noriko Ito and Toru Sugimoto

10 The components and structure of the context base, a database for computer text generation 324
Yusuke Takahashi, Ichiro Kobayashi and Michiaki Iwazume

Subject index 354

List of Contributors

William S. Armour is a Honorary Senior Lecturer in Japanese Studies at UNSW, Australia. He has taught courses in Japanese language, Japanese popular culture and intercultural communication. He researches on a variety of topics, including cross-cultural adaptation, how learning an additional language impacts on identity, and *manga* and *anime*. A recent publication is Armour, W. (2011) Learning Japanese by Reading 'manga': The Rise of 'Soft Power Pedagogy', *RELC Journal* 42(2): 125–140.

Christopher Barnard is a Professor in the Department of English, Teikyo University, Japan. His interests include Japanese linguistics and Japanese/English lexicography. Among his publications is Barnard, C. (2003) *Language, Ideology, and Japanese History Textbooks* London: RoutledgeCurzon.

Nagisa Fukui is a Lecturer in Japanese Studies at UNSW, Australia. Her research interests include the description of Japanese lexico-grammatical systems especially of the interpersonal metafunction, using the systemic functional approach. Among her publications is Thomson, E.A., Fukui, N. and White, P.R.R. (2008) Evaluating 'Reporter Voice' in two Japanese front-page lead stories. In E.A.Thomson and P.R.R. White (eds) *Communicating Conflict* 65–98. London: Continuum.

Reiko Furuya is a Senior Advisor for international students at Nagoya University, Japan. Her research interests include how cross-cultural adaption influences the acquisition of an additional language.

Chie Hayakawa is a Lecturer at Nagoya University of Arts, Japan. She teaches courses in general English. Her research interests lie in the functions of scientific and academic discourse, the language of education and the comparative analysis of Japanese and English texts. Among her publications is Hayakawa, C., Sano, M., Mizusawa, Y. and Ito, N. (2011) Identification of some problems with clause segmentation and a proposal of possible criteria in the view of the systemic functional theory. *Japanese Journal of Systemic Functional Linguistics*. vol. 6: 17–58.

Noriko Ito is an Associate Professor at Doshisha University, Japan. She researches systemic functional linguistics. An important publication is Ito, N.,

Sugimoto, T., Iwashita, S., Kobayashi, I. and Sugeno M. (2007) An analysis of rhetorical structure of Japanese instructional texts and its application to dialogue-based question answering systems. *Japanese Journal of Systemic Functional Linguistics* vol 4: 83–104.

Michiaki Iwazume is the Managing Director at Universal Communication Research Institute, National Institute of Information and Communications Technology (NICT), Japan. His main interests include artificial intelligence, knowledge-based systems, ontology-based applications, web intelligence. Among his collaborative publications is Iwazume, M., Kobayashi, I. and Sugeno, M. (2006) Natural Language Mediated Software Agentification, *Journal of Advanced Computational Intelligence and Intelligent Informatics (JACIII),* vol. 10 no. 6: 802–810.

Ichiro Kobayashi is a Professor of Advanced Sciences, Graduate School of Humanities and Sciences, Ochanomizu University in Japan. His main interests include natural language processing, artificial intelligence, and systemic functional linguistics. A recent publication is Kobayashi, I., Sugeno, M., Sugimoto, T., Iwashita, S., Iwazume, M. and Takahashi, Y. (2006) Everyday Language Computing Project Overview, *Journal of Advanced Computational Intelligence and Intelligent Informatics* vol. 10 no. 6: 773–781.

Yuko Ramzan is an Associate Professor at Ritsumeikan University, Japan. Her research interests include Japanese education, foreign language education, pedagogy and educational sociology. Among her publications is Ramzan, Y. (2009) *The construction of interculturality and foreign language education: Japanese language learning in Australian schools.* Germany: Verlag.

Motoki Sano is a Researcher at the National Institute for Information and Communication Technology, Japan. His research interest lies primarily in descriptions of Japanese grammar and semantics from a systemic functional perspective. Among his publications is Sano, M. (2012) The Classification of Japanese Evaluative Expressions and the Construction of a Dictionary of Attitudinal Lexis: An Interpretation from Appraisal Perspective, *NIJAL Research Papers,* vol. 3: 53–83.

Toru Sugimoto is a Professor at Shibaura Institute of Technology, Japan. He researches in the area of natural language processing. A recent important publication is Sugimoto, T., Ito N. and Iwashita, S. (2007) A proposal of a language-based context-sensitive programming system. *Journal of Advanced Computational Intelligence and Intelligent Informatics* vol. 11 no. 8: 1015–1022.

Kinuko Sato (Suto) is formerly of Tohoku University, Japan. She now lives in Germany, raising her child while she researches English and Japanese persuasive texts, including political manifestos, academic texts, newspaper editorials, magazine ads, and narratives. Among her publications is Suto, K. (2004) Technocratic Discourse: Deploying Lexicogrammatical Resources for Technical Knowledge as Political Strategies. *JASFL Occasional Papers* Vol. 3: 105–156.

Yusuke Takahashi worked for Justsystems Corporation, a software development company in Japan. Unfortunately, he passed away unexpectedly in 2009. His interests included Japanese and English lexicogrammar and semantics for natural language processing, especially for sentiment analysis. A recent collaborative publication is Takahashi, Y., Kobayashi, I., Iwazume, M., Ito, N. and Sugeno, M. (2004) The Contents and Structure of the Context Base, and Its Application. *Proceedings of 4th International Conference (EsTAL 2004)*: 103–114.

Elizabeth A. Thomson is a Visiting Fellow at UNSW, Canberra and the Academic Research Officer, Centre for Defence Research, Australian Defence College. Her research interests are in the areas of descriptive grammar within the tradition of systemic functional linguistics, applied linguistics, language for specific purposes, discourse analysis and interculturality. A recent publication is the book, Thomson, E.A. and Droga, L. (2012) *Effective Academic Writing*. Sydney: Phoenix Education.

Foreword

Theory and application nourish each other, and one cannot grow without the other. This very property has been imbued in Systemic Functional Theory since its birth half a century ago. In linguistic practices, 'application' means grammatical descriptions of linguistic items of various levels and dimensions on the one hand, and their utilization for a varied range of purposes on the other, although these are closely interrelated. Systemic Functional Theory (or perhaps Theories) has been being nourished and grown by such various kinds of applications as grammatical descriptions of English and other non-English languages, critical analyses of culturally or ideologically skewed ways of meaning in texts, explorations in socialization and child language development, studies of non-linguistic semiotics, natural language processing, studies of language and knowledge construction/ transmission, teaching of English as a first/ second language, and the like. Thus, Systemic Functional Theory is an ever-growing theory (never to be grown-up), responding always to the new applicational demands made upon it. In response to these demands, the theory expands the width and depth of its applicational potentialities. This co-nourishing relationship between a theory and its applications metaphorically parallels that between a linguistic system as potential meaning resources and texts as actual meaning instances, with new demands on meaning always pressuring the system to expand its meaning potentialities.

This new book edited by Elizabeth A. Thomson and William S. Armour is undoubtedly a significant contribution to this theory-application co-nourishing process in Systemic Functional Linguistic practices, as well as to studies of Japanese in general. All of the nine papers included in this volume are 'applicational' studies of the Japanese language and its related areas, within the theoretical and descriptive framework of Systemic Functional Linguistics.

Systemic Functional Linguistics equips researchers with such theoretical categories as Metafunctions (Ideational: Transitivity, Interpersonal: Mood, and Textual: Theme), Logico-semantic Relations (Elaboration, Extension, and Enhancement), Grammatical Metaphor (nominalisation) and so on. These theoretical categories have enabled the contributors to **describe** Japanese ways of meaning in such different semiotic dimensions as persuasion, speech functions, fact and story telling, scientific classification of natural phenomena, and grammatical gradation of negotiability. The descriptions of Japanese may, more often than not, require the redefinition of descriptive categories and the setting-up of new realisational relations between semantics and lexicogrammar, which tends to result in descriptive make-ups different from those found in English or other languages. And this, indeed, occurs in the contributors' descriptive practices. Such new descriptions are bound to nourish the overall organism of Systemic Functional Linguistics.

Although the descriptive practices mentioned above are already sufficiently applicational, there can be more or secondary applicational dimensions in Systemic Functional Linguistics. That is, the descriptions are **applied** to do something else: (in this volume) to help teach and learn how to write or speak Japanese as a foreign language, and to computer-process certain domains of daily verbal interactions in Japanese. These are areas where trade-off occurs between theory and application, and theoretical rigidity and descriptive precision tend to give way to applicational effectiveness and practical usefulness as well as technological feasibility. Results of these secondary applications may be turned back on the theory and make it more applicable. An example of this is the new theoretical architecture including 'semiotic base' and its components presented by the Everyday Language Computing Project team at Riken (The Institute of Physical and Chemical Research) in Japan. Such applicational reworking of the theory is again bound to nourish the overall organism of Systemic Functional Linguistics.

This well-organized book of chapters on the Japanese language and texts, along with an illuminative introductory chapter of a brief grounding exposition of Systemic Functional Theory, will find itself, on the one hand, to be a worthy contribution to the studies of Japanese and perhaps to the studies of other languages within the Systemic Functional Linguistic circle, and on the other hand, to the studies of Japanese outside the circle, especially in Japan. Firstly, notwithstanding its long history, Systemic Functional Linguistics has seen rather a limited number of sporadic studies of Japanese published in Japanese or English, although gradually increasing. Thus, this volume can be one of the most important frames of reference for linguists, students, or teachers interested in Japanese itself or in comparative/ typological studies between Japanese and other languages. Secondly, the studies of Japanese in Japan have fairly long established traditions, classical or modern (including Euro-American influences), which have built up the kinds of linguistic landscapes that their conventional reasoning and theorizing have allowed them to. The Systemic Functional studies of Japanese in this volume might at first disturb these comfortably familiar landscapes, but eventually it will surely turn out that this disturbance opens up refreshingly new and revealing perspectives on the Japanese linguistic system and texts.

Yamaguchi Noboru

Tohoku University, Sendai, Japan
July 2012

1 Systemic Functional theory: description and application

Elizabeth A. Thomson and William S. Armour
UNSW, Canberra
UNSW, Australia

Introduction

Systemic Functional (SF) Theory is a general linguistic theory developed by Michael Halliday and colleagues over the last 60 years, which, in its nascent form, was used to describe the system and structure of a fourteenth century early Mandarin translation of a Mongolian biography on Genghis Khan. This study formed Halliday's PhD in modern Chinese from Cambridge University, inspired and supervised by the influential linguist, J.R. Firth (Webster, 2005).

The theoretical architecture of SF Theory, as devised by Halliday, is organised around abstract categories and it is this feature that makes it applicable to the description of any language. Halliday did not describe his mother tongue, rather he used the theory to describe the grammar and tones of a foreign language that he learnt as a young adult both in London and China. The experience of learning a foreign language, of trying to understand and then later, teach its system and structure was the impetus behind Halliday's thinking about language and its use.

Staying true to Halliday's example, this book represents a body of work describing the system and structure of another Asian language, that of Japanese, both from a second/foreign language as well as a mother tongue point of view. Halliday (1980) has said that it has always been his view that 'what was needed in linguistics was not so much new theories as new descriptions' (p.vii). There are an increasing number of descriptions of languages other than English including, but not limited to, the following: Arabic (Ali Bardi, 2008), Chinese (McDonald, 1998; Halliday 1956 in 2006; Li 2007), French (Cafferal 2006), German (Steiner & Teich, 2004), Japanese (Teruya. 2007), Òkó (Akerejola 2005), Pitjantjatajra (Rose, 2004), Spanish (Lavid et al., 2010), Tagalog (Martin. 2004), Telugu (Prakasam 2004), Thai (Patpong. 2006), Vietnamese (Thai. 1998). According to Kim and McDonald (2012), 'there is so far no overall description in SFL terms of languages such as Indonesian and Russian' (p.95). Excluding Chinese much of this work is in its early stage of development in that only one or two people have developed the descriptions. SF work on Japanese has now reached a point where there are more than enough scholars using the theory to warrant a book such as this, that brings together the breadth of SF scholarship on Japanese.

This book is a compilation of some of these descriptions of Japanese from a Systemic Functional perspective, representing work conducted in Australia and Japan, by both native and non-native speakers of Japanese.

In Japan, the development of SF descriptions of Japanese has been nurtured by the Japan Association of Systemic Functional Linguistics (JASFL). The genesis of JASFL began with a number of scholars, Professors Yamaguchi Noboru and Tatsuki Masaaki included, venturing overseas to study under M.A.K. Halliday and Robin Fawcett. It was not until the early 1990s, however, when interest in SF Theory was expanding, that the Japanese Association of Systemic Functional Linguistics (JASFL) was formed. The inaugural meeting was held at Doshisha University, Kyoto in November 1993. Since that meeting, JASFL has fostered SF research into both English and Japanese, holding annual Autumn and Spring meetings, launching an Occasional Papers Series (now called Japanese Journal of Systemic Functional Linguistics) in 1998, and establishing a website in July 2000. The work of JASFL over the past 19 years has directly contributed to the exchange of ideas and development of the research profiles of many academics and postgraduate students. JASFL has fostered this endeavour to the extent that there is now a vibrant community of scholars and postgraduate students using SF Theory to describe Japanese and to apply these new descriptions to areas outside of general linguistics, providing new and exciting ways of using language in other disciplinary contexts. This book reproduces some of these descriptions and applications, with the specific purpose of contributing to our understanding of the Japanese language from the perspective of SF Linguistics.

The organisation of this book is as follows. Divided into two sections, *Part 1: Description*, includes SF descriptions of Japanese ranging across the three metafunctions of ideational, interpersonal and textual meanings. The second section, *Part 2: Applications*, applies these descriptions to three significant areas of social science, namely, Second Language Development, Education and Computer Science.

By way of introducing the two parts of the book, the following section will look at the task of linguistic description, outlining the principles inherent in SF theory and upon which the research described in this volume is based. A brief summary of each of the chapters in Part 1 follows. *Part 2: Applications* contains a concise overview of the applications of linguistic description, which includes summaries of the chapters.

Part 1: Description

> The object of linguistics analysis as here understood is to make statements of meaning so that we may see how we use language to live. (Firth, 1957 in Halliday, 1961:241)

The development of Halliday's Systemic Functional theory of language arises out of Firth's view that linguistic analyses are about understanding how we use language to live. In other words, the theoretical underpinning dictates the nature of the analyses. Consequently, Halliday stated that:

> one part of General Linguistic Theory is a theory of how language works. It is from this that the methods of Descriptive Linguistics are derived. (1961:242)

So what are the principals of Systemic Functional theory? In other words, what underpins the array of descriptive methodologies that are used to describe Japanese in this collection? While there are many principals on which SF theory is based, for our purposes, we highlight just four which relate directly to this collection. They are:

> SF theory can be used to describe any language in its own terms. The definitions are all relational within the framework of the language under investigation.
>
> SF theory assumes that language is a form of social behaviour and functions to serve a range of social purposes within the contexts of situation and culture.
>
> SF theory is organised stratally to reflect the enabling role of the lexicogrammar in enacting our social meanings.
>
> SF theory privileges paradigmatic choices thereby mimicking the nature of natural language as a system of choice and meaning potential.
>
> (adapted from Halliday, 1996)

Principle 1: SF theory can be used to describe any language in its own terms.

Halliday (1961) argues that a General Linguistic theory should be a theory that can be applied to any language. However, a General Linguistic theory is not a theory concerned with structural universality in a Chomskyan sense, but rather, it is one concerned with abstracted functional categories that are applicable to particular linguistic descriptions. This was first articulated by Firth when he stated,

> what is being sketched here is *a general linguistic theory* applicable to *particular linguistic descriptions,* not *a theory of universals* for *general linguistic description.* (Firth, 1957; Firth's emphasis, in Halliday, 1996:33)

In this sense, a theory can be used to describe any language. However, the description of a specific language is not in itself the theory. The theory is the theoretical framework in which the language is described. Further, different theoretical traditions will produce different descriptions 'which derive from, and are answerable to, that theory' (Halliday, 1961:241).

A General Linguistic theory generates methods of description which are based on 'a scheme of interrelated categories which are set up to account for the data' (Halliday, 1961:243). These categories, or the metalanguage of the theory, operate under two provisos. Firstly, each theory develops (within its own paradigm) a set of terms and notions whose meanings are defined by their relationship to each other within the theoretical framework (Halliday, 1996). The description which arises out of the observation of the phenomenon is then understandable within the theoretical categories that have been set up. Consider the term **subject** as an example. Within a Systemic Functional description of English, this term, in conjunction with the Finite element, is defined by its role in the MOOD structure. It is the nuclear participant which carries forward the information exchange in dialogue (Matthiessen, 1995:410–420). Alternatively, Halliday (1994) defines the grammatical subject as 'the warranty of exchange. It is the element the speaker makes responsible for the validity of what he is saying' (p.34). However, the term **subject**, which is readily used in other theoretical linguistic traditions, can have other meanings. This is evident in the use of **subject** in one manifestation of Universal Grammar. Li and Thompson (1976) define **subject** in relation to **topic** in terms of the degree of grammaticalization, 'Subjects are essentially grammaticalised topics' (p.484). To understand what **subject** means in this context, it is necessary to understand the notion of grammaticalization and how it is applied in Universal Grammar.

Secondly, metalanguage is interpretable within the particular linguistic environment of each individual language. As Halliday (1996) puts it, 'each language its own metalanguage' (p.33). In this instance, the term **subject** is understood as it operates in English, or in Japanese, or any other language. Therefore, according to SF theory, **subject** in English is that which enacts MOOD selection, while in Japanese it has been shown *not* to contribute to the grammar of MOOD.

> It seems obvious that in Japanese the element comparable in function to the English Mood includes not only primary tense and modality but also the main verb, sentence final particles and other items like adjectives and adverbs depending on the content, **the one thing that is not present in such an element is the Subject.** (Hori, 1995:165) [Emphasis added]

There is no doubt that Japanese clauses select for MOOD. However, the constituents of MOOD defined in English as the elements that are tossed

> back and forth to keep the discourse going, are not Subject and Finite in the case of Japanese. (Fukui, 1998:6)

Consensus has yet to be reached within the Systemic Functional community as to the function of **subject** in Japanese, but what is agreed is that **subject** in Japanese functions differently to **subject** in English (see Hori, 1995; Fukui, 1998; Teruya, 1998).

Returning to the issue of theory and description, it is pertinent to reiterate that the metalanguage used in this collection is that which arises out of the theoretical framework of SF Linguistics, but which also is defined within its language-specific environment. In other words, the Theory is centred around abstract categories and thus is, logocentric. The description of Japanese, on the other hand, is centred around specific realisations of abstract categorisation and is thus, glottocentric – privileging the language under description (Halliday, 1996:33). A Systemic Functional description of language is thus a description located within a specific theoretical architecture where the categories used to describe the language are defined in relation to each other within the bounds of that theoretical architecture. The description is not theory neutral (Matthiessen and Nesbitt, 1996).

Principle 2: SF theory assumes that language is a form of social behaviour and functions to serve a range of social purposes.

SF Theory views language as a form of social behaviour, albeit, a very complex and sophisticated form (Halliday, 1978:36–39). In this context, what is important about language is that it is instrumental in enacting our social relationships and social behaviour (Halliday, 1973:11). Language is used to accomplish things. For example, children use it to regulate their environment, to interact with others, to shape their identity, to explore their environment and to create imaginary worlds (Halliday, 1973). This 'use' of language as behaviour is purposeful and therefore fulfils a social function.

> Learning one's mother tongue is learning the uses of language, and the meanings, or rather the meaning potential, associated with them. The structures, the words and the sounds are the realisation of this meaning potential. Learning language is learning how to mean. (Halliday, 1973:24)

This meaning making potential is technically the semantic potential of language. The potential to make meaning is realised by the set of linguistic resources that are available within a language. These resources are within the lexicogrammatical system of the language, where lexicogrammar refers to the 'combination of grammar and lexis (vocabulary); the resources for expressing meanings as wordings' (Matthiessen, 1995:785). The capacity to make both linguistic and non-linguistic meanings combine to construe the totality of a society's semiotic potential. From an SF perspective then, the lexicogrammar functions to realise the meaning making potential of the semantic plane. Language therefore, constitutes human experience, social processes and the social order, the grammar transforming experience into meaning (Halliday, 1996).

Furthermore, our relationships and behaviour are dictated by cultural paradigms, that is, 'culture and language co-evolve in the same relationship as that in which, within language, meaning and expression co-evolve' (Halliday, 1992: 11). As such, each culture embodies a set of behavioural choices which are all 'potentially' possible, 'potentially' acceptable. This potentiality applies to all forms of behaviour including linguistic behaviour. In this behavioural sense, language is viewed as a resource for making meaning within the constraints of the culture in which it is embedded. SF Theory is thus a theory of human experience (Halliday, 1992:10), whereby we act out our meanings in language, with each individual linguistic act being an instance of the overall meaning potential (Halliday, 1996:32) within a cultural paradigm.

Furthermore, SF theory highlights that language as text is never without a context. The context is of two types: the context of the local surrounding text, that is the instantial context known as the Context of Situation; and the larger context of language in which the text is construed, known as the Context of Culture. Taking the social act of persuasion as an example, it is reasonable to speculate that there is more than one way to persuade and that the persuasive purpose and strategy used in different languages is determined by the cultural context of the language in question. For example, according to Sano (2006) persuasion in Japanese is different to persuasion in English. The social purpose, the generic elements and the language features are different. Why? Because culture motivates the difference. Sano explains that persuasion in Japanese culture has a tendency towards homologisation, the idea that 'anything and everything deserves to be given its own proper place within the whole culture scheme' (Ikegami, 1991:15). Homologisation is the strategy to reduce conflict by relativising contradictory phenomena through superordinate categories which are semantically empty. So the idea when you persuade in Japanese is 'to present an argument and ask the reader to share the same idea with the writer' (Sano and Thomson this volume). The argument deserves its proper place in the debate and the reader is invited to share the argument. This is in contrast with the social purpose of persuasion in English. As Butt et. al (1995) states, the social purpose of persuasion is 'to advance or justify an argument or put forward a particular point of view' (p.17). This act of persuasion does not acknowledge the sensitivities of the reader/listener in the way that the Japanese act does. Culturally, the English act is more concerned with advancing an argument rather than empathising with the reader and mitigating potential conflict. In other words, the cultural values of Japan dictate the social behaviour, which in turn dictates the kinds of persuasive meanings which are potentially possible, and which dictate the language selections used to realise the meanings.

Principle 3: The stratal architecture of the Systemic Functional model of language.

In keeping with Hjelmslev (1961), SF Theory is organised into a content and expression plane which is connected through an arbitrary relation. The expression plane is the phonology and graphology of language, while the content plane includes the potential set of meanings to be made by language. In SF Theory, the content plane has been divided further into semantic and lexicogrammatical strata. The semantic stratum sits 'above' the lexicogrammatical stratum. The lexicogrammar functions to realise the meanings located above in the semantics. The model is thus built around a tri-stratal architecture consisting of phonology/graphology, lexicogrammar, and semantics.

The semantic stratum is organised according to how language is put to use. We use language in three ways, that is, language has three distinct functions: the ideational, the interpersonal and the textual functions. These functions are, in a sense, macro, in that within them lie many permutations of that same function. Two of these macro, or more precisely, metafunctions, relate to phenomena outside language. One of these two, named the ideational, serves to *construe* our experience in and of the world. Further, the respective structures of the metafunctions differ in type. Within the ideational metafunction, experiential meanings are built up through a part/whole relation, a constituency relation, whereby the 'whole' is bounded, with the parts or constituents playing distinctive roles (Martin, 1995:195), such as participant, circumstance and process. This is a multivariate, particle-like structure.

While the ideational metafunction construes our experience in and of the world, it also relates this representation of the world in logical terms. In other words, there are two components to the ideational metafunction: the experiential and the logical. The logical metafunction defines complex units in the grammar, considering both the nature of dependency and the semantic function of the units within a complex. Logical structures are iterative or univariate in that the limited set of logical relations repeats itself throughout the grammar.

The experiential metafunction represents experience in language as happenings, entities and circumstantial features, while the logical metafunction represents experience in terms of logical relations between happenings and entities. Essentially, the experiential category represents experience directly, while the logical represents it indirectly (Halliday, 1979:59).

The other metafunction, which relates to phenomena outside of language, that is, the interpersonal metafunction, serves to *enact* our social roles and more particularly, our speech roles. Within the interpersonal metafunction, prosodic principles of structure are utilised. This kind of structure is 'a melodic line mapped on to the clause as a whole, running through from beginning to end' (Halliday, 1979:66) which expresses the particular tone or tenor of the speaker. Meanings of assertion, query, hesitation, doubt, wonderment and so on are made manifest through the intonation contour as it maps onto the clause. This is a field-like structure.

The third metafunction, the textual metafunction, serves to *enable* the ideational and the interpersonal to be presented 'as information that can be shared by speaker and listener in text unfolding in context' (Matthiessen and Halliday, 1997:13). The textual metafunction is that part of the grammar which enables the development of a parallel linguistic universe through which we can share our experiences and relationships. In other words, language creates its own world of meaning. Halliday summarises this as follows:

> The grammar creates its own 'world three' which is a world that is made of meaning, the semiotic counterpart of our worlds of reflection and of action. (Halliday, 1992:15)

The textual metafunction utilises a syntagmatic structure of periodic peaks of prominence. Peaks of thematic prominence and newsworthy prominence serve to organise the discourse into message units with the thematic peak signalling what it is that the speaker is concerned with, and with the newsworthy peak signalling what new information the hearer needs to attend to (Halliday, 1979: 68). This is a wave-like structure.

The stratification of the SF model of language allows speakers to construe experience through meanings (the semantic stratum), which are realised through wordings (the lexicogrammatical stratum), which are, in turn, realised through soundings (the phonological stratum). The semantic stratum interfaces with context and the phonological stratum interfaces with our physiological articulatory and auditory capability.

However, the lexicogrammatical stratum is the only one of the three which is 'purely internal to the linguistic system' (Matthiessen and Halliday, 1997:37). It is unique in that it can serve to realise the semantic plane and yet it is concurrently realised by the phonological plane. It is this kind of stratified semiotic system which enables constituency and produces myriads of open-ended acts of meaning:

> The stratal pattern of organisation, with an entirely substance-free stratum of grammar at its core, makes it possible to construct complex, open-ended networks of semantic potential in which meanings are defined

> relative to one another and hence can modify each other and also can change in interaction with changes in the ongoing (semiotic and material) environment. (Halliday, 1996:7)

The advantage of using a stratified theory is that the SF linguist has a resource for looking at the grammar from three perspectives. Halliday has called this the 'trinocular' view of grammar (Halliday. 1996:26). This view allows the linguist to characterise grammar 'from above', that is, from the viewpoint of semantics; 'from below', from the viewpoint of phonology, and 'from roundabout', from its own lexicogrammatical position. This ability arises from the theory having an abstract categorisation that mirrors the grammar and manifests the trinocular perspectives. For example, by taking the viewpoint of semantics, that is, 'from above' it is possible to look at how lexicogrammatical resources combine together to realise the rhetorical purpose of the text. Hayakawa (this volume) demonstrates this approach in her study of the ideational meanings of classification in Japanese Science high school textbooks. In contrast, the Thomson study (this volume) explores the textual metafunction by looking at the grammar of Theme 'from roundabout'. It is a quantitative and qualitative study of the order of lexicogrammatical constituents in the Theme unit, illustrating that the constituents in first position function to realise the point of departure of the message, that is, to realise Theme.

Further, the stratal principle provides a framework for looking at how different languages realise the metafunctions using different lexicogrammatical resources. The stratal architecture accounts for differences in form. For example, both English and Japanese select for Mood. Each language can construe questions, statements, commands and offers. However, the grammatical forms that do this are very different. In the Fukui chapter, the lexicogrammatical resources for Mood are detailed, demonstrating that Mood choices in Japanese are realised by the Predicate and Negotiatory markers, while in English, Mood type is realised by the presence and ordering of Subject and Finite.

Principle 4: Systemic Functional theory privileges paradigmatic choices.

As explained above, the lexicogrammar is that which realises the semantics. This realisational characteristic relies on linguistic choice – one meaning arises out of one or more set of choices, while another arises out of other choices. As mentioned, choice is a central feature of the theory. At any point in the instantiation of a text, there is a choice in what to select. Each choice will affect the meaning of the text. For example, in the clause, *My dog eats biscuits*, it is possible to change the constituent at each point in the clause by selecting other constituents from the selected set of possibilities. Instead of *my* it could be *the*, instead of *dog*, it could be *dinosaur*, instead of *eat* it could be *dig* and instead of *biscuits* it could be *holes* which results in a new clause, *The dinosaur digs holes*. This kind of choice, which selects from paradigmatic sets of constituents, is focal in the system.

SF Theory focuses on the paradigmatic axis for a number of reasons, which relate to the way the lexicogrammar is constitutive of the semantics. Paradigmatic representation:

> 'frees' the grammar from the rules of syntax;
>
> defines description as a relational phenomenon;
>
> represents language as a resource not as an inventory;
>
> predicts probabilistic semantic clustering; and
>
> shapes natural language into a lexicogrammar. (Halliday. 1996:21)

The lexicogrammar combines what is considered as two distinct orders of phenomena in other theories of language, that of the lexis and that of grammar. In SF Theory these are not treated as distinct but rather as a type of complementarity; lexis and grammar are seen as one resource existing on a cline with the most 'grammatical' idealised as generalisations, while lexis is idealised as the most lexicalised, delicate form of grammar. This is illustrated by the system network which moves from most grammatical and generalised on the left through a network of 'wiring' choices to the most lexicalised and specific on the right. The example below in Figure 1 is the network of MOOD systems in English taken from Matthiessen and Halliday (1997:6).

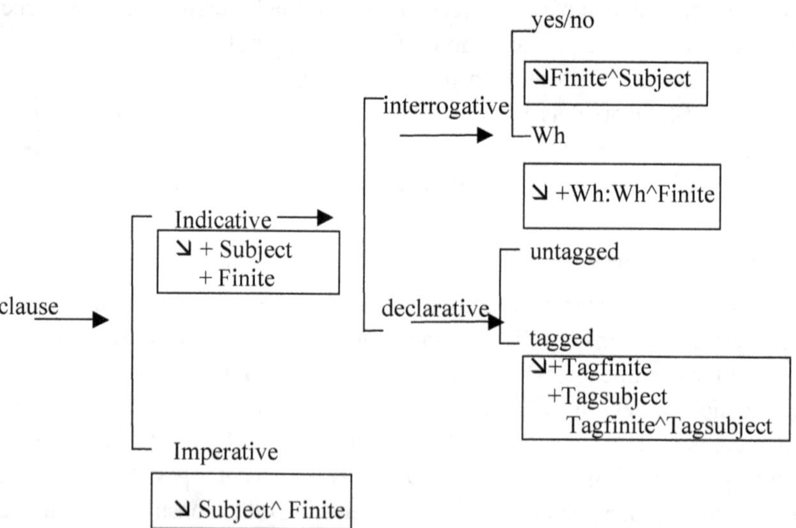

Figure 1: Network of MOOD systems in English

In this formulation, lexis and grammar are considered as the one phenomenon which can be viewed from different standpoints along the cline (Halliday, 1996). Movement along the system network notation (as in Figure 1) from generalisation on the left through to delicacy on the right is a consequence of the privileging of the paradigmatic axis within the theory. As choice within the system unfolds, the realisations become more and more word-like and may even move into the morphology.

Another way of understanding grammar is that, according to Halliday (1961:246), 'grammar is that level of linguistic form at which operate closed systems'. In other words, if you are describing a closed system in any language, you are describing the grammar of that language, for if you were to describe an open system, you would be describing its lexis. This is the distinguishing difference between grammar and lexis. Classes exist in open sets, while grammar is organised in closed sets or closed systems. Halliday (1961) has defined a closed system as follows:

> A closed system is a set of terms with these characteristics:
>
> (a) the number of terms is finite: they can be listed as A B C D, and all other items E... are outside the system.
>
> (b) each term is exclusive of all the others: a given term A cannot be identical with B or C or D.
>
> (c) if a new term is added to the system this changes the meaning of all the others (p.247).

As suggested above, another way of looking at closed systems is to consider them as paradigmatic relations, relations between competing possibilities. As a sentence is formulated, as every structure unfolds, the writer/speaker is choosing from the set of limited possibilities. This set of limited possibilities is the system. Within SF Theory, language is therefore not seen as a set of structures but rather as a network of systems which are interrelated sets of options for making meaning. Such options are not defined by reference to structure; they are purely abstract features, and structure comes in as the means whereby they are put into effect, or 'realised' (Halliday, 1994:15). These systems are abstract, however the realisation(s) of these systems are those which appear as structure in an actual instantiation of language, that is, in a text.

The full set of choices is what is considered the *system* of language, while a text is one *instance* or one possible output of the *system*. Japanese for example, has its own set of system networks. These networks have yet to be comprehensively mapped, however, enough is known about them to incorporate them into a computational model of Japanese which can understand and generate natural language. As Ito (this volume) explains, 'SFL provides a unified way of modeling language use in context by means of system networks with realisation statements... The stratal organisation and systemic sets of choices of the SF model lend themselves to computation application' (see p.275).

A final comment on the paradigmatic axis in SF Theory relates to the relationship between the two notions of *system* and *instance,* which are located at opposite ends of a cline of instantiation and form a complementarity of perspective. Language variation inherently depends on social phenomena, geographical location and registerial constraints. Such constraints locate instances of language in clusters somewhere between the full potential of the system and each individual instance or realisation of the system. This illustrates how system and instance exist on a cline of instantiation. A particular variety of language can be viewed from the system end of the cline and interpreted as a language sub-type, or else it can be viewed from the instance end of the cline and interpreted as a text type or genre. The interpretation depends on the perspective of the observer (Halliday, 1996:30). Looking from the point of view of instance, Japanese can be seen to be organised into genres. Within this volume, a number of genres such as exposition, information report, biographical recount etc. are investigated. Understanding these genres and others is one way of mapping cultural practices and revealing cultural values.

In summary, all languages have a *system* which is representable by system network notation, and all languages are functional, drawing on ideational, interpersonal and textual meanings. Thus using SF Theory enables comparisons between languages. SF descriptions allow similarities and differences between languages to be observable through system networks. It is possible within system networks to observe differences in the division of labour between features; in the probabilities of selections; in the degrees of differentiation; and in the levels of delicacy. Yet, at the same time, it is possible to observe similarities in social purpose and metafunctional meanings. For example, from the study by Sano (this volume), it is clear that both English and Japanese have a system of logico-semantic relations. Both languages have expansion and projection and within expansion, both have elaborating, extending and enhancing types of expansion. However, the choices begin to diverge within the sub-systems of elaboration, extension and enhancement as the two system networks generate different selection choices at increasing levels of delicacy.

It is these four principals along with, of course, others within the theory that shape linguistic description in Systemic Functional Theory. However, the four outlined above are particularly pertinent to the descriptions in this collection. In *Part 1: Description*, each chapter problematises a particular feature of Japanese and sets about providing a linguistic description and justifying the feature from the point of view of social purpose. In other words, the presence of these 'characteristic' language features is motivated by a desire to get things done in a social context.

There are five chapters in Part 1, organised according to metafunction. Sano and Thomson (Chapter 2) explores the *ideational* metafunction by describing the system of LOGICO-SEMANTIC RELATIONS within a set of persuasive texts. The chapter details the lexicogrammatical forms which realise the logico-semantic relations (LSRs), demonstrating: i) that Enhancement is the most frequently selected type of relation; ii) that the LSRs between each generic element in the texts are constant, suggesting a motivated rhetorical pattern of persuasion; iii) that the 'paragraph' in these texts functions to isolate logico-semantic clause clusters; and finally iv) that logico-semantic ambiguity is often a feature of persuasion to enable the reader an opportunity to arrive at the writer's idea of their own accord by interpreting the more delicate LSR choices in the network themselves. This study suggests that the art of persuasion in Japanese is motivated by social norms which avoid directness.

Fukui (Chapter 3) investigates *interpersonal* meaning by describing the system of MOOD in a set of dialogic texts. The chapter describes the congruent lexicogrammatical resources for realising the speech functions of statement, question, offer and command: Statement is realised by declarative; Question by interrogative; Command by imperative; and unlike English, Offer is realised by the distinctive oblative form. The chapter presents the system network of MOOD with output statements for the congruent forms, but also lists incongruent realisations for the four speech functions. In Fukui's data, the declarative form is used incongruently to realise all four speech functions, while the interrogative form is used to incongruently realise a statement.

Thomson (Chapter 4) investigates the *textual* metafunction by describing the system of THEME from a corpus of factual and storytelling genres. The description accounts for single and multiple Themes, noting that the multiple Theme configurations in the corpus do not produce an example of a multiple theme consisting of all three metafunctions, which is unlike English. The types of single Themes are classified and quantified, producing quantitative evidence for marked and unmarked Themes. Further, while Theme is the first constituent in the unit, the unit is not the clause. Rather, the unit is the Theme unit which is defined grammatically as a co-referential string which may, but need not, conflate with a clause. Semantically, the Theme unit can be defined as one phase of continuous thematic progression (refer to Thomson, 2005). The presence of such a unit in Japanese relates to the operation of ellipsis as a cohesive resource within the language.

Chapters 5 and 6 are not dedicated to one metafunction as such, rather they take a number of lexicogrammatical resources and describe how these function in particular genres. Hayakawa (Chapter 5) is a case study that investigates ideational and textual lexicogrammatical resources for classifying natural phenomena in a high school science textbook. The study demonstrates that classification is achieved through a range of lexicogrammatical resources such as logico-semantic relations between clauses, through particular process types in the transitivity structure and through the experiential structure of the nominal group. Further, Hayakawa demonstrates the method of development of the text through an analysis of the Themes and thematic progression patterns using the Theme unit as described by Thomson (2005).

Sato (Suto) and Barnard (Chapter 6) take a creative look at the lexicogrammatical resource of nominalisation by construing a cline which shows the degrees of nominalisation between the two congruent forms of verb as Event, and noun as Thing. Essentially, the process of nominalisation is a graded process shifting away from ranked clauses, to projections, to rankshifted clauses or embedded acts, to nominalisations and finally, to nouns. At the most nominalised end of the cline, the degree of negotiability of the proposition and the specificity of the transitivity roles of the original proposition are reduced, thereby preventing the proposition from being contestable or modally responsible. This loss of contestability and modal responsibility is used within political party manifestos as a strategy to construe the policies of the party as good and those of the opposition parties as bad. The more nominalised the policy statements become, the less contestable the evaluations. This strategy, which functions to persuade, enables the political parties to make bare, uncontestable assertions about party policies.

Part 2: Application

The second section of the book introduces how several researchers have *applied* SF theory to the areas of foreign language education, second or additional language development, and computational linguistics. Application of theory is important because it is in the application of a theory that a theory gets tested, improved, elaborated and re-theorised. Theory and application form a two-way street, and research that uses one without the other is an impoverished exercise. This book attempts to do both. For example, in the Suto and Barnard chapter, political manifestos are investigated for their strategic use of nominalisation. In the process of applying the theory of nominalisation, they depict it as a process of degrees, representing it as a cline from less noun-like to more noun-like, the point being to demonstrate how the more noun-like a proposition becomes, the less the opportunity occurs to contest, negotiate or specify the proposition. Using the innovation of the cline helps demonstrate the process. As the cline is an innovation of theory, it is an example of how application informs theory.

According to Halliday (1994) there are 21 possible applications of SF Theory. Halliday notes that a 'theory is a means of action, and there are many very different kinds of action one may want to take involving language' (pp. xxix-xxx). SF Theory, therefore, is to be treated as a means of action, and in this volume, it has been used to describe the three metafunctions and how they work in the context of the Japanese language. Halliday (1994) suggests that '[A]pplications of linguistics range from research applications of a theoretical nature to quite practical tasks where problems have to be solved' (p. xxix). In the four chapters of Part 2, we can see how SF Theory is put into operation, made relevant, and put to practical use by understanding how adults develop Japanese as an additional language; helping students learn Japanese as a foreign language; and designing computer models that will eventually understand and produce text.

Armour and Furuya (Chapter 7) apply SF Theory to the development of Japanese as an additional language. Interestingly, SF Linguistics has had less to say on learning languages other than the mother tongue. In this chapter, *Principles 2* and *4*, which were mentioned above seem to be the most relevant to apply. The purpose of their contribution is to understand how meaning is made collaboratively in a Second Language Development context. While in each data set, 'errors' which were made by the five Japanese as an additional language learners have been foregrounded, these errors act as an aside to understanding what actually happened in their tape recorded conversations with a Japanese national. The researchers, Armour and Furuya were interested in understanding the set of the linguistic and behavioural choices which, as *Principle 2* above notes, are both potentially possible and acceptable. One conclusion that Armour and Furuya have made is that there appears to be an interpersonal requirement that adult learners of an additional language need to have to enable their entry into the initial stages of L2 development. It is claimed that each 'expert' interlocutor literally becomes or is positioned as a 'parent' to the L2 learner whether she or he likes it or not. Therefore, it is the collaboration between interlocutors that is most likely to be crucial to how the novice actually develops his or her meaning potential. The novice cannot simply resolve a meaning making problem *in situ* without the help of the expert.

Ramzan and Thomson (Chapter 8) apply SF Theory to foreign language education by introducing an alternative method of teaching the skill of writing in Japanese. *Principle 4* above highlights the importance of linguistic choice. The writing skill tends to be the most difficult of the four language skills of speaking, listening, reading and writing to develop, and yet writing tends to be given the least amount of time. Given the time devoted to teaching and learning how to speak Japanese and how to read and write *hiragana*, *katakana*, and *kanji,* most typically without regard to the context of the text, it is little surprise that L2 learners do not write meaningful texts in Japanese. There seems to be a folkloric assumption that the ability to make oral meaning will in some way enable the making of graphological meaning. Given this assumption, Ramzan and Thomson suggest a method based on the Genre Approach, used to teach writing skills to English as a first language learners. This chapter presents an argument justifying such a move as well as setting out a procedure that was piloted in an actual Japanese language classroom. While more research needs to be done to evaluate the success of such a treatment, the authors approach the teaching of the writing skill using the trinocular view of language discussed above, combining this with the strategy of introducing Japanese language learners to the notion of genre and how genre choices ultimately influence what can or cannot be written in any given context.

The final two chapters in the volume describe computer software which has been developed, based on the SF model of language. Part of a larger research project called the *Everyday Language Computing Project,* it was carried out at the Rikagaku Kenkyujo (RIKEN) in Japan. The chapters describe two sides of the same coin in the sense that Ito and Sugimoto (Chapter 9) describe the algorithm for Japanese language text *understanding,* based on a *Semiotic Base*, while Takahashi, Kobayashi, and Iwazume (Chapter 10) describe the algorithm for Japanese language *generation*. These two chapters contribute to our understanding of how SF Theory can be applied to computer science.

In Chapter 9, Ito and Sugimoto deal with how context and its influences on language can be modelled, and how these influences can be represented systematically in a computational form. The *Semiotic Base* that was developed consists of four other databases: *the Context Base*, *the Meaning Base*, *the Wording Base*, and *the Expression Base.* In the construction of the algorithm, Ito and Sugimoto have not only based their research on the WAG systemic parser as described in O'Donnell (1994) but significantly extended it to integrate the results of a non-systemic parser as well as a machine readable dictionary.

Takahashi, Kobayashi, and Iwazume (Chapter 10) report on how they have developed the text generation process based on SF Theory (Halliday and Matthiessen, 1999, 2004) using *the Semiotic Base*. The authors demonstrate that by using *the Semiotic Base*, a computer can generate text strings as a response to an inquiry or request from a user, providing several examples of text generation created through their model.

While the actualisation of text processing based on natural language is still in the development stages, the contribution that these researchers have made so far indicates how innovatively SF Theory can be applied. Given the newness of such research and subsequent application, the authors of both chapters conclude by noting both advantages and limitations of their computational model. Both chapters complement each other by showing the significant advances that have been made in terms of applying SF Theory to computer science. And importantly, in the process of application to the context of computer science, they have made some interesting innovations to the theory, most notably, in the relationship between the context and semantics.

It has not been possible to publish all the work that has been or is being conducted regarding either descriptions of Japanese or applications of SF Theory to aspects in which the Japanese language is involved. The editors acknowledge that many other scholars and researchers of Japanese are working on exciting and innovative projects. This book represents a small collection of work, demonstrating how SF Theory has been used to describe Japanese and to demonstrate these descriptions in contexts of application.

This volume would not have eventuated without the help of many colleagues and friends. Firstly, the JASFL network brought the contributors of this book together. The editors of this volume would like to acknowledge the work of JASFL and thank them for nurturing the introduction of SF Theory to Japan. We encourage the organisation to continue to foster and grow SF descriptions of Japanese. Secondly, we would like to thank all the contributors who have been patient with us as editors, meeting deadlines, and producing papers which have fulfilled our intentions. Thirdly, we would like to thank all those who have helped us with proof reading, insightful comments on papers, and the finer points of book editing. Their contributions were invaluable. We would also like to thank the University of Wollongong for the financial and in-kind support with the indexing process and the preparation of the final manuscript. Lastly, we would like to thank the publisher for the much needed support and guidance throughout the entire process.

In closing, we would like to invite you, the reader, to engage with and critique the research in the volume. One of the many frustrations that researchers often voice is that they do not really know what impact their ideas have had or how their ideas are being used by those who read their work. Like the view taken in this monograph that theory and application are linked, the writers of these chapters wish to link and engage with the readers. We would encourage you to further develop the ideas offered in this book, so that the tradition of using Systemic Functional Theory to expand and offer new understandings of Languages Other than English (LOTEs) continues.

References

Akerejola, E. (2005) *A text-based lexicogrammatical description of Òkó.* PhD Dissertation, Division of Linguistics & Psychology, Department of Linguistics, Macquarie University, Sydney.

Ali Bardi, M. (2008) *A systematic functional description of the grammar of Arabic.* PhD Dissertation, Division of Linguistics & Psychology, Department of Linguistics, Macquarie University, Sydney.

Butt, D., Fahey, R., Feez, S., Spinks, S. and Yallop, C. (1995) *Using Functional Grammar: An Explorer's Guide*, National Centre for English Language Teaching and Research, Macquarie University: Sydney.

Cafferal, A. (2006) *A Systemic Functional Grammar of French,* London: Continuum.

Fukui, N. (1998) A Description of the Mood System of a set of Japanese spoken dialogic texts. MA. Dissertation, School of Linguistics, University of NSW, Sydney.

Halliday. M.A.K. (1956 in 2006) *Studies in Chinese Language,* London: Continuum.

Halliday, M. A. K. (1961) Categories of the Theory of Grammar. *Word* 17(3): 241–292.

Halliday, M. A. K. (1973) *Explorations in the Functions of Language*. London: Edward Arnold Publishers.

Halliday, M. A. K. (1978) *Language as Social Semiotic*. London: Edward Arnold Publishers.

Halliday, M. A. K. (1979) Modes of meaning and modes of expression: types of grammatical structure, and their determination by different semantic functions. In D. J. Allerton, E. Carney and D. Holdcroft (eds) *Functional and Context in Linguistic Analysis*. Cambridge: Cambridge University Press.

Halliday, M. A. K. (1980) Foreword to *Terms in Systemic Linguistics: A Guide to Halliday* vii. Foreword by A. de Joia and A. Stenton. London: Batsford Academic and Educational Ltd.

Halliday, M. A. K. (1992a) The act of meaning. *Georgetown University Round Table on Languages and Linguistics*. Georgetown University Press: Washington D.C.

Halliday, M. A. K. (1994) *An Introduction to Functional Grammar*. 2nd Edition. London: Edward Arnold Publishers.

Halliday, M. A. K. (1996) On Grammar and Grammatics. In R. Hasan, C. Cloran and D. Butt (eds) *Functional Descriptions: Theory in Practice*. Amsterdam: John Benjamins Publishing Company.

Halliday, M. A. K. and Matthiessen, C. M. I. M. (1999) *Construing Experience through Meaning: A Language-Based Approach to Cognition*. London: Cassell.

Halliday, M. A. K. and Matthiessen, C. M. I. M. (2004) *An Introduction to Functional Grammar*. 3rd Edition. London: Edward Arnold Publishers.

Hjelmslev, L. (1961) *Prolegomena to a Theory of Language*. Madison: University of Wisconsin Press.

Hori, M. (1995) Subjectlessness and Honourifics in Japanese: A Case of Textual Construal. In R. Hasan and P. Fries (eds) *On Subject and Theme: A Discourse Functional Perspective*. Amsterdam: John Benjamins Publishing Company.

Ikegami, Y. (1991) Introduction: Semiotics and Culture. In Y. Ikegami (ed.) *The Empire of Signs* 1–24. Amsterdam: John Benjamins Publishing Company.

Kim, M. & McDonald, E. (2012) SFL-based text analysis for translator education. In Knox, J (ed.) *To boldly go, Proceedings of the 39th International Systemic Functional Congress*, Sydney.

Lavid, J., Arus, J. & Zamorano, J.R. (2010) *Systemic Functional Grammar of Spanish: A Contrastive Study with English.* London: Continuum.

Li, E. (2007) *A Systemic Functional Grammar of Chinese*. London: Continuum.

Li, C. N. and Thompson, S. A. (1976) Subject and Topic: A New Typology of Language. In C. N. Li (ed.) *Subject and Topic*. Academic Press Inc: New York.

McDonald, E. (1998) *Clause and verbal group systems in Chinese: a text-based functional approach*. PhD Dissertation, Division of Linguistics & Psychology, Department of Linguistics, Macquarie University, Sydney.

Martin, J. (1995) Logical meaning, interdependency and the linking particle {na/-ng} in Tagalog, *Functions of Language* 2(2): 189–228.

Martin, J.R. (2004) Metafunctional profile of the grammar of Tagalog. In Caffarel, A. Martin, J.R. & Matthiessen, C.M.I.M (eds.) *Language Typology, A functional perspective*, London: John Benjamins.

Matthiessen, C. M. I. M. and Halliday, M. A. K. (1997) *Systemic Functional Grammar: A first step into the theory*. (Unpublished draft manuscript.)

Matthiessen, C. M. I. M. and Nesbitt, C. (1996) On the Idea of Theory-Neutral Descriptions. In R. Hasan, C. Cloran and D. Butt (eds) *Functional Descriptions: Theory in Practice*. John Benjamins Publishing Company, Amsterdam.

Matthiessen, C. (1995a) *Lexicogrammatical Cartography: English Systems*. Tokyo: International Language Sciences Publishers.

O'Donnell, M. (1994) *Sentence Analysis and Generation: A Systemic Perspective*. PhD Dissertation, University of Sydney.

Patpong, P. (2006) *A systemic functional interpretation of Thai grammar: an exploration of Thai narrative discourse.* PhD Dissertation. Division of Linguistics & Psychology, Department of Linguistics, Macquarie University, Sydney.

Prakasam, V. (2004) Metafunctional Profile of the grammar of Telugu. In Caffarel, A. Martin, J.R. & Matthiessen, C.M.I.M (eds.) *Language Typology, A functional perspective*, London: John Benjamins.

Rose, D. (2004) Metafunctional Profile of the grammar of Pitjantjatjara. In Caffarel, A. Martin, J.R. & Matthiessen, C.M.I.M (eds.) *Language Typology, A functional perspective*, London: John Benjamins.

Sano, M. (forthcoming 2007) *A Linguistic Exploration of Persuasion in Japanese Culture* (tentative title). PhD Dissertation, School of English Literatures, Philosophy and Languages, Faculty of Arts, University of Wollongong.

Steiner, E & Teich, E. (2004) Metafunctional Profile of the grammar of German. In Caffarel, A. Martin, J.R. & Matthiessen, C.M.I.M (eds.) *Language Typology, A functional perspective,* London: John Benjamins.

Teruya, K. (1998) *An Exploration into the World of Experience: A Systemic Functional Interpretation of the Grammar of Japanese.* PhD Dissertation, School of English, Linguistics and Media, Macquarie University, Sydney.

Teruya, K. (2007), *A systemic Functional Grammar of Japanese.* London: Continuum.

Thai, M.D. (1998) *A systemic functional interpretation of Vietnamese grammar.* PhD Dissertation, Division of Linguistics & Psychology, Department of Linguistics, Macquarie University, Sydney.

Thibault, P. J. (2004) *Brain, Mind and the Signifying Body: An Ecosocial Semiotic Theory.* London and New York: Continuum.

Thomson, E. (2005) Theme Unit Analysis: A systemic functional treatment of textual meanings in Japanese. *Functions of Language* 12(2): 152–180.

Webster, J. (2005) M. A. K. Halliday: the early years, 1925–1970. In R. Hasan, C. M. I. M. Matthiessen and J. Webster (eds) *Continuing Discourse on Language: A Functional Perspective* vol. 1. 3–14. London: Equinox Publishing Ltd.

2 How to argue in Japanese: a systemic functional interpretation of the logico-semantic relations in Japanese exposition

Motoki Sano and Elizabeth A. Thomson
University of Wollongong, Australia
UNSW, Canberra

This paper presents a case study of the logico-semantic relations in a set of selected Japanese expository texts. The logico-semantic relations are classified according to Halliday's (1994) categorisation. The study shows that the logico-semantic relation of 'enhancement' plays a central role in the method of development of exposition. Furthermore, it sheds light on the social purpose of Japanese exposition – 'to present an argument and ask the reader to share the same idea with the writer'. Although paragraphing in Japanese is often considered very flexible and up to the writer, the study shows that the boundaries between paragraphs often correlate with the boundaries between groups that are connected by logico-semantic relations.

Introduction

In Japanese, as in other languages, a text forms a coherent whole partly due to the logical and semantic connections which exist between the clauses and clusters of clauses in the text. In the theory of Systemic Functional (SF) Linguistics, one crucial system that constitutes such logical and semantic connections is known as the system of LOGICO-SEMANTIC RELATIONS, which is one of the systems of language from which choices are made to establish and develop an argument (Halliday, 1994). And so, inter alia, if we want to understand how to argue in Japanese, we need to understand the patterns of choices which are made within the system of LOGICO-SEMANTIC RELATIONS.

Logico-Semantic Relations in Japanese has already been studied by Thomson (2001) and Teruya (1998, 2003). Thomson (2001) studied the logico-semantic relations between generic stages in the genres of news stories, nursery tales and narratives. Teruya (1998) studied the logico-semantic relation of projection in his account of verbal and mental processes in Japanese. The work of Teruya (2003) also presents a categorisation of logico-semantic relations in Japanese. Building on these works, this study will further contribute to the expansion of our understanding of the system of LOGICO-SEMANTIC RELATIONS as it is realised in Japanese.

This paper aims to describe how the system of LOGICO-SEMANTIC RELATIONS is utilised in a set of selected Japanese expository texts. In these expository texts, the system of LOGICO-SEMANTIC RELATIONS contributes to the rhetorical organisation of the text via:

a) the frequent use of ENHANCEMENT;

b) the writers' selection of different degrees of differentiation in the realisation of the enhancing relations; and

c) particular and predictable patterns of logico-semantic relations between and within generic elements.

In part, it is through these particular configurations that the social purpose of the genre and the functions of the generic elements are realised.

Additionally, this study also sheds light on how a text is divided into paragraphs in Japanese. According to the result of the study, the paragraph boundaries in the corpus typically conflate with the boundaries between clusters of clauses that are connected by a particular logico-semantic relation. This may imply that the purpose of paragraphing in Japanese is to isolate logico-semantically connected clauses and/or clause clusters.

This paper begins with a description of the texts in the corpus, outlining their generic elements and structures. This is followed by an explanation of the method used to identify and classify the types of logico-semantic relations, and an illustration of how these relations connect clauses in the texts. The paper subsequently presents both the classification and the salient characteristics of the logico-semantic relations in the analysed texts, and concludes with a discussion on the possible reasons for the presence and function of these characteristics in constructing Japanese exposition.

The corpus

The corpus of the present study is composed of three texts:[1]

1) *Kyooiku kihonhoo – risoo moteasobu hima wa nai* (The Fundamentals of the Education Act – there is no time for playing around with ideals), *Asahi Shimbun* (Asahi Newspaper), 15 Nov 2002.

2) Kawai, H. 2001 '*Nihonjin to kosei*' (Japanese and Individuality), *Taiwa suru ningen* (*Humans in conversations*), Kodansha, Tokyo, pp.153–156.

3) Sasaki, M. 1994 '*Nihonjin rashisa to iu koto*' (The meaning of being Japanese), *Gaikokugo to shite no nihongo* (Japanese as a foreign language), Kodansha, Tokyo, pp.234–237.

Kyooiku kihonhoo, Nihonjin to Kosei, Nihonjin rashisa to iu koto will be referred to as the 'Asahi', the 'Kawai', the 'Sasaki' texts respectively.

Each of these texts serves the social purpose of persuasion. The *Asahi* text is from the editorial section of the Asahi Newspaper. This text proposes that although the Central Education Discussion Group revised the Fundamentals of Education Act, the revised version of the Act is not effective for the improvement of the current situation in education. The *Kawai* text is from a book written by an academic for public consumption. It claimes that the nature and meaning of individuality (*kosei*) in Japan should be discussed more carefully when the notion is applied to education. The Sasaki text, like the Kawai text, is also from a book written by an academic for public consumption. This text suggests that the purpose of Japanese language education for non-native speakers is to create the opportunity for them to understand the Japanese world through the Japanese language and to help them with problems of interculturality.

The generic elements of the three texts

An analysis of the generic elements of the texts in the corpus shows four generic elements. These are:

1) Orientation (O)
2) Argument (A)
3) Thesis (T) and
4) Concession (C)

The Orientation element sets the scene of each text and provides the background for the understanding of other elements. The Argument element provides the supporting arguments for the claim. The Thesis element proposes the main position or the claim of the writer. The Concession element presents concessive or counter arguments of the main arguments to acknowledge the existence of oppositions or particular conditions, with a view to discounting their importance. Unlike the other elements which were common to all three texts, the Concession element was the only element not evident in all the texts. The generic structures of each text are represented in Table 1.

All three texts begin with an Orientation. In the Asahi text, the Orientaion is followed by one Concession, two Argument elements and a Thesis. In the Kawai text, the Orientation is followed by one Argument element, one Concession and a Thesis. In the Sasaki Text, the Orientation is followed by one Argument element and a Thesis. This is the text that has no Concession element.

Table 1: The actual generic structures of the three texts

Asahi text	O^C^A1^A2^T
Kawai text	O^A^C^T
Sasaki text	O^A^T

Methodology

There were two major steps in this study. The first step was to identify the presence of the logico-semantic relations. In total, 175 logico-semantic relations were identified and these relations were classified. The second step was to explore their role in the rhetorical organisation of each text.

The classification of the logico-semantic relations

The relations were classified according to Halliday's (1994) categorisation of logico-semantic relations. However, it was not assumed that the kinds of logico-semantic relations found by Halliday to be operating in English would be necessarily the same in Japanese. Despite this, Halliday's classification served as a good starting point, so the relations within the three texts were classified into Expansion and Projection types and then into the relevant subsystems, as appropriate.

As part of this process, the study identified which conjunctive elements indicated which relations. In Japanese, there are two types of conjunctives: structural and non-structural conjunctives (Thomson, 2001). The structural conjunctives are grammaticalised conjunctives that create cohesion between clauses and within clause complexes. They include types of verbal inflections such as the 'stem form' and '*te* form' that link clauses in clause complexes; postpositions such as '*~ga*' (but); grammaticalised verbal postpositions such as '*ni tsuite*'(about), '*ni kanshite*' (in relation to); and the combination of a verbal inflection and postposition such as '*~ te mo*' (although).

The nonstructural conjunctives create cohesion between sentences and paragraphs. In other words, they can function above the clause structure. In this sense, they are not constitutive of clause structure and are therefore non-structural. Examples include conjunctions like '*tatoeba*' (for example) and *shitagatte* (consequently).

Apart from logico-semantic relations being indicated by conjunctives, they can also be expressed by implication. That is to say, the relation can be indicated by simply locating logico-semantically related elements in the same neighbourhood as each other without using any explicit resource. The existence of implicit logico-semantic relations can be confirmed by testing whether the relation can be explicitly expressed by a conjunctive or not (Martin, 1992). If a conjunctive can represent the relation, then there is an implicit relation. It is necessary to test whether it's possible to insert one so that we do not assume that they are there, when in fact they may not be, which is called 'reading too much into the text' (Halliday, 1994; Martin, 1992). Examples of implicit relations can be found in the Result Section of the chapter.

Examination of the logico-semantic relations between clauses and clusters

In order to illustrate a graphic representation of the logico-semantic relations between clauses and clause clusters, the RST tool (O'Donnell, 2003) software is utilised. An example of the representation is in Figure 1. The numbers under the bar indicate unit numbers. The units analysed in this study are *typically* a clause or a cluster of clauses. When a unit is composed of a clause, the number under the bar is called a clause number. When the unit is composed of a cluster of clauses, it is referred as a cluster number. In the Figure, the numbers '1, 2, 3, 4' are the clause numbers. The type of logico-semantic relation is indicated above the curved arrow by relation labels.[2] In Figure 1, 'Enh' (enhancement) and 'Enh:cond:pos:hyp' (enhancement: condition: positive: hypothetical) refer to the type of logico-semantic relation.

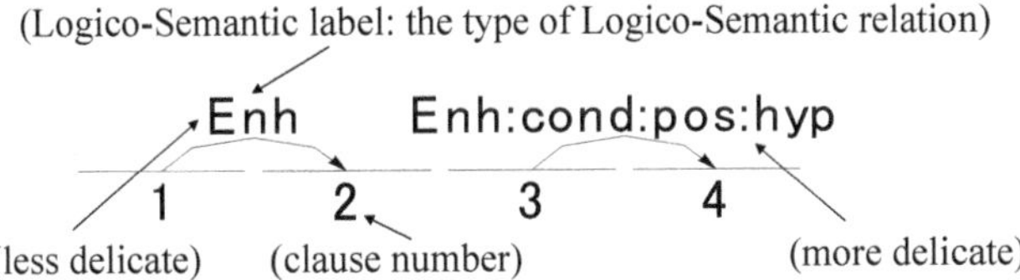

Figure 1: Example of the analysis of logico-semantic relations between clauses in clause complexes

The relation labels also indicate the degree of differentiation of a relation. If the relation is relatively *undifferentiated*, then the relation label is less specified. If the relation is *highly differentiated*, then the label is more delicate and highly specified. For example, in Figure 1, if we compare the relation between Clauses 1 & 2 and Clauses 3 & 4, the relation between Clause 3 and 4 is far more specific. In other words, it is more delicately differentiated. This more delicate relation is labelled, 'Enh: cond: pos: hyp', which refers to a highly specific relation of 'Enhancement: condition: positive: hypothetical', unlike the less delicate relation between Clause 1 and 2, which is simply labelled as 'Enh', referring to 'enhancement'.

Note that the direction of the curved arrow indicates which clause expands or projects the other. When one clause or cluster expands another, the curved arrow starts from the expanding clause and ends at the expanded clause. When one clause or cluster projects the other, the arrow starts from the projected clause and ends at the projecting clause. For example, in the enhancement relationship between Clause 1 and 2, the curved arrow starts at the expanding Clause 1, and ends at the expanded Clause 2.

Having identified the relations between clauses in a clause complex, the next step was to examine the relations between the groups or clusters of clauses as they entered into logico-semantic relations with other clauses or clusters. For example, in Figure 2, the relations between the cluster composed of Clauses 1 and 2, and the other cluster composed of Clauses 3 and 4 is identified. The logico-semantic relations between clusters were represented in a similar manner to that of clauses.

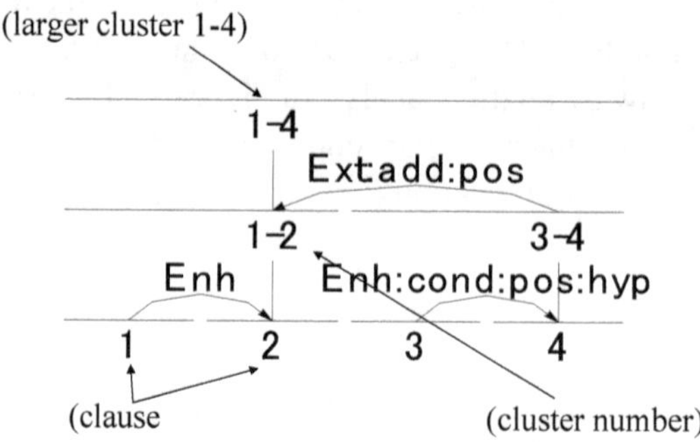

Figure 2: Example of logico-semantic relations between clusters

An analysis of an entire text produces a graphical representation of all the logico-semantic relations between clauses and clusters as in Figure 3. The Figure represents how the nine clauses are logico-semantically connected thereby producing a coherent text through the formation of various logico-semantic clusters.

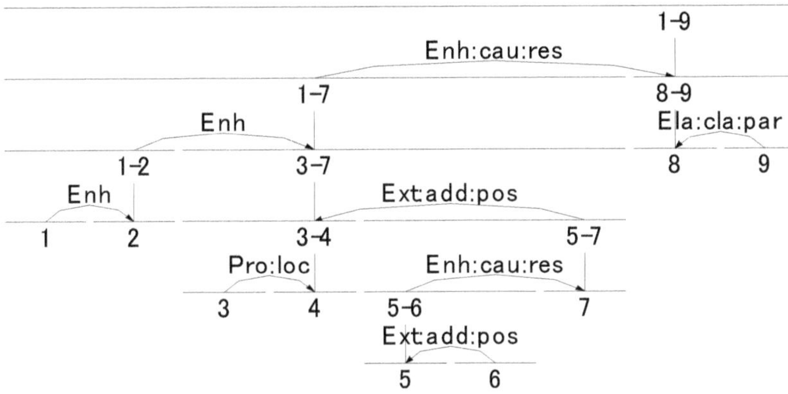

Figure 3: Example of an analysis of an entire text

Results

The results are organised into three sections: a description of the system network of the logico-semantic relations in the corpus; the identification of the dominant logico-semantic relation; and a description of the patterns of logico-semantic progression that exist in each of the three texts.

The system network of the logico-semantic relations in the corpus

The logico-semantic relations in the corpus were classified and represented as a system network, as reproduced in Figure 4. The relations are classified into either a) the system of EXPANSION – the relation where one clause or cluster expands the other by i) elaborating, ii) extending or iii) enhancing, or b) PROJECTION – the relation where one clause projects the other either by i) idea or ii) locution (Halliday, 1994). Each system has several subcategories, as is explained below. At the point of entry of the system, where the choices are more generalised, English and Japanese are the same. However, as more specified relations are selected, the kind of relations that occur in Japanese differ from those in English.

The entry condition for the system network is nexus, that is, the presence of a logical and semantic bond between clauses or clusters. In some of the examples, some conjunctions are bracketed with '( )'. These are conjunctions which do not originally appear in the texts, but are inserted to make explicit the implicit conjunctive relations. In other words, they were inserted to test the existence of implicit relations. The brackets '<< >>' are used to indicate included clauses.

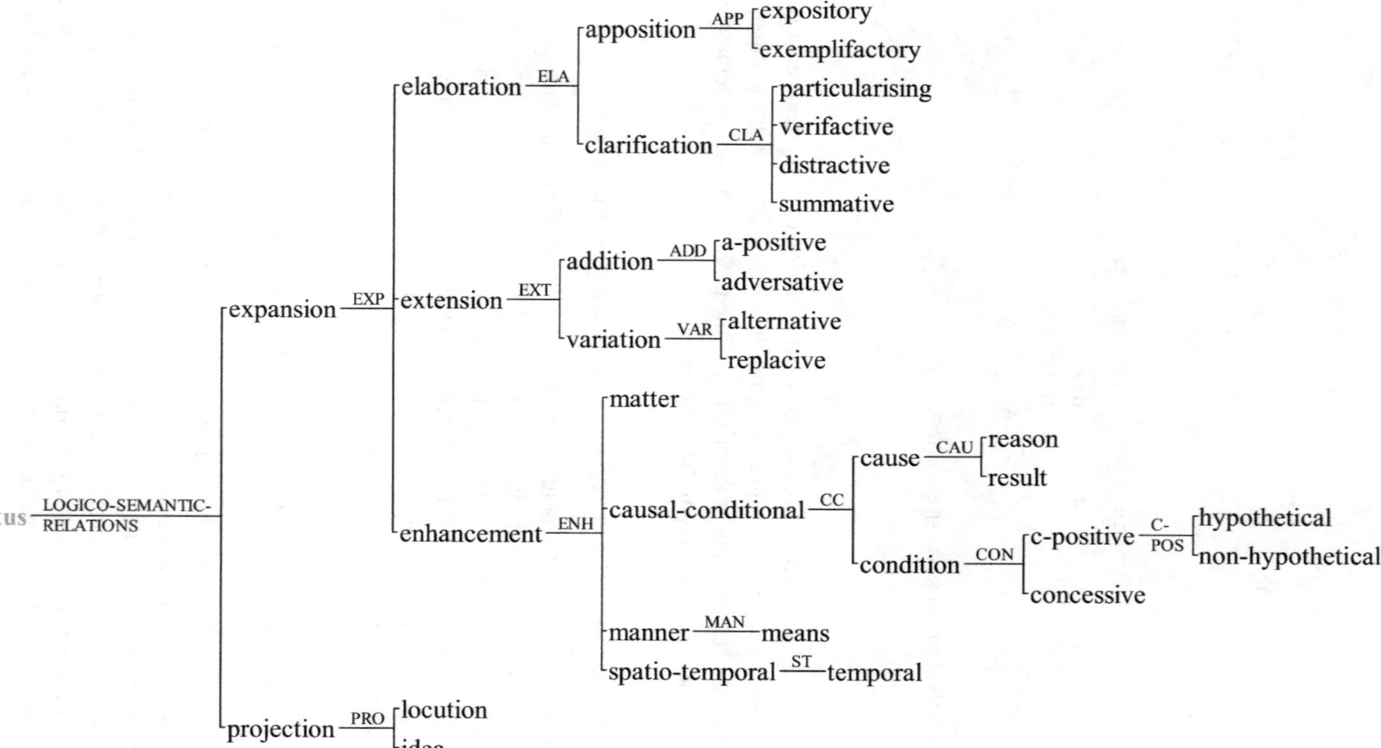

Figure 4: The system network of LOGICO-SEMANTIC RELATIONS in the three expository texts

Expansion

If the nexus is one of EXPANSION, then there are three choices. These are ELABORATION, EXTENSION and ENHANCEMENT.

Elaboration

ELABORATION is the relation where one clause or cluster elaborates the other (Halliday, 1994). In the corpus, elaboration is often expressed by nonstructural conjunctives rather than structural ones. ELABORATION has two subsystems: APPOSITION and CLARIFICATION.

APPOSITION is a relation where one clause or cluster restates the other (Halliday, 1994). Apposition can further be classified into two subsystems: EXPOSITORY and EXEMPLIFACTORY. An expository relation occurs where one clause or cluster restates the other by providing *further explanation*. In Example 1, the preceding clause is elaborated by the following clause which provides a further interpretation of the Imanishi group's characteristics presented in the preceding clause by means of a relation of restatement. The relation is indicated by the conjunctive *tsumari* (that is to say).

(1) (a) *imanishi guruupu wa zentaishugiteki de hikoseiteki de naika,*
Imanishi group-WA group oriented and nonindividualistic COP-PRO,
the researchers in the Imanishi group were group-orientated and 'non-individualist',

(b) ***tsumari,*** *guruupu no kakujin ga*
CONJ, the group NO each member GA

sootoo ni kakuitsuteki na sonzai dewanaika to…
very uniform existence COP-PRO. TO.
that is to say, the group members were assumed to be uniform…

(the *Kawai text*)

An exemplifactory relation exists where one clause or cluster restates the other by providing *an example*. In Example 2, the preceding clause is elaborated by the following cluster which exemplifies the argument presented in the preceding clause. The conjunctive *tatoeba* (for example) was inserted to confirm the implicit relation between them.

(2) (a) *sudeni shinpai sareru ugoki mo deteiru.*
Already worry-PASS movement MO emerge-ASP.
Such a worrying movement is already emerging.

(b) ***(tatoeba)*** *fukuokashinai no shoogakkoo dewa,*
(**CONJ**) in Fukuoka-city NO primary school DE WA,

tsuuchihyoo ni kuni o aisuru shinjo, sekai no naka no nihonjin no jikaku ni tsuite
grade record at nation O love feeling, world NO inside NO Japanese NO awareness about

hyoka suru komoku o moketeiru tokoro ga kanari aru.
assess section O implement-ASP places GA many exist.

shizen ni wakiokorubeki kokyoo ya kuni o aisuru kokoro o seiseki to shite chekku sure ba,
naturally occur-OBL home country and nation O love feeling O grade as mark-CND,

ii seiseki o toritai kodomo wa kyooshi no shidoo ni shitagaudaroo.
good grade O achieve child WA teacher NO instruction NI obey-PRO.

shikashi, sore de kokyoo ya kuni o aisuru kokoro ga hontoo ni sodatsudarooka.
However, that by home town and nation O love feeling GA really develop-PRO-Q.

(For example) At primary schools in Fukuoka City, (many schools have established) a section in the grade record that assesses how much the students love their country and their level of awareness as Japanese in the world. If teachers mark how much the students love their nation, (which should develop naturally), the students who'd like to achieve a high mark would follow the teacher's instruction. However, would this really contribute to the development of a love for one's nation?

(the *Asahi text*)

Clarification, which is the other subsystem of Elaboration, is a relation where one clause or cluster clarifies the other. There are four kinds: Particularising, Verifactive, Distractive and Summative. A particularising relation exists where one clause or cluster clarifies the other by providing specific items, events or arguments, etc. (subclasses) of the superordinate element which is presented in an elaborated clause or cluster. In Example 3, the following clause provides the subclasses such as *dentoo ya bunka no sonchoo* (the respect for the tradition and culture) of the superordinate element '*kokyoo ni kansuru kihan*' (the community ideals). The conjunctive *tokuni* (in particular) was inserted.

(3) (a) *hookoku niwa, kihonhoo ni aru 'kojin no songen' ya*
the report at WA, the Fundamentals of Education Act at exist 'individual NO dignity' and

'jinkaku no kansei' no rinen wa korekara mo taisetsu da ga,
'identity NO perfection' NO ideals WA after this MO important COP-but,

aratana rinen ya gensoku to shite, daigakukaikaku no sokushin ya
new ideal and principle as, the reformation of university NO promotion and

katee no kyooikuryoku no kaifuku no hoka, 'kokyo' ni kansuru kihan no
home NO educational power NO restoration NO else, 'community' about ideals NO

saikoochiku nado o morikomuyoo motometa.
reconstruction and so on O incorporate-VOL demand-PST.

The report recommends university reform and improvements in raising children as well as redefining community ideals in the Act, although the report also commented that the existing ideals of 'individual dignity' and 'mature identity' are important for the future.

(b) ***(toku ni)*** *kokyoo ni kansuru kihan ni wa, dentoo ya bunka no soncho,*
CONJ home town about principle NI WA, tradition and culture NO respect,

kyoodo ya kuni o aisuru kokoro, kokusaisei no shiten mo fukumareru.
home town and nation O love feeling, internaltional NO prospect MO include-PASS.

(In particular) In redefining community ideals, ideals such as respect for tradition and culture, the development of patriotism and the development of an international outlook need to be incorporated.

(the *Asahi text*)

A verifactive relation is where one clause or cluster clarifies the other by supplying the evidence of an occurrence or happening. In Example 4, the preceding cluster is clarified by the following cluster by presenting an actual event which occurred in Western culture. The relation is indicated by the conjunctive *jitsu no tokoro* (as a matter of fact).

(4) (a) *nihonjin dakara nihonjin rashii tokusei o hakkishite...*
Japanese COP-because Japanese like characteristics O utilise-SUSP...

nado to iu kechikusai ryoken de wa naku,
such TO IU small-minded prospect COP-NEG-SUSP,

Let's not take the small-minded notion that the Japanese are uniquely Japanese,

(b) ***jitsu no tokoro,*** *obei ni oitemo seiyookindaikagaku no minaoshi,*
CONJ Europe and the US at modern Western science NO reconsideration

kojinshugi no minaoshi wa hajimaritsutsuaru no de aru.
individualism NO reexamination WA start-ASP.

as a matter of fact, the nature of individuality and modern science is being reconsidered in the West.

(the *Kawai text*)

A distractive relation is where one clause or cluster clarifies the other by providing distractive comments, events or phenomena. In Example 5, the preceding cluster is distracted by the following cluster that changes a topic from the description of Imanishi group to a story of the Western scientist. The relation is indicated by the conjunctive *tokoro de* (by the way).

(5) (a) *Imanishi kinji hakushi o chooten to suru, nihon no reichooruikenkyuu wa*
Imanishi Kinji Doctor o top locate, Japan NO the study of primates WA

kokusaiteki ni takai hyooka o eteiru koto wa shuuchi no toori de aru.
International NI high reputation O achieve-ASP NOMZ WA well known NO way-COP.

It is well known that the Japanese research group studying primates, led by Imanishi Kinji has an internationally high reputation.

(b) ***tokoro de*** *oobei no aru gakusha wa, imanishi hakushi no riron ya,*
CONJ Europe and the US NO certain scientist WA, Imanishi Doctor NO theory and,

(sore wa seibutsu no shu o zentai to shite miyoo to suru kihonteki shisei o motsu)
that WA species NO kinds O whole as see-VOL fundamental attitude O have

nihonjin no ippanteki tokusei nado kara ruisoku shite,
Japanese NO general characteristics and so on from infer-SUSP,

imanishi guruupu wa zentaitekishugi de hikoseiteki de naika,
Imanishi group-WA group oriented and nonindividualistic COP-CJT,

tsumari guruupu no kakujin ga
CONJ, the group NO each member GA

Sootoo ni kakuitsuteki na sonzai dewanaika to kangaete rainichishita.
very uniform existence COP-CJT TO think-SUSP arrive-Japan-PST.

By the way, basing his views on the Imanishi group's research and on his knowledge of the general characteristics of the Japanese, a Western scientist visiting Japan assumed that the researchers in the Imanishi group were group-orientated and 'non-individualist', that is to say, the group members were assumed to be uniform.

(the *Kawai text*)

A summative relation is where one clause or cluster clarifies the other by summarising an elaborated clause or cluster. The relations can be indicated by conjunctives such as *ryakusuto* (in brief) and *tsumari* (in sum).[3] An example is the relation between Cluster 39~48 and Cluster 49~53 in the Kawai text (see Appendix for example). Cluster 39~48 discusses the reason why a Western scientist wrongly anticipated the characteristics of the Imanishi group. Cluster 49~53 summarises the discussion.

Extension

The second subsystem of Expansion is Extension. Extension is the relation where one clause or cluster extends the other (Halliday, 1994). In the relation of extension, both structural and non-structural conjunctives are used. There are two types of Extention: Addition and Variation.

Addition is the relation where one clause or cluster extends the other by *adding* something further. Depending on how a clause or cluster is extended by addition, the relation of addition can further be classified into either i) Positive or ii) Adversative. A positive relation occurs when one clause or cluster extends the other positively by adding a comment, event, phenomenon, etc. In a positive relation, the polarities in the two clauses or clusters are positive. In Example 6, the preceding clause is extended by the following clause which provides the additional comment. The polarities of both clauses are positive (*yasukatta*: was cheap, *shimeshita*: did show). The relation is indicated by the postposition *~shi* (and).

(6) (a) *nedan mo yasukatta* ***shi***,
Price MO cheap-COP-and,
Because the price was very cheap, and

(b) *ryuugakuseitachi mo kyoomi o shimeshita ...*
overseas-students MO interest O show-PST ...
the overseas students showed an interest,

(the *Sasaki text*)

An adversative relation is where one clause or cluster extends the other by adding a comment, event or phenomenon adversatively. In Example 7, the preceding clause is adversatively extended by the following clause. The relation is indicated by postposition *~ga* (but).

(7) (a) *sonotameni, sono hito wa imanishi guruupu no hitotachi no kenkyuu o hajimeyoo to suru no da* ***ga,***
CONJ, that person WA Imanishi group NO people NO study O start-VOL-**CONJ**,

As a result of the mis-match in terms of individuality, the Western scientist began to research the Imanishi group, **but**

(b) *sono ten ni tsuite wa shooryakusuru.*
that part about WA omit.
apart from this I won't elaborate further.

(the *Kawai text*)

The other type of Extension is Variation. The relation of variation exists where one clause or cluster extends the other by varying it (Halliday, 1994). Variation has two kinds: Alternative and Replacive. An alternative relation is where one clause or cluster extends the other by providing an alternative. In Example 8, the preceding clause is extended by the following clause which provides an alternative interpretation. The relation is indicated by the conjunction *aruiwa* (or).

(8) (a) *seito no kosei o nobasu kyooiku o shinakute wa naranai,*
student NO individuality O improve education O do-OBL,
(We) need to provide the education that develops students' individuality.

(b) ***arui wa**, seito no kosei o tsubusuyoona kakuitsushugi no kyooiku wa ikenai ...*
CONJ, student NO individuality O destroy-like uniform. NO education. WA harmful-COP...
or, at least should not hamper the development of a student's individuality through a uniform education.

(the *Kawai text*)

A replacive relation exists where one clause or cluster extends the other by replacing the comment, events or phenomenon that is presented in an elaborated clause or cluster. In Example 9, the comment presented in the preceding clause is extended by the following clause that provides the replacive comment of the preceding one. The relation is indicated by the postposition *~yori* (rather than).

(9) (a) *bunshoo o ijiru **yori,***
text O play rather,
Rather than just play with the words in the Act.

(b) *hooritsu no mokuteki o jitsugensuru gutaitekina hoosaku o saguru no ga senketsu da...*
Law NO aim O realise concrete strategy O find NOMZ GA first-COP.
they should first determine the strategies that need to be in place to realise the aims of the Act.

(the *Asahi text*)

Enhancement

The third and last subsystem of EXPANSION is ENHANCEMENT. Enhancement is the relation where one clause or cluster enhances the other by qualifying it with some circumstantial features such as i) MATTER (what it is about), ii) CAUSAL-CONDITIONAL (what the cause is, and under which conditions), iii) MANNER (how) and iv) SPATIO-TEMPORAL (where and when) (Halliday, 1994).

In the relation of matter, one clause or cluster enhances the other by providing the theme, background or scene of the event, claim or argument which is presented in the enhanced clause. In Example 10, the preceding clause specifies the matter of the following clause. The relation is indicated by the postposition *~ni tsuite* (about).

(10)(a) *kokode naze sonoyoona gokai ga shoojitaka **ni tsuite**,*
At this point why such misunderstanding GA occur-PST-Q **about**,
About the reasons why such a misunderstanding occurred,

(b) *hissya no kangae o shirushite miru.*
Author NO idea. O describe-ASP.
I will attempt to explain my idea.

(the *Kawai text*)

A causal-conditional relation is the relation where one clause or cluster enhances the other by providing the cause or condition of the enhanced clause or cluster. If the relation is enhanced by providing a cause, two clauses or clusters have the relation of CAUSE. If the relation is enhanced by providing a condition, the relation is one of CONDITION. The causal relation can further be categorised into REASON or RESULT. A relation of reason occurs where an enhancing clause or cluster provides a reason. In Example 11, the preceding clause provides the reason of the action presented in the following clause, which is indicated by the postposition *~node* (because).

(11)(a) *nedan mo yasukatta shi, ryuugakusei tachi mo kyoomi o shimeshita* ***node,***
price MO cheap-COP-and, overseas-students MO interest O show-PST **because**,
Because the price was very cheap, and the overseas students showed an interest,

(b) *kekkyoku karen kara risan made, tochuu no gaido o kanete noru koto ni shita.*
in the end Karen from Risan to, on the way NO guide O combine get on-PAST.
I decided he could be our guide from Karen to Risan and so let him pick us up.

(the *Sasaki text*)

The relation of result occurs when a clause or cluster provides a result of the actions, arguments or phenomena presented in the other clause or cluster. In Example 12, the following cluster provides the potential result of the action presented in the preceding cluster. The relation can be indicated by conjunctions such as *kekkateki ni* (consequently).

(12)(a) *rinen dake no hanashinara kaiseeshite mo gai wa nai to iu iken mo arukamoshirenai.*
ideal only NO talk-CJT revise MO harm WA exist-NEG TO IU opinion MO exist-CJT.

daga, hokoku wa kokkashijooshugiteki ni nattewa naranai to shitsutsumo,
however, the report WA nationalistic NI become-NEG-OBL-CJT-and MO,

'nihonjin' ya 'kokoro' ga kyoochoo sareteiru koto ga kininaru.
'Japanese' and 'Japanese feeling' GA emphasise-PASS NOMZ GA worry.

Some may say that there will be no harm done if only the ideals in the Act are changed. However, although the reports says that the change is not about evoking a strong sense of nationalism, we are concerned that it over emphasises feelings of 'Japanese-ness'.

(b) ***(kekkateki ni,)*** *hokano rinen ni kurabete kinkoo o*
CONJ other ideal NI compare balance O

kaku hodo toshutsu sure ba, ikisugi ni narikanenai.
lack to extent stand out-CND, going too far NI become-CJT.

(Consequently,) If they over emphasise this ideal in relation to others, this could become a great problem.

(the *Asahi text*)

The other type of causal-conditional relation is Condition. The relation of condition occurs when one clause or cluster enhances the comments, events or phenomena presented in the other clause or cluster by providing a condition to them. The relation of condition has two kinds: Positive or Concessive. Positive condition can further be divided into Hypothetical and Nonhypothetical. A hypothetical relation occurs where a condition presented in the enhancing clause or cluster is hypothetical. The polarity in the enhancing clause is positive (e.g. *mireba*, if one sees) as opposed to negative (e.g. *minakereba*, if one does not see). If the relation is hypothetical, the term *moshimo* (if) can be inserted before the enhancing clause or cluster. In Example 13, the included clause provides the hypothetical condition for the argument presented in the other clause to be the case. The relation is indicated by the verbal inflection *~ba.*

(13)(a) *kihonhoo ni morikomoo to suru koomoku wa, <<A>> unazukeru mono ga hotondo da.*
the Acts ni incorporate-VOL items WA, <<A>> acceptable item GA most-COP.
The items that are attempted to be incorporated in the Act, <<A>> are mostly acceptable.

(b) <<A>> = *<<(moshimo) hitotsu hitotsu o mire* ***ba,***>>
(CONJ) each individual O consider-CJT
if you consider the incorporation of each of these ideals individually,

(the *Asahi text*)

In a nonhypothetical relation, on the other hand, the condition that is presented in the enhancing clause is realis. In Example 14, the preceding clause provides the condition that was necessary for the event presented in the following clause to have occurred, and is indicated by the verbal inflection, *te* form. The term *moshimo* (if) cannot be attached for a nonhypothetical relation.

(14)(a) *busshitsu to seishin o setsuzen to wakeru dekarutoteki shikoo ni sasaerare* ***te,***
matter TO mind O clearly TO divide Descartian paradigm NI sustain-PASS-**SUSP**,
Sustained by Descartian philosophy which clearly separates the body and the soul,

(b) *kindaikagaku no taikee ga dekiagattekita.*
Modern science NO system GA established-PER-ASP.
the system of modern science developed.

(the *Kawai text*)

A concessive relation occurs when one clause or cluster enhances the other by providing a concessive argument or comment, etc. In Example 15, the preceding clause provides the concessive argument for the comment presented in the following cluster, and is indicated by the postposition *mo* in combination with the verbal inflection *te* form.

(15)(a) *eigo de hanashiteite* ***mo***
English by speak-ASP-**SUSP-CND**
even though (she) was speaking in English,

(b) *zettai, nihonjin ni chigainai*
without any doubt, Japanese NI-COP-PRO
without any doubt, (she) must be Japanese.

(the *Sasaki text*)

Another relation of ENHANCEMENT is the system of MANNER. The only type of manner presented in this corpus is MEANS. In the relation of means, a clause or cluster enhances the other by referring to means. In Example 15, the preceding clause enhances the following cluster by referring to the means of explanation. This is indicated by the verbal group plus the postposition *mochiirunara* (by using).

(16)(a) *kokode kiwamete tantekina hyoogen o* ***mochiiru nara,***
At this point, extremely short expression O **use-CND**,
By using a short expression, (it can be said that)

(b) *seiyooryuu no bunkatsu ni taishite, nihonryuu no tsunagari ga koo o sooshita node aru.*
Western way NO dividing toward, Japanese way NO networking GA the key to success-COP.
in comparison with the Western way of 'separating', the Japanese way of 'networking' was the key to success.

(the *Kawai text*)

The fourth and final subsystem of ENHANCEMENT is the relation of SPATIO-TEMPORAL. In this relation, a clause or cluster enhances the other by indicating the space or time in which the event occured. However, in this corpus, the relations of space and time are often expressed within a clause, as a circumstance in the transitivity structure rather than between clauses in a clause complex. However, although it was rare, the relation is sometimes expressed between clauses or clusters.

One type of the spatio-temporal type of relation is TIME. In this relation, the enhancing clause provides the time which the events presented in the enhanced clause occurred. In Example 17, the preceding clause provides the time when a taxi driver approached the writer and her students. The relation is indicated implicitly by the nonstructural connective *sono toki* (at that time).

(17)(a) *taihoku kara kisha ni nori, karen no eki ni oritatta toki no kotoda.*
Taihoku from train NI get on-PST, Karen NO station at get off-PST time NO event-COP.
It happened when we arrived a Karen station.

(b) ***(sono toki)*** *ryuugakusei to issho ni eigo de hanashiteiru watashi no sobade*
CONJ the overseas-students with together English DE speak I NO near-DE

'nee, nihonjin desho, wakarimasuyo. nottekudasaiyo' to
Hey, Japanese-COP-Q, (I) know-INT. get on-FOR-INT' TO

watashitachi ni tsukimatotte hanarenai takushii no untenshu ga ita.
we NI follow-SUSP leave-NEG taxi NO driver GA exist.

(at that time) There was a taxi driver who persistently followed us and when I was talking to the overseas students in English, and he said, 'You are Japanese, right? I knew it. Please take (my taxi)'.

(the *Sasaki text*)

Projection

At the entry of the nexus, the other most general type of logico-semantic relation is that of Projection. There are two types of Projection: Locution and Idea.

Locution

In the relation of locution, one clause projects another clause or clauses via 'a construction of *wording*', which is what is said or written (Halliday, 1994). It is often expressed by the quotative postposition: *~to* along with a *verbal* process. In Example 18, the following clause projects the preceding clause that presents what was said.

(18)(a) *'sore wa, watashi no eigo ga nihonjin no hanasu yoona eigo datta kara desuka'* ***to***
'that WA, I NO English GA Japanese NO talk-like English-COP-PST because-COP-Q **TO**
'Is that because my English is like the English that the Japanese speak?',

(b) *kiku...*
ask
(I) ask.

(the *Sasaki text*)

Idea

In the relation of idea, one clause projects another clause or clauses that presents the 'construction of *meaning*', which is 'what is thought' (Halliday, 1994). The relation is often expressed by the quotative postposition *~to* along with a *mental* process. In Example 19, the preceding clause is projected by the following one. The preceding clause presents what was thought.

(19)(a) *'kao wa nihonjin no yoodaga, nikkeijin ni chigainai'* ***to***
'face WA Japanese NO like-COP-CNJ, Japanese NI-COP-PRO' **TO**
'her face is like a Japanese, so she must be of Japanese descent'

(b) *omotta sooda.*
think-PST-TPI.
(I heard that he) thought.

(the *Sasaki text*)

Conjunctives in the corpus

Having now described the system network, it is possible to summarise the full set of conjunctives in the corpus that are used to indicate each kind of relation. This is illustrated in Table 2. The conjunctives in the table are only those examples which appeared in the corpus and are not an exhaustive list of conjunctive choices in Japanese.

The dominant logico-semantic relation in the corpus

In this corpus, the most frequent logio-semantic relation is ENHANCEMENT, which accounts for 53.7 % of the total relations. This number is far greater than those of any other logico-semantic relation, as shown in Figure 5.

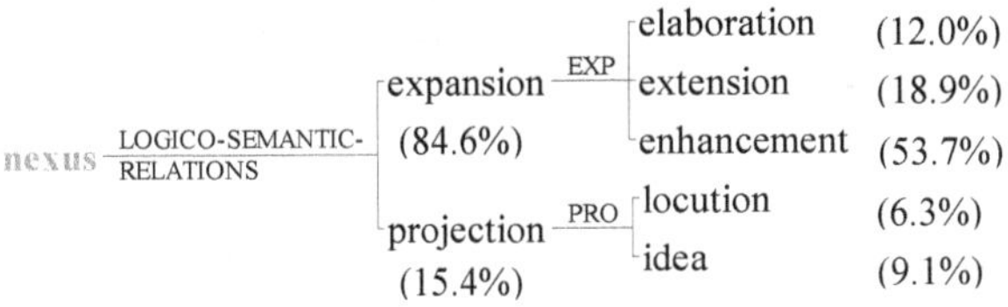

Figure 5: The frequency of the instances of the logico-semantic relations

Within the relations of enhancement, it is the causal-conditional type, especially the relations of reason and concessive, that occurs most frequently, as shown in Figure 6.

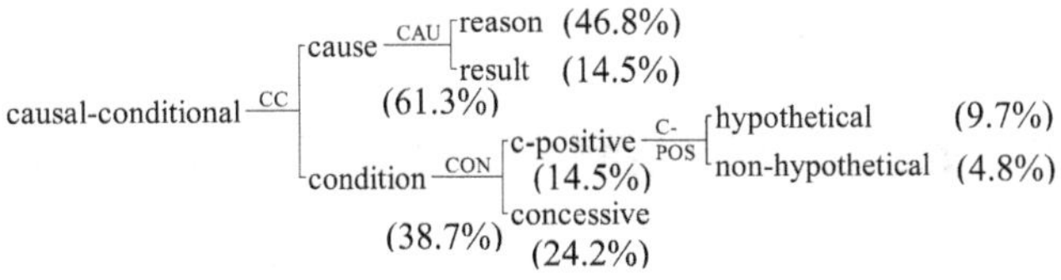

Figure 6: The frequency of the instances of causal-conditional types

Table 2: Conjunctive indication of the relations in the corpus

Categorisation of Logico-Semantic Relations			
Relations		recognition criteria: conjunctives	
		e.g. structural	e.g. non-structural
EXPANSION			
Elaboration (Ela)			
(a) appoisition (app)			
	expository (exp)		*tsumari*
	exemplifying (exe)		*tatoeba*
(b)clarification			
	particularising (par)		*tokuni*
	verifactive (ver)		*jitsunotokoro, jitsuwa*
	distractive (dis)		*tokorode*
	summative (sum)		Clause 49 in the Kawai text
Extension (Ext)			
(a) addition (add)			
	positive (pos)	*te-form, stem-form, -shi*	*mashiteya*
	adversative (adv)	*-ga, -keredomo, -keredo*	*shikashi, tokoroga*
(b) variation (var)			
	alternative (alt)		*aruiwa*
	replacive (rep)	*-yori*	
Enhancement (Enh)			
(a)matter (mat)		*-ni tsuite, -ni atatte*	
(b) causal-conditional			
cause (cau)			
	(1)reason (rea)	*te-form, stem-form, -to, -node, -kara*	*nazenara*
	(2)result (res)		*shitagatte, yueni, kekka to shite*
condition (cond)			
	(1)positive (pos)		
	(i)hypothetical (hyp)	*-ba, -nara*	*moshimo*
	(ii)non-hypothetical (non-hy)	te-form, -to	
	(2)concessive (conc)	*-ga, -mo with te-form, -nimokakawarazu, -daga, -noni*	*tokoroga*
(c) manner (man)			
	means (mea)	*-nara*	
(d)spatio-temporal			
temporal (tem)			*sonotoki*
PROJECTION (Pro)			
locution (loc)		*- to with verbal process*	
idea (idea)		*-to with mental process*	

Patterns of logico-semantic progression

Further, the logico-semantic relations in the corpus are patterned in four specific ways: the *right accumulative*, the *left accumulative*, the *stem accumulative* and the *nesting pattern*. Graphical representations of each pattern are provided in Figures 7~10.

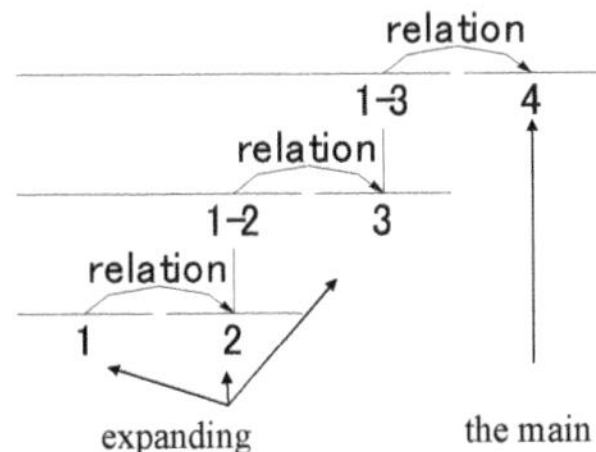

Figure 7: Right accumulative pattern

The right accumulative pattern is the progression type where a main clause or cluster, which is located ***at the end of the progression***, is expanded by a preceding clause or cluster that is further expanded by other preceding ones as in Figure 7. Accumulation builds towards the right. Expansion by preceding clauses or clusters may occur iteratively. This type is used when one event, argument or phenomenon leads to another and then another, culminating in the main clause. In Figure 7, Clause 1 leads to 2, Cluster 1–2 leads to Clause 3, and Cluster 1–3 leads to the main clause, which is Clause 4.

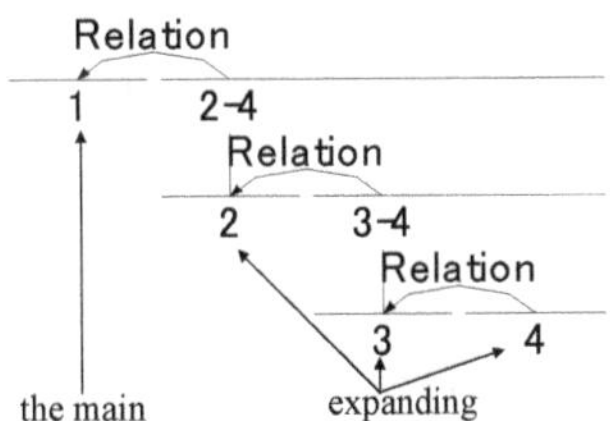

Figure 8: Left accumulative pattern

The left accumulative pattern is the progression type where the main clause or cluster, which is located ***at the beginning of the progression***, is expanded by the following clauses or clusters that are further expanded by other subsequent ones, as in Figure 8. In other words, the accumulation occurs towards the left. Like right accumulative progression, the expansion by subsequent clauses or clusters may occur iteratively. In Figure 8, Clause 1, which is the main clause, is expanded by Cluster 2–4; Clause 2 is expanded by Cluster 3–4; and Clause 3 is expanded by Clause 4.

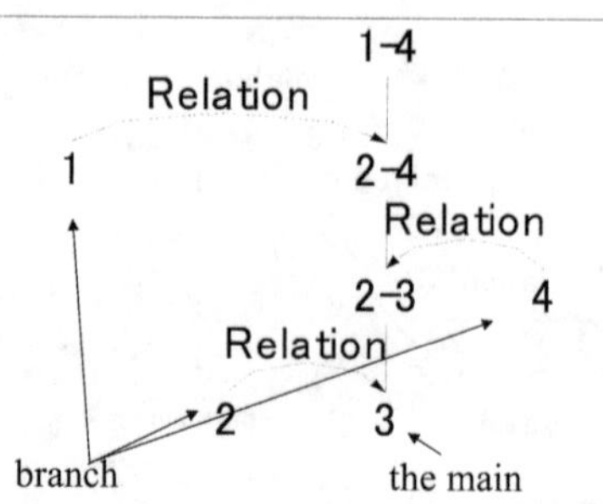

Figure 9: Stem accumulative pattern

The stem accumulative pattern is the progression type where a main clause or cluster acts as a stem. This stem is expanded by the other clauses which are further expanded up the stem as in Figure 9. This pattern is named stem accumulative because the main clause acts like the stem of a plant. The expanding clauses connect to the main stem on either the left or right side, and the accumulation builds from the bottom to the top. The accumulation can also occur iteratively. The expanding clauses or cluster may precede or follow the stem, although the expansion by preceding ones occurs more frequently in this corpus. In Figure 9, the stem is Clause 3, which is expanded by Clause 2. Cluster 2–3 is further expanded by Clause 4 and Cluster 2–4 is expanded by Clause1.

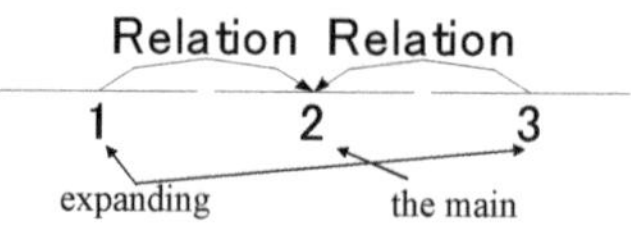

Figure 10: Nesting pattern

The nesting pattern is the progression type where a main clause or group of clauses is enhanced by more than one preceding or following clauses or clusters without accumulation, as seen in Figure 10. This progression type is different from the others in the sense that only one clause or one group of clauses is enhanced by others. It is used, for example, when a main argument is expanded with several circumstantial features. In Figure 10, Clause 2 is the main clause and it is expanded by Clause 1 and 3. This nesting represents a kind of localised pattern.

Among the four types, the patterns that are most prominent are the stem accumulative (57.7%) and right accumulative (32.1%), as shown in Figure 11. Left accumulative and Nesting rarely occur (Left accumulative pattern 7.7%, Nesting pattern 2.6%). The frequent use of the right and stem patterns occurs because the expanding clauses or clusters, which serve to accumulate evidence in support of the writer's arguments, typically precede the expanded clauses or clusters.

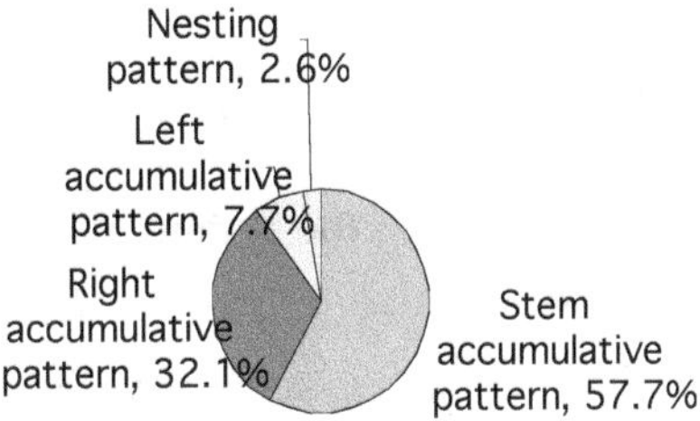

Figure 11: The percentage of the instances of progression patterns

There is a further pattern in the logico-semantic organisation of these texts which relates to the conflation of logico-semantic clusters with paragraphs. In this corpus, the boundaries between the logico-semantic clusters often correlate with the boundaries of paragraphs. For example, the logico-semantic clusters in the Asahi text match with all the paragraphs, except for Paragraph 13, as shown in Figure 12.[4] This finding is significant in the sense that it suggests that paragraphs in Japanese have a semantic function, which is in contrast to the common view that paragraphs in Japanese do not have a specific function. Rather paragraphs are available to be constructed at the creative whim of the writer (Okuma, 1992; Maynard, 1998). This research suggests compelling evidence to the contrary.

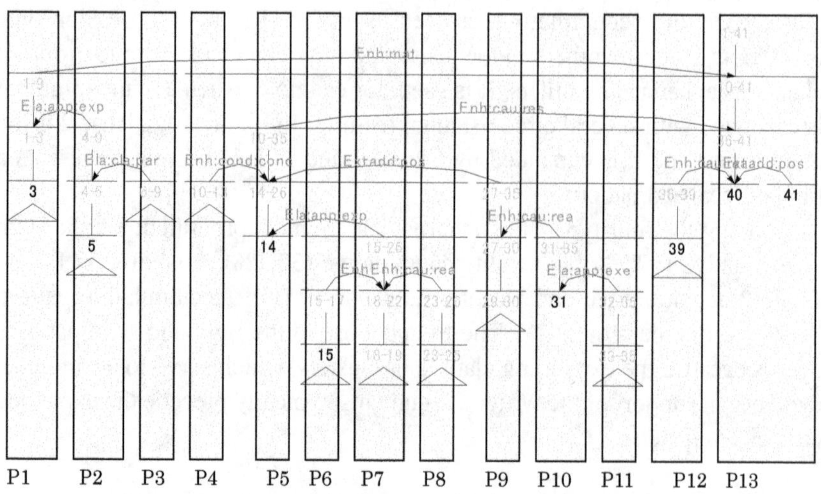

Figure 12: The correlation between paragraphs and logico-semantic groups

How to argue in Japanese: realising the system of logico-semantic relations in the expository texts

The previous section described the system network of the logico-semantic relations in the corpus and the patterns of logico-semantic progression. This section will discuss some of the salient characteristics of selections within that system and the patterns of progression which, in part, contribute to the social purpose of exposition. The discussion will demonstrate how an argument is constructed in Japanese by using the three expository texts as examples.

The results of the analysis give rise to a number of issues. The first relates to the social purpose of exposition in Japanese, which the analysis suggests may serve a different function to an exposition in English. In English, the social purpose is often defined using terms such as to 'convince' or to 'justify'. For example, Butt et al. (1995, p.17) defines it as 'to advance or justify an argument or put forward a particular point of view'.

In Japanese, it seems to be more appropriate to describe the social purpose of exposition as an opportunity to present an argument and ask readers to either share the same idea with the writer or merely to accept the writer's position. The social purpose is defined in this way because, unlike in English expositions, in this corpus, the writers gently or indirectly present their position for the readers' acceptance. The writers do not force their arguments upon the reader. The evidence of this can be seen in the writer's selection of the degree of differentiation of the logico-semantic relation. That is to say, the system of LOGICO- SEMANTIC RELATIONS is realised either with or without making delicate or less delicate choices. For example, in the Sasaki text, some instances of the relations are very specific, while others are more general or less delicate. In the example in Figure 13, the Sasaki text's writer made specific choices in actualising the system in the relations between Clause 40 and 41, where the relation type is 'enhancement: causal-conditional: cause: reason'. Here, the writer selected the highest degree of delicacy, which is that of 'reason'. The writer wanted to make it clear to the reader that the differentiated relation of 'reason' is salient in relation to the developing argument. This tendency occurs consistently between generic elements in the corpus, as these are the sites where the writer wants to be explicit and clear about the logical connections between the functions of the generic elements and the development of the rhetorical organisation.

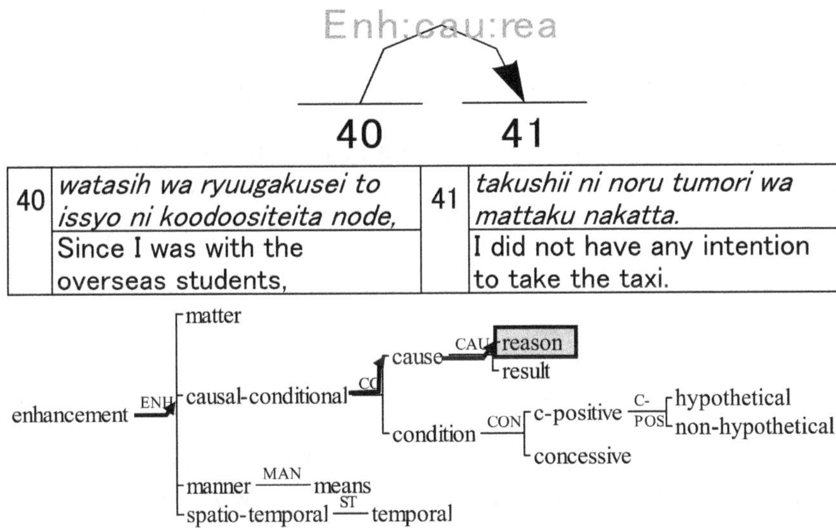

Figure 13: The writer's choices for the delicate relation between Clause 40 and 41

On the other hand, in the example in Figure 14, the writer selected a lower degree of differentiation in the relation of 'enhancement' between Clause 7 and 8, which is enhancement: causal-conditional. As the writer made the choice only to the point of 'causal-conditional', the enhancing relation between Clause 7 and 8 is ambiguous. Thus, the choice between 'reason' and 'condition' is left unclear.

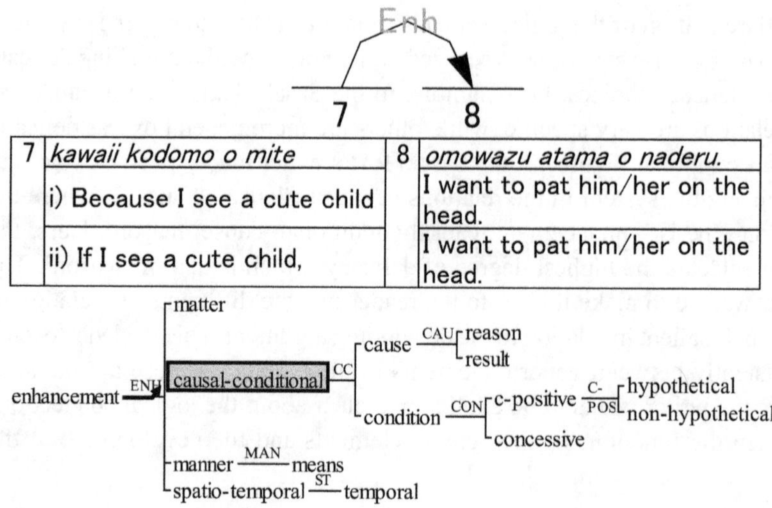

Figure 14: The writer's choice for the less delicate relation between Clause 7 and 8

When the writer does not differentiate, making less delicate choices, she or he leaves the option open for the reader to interpret the relation as they wish. The reader can either make the more delicate choices themselves or accept the ambiguous relation as it is. In either case, the reader is given an opportunity to infer their own meaning. This is typically found at the local level, that is to say, within generic elements but not between them. This is a less forceful way of stating one's point, giving the reader the opportunity to arrive at the writer's idea of their own accord, and is very different from the more direct strategy, which is typical of English exposition.

It is this ambiguous and indirect presentation of the position which is, in part, realised by the selection of the degree of differentiation, which allows the writer to provide some space for the reader to interpret the logico-semantic relations. In short, the writers select delicate relations when they need a clear and explicit logical construction, but when they need to avoid being too obvious with their logical construction so that they do not force their argument, the writers use the less delicate relations to ensure ambiguity.

A similar argument is claimed by Miyakoshi (1987), who states that in Japanese, a writer avoids arguing too clearly or obviously, since it might give the impression that the writer is forcing the reader to accept his or her argument. Instead, the writer just implies the logic and leaves it to the reader to arrive at the conclusion in their own way. As this strategy is employed by each text in the corpus, it may be possible to generalise and suggest that in Japanese exposition has an ambiguous and indirect logical structure which contributes to the social purpose of exposition as an opportunity to present an argument and ask readers to either share the same idea with the writer or merely to ask for acceptance of the writer's position.

The second issue arising out of the analysis is that all three expositions rely on the logico-semantic relation of enhancement in order to build up logical connections within each text. This would imply that the frequent realisation of enhancement is, more than likely, a generic feature of Japanese exposition. But what is more salient about the use of enhancement in the texts is the fact that it is strategically utilised **between** generic elements.

This strategic use is best seen through the lens of Generic Structure Potential. As described earlier, the three texts share the following common generic elements which are illustrated in Figure 15 using Hasan's (1984/96) GSP notation. [5]

Orientation ^ Argument • (Concession) ^ Thesis

Figure 15: The Generic Structure Potential of the three texts

In brief, the GSP of the three texts illustrates that:

1) The three expository texts share the generic elements of Orientation, Argument and Thesis. These elements can therefore be said to be obligatory;
2) The Concession element is optional, that is to say, it can occur but does not have to occur in an expository text;
3) The Argument element is iterative, that is to say, it can occur more than once;
4) The Orientation element, which is situated at the beginning of the text is followed by either the Argument(s) or Concession;
5) The Argument(s) and Concession element can change their position but they do not occur before the Orientation or after the Thesis; and
6) The Thesis is located last.

The point here is that the logical relations **between** the generic stages are **types of enhancement**. The three texts share both the same types of enhancement between the generic elements and also the same pattern of logico-semantic progression to link the other elements to the Thesis. This is illustrated in Figures 16–18.

The **Argument and Thesis** elements in the all three texts are connected by the relation of **reason**. The **Concessive and Argument** elements in the Kawai and the Asahi texts, which have a Concession, are connected by a **concessive** relation. The **Orientation elements and the remainder** of the each of the texts are connected by a relation of **matter.** The relations of reason, concession and matter are all kinds of enhancement. It is these choices within the system of ENHANCEMENT that serve to construe the logical development of an argument.

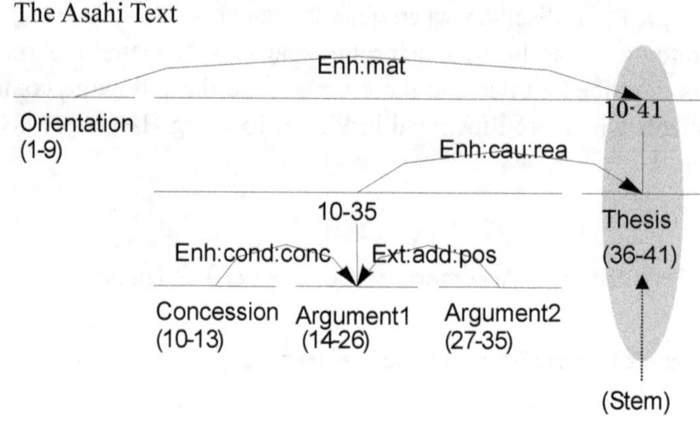

Figure 16: The logico-semantic relations between the generic stages (Asahi text)

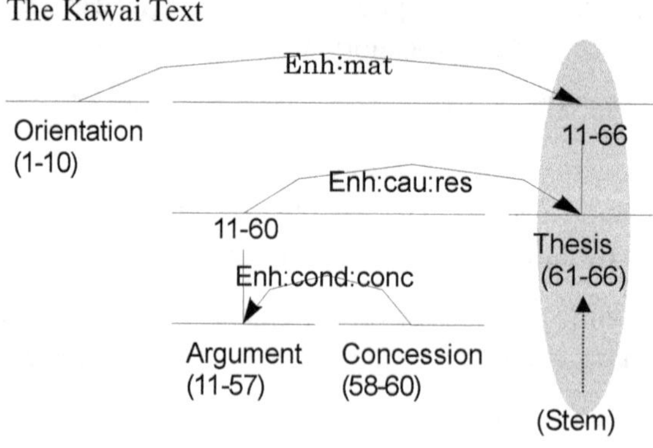

Figure 17: The logico-semantic relations between the generic stages (Kawai text)

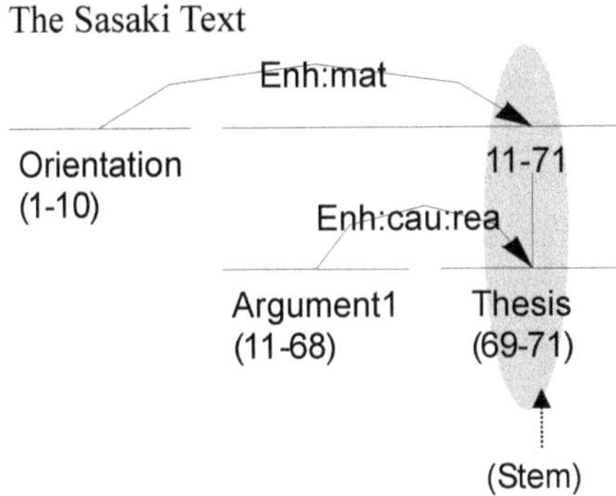

Figure 18: The logico-semantic relations between the generic stages (Sasaki text)

Another commonality between the texts is the fact that in each case, the **Thesis** element is logically developed using the **stem accumulative pattern** of logico-semantic progression. This is also illustrated in Figures 16–18. The Thesis is expanded by the other generic elements. In all the texts, the Thesis stage acts as the stem. The stem is enhanced by the other generic elements: in other words, the Orientation, Argument(s) and Concession logically support the Thesis.

In summary, the texts all share a common rhetorical organisation which serves to construe each text as an exposition. This commonality relates to the logical connections of enhancement between the generic elements and the choice of the stem pattern of logico-semantic progression building up to the Thesis. This is summarised in Table 3.

In addition, the common relations between generic elements serve to realise, in part, the functions of the elements. The relation of matter serves to realise the function of the Orientation, which is to provide the background or to set the scene for the ensuing discussion. The relation of reason serves to realise the function of the Argument(s), which is to provide justifiable reasons for the claim or Thesis. And similarly, the relation of concession serves to realise the function of the Concession element, which is to acknowledge the concessive or counter arguments in order to discount them in favour of the writer's arguments. In other words, there is a natural resonance between the function of the generic elements and the logico-semantic relations which link them to other elements. In this fashion, the logico-semantic relations between stages are naturally organised.

Apart from the logico-semantic relations between the generic elements contributing, in part, to the function of each element, there are also the choices of logico-semantic relations within each generic element which also serve, in part, to realise each of their respective functions. This is summarised in Table 3.

Table 3: How to argue in Japanese: A Systemic Functional Description of the selected Japanese expository texts

How to argue in Japanese – A Systemic Functional Description of Japanese exposition			
Social Purpose	To present an argument and ask readers to either share the same idea with the writer or to ask for acceptance of the writer's position		
Generic Structure	Orientation ^[Argument・(Concession)]^Thesis		
The system of LOGICO-SEMANTIC RELATIONS in the Japanese expository texts			
Between Generic Stages	The relations between generic stages • Orientation – the rest of stages : Matter • Argument- Thesis : Reason • Concession – Argument: Concessive • stem accumulative pattern		
Within Generic Stages	*Generic Stages*	*the types of Logico-semantic relations that occur in all the stages of the three texts*	*The pattern of Logico-Semantic Progression occurs in the all stages of the three texts*
	Orientation	Ela:app: exp Pro: loc	Stem accumulative pattern Right accumulative pattern
	Argument	Ela: app: exp Ext: add: adv Enh Enh: cau-con: cau: rea Enh: cau-con: cau: res Enh: cau-con: cau: conc Enh: cau-con: cond: pos Pro : idea Pro : loc	Stem accumulative pattern Right accumulative pattern Left accumulative pattern
	Thesis	Enhancement	Stem accumulative pattern
	Concession	Ext: add: pos	

The logico-semantic choices which may serve to realise the function of the Orientations in the three texts are the cause/conditional enhancing relations, the expository elaborating relation and the projecting relation of locution as illustrated in Figure 19.

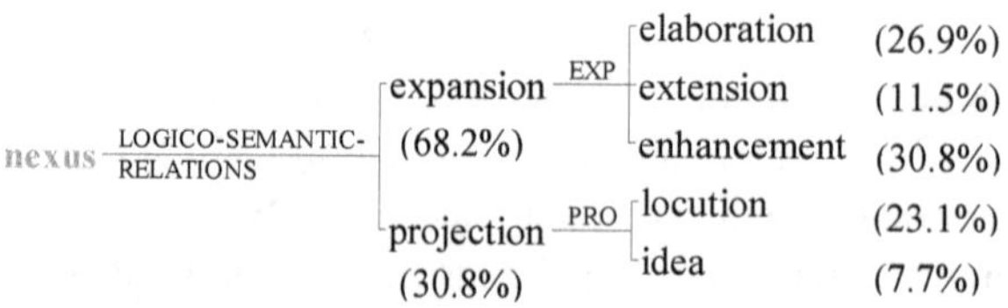

nexus — LOGICO-SEMANTIC-RELATIONS
- expansion (68.2%) — EXP
  - elaboration (26.9%)
  - extension (11.5%)
  - enhancement (30.8%)
- projection (30.8%) — PRO
  - locution (23.1%)
  - idea (7.7%)

Figure 19: The logico-semantic relations in the Orientation in all the texts

These relations play a role in providing the background or in setting the scene for the ensuing discussion in the following manner. The enhancing relations establish some kind of cause and effect which arises out of a description. The description is introduced using a projecting relation of locution which is further detailed by the expository elaborating relation.

The logico-semantic choices which may serve to realise the function of the Arguments in the three texts are from the system of ENHANCEMENT, as illustrated in Figure 20.

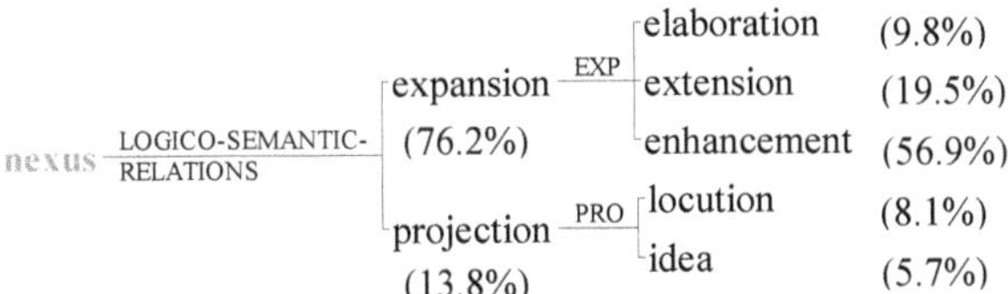

Figure 20: The logico-semantic relations in the Argument in the all the texts

Typically, each text employs either undifferentiated enhancement choices or more delicate choices of reason, concession or condition. These relations play a significant role in building up justifiable reasons for the claim or Thesis.

And similarly, the Thesis element typically includes relations of enhancement, particularly the relation of reason as in Figure 21.

nexus
LOGICO-SEMANTIC-RELATIONS
expansion (83.3%)
projection (16.7%)
EXP
PRO
elaboration (8.3%)
extension (25.0%)
enhancement (50.0%)
locution (0.0%)
idea (16.7%)

Figure 21: The logico-semantic relations in the Thesis in the all the texts

Again, this choice of relation serves to establish the writer's claim by logically connecting their position with their reason.

A final issue arising out of the analysis of the logico-semantic relations of the three expository texts is the conflation of logico-semantic clusters with paragraphs. This may imply that the boundaries between paragraphs are not random but oriented partially by the system of LOGICO-SEMANTIC RELATIONS. As previously mentioned, other studies (Okuma, 1992; Maynard, 1998) have suggested that the Japanese paragraph is flexible and that paragraph boundaries and paragraph size are random and depend on the writer's purposes. In other words, the size and the limit of paragraphs boundaries differ from text to text, so it is therefore hard to make any generalisations about the function of the paragraph in Japanese. However, the findings of this study suggest otherwise. In so far as the three expository texts are concerned, the paragraphing functions to delimit logico-semantically clustered clauses. This clustering, that is, the paragraphing, serves to isolate the logical relations which build the generic elements and which collectively construe the social purpose of persuasion. There is nothing at all random about this. It is highly motivated: the size of the paragraph depends on the number of clauses in the logico-semantic cluster; and the function of the paragraph depends on where the paragraph is located in the generic structure of the text.

Conclusion

This paper has illustrated how the system of LOGICO-SEMANTIC RELATIONS is used in three instances of Japanese exposition. In these texts, the system contributes to: i) the overall social purpose of the text; ii) the generic structure of the text; iii) the organisation of the generic elements within the text; and iv) to the structure and function of paragraphs.

The clauses in these texts are typically logically connected by the relation of enhancement. They cluster into logico-semantic sets which pattern in predictable ways. The most common patterns of clause clustering are the right accumulative and stem accumulative progression patterns. These patterns occur most frequently because the enhancing clauses or clusters tend to precede the enhanced clause or cluster.

Between the generic elements, the same types of logico-semantic relations and patterns of progression are found. The choice of relation is consistent with the function of the generic elements. These choices and the patterns in which they operate serve to construe the texts as expositions. However, unlike the relations between the generic elements which are common across the three texts, the choice of relations and patterns of progression within the generic stages are more varied. While the relation of enhancement and stem and right accumulative patterns of progression are dominant, there are other types of relations and patterns of progression which are not shared across the texts. This suggests that the individual style of a text can be found in the choices and patterns within the generic elements rather than between them. In a sense, it could be said that the genre is built up by the relations and patterns between the elements, while the individual style of the writer is built up by the relations and patterns within the elements. In addition, the system of logico-semantic relations appears to influence the process of paragraphing in Japanese. A logico-semantic cluster conflates with the paragraph.

So, how do you argue in Japanese? It seems that were you to model an exposition on the patterns evident in these three texts, then you would 'argue' using relations of enhancement, which are consistent and predictable between generic elements and which include an Orientation, Argument(s), a Thesis and sometimes a Concession. The generic elements occur in a fixed order: the Orientation is followed by Arguments(s), which is followed by the Thesis element, however, an optional Concessive element may occur before or after the Argument. The enhancing relation between the Orientation and the rest of the text is one of Matter; the enhancing relation between the Argument(s) and the Thesis is one of Reason; while the enhancing relation between a Concession element and the Argument is a concessive relation. You also need to be aware of how forcefully you make your point. It seems it is better to be ambiguous and indirect by making undifferentiated choices of cause/condition, rather than highly differentiated ones. And finally, you need to isolate the logico-semantic clusters as paragraphs both within generic elements and/or as complete generic elements.

Notes

1 The romanised versions and English translations of the three texts appear at the end of the chapter.

2 The abbreviations of the types are described in Table 2.

3 *ryakusuto* can alternatively be analysed as a clause rather than a conjunctive. However, in this case, *ryakusuto* is treated as a conjunctive since it is grammaticalised and functions as a grammatical item indicating a summarising relation rather than as a lexical item.

4 The reason why Paragraph 13 is not correlated with logico-semantic cluster is because the writer did not include the reason for the main argument presented in Paragraph 13 as a part of it, but separated as another paragraph as Paragraph 12. However, other than this, the paragraphs conflate with the logico-semantic clusters.

5 GSP represents the varieties of text structures under a particular situational type, or under what Hasan calls a 'contextual configuration', which is a configuration of the discourse of Field, Tenor and Mode (Hasan, 1984/96, Matthiessen, 1995). Hasan's notion of Generic Structure Potential (GSP) is used to account for the expected variation of the generic structures within the three persuasive texts of the corpus.

Acknowledgement

This study was conducted as a part of BA(Honours) and Ph.D research work at University of Wollongong. We would like to thank Faculty of Arts, University of Wollongong for their financial assistance in the form of conference support which contributed to the development of this study.

We are grateful to Asahi Newspaper for allowing us to describe and discuss their editorial in this chapter.

Notations Key

ASP: aspect, CJT: conjecture, CND: condition, CONJ: conjunctive, COP: copula, DE: enhancement marker, FOR: formal form of the verb, GA: particle *ga*, INT: interpersonal key, MO: additional referntial marker, NEG: negation, NI: particle *ni*, NO: nominal marker, NOMZ: nominaliser, O: particle *o*, OBL: obligation (e.g. *–subeki*), PASS: passive, PER: perfect, PRO: probability, PST: past, Q: question marker (e.g. *–ka*), SUSP: suspensive form, TO: postpositional quotative particle, TO IU: definig modifier, TPI: third party information (e.g. *-sooda*) VOL: volitional marker, WA: particle *wa*

Appendix

Kyoiku kihonhoo – riso moteasobu hima wa nai (The Fundamentals of the Education Act – there is no time for playing around with ideals), _Asahi Shimbun_ (Asahi Newspaper), 15 Nov 2002

Note: the number in the '( )' indicates unit number, which are *typically* clauses.

Japanese	Translation
¶1(1)'21seeki o kirihiraku kokoro yutaka de takumashii nihonjin o sodateru'. (2)sore ga aratana kyooiku no mokuhyoo da, to (3)chuuoo-kyooiku-shingikai ga chuukan hookoku o matometa.	¶1(1)'Raising broadminded and strong Japanese young people who can explore the 21st century'. (2) This is the new aim of education (3)as concluded by the Central Education Discussion group in their interim report.
¶2(4)sono mokuhyoo jitsugen no tame kyooiku kihonhoo o kaiseeshinakerebanaranai, to (5) iunodearu.	¶2(5)The CED says (4)that we have to revise the Act in order to realise the new aim.
¶3(6)hokoku wa, (7)<<kihonhoo ni aru 'kojin no songen' ya 'jinkaku no kansei' no rinen wa korekara mo taisetsu daga,>>(8)<<aratana rinen ya gensoku to shite, daigaku kaikaku no sokushin ya katei no kyooiku-ryoku no kaifuku no hoka, 'kookyoo' ni kansuru kihan no saikoochiku nado o morikomuyoo>> motometa. (9)kookyoo ni kansuru kihan ni wa, dentoo ya bunka no sonchoo, kyoodo ya kuni o aisuru kokoro, kokusaisei no shiten mo fukumareru.	¶3(6)The report recommends (8)university reform and improvements in raising children as well as redefining community ideals in the Act, (7)although the report also commented that the existing ideals of 'individual dignity'and 'mature identity' are important for the future. (9)In redefining community ideals, ideals such as respect for tradition and culture, the development of patriotism and the development of an international outlook need to be incorporated.
¶4(10)kihonhoo ni morikomootosuru koomoku wa, (11)<<hitotsu hitotsu o mireba,>> unazukeru mono ga hotondoda. (12)umare-sodatta tochi no dentoo ya bunka o taisetsu ni suru no wa darenimo iron wa arumai. (13)kyoodo ya kuni o aisuru no mo shizenna kokoro-daroo.	¶4(11)If you consider the incorporation of each of these ideals individually, (10)then they are mostly acceptable. (12)Nobody would object to taking good care of their tradition and culture. (13)It is natural to love one's own home and country.
¶5(14)mazu mondai wa, rinen o kihonhoo ni kuwaeru koto de, kodomo tachi o torimaku shinkokuna jookyoo o kooten-saserareruka doo ka dearu.	¶5(14)The problem is the fact that we do not know for sure whether we can improve the education of children by simply adding new ideals or principals to the Act.

Japanese	Translation
¶6(15)watashitachi wa koremade, (16)<<bunshoo o ijiru yori,>> (17)<<hooritsu no mokuteki o jitsugensuru gutaitekina hoosaku o saguru no ga senketsu da, to >> shuchooshitekita.	¶6(15)Those of us at Asahi have been saying (17)that they should first determine the strategies that need to be in place to realise the aims of the Act, (16)rather than just play with the words in the Act.
¶7(18)konkai matomatta hookoku o yonde mo, (19) sonokangae wa kawaranai. (20)inshitsuna ijime ya gakkyuuhookai, benkyoo o suru iyoku no teika, aruiwa tanin o omoiyaru kokoro no nai koto nado, kaiketsusubeki mondai wa yamahodo aru noni, (21)konkai no hookoku ga kimete ni naru towa (22)omoenai.	¶7(18)Even though, we have read the interim report, (19)our view has not changed. (20)While ever there remains no solution to the problems of insidious bullying, classroom disruption, the decline in the motivation to study and the loss of duty of care to others, (22)we cannot believe (21)that the report will be the key to improving the situation.
¶8(23)genkoo no kihonhoo wa, sekinin ya kinroo, seigi, bunka o omonjiru shisei o meikaku ni shiteiru. (24)sorera ga kichinto jitsugensareteireba, (25)kyooiku ga konnani koohaisuru koto wa nakattanoda. (26)shingi de wa, kako no kyooiku-gyoosei no kenshoo ya hansei, bunseki wa juubun-dewa-nakatta.	¶8(23)The current Act clearly emphasizes the importance of responsibility, diligence, justice and culture. (24)Had these been properly realized, (25)the decline in education standards would not have happened. (26)In the CED's discussion, the verification, re-examination and analysis of the past administration of education were not satisfactory.
¶9 (27)rinen dake no hanashinara kaisee shitemo gai wa nai to iu iken mo arukamoshirenai. (28) daga, hookoku wa kokka-shijoo-shugi-teki ni nattewanaranai to shitsutsu mo, 'nihonjin' ya 'kokoro' ga kyoochoosareteiru koto ga kininaru. (29)hokano rinen ni kurabete kinkoo o kaku hodo tosshutsu sureba, (30)ikisugi ni narikanenai.	¶9(27)Some may say that there will be no harm done if only the ideals in the Act are changed. (28) However, although the reports says that the change is not about evoking a strong sense of nationalism, we are concerned that it over emphasizes feelings of 'Japanese-ness'. (29)If they over emphasise this ideal in relation to others, (30)this could become a great problem.
¶10(31)sudeni shinpaisareru ugoki mo deteiru.	¶10(31)Such a worrying movement is already emerging.
¶11(32)fukuoka-shinai no shoogakkoo de wa, tsuuchihyoo ni kuni o aisuru shinjoo, sekai no naka no nihonjin no jikaku ni tsuite hyooka suru koomoku o mooketeiru tokoro ga kanari aru. (33) shizen ni waki okorubeki kokyoo ya kuni o aisuru kokoro o seiseki toshite chekku sureba, (34)ii seiseki o toritai kodomo wa kyooshi no shidoo ni shitagau daroo. (35)shikashi, sore de kokyoo ya kuni o aisuru kokoro ga hontoo ni sodatsudarooka.	¶11(32)At primary schools in Fukuoka City, (many schools have established) a section in the grade record that assesses how much the students love their country and their level of awareness as Japanese in the world. (33)If teachers mark how much the students love their nation, (which should develop naturally), (34) the students who'd like to achieve a high mark would follow the teacher's instruction. (35)However, would this really contribute to the development of a love for one's nation?
¶12(36)monbu kagakushoo no shudoo de hookoku wa konomama tooshin ni kawari, (37)kaisei-kihon-hooan-zukuri ni susumikanenai. (38)sore wa yagate shidoo-yooryoo no kaitei ya koremade ijoo no kyooiku-genba e no tettei to naru. (39)rinen wa rinen ni todomarazu, baai ni yotte wa yugami o shoozuru koto mo aru.	¶12(36)If the Ministry of Education, Culture, Sports, Science and Technology follows the recommendations of the CED, (37)the report could become official and the government could proceed to rewrite the Fundamentals of Education Act. (38)This would eventually result in the revision of the teaching curriculum and the enforcement of the ideals in the classroom and elsewhere. (39)There will be cases where the interpretation of these ideals will differ and create problems.
¶13 (40)kyooiku no genjoo o dakai-suru no ni, yuukoona shohoosen to wa ienai. (41)rinen o moteasondewaikenai.	¶13(40)Revising the Act is not going to effectively solve the problems in education. (41)The CED should not play with the ideals.

Kawai, H. 2001 '*Nihonjin to kosei*' (Japanese and Individuality), *Taiwa suru ningen* (Humans in conversations), Kodansha, Tokyo, pp.153–156

Japanese	Translation
¶1(1)rinji-kyooiku-shingikai (rinkyooshin) de 'kosei no sonchoo' to iu koto ga taisetsu na rondai to natte iru yoodearu. (2)seito no kosei o nobasu kyooiku o shinakute wa naranai, (3)arui wa, seito no kosei o tsubusu yoona kakuitsu-shugi no kyooiku wa ikenai, nado to (4)iwareru. (5)konoyoona iken ni taishite wa dare mo sansei suru de arooshi, (6) nijuuisseeki no kyooiku o kangaeru ue de, seito no kosei no sonchoo to iu koto ga taisetsu de aru koto niwa, dareshimo hantaishinaide aroo to (7)omowareru.	¶1(1)At the meeting of the EED group, the issue of 'the respect for the individual' was the heart of the discussion. (4)It is often said (2)that education should develop students' individuality (3)or, at least should not hamper the development of a student's individuality through a uniform education. (7)I think (5)that people would agree with this (6)and no-one would object to the idea that respect for the students' individuality is an important consideration in education in the 21st century.
¶2(8)konna ten mo atte, (9)'jiyuuka' nado to iu butsugi o kamoshi soo na kotoba ni kawatte, 'kosei no sonchoo' to iu kotoba ga rinkyooshin demo detekita to sae (10)omowareru no dearu.	¶2(10)I think that (8)because respect for the students' individuality is considered important in education in the 21st century, (9)the term, 'respect for individuality' was used at the EED meeting rather than a term like 'liberalisation', which potentially could cause controversy.
¶3(11)shikashi, kokode kiwamete juudai na mondai wa, (12)<<somosomo 'kosei' to wa nanika to iu ten ga aimai na mama ni hoochi sareru,>> (13)<<aruiwa, kosei to iu ten ni tsuite tagiteki na kaishaku ga sonzai suru mama,>> sore ga gutaiteki na kyooiku-seedo ya, kyooiku-hoohoo ni musubi tsukerareru osore ga aru to iu koto de aru.	¶3(11)However, the important issue here is that there is a danger in using the term individuality as it can affect the methods and practices in the education system (12)as the term is ambiguous (13)and open to multiple interpretations.
¶4(14)kosei to iu go o 'koojien' de hiku to, (15) sono shita ni wazawaza (individuality) to iu eigo ga kakareteiru. (16)konokoto wa, kono gainen ga seiyoo kara kita mono de ari, sono haigo ni seiyoo-kindai ni oite kakuritsu sareta 'kojin-shugi' to iu koto ga sonzai shiteiru koto o shimeshiteiru.	¶4(14)If I look up the term 'kosei' in the dictionary, (15)the English word, individuality is purposefully listed. (16)This fact implies that this concept came from the West, and that behind it, there is the notion of individualism which developed in modern Western culture.
¶5(17)kojin (individual) to iu kotoba wa ikura bunkatsushitemo, bunkatsushienai saisyoo-tani to iu kangae ga, sono eigo no tango kara sasserareru. (18)soshite, sore wa monogoto o 'bunkatsu' suru koto, 'kubetsu suru' koto ni omoki o oku shisei ni sasaerareteiru. (19)seiyoo-kindai no kagaku wa, kono 'bunkatsu' suru kinoo o furu ni hatarakaseru koto ni yotte ningen ga utitatetekita mono de aru.	¶5(17)The term 'individual' implies the notion that the individual is the smallest unit that cannot be further divided. (18)And this notion is sustained by the Western attitude that emphasises separation and distinction. (19)This separation or differentiation is the basis on which modern Western science was established.

Japanese	Translation
¶6(20)busshitsu to seishin o setsuzen to wakeru dekaruto-teki-shikoo ni sasaerarete (21) kindaikagaku no taikei ga dekiagatte kita. (22) konoyoona kagaku o hatten saseru shikoo to, ningen no 'ko'o sonchoo suru taido wa kittemo kirenai kankei ni aru. (23)shikashi jissai no tokoro, nihonjin wa seiyoojin to onaji imi ni okeru 'ko' o motteiru darooka. (24)hissha wa sono ten ni tsuite, oobeijin to nihonjin wa sootoo ni kotonaru to (25) kangaeteiru.	¶6(20)Sustained by Descartian philosophy which clearly separates the body and the soul, (21)the system of modern science developed. (22)There is an inseparable relationship between this type of thought found in Western science and respect for individuality. (23)However, when considering the reality, do Japanese and Western people share the same meaning of the term 'ko' (individual)? (25) I think (24)that the Japanese 'ko' and the Western 'individual' are distinctively different.
¶7(26)koko de higa no 'kosei' ni tsuite kangae saserareru hitotu no episoodo o shookai shiteokitai.	¶7(26)At this point, I'd like to introduce an episode that make us think about the difference between 'individuality' in Japan and the West.
¶8(27)imanishi kinji hakushi o chooten to suru, nihon no reichoorui-kenkyuu wa kokusaiteki ni takai hyooka o eteiru koto wa shuuchi no toori de aru. (28)tokorode oobei no aru gakusha wa, (29)<<imanishi-hakushi no riron ya, (30)<<(sore wa seibutsu no shu o zentai to shite miyootosuru kihonteki shisei o motsu)>> nihonjin no ippanteki tokusei nado kara ruisokusite,>> (31)<<imanishi guruupu wa zentaiteki-shugi de hi-koseiteki de naika,>> (32)<<tsumari, guruupu no kakujin ga sootoo ni kakuitsu-teki na sonzai de wa naika to>> kangaete (33)rainichishita.	¶8(27)It is well known that the Japanese research group studying primates, led by Imanishi Kinji has an internationally high reputation. (28–30) By the way, basing his views on the Imanishi group's research and on his knowledge of the general characteristics of the Japanese, (33)a Western scientist visiting Japan (31)assumed that the researchers in the Imanishi group were group-orientated and 'non-individualialist', (32)that is to say, the group members were assumed to be uniform.
¶9(34)yattekite sugu wakatta koto wa, imanishi guruupu no gakusha tachi wa kakuitsu-teki dokoroka, hitori hitori ga kiwamete dokusooteki de aru to iu koto de atta. (35)to ittemo, (36)sore wa seiyoojin ga kangaeru imi deno koseiteki to iu no demo nakatta. (37)sonotameni, sono hito wa imanishi guruupu no hito tachi no kenkyuu o hajimeyootosuru no daga, (38)sono ten ni tsuite wa shooryakusuru.	¶9(34)What he understood upon his arrival was that each member of the Imanishi group was very unique and not group-oriented at all. (35)Despite having understood this, (36)the Imanishi group were however, not individualistic in the Western sense. (37)As a result of the mis-match in terms of individuality, the Western scientist began to research the Imanishi group, (38)but apart from this I won't elaborate further.
¶10(39)kokode naze sonoyoona gokai ga shoojitaka ni tsuite, (40)hissha no kangae o shirushitemiru. (41)seiyoo no kindai-kagaku no konpon ni wa 'bunkatsu' ga aru to (42) nobeta. (43)shitagatte sore ni yorunaraba, ningen to saru to wa kotonaru sonzai de aru koto o mazu meikakunishi, kansatsu suru shutai to shite no ningen to, kansatsusareru kyakutai to shite no saru to no aida ni wa kakuzen to shita kubetsu ga sonzaisuru koto ni naru.	¶10(39–40)At this point, I will attempt to explain my idea about the reasons why such a misunderstanding occurred. (42)I mentioned (41) that there is the notion of separation underpinning modern Western science. (43)Thus, based on this idea, when a Western scientist approaches the task of researching, say for example, primates, there is a separation between the researcher who is observing and the object under investigation, in this case, the primate.

Japanese	Translation
¶11(44)shikashi, waga kuni no reichoorui-kenkyuu ga oobeijin no soozoo o dasshita kyoomibukai seika o ageta konpon ni wa, nihon no gakusha tachi ga sudeni nobeta yoona taido dewa naku, (45) kansatsusha to hi-kansatsusha tono bunkatsu o, dekirukagiri sukunakusuru yoona kihon-shisei o motteita kara nano de aru. (46)kokoni wa shoojutsu wa dekinaiga, (47)sore wa nihon no reichoorui-kenkyuu-guruupu no ronbun o yomeba (48) dareshimo kizuku koto dearu.	¶11(44)However, from the Japanese scientists' point of view, there is an attempt to reduce the gap as much as possible between observers and the observed objects. (45)This is a different style to the Western approach and is what surprised the Western scientist about the Imanishi group. (46) While not going into detail, (47)this is the thing that everyone notices when they read the Imanishi report.
¶12(49)kokode kiwamete tanteki na hyoogen o mochiiru nara, (50)seiyooryuu no bunkatsu ni taishite, nihonryuu no tsunagariga koo o sooshita node aru. (51)konoyoona ten ni nomi oobeijin ga chuumokusuru toki, (52)<<kono gakusha tachi wa individualistic dewa nai,>> (53)<<shitagatte zentaishugiteki da nado to>> sokudanshita node aroo.	¶12(49)By expressing it in a concise form, (50)in comparison with the Western way of 'separating', the Japanese way of 'networking' was the key to success in discovering the findings in relation to the primates. (51)The Western scientist observed the Imanishi group's methodology of networking (52)and concluded that they were non-individualistic and (53)hence group-oriented.
¶13(54)imanishi-guruupu no gakusha ga dokusooteki de aru koto wa seiyoojin mo mitomeru. (55)shikashi, kokode karera wa osoraku kojinteki (individualistic) to iu kotoba wa tsukawanaidearoo. (56)nooberu-shoo-jushoosha, fukui kenichi hakushi no chosho ni mo ('gakumon no soozoo'), 'shizen ni kumikomareta kagaku' 'shizen o sonkeisuru kagaku' o mokuhoo to shitai to iu kotoba ga mitomerareru. (57)kokonimo, ningen o shizen kara kirihanashi, sore o kansatsusuru to iu taido towa kotonaru shisei ga meiryoo ni mirareru nodearu.	¶13(54)Western people also acknowledge that the Imanishi group is unique. (55)However, they would not use the term individualistic to describe the group. (56)In the books written by Dr. Fukui Kenichi, who received the Nobel Prize, we find phrases such as 'the science embedded in nature' and 'constructing a science which respects nature'. (57)Here again, is an example of the attitude that is different from the one that separates humans as observers from nature.
¶14(58)nihonjin dakara nihonjin rashii tokusei o hakkishite . . . nado to iu kechikusai ryooken dewanaku, (59)jitsunotokoro, oobei ni oitemo seiyoo-kindai-kagaku no minaoshi, kojin-shugi no minaoshi wa hajimaritsutsuaru no dearu. (60) sudeni nobeta gakusha tachi ga kokusaiteki ni mitomerareru no mo, jitsuwa, oobei to kotonaru shiten o motsu kara nado to iu node wa naku, seiyoo-kindi o koete nijuuisseeki ni mukau kagakusha to shite, jidai o sakidorisuru mono o kanjisaseru kara de aru to iu hoo ga datoo de aroo.	¶14(58)Let's not take the small-minded notion that the Japanese are uniquely Japanese, (59)because, as a matter of fact, the nature of individuality and modern science is being reconsidered in the West. (60)It is appropriate to think that the reason why the scientists mentioned above (Dr. Imanishi and Dr. Fukui) are internationally accepted is, not because they have a different viewpoint from the West, but because they have a new attitude towards the 21st century surpassing that of modern Western science.
¶15(61)koo kangaeru to, (62)kosei to iu mono no honshitsu, sono imi ni tsuite sootoo na shisaku ga hitsuyoo to (63)omowareru. (64) mashiteya, jiyuu na kyoosoo ni yotte koso kosei ga migakareru, to iu seiyoo-kindai ni tuuyooshita moderu o nijuuisseeki no kyooiku o kangaeru ba de furimawashite mitemo, (65)sore wa amari minoarumono ni naru to wa (66) kangaerarenainodearu.	¶15(61)When you think like this, (62–63)it is necessary to consider the nature and meaning of individuality in depth. (64)Even more, (66)<<I cannot believe>> that using the typical modern Western concept of individuality, which develops through 'liberated competition', as suggested by certain educators, (65)will bear fruit.

Sasaki, M. 1994 *'Nihonjin rashisa to iu koto'* (The meaning of being Japanese), *Gaikokugo to shite no nihongo* (Japanese as a foreign language), Kodansha, Tokyo, pp.234–237

Japanese	Translation
¶1(1)kono shoo no saigo ni natta ga, (2)'nihonjin rashisa' towa nan nanoka ni tsuite kangaete mitai. (3) nihongo kyooiku towa, nihongo o oshieru koto ni yotte, nihonjin no gengo-koodoo o rikaisaseru koto da to (4)iwareru. (5)gengo-koodoo wa, sorezore ga kizokusuru koyuu no bunka ni yotte kotonaru.	¶1(1) Even though the chapter is at an end, (2) I'd like to take the opportunity to consider the meaning of Japanese-ness. (4)It is often said (3) that Japanese language education (for foreign students) is about understanding Japanese language behaviour. (5)That is, language behaviour is different depending on the culture in which one belongs.
¶2(6)sorede wa, wareware no gengokoodoo towa nannanodaroo. (7)kawaii kodomo o mite (8) omowazu atama o naderu. (9)nihon no shakai no naka dewa goku atarimae no kooi ga, aite ga taijin no baai niwa shitsurei na kooi ni ataru. (10)kooitta muishiki no koodoo ga, nihonjin-shakai no naka de seibetsu, nenrei, chiiki nado ni kakawarinaku okonawareru toki, sore o 'nihonjin no gengo-koodoo' to ittemo yoinodewa naidarooka.	¶2(6)Having said that, one wonders what our language behaviour is like? (7)For example, when looking at a cute child, (8)we feel like patting them on the head. (9)Although this is a natural behaviour for the Japanese, it is impolite behaviour for Thai people. (10)When this kind of natural behaviour occurs in Japanese society. we call it Japanese language behaviour regardless of sex, age and location.
¶3(11)nihonjin no gengo-koodoo ni tsuite kangaeru toki, kanarazu to itte yoi hodo omoidasu dekigoto ga aru. (12)suunin no ryuugakusei to issho ni taiwan o ryokooshita toki no, wasurerarenai kioku no hitokoma da.	¶3(11)When I think about Japanese language behaviour, there is an episode that I always recall. (12)It is a memory that I cannot forget – an episode where I went to Taiwan with a few overseas students.
¶4(13)taihoku kara kisha ni nori, karen no eki ni oritatta toki no kotoda. (14)ryuugakusei to issho ni eigo de hanashiteiru watashi no sobade 'nee, nihonjin desho, wakarimasuyo. nottekudasaiyo' to watashitachi ni tsukimatotte hanarenai takushii no untenshu ga ita. (15)saigo niwa konmakeshite, (16)sonotakushii de risan made iku koto ni shita ga, (17)joozu na nihongo de hanasu untenshu-san no hanashi wa, hijoo ni kyoomibukai mono datta.	¶4(13)It happened when we arrived a Karen station. (14)There was a taxi driver who persistently followed us when I was talking to the overseas students in English, and who said, 'You are Japanese, right? I knew it. Please take (my taxi)'. (15)In the end, I gave up rejecting him, (16)and decided to take his taxi to Risan, 917)but the conversation with the driver, who spoke Japanese very well, was very interesting.
¶5(18)hajime ryuugakusei to eigo de hanashiteiru watashi o mite, (19)'kao wa nihonjin no yoodaga, nikkeijin ni chigainai' to (20)omoatta sooda.	¶5(18)At first, as he watched me speaking English, (20)he thought, (19)'her face is like a Japanese, so she must be of Japanese descent'.

Japanese	Translation
¶6(21)tokoro ga, shibaraku watashi no yoosu o miteite, (22) eigo de hanashitewa ite mo (23)'zettai, nihonjin ni chigainai' to (24)omotta sooda. (25) 'sore wa, watashi no eigo ga nihonjin no hanasu yoona eigo datta kara desuka' to (26)kiku to, (27) 'watashi wa, eigo wa zenzen wakarimasen' to (28)ii, (29) miburi, jesuchaa ga nihonjin koyuu no mono datta node (30) nihonjin to kentoo o tsuketa noda to (31)iu.	¶6(21)However, after more watching, (24)he thought (22)that even though I was speaking in English, (23)without any doubt, I must be Japanese. (25)'Is that because my English is like the English that the Japanese speak?', (26) I asked. (27)'I don't understand English at all', (28)He said. (31)Rather, he said that (30) he guessed I was Japanese (29)because of my body language and gestures which he said, were 'unique' to the Japanese.
¶7(32)sono untenshu-san wa, nihon ga taiwan o tooji shiteita koro shoogakkoo datta to (33)iu. (34) umeboshi no haitta obentoo o tabe, (35)nihonjin no sensei ga jugyoo o tantooshita.	¶7(32)This driver was a primary school student when Japan had sovereignty over Taiwan. (33)So he said. (34)He ate a Japanese lunch of pickled plum and (35)had a Japanese teacher in charge of his class.
¶8(36)sonokoro oboeta nihongo wa shuusei minitsuki, (37)ima, nihongo ga hanaseru untenshu toshite nihonjin no okyakusan o sagashite wa (38)noserunoda to (39)iu.	¶8(39)He said (36)that Japanese was the language that he learnt at that time and that it has become a skill for life. (37)Now, as a taxi driver who can speak Japanese, he looks for Japanese customers and (38)picks them up.
¶9(40)watashi wa ryuugakusei to issho ni koodooshiteita node, (41)takushii ni noru tumori wa mattaku nakatta. (42)ryuugakusei tachi to eigo de hanashinagara, untenshu o furikitte arukitsuzukeru watashitachi o, sono untenshu wa shitsuyoo ni oikakete kite (43)'nee, nihonjin desho. (44) wakatteirundesuyo. (45)annaisasete kudasai yo' to (46)ittanoda. (47)nedan mo yasukatta shi, (48) ryuugakusei tachi mo kyoomi o shimeshita node, (49) kekkyoku karen kara risan made, tochuu no gaido o kanete (50)noru koto ni shita. (51)kare wa wareware no yado made sagashite kureta. (52) taiwan-toochi-jidai ga natsukashii to (53)kare wa nankai mo itteita. (54)watashi no motsu fuinki ga kareno omoo nihonjin rashisa ni gachishita noda tomo.	¶9(40)Since I was with the overseas students, (41)I didn't intend to take a taxi. (42)The taxi driver persistently followed me while I was talking with the students. I tried to turn him down and kept walking. (46)He said, (43)'You're Japanese, aren't you? (44)I knew it! (45)Please let me pick you up'. (47)Because the price was very cheap, and (47)the students showed an interest, (49–50)I decided he could be our guide from Karen to Risan and so let him pick us up. (51)Further, he kindly looked for a hotel for us to stay in. (53)He repeatedly said (52)that he felt nostalgic when he thought of the time when Taiwan was governed by Japan. (54) He also said that my behaviour matched with his views on what Japanese were like.
¶10(55)sono toki, watashi wa nihonjin no motteiru nihonjin rashisa towa, ittai nannanodaroo to kyoomi ni karareta no o oboeteiru.	¶10(55) I remembered at the time wondering about what it means to be Japanese.
¶11(56)tatoeba, gutaiteki ni dooitta jesuchaa o sasunoka to (57)kiitemo, (58)zannen na koto ni takushii no untenshu niwa setsumei dekinai. (59)sore wa doomo chokkanteki na mono rashikatta.	¶11(56)For example, what sort of gestures indicate Japanese-ness? (57)Even though I asked him, (58)the driver could not explain it. (59)It appeared to me that it was probably based on his intuition.

Japanese	Translation
¶12(60)kono 'chokkanteki na mono' o ryuugakusei ni oshieru no wa yooi dewa nai. (61)sore wa karera ga nihonjin no shakai no naka de shizen ni tsukamu mono de, (62)heta ni nihonjin wa kooitta bamen de, kooiu miburi ya koodoo o shigachi da to oshieru no wa, nihonjin no gengo-koodoo o sutereotaipu-ka-suru koto ni nari, (63) kiken konoue nai.	¶12(60)Teaching intuition to overseas students is not a simple task. (61)Intuition should develop naturally through the students' life in Japanese society. (62)Teaching how Japanese behave in a particular situation by saying, 'this is the way Japanese behave… etc..' only teaches stereotypes, thus, (63)it is very dangerous.
¶13(64)nihongo wa nihonjin o tsuujite, (65)sono gengo-koodoo ni made eikyoo o ataeteiru. (66)hanasu toki no aite tono kyori, unazuki kata, ojigi no shikata, waraikata, mesen, nihongo o bogo to suru hitotachi ni kyootsuu na gengo-koodoo mo 'nihonjin rashisa' ni ireru to suru nara, (67)totemo kyooshitsu no nihongo no jugyoo dewa kabaa dekinai bunya dato (68)omoo.	¶13(64)The Japanese people exchange Japanese language and (65)this exchange influences language behaviour. (66)If we include in the notion of Japanese-ness, language behaviours such as the distance between the speaker and 'others', nodding, bowing, laughing, eye contact, then (68)I think (68)it is too much to cover in the Japanese as a foreign language classroom.
¶14(69)'gaikokugo o manabu koto', sore wa, sorezore no bunka o haikei ni, kakuji no aidentyityi o ushinau koto naku, sono zure o ninshiki shi, choosei suru nooryoku o minitsukeru koto da.	¶14(69)'Learning a foreign language' means acquiring the ability to adjust and acknowledge the gap between one's own culture and that of Japan without losing one's own identity and background.
¶15 (70)'nihongo o oshieru koto', sore wa, nihongo to iu hitotsu no gengo o tsuujite, betsu na sekai o nozoku kikai o ryuugakusei tachi ni ataeru koto, soshite ryuugakusei tachi ga, bunka-masatsu no hazama no naka de kishikishi oto o tateteiru toki ni, karera no gengo-koodoo no kusshon no yakume o hatashite ageru koto da.	¶15(70)'Teaching Japanese' to overseas students means providing the opportunity to see a different world view via a different language. It also acts as a cushion when students are caught between two cultures.
¶16(71)sore wa kyooshi ni tottemo ryuugakusei dooshi ni tottemo, otagai no aidentyityi no naka kara, kotoba no kontei ni sonzai suru fuhenteki na sekai o kyooyuu suru koto ni hokanaranai daroo kara.	¶16 (71)What this means for both teachers and students is that between each of their identities, they find and share the common world which consists of a linguistic base.

References

Butt, D. et al. (1995) *Using Functional Grammar: An Explorer's Guide*. Sydney: National Centre for English Language Teaching and Research Macquarie University.

Halliday, M. A. K. (1994) *An Introduction to Functional Grammar*. London: Edward Arnold.

Hasan, R. (1984/96) The nursery tale as a genre. In C. Cloran, D. Butt and G. Williams (eds) *Ways of Saying Ways of Meaning* 51–72. London: Cassell.

Hasan, R. (1985) The structure of a text. In Halliday, M. A. K. and Hasan, R. *Language, Context and Text: Aspects of Language in a Social-Semiotic Perspective* 52–69. Waurn Ponds, Vic.: Deakin University.

Martin, J. R. (1992) *English Text: System and Structure*. Philadelphia: John Benjamins Pub. Co.

Martin, J. R., Christie, F. and Rothery, J. (1987) *Working Papers in Linguistics 5*. Department of Linguistics, University of Sydney. (Reprinted in *The*

Teaching of English, September 1987, English Teachers Association of New South Wales.)

Matthiessen, C. M. I. M. (1995) *Lexicogrammatical Cartography: English Systems.* Tokyo: International Language Sciences Publishers.

Maynard, S. (1998) *Principles of Japanese Discourse*. Cambridge: Cambridge University Press.

Metropolitan East Disadvantaged School's Program. (1992–1995) *Write It Right: Literacy in Industry Research Project.* Sydney: Write-it-right project, Metropolitan East Disadvantaged School's Program, NSW Dept. of School Education.

Miyakoshi, M. (1987) Nihonjin no gengo seikatsu (Japanese language activities). In *Gengo No Kenkyuu (Research on Language)* 115–125. Tokyo: Gagugei Tosyo Kabushiki Gaishya.

O'Donnell, M. (2003) *RSTtool 3.41.* Wagsoft from http://www.wagsoft.com/RSTTool/

Okuma, T. (1992) Gengo tani to shite no bunsyoo (Text as linguistic unit). *Nihongogaku (Japanese study)* 11(4): 20–25.

Teruya, K. (1998) *An Exploration into the World of Experience: A Systemic-Functional Interpretation of the Grammar of Japanese*. School of English, Linguistics and Media, Maquarie University.

Teruya, K. (2003) *Japanese-Ryukyuan Language Family: A Short Exploration. Paper presented at the Festival of Languages*: Systemic Functional Typology Symposium III, University of New South Wales.

Thomson, E. A. (2001) *Exploring the Textual Metafunction in Japanese*. Faculty of Education, University of Wollongong.

3 Description of MOOD in Japanese: examining Mood types in a selected set of texts

Nagisa Fukui
UNSW, Australia

The aim of this paper is to present a description of the Mood types in Japanese based on a selected set of texts. The description includes both congruent and some incongruent realisations of the four main speech functions: offer, command, statement and question. This paper also explores the nature of the constituents of MOOD[1] in each Mood type that realise the speech functions. The system network and realisation statements are described. There are three texts used to illustrate examples of each of the Mood types and their constituent structure, two spoken and one written.

Introduction

According to the Systemic Functional model of language (Halliday, 1994, 2004; Eggins, 1994, 2004; Mattheissen, 1995, 2004), language, or rather making meaning through language, is a form of social behaviour. Our social relationships are enacted through our lexicogrammatical choices within the MOOD system of the language. This has been illustrated in both Eggins's work (1994, 1997, 2004) and Matthiessen's work (1995) on casual conversation in English. The grammatical system of MOOD refers to variables such as the types of clause structure, modality (the degree of certainty or obligation expressed), negotiation (the tag usages in the case of English), vocatives etc. The work on Mood types in English has laid the groundwork for beginning the process of investigating the Mood types in Japanese.

There have been a number of fundamental works published on the description of Japanese language from the Systemic Functional point of view (Hori, 1995, 1997; Kato, 2007; Mizusawa, 2008; Sano, 2003, 2006 & 2008; Teruya, 1998, 2004; Thomson, 1996, 2001, 2005; Thomson, Fukui & White, 2008). However, not many of these studies focus on describing the MOOD system of Japanese. Thus this chapter, explores the system of MOOD in Japanese by taking examples from three different texts. This study will specifically focus on the types of clause structures that are used to realise the speech functions of statement, question, command and offer.

Mood type

Speech function

According to Halliday, each clause within a message has a particular role in indicating what a speaker or writer expects to receive from a listener or reader in return. For example, when we ask a question, we expect to receive an answer from a listener or a reader. In other words, we take on various speech roles when we engage in dialogue. Halliday (1994) states that 'the most fundamental types of speech role, which lie behind all the more specific types that we may eventually be able to recognise, are just two: 1) giving, and 2) demanding' (p.68). Further, Halliday divides the commodity being exchanged into two categories: goods-and-services and information. From these variables, four primary speech functions arise: statement, question, command and offer. A statement involves giving information; a question involves demanding information; a command involves demanding goods and services; and an offer involves giving goods and services. In English, each of these speech functions are identified by specific lexico-grammatical features (Halliday, 1994).

Mood types in English

Halliday (1994) notes that only particular constituents within a clause realise these four speech functions. In the case of English, the constituents, Subject and Finite, serve to realise the Mood types of a clause and together form the Mood elements. Both the presence and the order of these two key elements serve to define the specific Mood type. These Mood elements make up the lexico-grammar used for exchanging messages in English and are referred to as the grammar of propositions and proposals (Halliday, 1994). Table 1 is a partial summary of the realisation of the Mood types of English as described by Halliday (1994:74).

Table 1: A summary of two of the four speech functions in English

Speech Function	Mood type	Order of MOOD elements	Example
Statement	Declarative	Subject ^ (followed by) Finite	***I am*** *typing up my essay.*
Question	Yes/No interrogative	Finite ^ Subject	***Is this*** *an essay?*
	WH- interrogative (i) if WH is subject	Subject ^ Finite	***Who is*** *typing the essay?*
	WH- interrogative (ii) if WH isn't subject	Finite ^ Subject	*What* ***are you*** *typing?*

As indicated, within propositions the order of the MOOD elements realises a specific speech function. For example, the declarative Mood, which has the order Subject followed by Finite, is typically used for making a statement, and the interrogative Mood, which, apart from one exception has the order Finite followed by Subject, is typically used for making a question. However, Halliday also argues that there are unmarked Mood types or congruent realisations, and marked Mood types or incongruent realisations for each speech function. For example, a tagged declarative clause can realise a statement, as in '*The Bostonians* was Henry James' last novel, wasn't it?' (Eggins, 1994: 153). Further, making a choice between a marked or an unmarked realisation is influenced by contextual demands (Eggins, 1994).

Mood types in Japanese

There is no doubt that Japanese clauses also select for Mood. Japanese speakers use the declarative Mood when they are making a statement and the interrogative Mood when they are asking a question. However, the MOOD elements of Subject and Finite that are tossed back and forth to keep the discourse going in English are not the MOOD elements in the case of Japanese.

Hori's work (1995) made a fundamental contribution to our understanding of the MOOD system in Japanese. She demonstrated that the grammatical subject is not that which is bandied back and forth in order to carry the conversation forward. Instead, Hori argued, using a translation of Halliday's teapot text (Halliday, 1985:71), stating that 'the repeated items belong to two classes; (a) the conjugated forms of the main verb, and (b) the sentence final particle' (Hori, 1995:165). The MOOD elements that are bandied back and forth are the verb and the sentence final particles. However, Hori based her argument only on clauses ending in verbal predicates and did not discuss the clauses ending with nominal or adjectival predicates.

Research questions

Hori's findings suggest that some further questions need to be addressed for a more comprehensive understanding of the Japanese Mood system. These are:

1) What are the full set of MOOD elements and Mood types in Japanese?
2) Are there four primary Mood types which realise the four fundamental speech functions of offer, command, statement and question?
3) What are the congruent and incongruent realisations of each speech function?

The corpus

In order to answer these questions, this study analysed three Japanese texts. The first is taken from a corpus of spoken dialogue published by Real World Computing Partnership. It is a semi-natural dialogue, between two native Japanese speakers, one female and one male. They were asked to conduct a role-play without a written script and were informed that the conversation would be recorded for linguistic research purposes. They were told to talk for as long as they liked provided they maintained their roles. The constructed situation was located at a travel agency and the role of Speaker is that of the clerk at the agency, while the role of Speaker two is that of a customer. Before the recording, Speaker two was told to imagine planning an overseas trip and visiting an agency in order to make enquiries. The speakers had never met before. Speaker two was allowed to ask any kind of question which would be considered natural in the context. The recording was conducted in an audio room with recording equipment. Some brochures were prepared in case they were needed during the conversation. The recording was conducted only once and no one interrupted the conversation during the recording. The conversation is about half an hour long, but only a selected portion consisting of 66 turns was analysed for this study.

The second text is a naturally occurring conversation held at a coffee shop on the campus of a University between four native female Japanese speakers who were close friends and colleagues. It was recorded in December 1997 and the speakers were informed that the dialogue would be recorded. The whole conversation was conducted over one hour, however, due to the length, only a selected part consisting of 94 turns was chosen for analysis.

The third text is a story called *Momotaroo* taken from a Japanese children's book of nursery tales. The story was chosen to complement the dialogic texts in order to confirm the presence of the Mood types in both spoken and written mode.

Samples of the texts appear in Appendices A, B and C, which detail the textual analysis. In total, the corpus consists of 358 clauses.

Method

The analysis of the transcriptions follows the conventions from the book 'Casual Conversation' by Eggins and Slade. (See the description of transcription key, Eggins and Slade, 1997:1–5) Further, a notation key is attached at the end of the chapter which explains the interlinear gloss of the examples.

In the transcriptions, each speaker's new turn begins a new line, and each turn is divided up into clauses. The individual clauses are analysed for MOOD by labelling the constituents that determine the various Mood types as the MOOD elements, and labelling the remainder of the clauses as RESIDUE. The MOOD elements are further analysed morphologically. Each clause is analysed to identify: 1) its Predicate type; 2) Mood type; 3) speech function; and 4) congruence. (see Appendices A to C).

Results

The MOOD elements

The analysis shows that the clause constituents that are repeated to progress the conversation are the Predicate and the Negotiatory Marker. As the following examples in Example 1, 2 and 3 demonstrate, the Predicate is identified as a key element which must be repeated to keep the discourse going. The term Predicate is used here to mean the entire verbal group. This is in contrast to the Predicator, which in Halliday and Mathiessen (2004) refers to the 'verbal group minus the temporal or modal operator, which functions as Finite in the MOOD element' in English. In Japanese the entire verbal group, including the temporal or modal element is bandied back and forth. The entire verbal group is referred to as the Predicate. There are three kinds of Predicates in Japanese, which are explained below.

Ex. 1: Identifying the MOOD elements (1 – verbal group Predicate)

S2:

***Yon**da,*	*ano hon?*
read-pos- pst-inf	that book
PRED(Verbal group)	
MOOD	RESIDUE

Have you read that book?

Mada	***Yon**de nai deshoo?*
not yet	read- neg-pst-inc
	PRED(Verbal group)
RESIDUE	MOOD

You haven't read it, have you?

S3:

Yonde nai n da
read- neg-non-inf
PRED (Verbal group)
MOOD

No, I haven't.

Ex. 2: Identifying the Mood elements (2 – adjectival group Predicate)

S1:

Ookatta tokoro tte	***ooi***	*no ne.*
many-past place-TTE	many-pos-non-inf	NO NE
	PRED (Adjectival group)	NEG
RESIDUE	MOOD	

There are many of them (gay men) at places where (many women) work.

S2:

Un un	***ooi, ooi***
yes	many-pos-non-inf many-pos-non-inf
POL	PRED (Adjectival group)
MOOD	

Yes, there are many, many.

S3:

Dakara sensei mo	***ooi** n da*	*yo ne*
That's way teacher-MO	many-pos-non-inf-DA	YO NE
	PRED (Adjectival group)	NEG
RESIDUE	MOOD	

That's why, there are also many of them among teachers.

Ex. 3: Identifying the Mood elements (3 – nominal group Predicate)

S3:

A, Konjiki?
Umm, Konjiki-pos-non-inf
PRED (Nominal group)
MOOD

Isn't it Konjiki?

S2:

Soo	***Konjiki.***
Yes,	Konjiki-pos-non-inf
POL	PRED (Nominal group)
MOOD	

Yes, it's Konjiki.

Konjiki dakke?
Konjiki-pos-non-inf
PRED (Nominal group)
MOOD

Is it?

Note: Bold font in the examples highlights the part of the Predicate which is repeated back and forth.

As suggested, the Predicate is expressed by more that just a final verbal group. Other kinds of Predicates which are formed by other word classes also occur. The examples above demonstrate this.

In order to explain the different kinds of Predicates, I will briefly discuss 'class' in Japanese. Within the open[2] class of words, there are two primary Japanese classes. These are nominals and verbals (Thomson, 2001). Within the nominal class there is a *no*-nominal and a *na*-nominal, while in the verbal class, there is a *–ru* verbal and an *–i* verbal (see Thomson, 2001 for the full description of class in Japanese pp.31–32). As Thomson suggests, these four types serve different semantic functions in the clause and group units. The*–ru* verbal functions as the process in the clause; the *no* nominal functions as the participant in the clause and the Thing in the noun group, while the *–i* verbal and *na* nominal function as epithets in the noun group and as Attributes in Relational processes. As the *na*-nominal and *–i* verbal serve the same function,

I have classified them as one Predicate type, the adjectival type. The *–ru* verbal is classified as the verbal Predicate and the *no*-nominal as the nominal Predicate. Thus in the examples, Example 1 contains a verbal Predicate, Example 2 an adjectival Predicate and Example 3 contains a nominal Predicate.

In some instances, sentence-final particles as well as the Predicate participate in the process of progressing the discourse. These particles are known as the Negotiatory Markers (Teruya, 1998). 'The function the Negotiatory Marker enacts the negotiatory value of the proposition / proposal' (1998: p.50). These Negotiatory Markers, which follow the Predicate, have interpersonal potential. For example, the Interrogative Mood is realised by the Predicate and a Negotiatory Marker such as *ka, no*, or *kai*, in some cases, with rising intonation, as in the following example in Example 4. Here, the interrogative Mood in the first turn is realised by the presence of the Predicate and the Negotiatory Marker while in the second turn, the declarative is realised by the Predicate.

Ex. 4: Interrogative Mood: Predicate + Negotiatory Marker

SA:

Pasupooto	***omochi desu***	*ka.*
Passport	have-pos-non-hon	KA
	PRED (N)	NEG
RESIDUE	MOOD	

Do you have your passport?

SB:

A, ima	***motte masen.***
Umm, now	Carry-ssp have –neg-non-fml
	PRED (V)
RESIDUE	MOOD

I don't have one now.

Thus, in the case of Japanese, the MOOD elements are the Predicate and the Negotiatory Marker. The remaining elements of the clause form the RESIDUE. The Subject is, therefore, one of the RESIDUE elements, not one of the MOOD elements. In the following section, the full set of Mood types will be described.

Mood types in Japanese and their congruent realisations

In the corpus, four different Mood types of the major clause are identified. They are declarative, interrogative, imperative and oblative.[3] Further, these four Mood types typically realise 'the four primary speech functions of STATEMENT, QUESTION, COMMAND and OFFER' (Halliday, 1994:69).

Declarative Mood

The declarative Mood is the most common Mood type which appears in the corpus, and the three types of Predicate – verbal, adjectival, and nominal are deployed in these clauses. The declarative Mood is realised by the 'dictionary' form[4] of the verb or its formal equivalent, the *desu/-masu* form.[5] Examples are below in Table 2: Note that verbal Predicates and some of adjectival type Predicates, which are formed by *–i* verbals, select Mood through morphological change. For example, the form of the verb *yomu* is *yomimasu*, realised by a morphological change on the final vowel in the dictionary form '*u*'. In contrast, the nominal Predicate and the *na* nominal adjectival Predicate select for Mood through the addition of the copula verb '*da*' (to be).

The declarative form can occur in either a modal or non-modal structure. In other words, the modal form can express degrees of probability, usuality, certainty etc, while the non-modal forms, select for tense and do not express any modal meanings.

Table 2: Dictionary form and masu/desu form

Predicate type	Dictionary form	Formal form
Verbal		
• Group 1	*yomu* VERB (someone) reads.	*yomimasu* VERB (someone) reads.
• Group 2	*taberu* VERB (someone) eats.	*tabemasu* VERB (someone) eats.
• Irregular	*suru* VERB (someone) does.	*shimasu* VERB (someone) does.
Adjectival:		
• Verb-like, *~i* type	*ii* ADJ (something) is good.	*ii desu* ADJ FOR (something) is good.
• Noun-like, *~na* type	*kirei da* ADJ COP (something) is pretty.	*kirei desu* ADJ COP (something) is pretty.
Nominal		
	hon da NOUN COP (It) is a book.	*hon desu* NOUN COP (It) is a book.

Interrogative Mood

As is the case in English, Japanese has two different types of interrogatives. They are polar and wh- interrogatives which typically realise the speech function of Question. The polar interrogative is realised by the Negotiatory Marker which follows the verbal group Predicate of the declarative clause. Moreover, rising intonation also accompanies the Negotiatory Marker. The Negotiatory marker *ka* is probably the most well known of the question markers. Others include *no kai*, *no* and *kai*. Example 5 and 6 illustrate the declarative and the polar interrogative Moods respectively.

Ex. 5a: Declarative Mood realised by nominal group Predicate

Eaazurokku desu.
The Ayres Rock-pos-non-fml-ccl
PRED (N)
MOOD

It is Uluru (Ayres Rock)

Ex. 5b: Declarative Mood realised by verbal group Predicate

Momotaroo to namae o	*tsukemashita.*
Momotaroo TO name O	deicide-pos-pst-fml
	PRED.(V)
RESIDUE	MOOD

(Someone) decided the name, 'Momotaroo'.

***Ex. 6: Polar (positive) interrogative clause realised by Negotiatory Marker** KA*

Eaazurokku desu	*ka.*
The Airs Rock-pos-non-fml-ccl	KA
PRED.(Nominal)	NEG.
MOOD	

Is it Uluru (Ayres Rock)?

The other type of interrogative is the wh- interrogative type. It is realised by the presence of D-words (equivalent to wh- in English) and by the Negotiatory

Marker at the end of a clause. D-words[6] are named so after the initial letter of some interrogative words such as *dare* (who), *doko* (where), *doo* (how), *dochira* (where) and *donna* (what kind). Examples are provided in Example 7 and 8.

***Ex. 7: wh- interrogative clause realised by D-word and** KA*

***Donna** kanji no ga*	*aru deshoo*	***ka.***
what kind ones (tour)-GA	have-pos-non-fml-inc	KA
	PRED.(V)	KA
RESIDUE	MOOD	

What kind of tour do you have?

*Daitai **dono** gurai ni*	*narisoo deshoo*	***ka***
about how long-NI	seems become-pos-non-fml-inc	KA
	PRED.(V)	NEG.
RESIDUE	MOOD	

About how much will it cost?

Ex. 8: A clause with D-word which realises declarative Mood

***Dare** ka*	*wasureta*
Who KA	forget-pos-pst-fnf
	PRED.(V)
RESIDUE	MOOD

I forgot who it was.

According to Teruya, 'D- interrogative is realised by D-words being inserted where an element of transitivity structure (participant or circumstance) is queried.' (1998 p.51) An important point is that the presence of D-words does not realise the Mood type as the interrogative Mood as Example 7 shows, instead the Negotiatory Markers with rising intonation typically determine the Mood type. However, the presence of D-words in the clause realises the wh-interrogative Mood and this is what differentiates it from the polar interrogative Mood.

An important point to note is that in the clauses that are expressed by adjectival or nominal Predicates, only the declarative and interrogative Moods are possible. However, in the case of a verbal Predicate, other Mood types are possible and these are realised by the morphological system of the verb class.

Imperative Mood

Only the verbal group Predicate can realise the imperative Mood, the grammar of the speech function Command. This is because the nature of imperative Mood is established by the volition of the speaker. The imperative Mood is established when the speaker would like the listener to do something, and that speaker's volition is expressed in the clause. Only the verbal group can realise this volition via morphological change. The nominal and the adjectival groups are not able to realise speakers' volition.

The imperative Mood has two types: positive and negative, each of which entails a morphological change on the last syllable of the verb. The positive imperative which is realised by final *–e* or *–o*, depends on the verb type. For example, *yomu* (to read – declarative) is a group 1 verb with the imperative Mood form, ***yome*** (Read it), and *taberu* (to eat –declarative) is a group 2 verb with the imperative Mood form, ***tabero*** (Eat it), while *suru* (to do –declarative) is an irregular verb with imperative Mood, ***shiro*** (Do it). The negative imperative or prohibitive is realised by the negative suffix *–na* which is added to the dictionary form of the verbs, for example, ***yomuna*** (Don't read it) and ***suruna*** (Don't do it). The negative suffix *–na* attaches to all classes of verbs, Groups 1 and 2, and the irregular set.

Further, many imperatives in Japanese are formed using the verb *kudasaru* ([It] is given to me – declarative) or *choodai suru* (I receive it – declarative) in their imperative form, *kudasai*[7] or *choodai*[8] combined with another process in a verbal group complex, for example, *yonde kudasai* (Give me a reading or Please read). In the example in Example 9, the imperative Mood element, *kudasai* is elided leaving only the lexical verb in the verbal group complex, *yonde*. The ellipsis of the imperative Mood constituent in the Predicate in this example is a feature of casual conversation. It is an imperative Mood choice which is less 'commanding'. The *te*-form (suspensive form), *yonde* (read it) along with the elided imperative form, *kudasai* in Example 9 realises the imperative Mood choice found in the corpus.

Typically, the positive or negative imperative forms are used by a speaker who has more power over a listener, such as in a mother/child or teacher/student relationship. Therefore, analysing other registers is required to reveal further details of these forms since the choice of these forms is influenced by the tenor of the context of situation.

Ex. 9: Imperative Mood realised by te-from or suspensive form

Hayaku	*yonde.*
quickly	read-ssp
	PRED.(V)
RESIDUE	MOOD

Read it quickly.

Oblative Mood

Like the imperative Mood, the oblative Mood is only realised by the verbal group Predicate. It is typically realised by the volitional suffix, such as *-oo* such as in the example, *shiyoo* (…offer to do...), *yomoo* (…offer to read..) or the formal *-masu* equivalent, *-mashoo,* as in *yomimashoo* (…offer to read…). The difference between the two forms is the degree of politeness. The relationship between interactants and the situation affects the choice of the form. Further, the Negotiatory Marker *ka* can be added to *-mashoo / -oo* for expressing suggestive offers. Example 10 shows two examples of the oblative Mood, the suggestive and the direct.

Ex. 10: Oblative Mood realised by the volitional suffix –oo

1) Direct type

Uchi no ko ni	*shimashoo*
Our home No child NI	Do-pos-for
	PRED.(V)
RESIDUE	MOOD

Let's adopt him as our child.

2) Suggestive type

Dewa	*itadakimashoo*	*ka*
then	receive-pos-hon	KA
	PRED.(V)	NEG
RESIDUE	MOOD	

Shall we eat it?

Summary of Mood type

Having described the four Mood types, the following is a summary of the typical or congruent realisations in Japanese organised according to speech function:

1) STATEMENT: realised by Declarative Mood which is expressed by a verbal, nominal or adjectival Predicate in the dictionary form or the equivalent formal, *desu/-masu* forms.

2) QUESTION: realised by Interrogative Mood which is expressed by a verbal, nominal or adjectival Predicate followed by a Negotiatory Marker, such as *ka* with rising intonation.

3) COMMAND: realised by Imperative Mood which is expressed by only a verbal Predicate either positively using *–i* or *–e* suffixes, or negatively using the dictionary form followed by the negative suffix, *na.* Often the imperative Mood element *kudasai* is elided in a verbal group complex such as *yonde* ([give me] reading)

4) OFFER: realised by Oblative Mood which is expressed by only a verbal Predicate using the *–oo* or formal, *-mashoo* suffixes with or without Negotiatory Marker, *ka.*

Importantly, the nominal and adjectival Predicates do not express imperative or oblative Moods. These grammatical forms are limited to the expression of indicative (declarative and interrogative) Mood.

The system network of Mood type

Having summarised the Mood types, it is useful to consider how they are organised as a system network. Figure 1 presents the system network of Mood type. In addition to Mood type, all major finite clauses in Japanese can select for two other systems: FORMALITY and HONOURIFICATION. The two systems are separate from the system of Mood type and are not the subject of this paper.

Within the system of Mood type, the first choice is between oblative and non-oblative forms. This distinction is made based on the fact that oblative forms do not select for polarity. In other words, there is no negative oblative. However, within the oblative type, there are two choices: that of suggestive, realised by a verbal Predicate ending in the oblative suffix,– *oo ka*, and that of direct, realised by a verbal Predicate ending in the oblative suffix – *oo*.

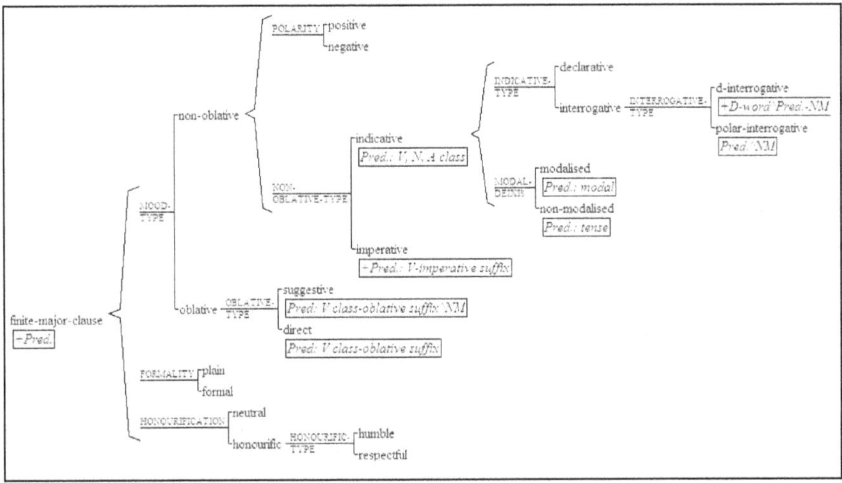

Figure 1: The system network of Mood type

The other remaining Mood types all select for polarity and are clustered together as the 'non-oblative' set. As the above description suggests, there are two simultaneous systems when selecting the non-oblative feature: that of either positive or negative polarity; and that of non-oblative Mood types. The choice here is between imperative and indicative.

The imperative is realised by a verbal Predicate ending in the imperative suffixes which depend on verb class: either group 1 taking the suffix – *e,* group 2 taking the suffix, – *o* or the irregular verbs taking an irregular suffix. If negative polarity is selected, then the negative imperative is realised by the verbal suffix, -*na*.

The indicative is realised by any class of Predicate and involves two simultaneous systems: that of modal deixis; and that of indicative Mood type. Modal deixis is a choice between a modalised form realised by a modal auxiliary (*kamoshirenai* – may) or a modal nominal suffix in the verbal group (*tsumori desu* – intending) and the non-modalised form realised by an indicative Predicate selecting for tense.

The indicative type has two options: that of declarative and interrogative. The interrogative type has a further two options: that of d-interrogative realised by a D-word followed by a Predicate and Negotiatory Marker such as *ka;* and that of polar-interrogative realised by just a Predicate followed by a Negotiatory Marker.

Examples of the output of the system of Mood type are provided in the Table 3.

Table 3: Outputs of the system network of MOOD types

	example	translation
Oblative: suggestive	*tabeyoo ka*	Shall we eat?
Oblative:Direct	*tabeyoo*	Let's eat.
Imperative: positive type Group 1 verb	*kike*	Listen!
Imperative: positive type Group 2 verb	*miro*	Look!
Imperative: positive irregular verb	*koi*	Come!
Imperative: negative type Group 1 verb	*kikuna*	Don't listen!
Imperative: negative type Group 2 verb	*miruna*	Don't look!
Imperative: negative type irregular verb	*kuruna*	Don't come
Indicative: Declarative: Positive: non modalised	*taberu*	(1) eat
Indicative: Declarative: Positive: modalised	*taberu kamoshirenai*	(I) might eat
Indicative: Declarative: Negative: non modalised	*tabenai*	(I) don't eat
Indicative: Declarative: Negative: modalised	*tabenai kamoshirenai*	(I) might not eat
Indicative: d-interrogative: Positive: non modalised	*Doko ni ikimasu ka*	Where are (you) going?
Indicative: d-interrogative: Positive: modalised	*Doko ni iku tsumori desu ka*	Where do (you) intend to go?
Indicative: d-interrogative: Negative: non modalised	*Dare ga konakatta no ka*	Who didn't come?
Indicative: d-interrogative: Negative: modalised	*Dare ga konai'n daroo ka*	Who might not come?
Indicative: polar-interrogative: Positive: non modalised	*Ikimashita ka*	Did (you) go?
Indicative: polar-interrogative: Positive: modalised	*Iku daroo ka*	Will (I) go?
Indicative: polar-interrogative: Negative: non modalised	*Ikanakatta no ka*	Didn't (you) go?
Indicative: polar-interrogative: Negative: modalised	*Ikanai kamoshirenai no?*	You might not be going?

Incongruent realisations

From the discussion so far, only congruent realisation patterns of the Mood types and the speech functions in Japanese have been described, however, the realisation patterns are not limited to the congruent options alone. There is an extensive set of non-typical or incongruent options as well. This section discusses some of the incongruent realisations of the speech functions which have been identified in the corpus.

In the first text, the simulated travel agency conversation, two different patterns are identified. The first one is the omission of the interrogative Predicate when asking a question. The typical Mood type used for a question is the interrogative Mood which is expressed by the presence of the Predicate plus the Negotiatory Marker. However, one of the incongruent realisations of the interrogative Mood is the ellipsis of the entire set of interrogative Mood elements, that is both the Predicate and Negotiatory Marker, yet the clause most definitely selects for interrogative Mood as there is a D-word, *itsugoro-ni* (about when) in the Residue. This is illustrated in Example 11.

Ex. 11: Incongruent realisation from text 1

SB:

Shinkon-ryokoo daitai itsu-goro ni	*(irasshaimasu*	*ka)*
honeymoon roughly whne-about NI	go-pos-pres-hon-for	KA
	Predicate (V) NEG	
RESIDUE	MOOD	

Roughly, when (will) your honeymoon (be)?

SA:

Aki gurai ni	*(ikimasu).*
Autumn about NI	go-pos-pre-for
	Predicate (V)
RESIDUE	MOOD

(It will be) about autumn.

The reason why both speakers understand the Mood selection relates to their mutual understanding of the redundancy in the grammar of Japanese. This is called formal exophoric reference (Hasan (1996) cited in Thomson, 2005). The missing information is retrievable from the speakers' mutual understanding of the grammar of Japanese. They both 'know' that the verb, *irasshaimasu* plus the Negotiatory Marker, *ka* are operative but not articulated. In the recording the rising intonation is not present. Again both interactants 'know' due to the presence of D-word, *itsu goro ni*, that the Mood selection is interrogative and therefore rising intonation is also redundant.

The other incongruent pattern evident in the travel agent text is the deployment of the declarative Mood to realise a command as indicated in Example 12. The form *'~n desu'* in *negaitai'n desu* (…want to request you…) realises declarative Mood, and therefore, the speech function of statement, however, in this case the clause realises a command. In a formal situation, the declarative Mood is often employed to command. In the case of the example in Example 12 thc Mood type is lexicalised in the sense that the speech function of command rests in the meaning of the verb, *negau* (to request), while the Mood selection is declarative realising the speech function of statement. However, in this case, the speech function is not that of statement but rather, that of command. It is a politer way of making a request.

Ex. 12: Incongruent realisation from text 1

S2:

O-kikase negaitai n desu	*keredomo.*
listen-caus-hon want to request- pos-non-fml	but
PRED.(V)	
MOOD	

I would like to request you to tell me (about it).

In the second text, the casual conversation about gay men, the declarative Mood is used incongruently to realise the speech function of question. This is a rather common pattern in the text and is illustrated in Example 13 and 14.

Ex. 13: Incongruent realisation from text 2 (1)

Yonde nai deshoo,	*mada?*
read- neg-non-fml-inc	yet
PRED.(V)	
MOOD	

(You) haven't read it yet?

Ex. 14: Incongruent realisation from text 2 (2)

Koko dake da to	*omotta?*
[here only-pos-non TO]*	PRED.(V)
[PRED.(N) TO]	PRED.(V)
MOOD	MOOD

Did (you) think (it)'s only here?

**projected clause*

This occurs because many clauses can depend on the intonation for the realisation of the speech functions. The Negotiatory Marker which acts as the question mark is elided in many cases as in the examples above. These clauses are declarative clauses, but because of a rising intonation pattern, they realise a Question. They would realise a Statement if the intonation pattern fell. According to Eggins (1997), the dependence on the intonation for the realisation of speech function is one of the characteristic features of casual conversation in English. It seems that this pattern is also applicable to the case of Japanese as well.

Another incongruent pattern which is evident in text 2 is the use of the declarative type to realise an OFFER. Consider the examples in Example 15.

Ex. 15: Offer, realised by declarative mood

S3:

kondo	*motte kuru*	*yo*
Next time	bring-pos-non-inf	YO
	PRED.(V)	NEG
RESIDUE	MOOD	

I'll bring it next time.

In the example, the sentence final particle, *yo,* functions to emphasise the declarative Predicate. Through the emphasis achieved via the particle, *yo*, the declarative Mood realises an OFFER.

An incongruent pattern found in the *Momotaroo* text is the use of an interrogative type to realise a STATEMENT. '*~ dewa arimasen ka*' from the sentence, *Wareta momo no naka kara otoko no ko ga tobidashita dewa arimasen ka* (From the cracked peach, out jumped a child.) is used to construe a statement which is a surprise, and does not realise a Question despite the presence of the Negotiatory Marker, *ka.*

Both the congruent and incongruent realisations that are found in the corpus are summarised in Table 4.

Table 4: Congruent and incongruent realisation of speech functions in the corpus

Speech Function	**Congruent clause mood**	**Incongruent clause mood**
Command	imperative	declarative with a specific lexical verb of request
Question	interrogative	declarative with rising intonation
Offer	oblative	declarative
Statement	declarative	interrogative using Negotiatory Marker, *ka*

Conclusion

This chapter has described the grammatical elements of Japanese that are involved in realising the speech functions within the interpersonal metafunction. These speech functions relate directly to the tenor of the context of situation. They enact our social relationships in terms of our approach to communication. When we communicate we choose between giving or demanding either information or goods and services. The lexicogrammatical resources for construing these meanings in Japanese, that is, the Mood selection of the clause has been investigated and described in this chapter.

Japanese clauses select for Mood. The Predicate and the Negotiatory Markers are the elements which determine the Mood types. These two elements typically occur at the end of a clause, thus the end of a clause makes a significant contribution to the MOOD system in Japanese. This represents a significant difference between English and Japanese in that the MOOD elements in English typically occur clause initially, while in Japanese they occur clause finally. Further, the MOOD elements in Japanese are not Subject and Finite as they are in English.

Four different Mood types of the major clause are identified in the corpus. They are declarative, interrogative, imperative and oblative. These four Mood types typically realise Halliday's ' four primary speech functions' of STATEMENT, QUESTION, COMMAND and OFFER respectively. The order of the MOOD elements determine Mood types in the case of English, but this is not so in the case of Japanese. Rather, Mood types are realised by Predicate type combined with or without the Negotiatory Marker. The Predicate can be verbal, adjectival or nominal in form. However, only the verbal Predicate can select for the four Mood types of declarative, interrogative, oblative and imperative. The adjectival and nominal Predicates are limited to only declarative and interrogative Mood. The declarative Mood is realised by a verbal, nominal or adjectival Predicate in the dictionary form or the equivalent formal, *desu/masu* forms. The interrogative Mood is realised by a verbal, nominal or adjectival Predicate followed by a Negotiatory Marker, such as *ka*. The imperative Mood is realised by only a verbal Predicate either positively using *–i* or *–e* suffixes, for regular verbs with irregular verbs having their own idiosyncratic forms or negatively using the dictionary form followed by the negative suffix, *na.* Often the imperative Mood element is elided in a verbal group complex where the lexical verb occurs in the suspensive *–te* form such as *yonde* ([give me] reading) And finally, the oblative Mood is realised by only a verbal Predicate using the *–oo* or formal, *-mashoo* suffixes for the direct kind, and *–oo ka* for the suggestive type.

However, the realisation patterns of these speech functions are not the only possibilities. These are only typical patterns. Some incongruent realisation patterns are also identified in the corpus. Since only three different texts are analysed for this project, it is not appropriate to generalise the findings, but it is interesting to note that the declarative Mood can be used to realise all four speech functions. This result is the same as the result of Eggins's work in analysing English conversations. (Eggins, 1997:184)

There are many other factors which need to be identified and pursued in order to explore the system of Mood in Japanese. This project, with its focus on the identification of MOOD elements, and the Mood types, is just a starting point for the exploration and points to further studies.

First of all, the constituents of the RESIDUE need to be described. While they do not play a role in defining the type of Mood, they still play a role in expressing interpersonal meanings. For example, Modal Adjuncts which reside in the Residue add interpersonal meanings to the clause. Eggins (1994) explains these as follows, 'Modal Adjuncts add meanings which are somehow connected to the creation and maintenance of the dialogue. They can do this either by impacting directly on the MOOD element or indirectly' (p.166). Thus the elements of the RESIDUE in Japanese need to be identified and their functions defined.

Moreover, as the Subject is not a MOOD element in the case of Japanese, its function in relation to interpersonal meaning also needs to be further researched. This raises the issue of modal responsibility (refer to Teruya, 1998: 2–65 for a brief description on modal responsibility in Japanese).

Moreover, the function of the Negotiatory Marker needs to be further defined. I have discussed one of the aspects of the Negotiatory Marker which functions as a question marker, however, other aspects which contribute to the interpersonal meanings such as confirming, empathising, and asserting, have not been addressed.

As mentioned, the systems of Polarity, Formality, Honourification and Modality are key interpersonal systems. How these meanings are realised in the grammar has yet to be described in Systemic Functional terms.

Finally, further study into intonation is needed to reveal the prosodic resources for the expression of interpersonal meaning in spoken texts. From the texts used in this project, we observed that the identification of the interrogative Mood was not only via the Negotiatory Marker but also via patterns of intonation. Emphasis, meanings of suspicion, distrust and confirmation etc. can be expressed by the combination of the Negotiatory Marker and intonation. This also needs further description.

Notes

1 We use capital letters to differentiate the MOOD constituent of the clause and the MOOD system from the general term, Mood, which describes the overall structure of the clause.

2 An *open* class is a non-finite lexical set (Halliday, 1961:245).

3 'Oblative' derives form Latin *oblaio* meaning 'offer' (Macquarie Dictionary 1994).

4 The dictionary form is the form of the verb or adjective as it appears in the dictionary. For the class of verb, there are three kinds, Group 1, Group 2 and the irregular set. All verbs fall into these categories. For the class of – *i* adjectives, the dictionary form is the form ending in ~*i*.

5 The *desu*/-*masu* form is the formal equivalent of the dictionary form. '*desu*' is the formal of the copula '*da*' (to be), while ~*masu* is the formal morphological ending of the three verb types.

6 The term 'd-word' was coined by Teruya (1996).

7 *Kudasaru* is an irregular verb and thus has its own imperative form, *kudasai*.

8 Similarly, *choodai suru* is also irregular, forming its own imperative form by dropping *suru*.

Notation key

Notation	Meaning	Form and some Examples
PRED(A)	Predicate, adjectival group	eg: *kanari koosu ga* ***sukunai'n desu*** quite courses GA **a few**
PRED(N)	Predicate, nominal group	eg: *genchi kakariin tte yuu no wa* ***Nihon-go no hanaseru kata ?*** local person in charge NO WA **person who can speak Japanese?**
PRED(V)	Predicate, verbal group	eg: *soko made* ***ikanakatta*** *wa.* there till **did not go** WA.
ccl	conclusive	*-da, -dewa/jya nai, -desu, -dewa/jya arimasen, -datta, -dewa/jya nakatta, -dewa/jya arimasendeshita*
fml	formal	*-desu, -deshita, -dewa/jya arimasen, -dewa/jya arimasen deshita* *-masu, -masen, -mashita, -masen deshita*
hon	honorific	eg: *omochi desu ka*
imp	imperative	*-e, -ro* eg: *yome, tabero*

Notation	Meaning	Form and some Examples
inc	suppositive (inconclusive)	*-daroo, -dewa/jya nai daroo, -de shoo, -dewa/jya nai deshoo, -datta daroo, -dewa/jyani daroo, -datta deshoo, -dewa/jya nakatta deshoo*
inf	informal	*-ru, -ta, -nai, -nakatta, -da, -dewa/jya nai, -datta, -dewa/jya nakatta*
neg	negative	*-nai, -naktta, –masen, -masen deshita, –dewa/jya nai, -dewa/jya naktta, -dewa/jya arimasen, -dewa/jya arimasen deshita*
neg	Negotiatory Marker	*ka, yo, ne, wa, no, ze, sa, yo ne, no ne, no yo ne, no ka/kai, ka na, na no, kai, ka ne, no sa*
non	non past	*-ru, -nai, –masu, -masen, –da, -dewa/jya nai, –desu, -dewa/jya arimasen*
pos	positive	*-ru, -ta, -masu, -mashita, –da, -datta, -desu, -deshita*
prh	prohibitive	*-na* eg*: yomuna*
pst	past	*-ta, -nakatta, -mashita, -masen deshita, -datta, -dewa/jya nakatta, -deshita, -dewa/jya arimasen deshita*
ssp	suspensive or *te*-form	*-te, -nai de* eg*; yonde*
vol	volitional	*-oo, -shoo* eg*: yomoo, yomimashoo*

(adapted from Teruya ,1998:xxiii and Thomson, 2005:177)

References

Primary sources

Kodansha (1993) *Nihon Mukashi-banashi, Sansai no Hon 10* 20–25. (Japanese Folk Tales, Books for 3yrs olds no. 10), Kodansha, Tokyo.

Travel agent: *Spoken Dialogue Corps, Real World Computing Partnership,* Travel. Text 1 F_06. Tokyo.

Four women chatting: (1997) a naturally occurred conversation recorded by Nagisa Fukui, Sydney.

Secondary sources

Eggins, S. (1994) *An Introduction to Systemic Functional Linguistics*. London: Pinter Publishers Ltd.

Eggins, S. and Slade, D. (1997) *Analysing Casual Conversation.* London: Cassell.

Eggins, S. (2004) *An Introduction to Systemic Functional Linguistics*. 2nd ed. New York: Continuum.

Halliday, M. A. K. (1961) 'Categories on the Theory of Grammar'. *Word* 17(3).

Halliday, M. A. K. (1985) *Spoken and Written Language*. Victoria: Deakin University.

Halliday, M. A. K. (1994) *An Introduction to Functional Grammar*. 2nd ed. London: Edward Arnold Press.

Halliday, M. A. K. and Matthiessen, C. M. I. M. (2004) *An Introduction to Functional Grammar*. 3rd ed. London: Arnold.

Hori, M. (1995) Subjectlessness and Honourifics in Japanese: A Case of Textual Construal. In R. Hasan and P. H. Fries (ed.) *On Subject and Theme. A Discourse Functional Perspective* 151–186. Amsterdam: John Benjamins Publishing Com.

Hori, M. (1997) *Mood Structure in Spoken vs. Written Japanese*. Presented at the ASFLA Conference, October 1997, University Of Wollongong, Australia. (Unpublished.)

Kato, K. (2007) *Exploring the Structure and Meaning of the Family of Procedural (How to) Texts in Japanese,* Honours dissertation, Faculty of Arts, University of Wollongong, Australia.

Matthiessen, C. M. I. M. (1995) *Lexicogrammatical Cartography: English system*. Tokyo: International Science Publishers.

Mizusawa, Y. (2008) *Investigating the Directive genre in the Japanese and Australian workplace: A Systemic Functional Approach,* PhD dissertation, Faculty of Arts, University of Wollongong, Australia.

Sano, M. (2003) *Uncovering the Logico-Semantic Relations of Japanese: A Systemic Functional Interpretation of Selected Expository texts,* Honours dissertation, Faculty of Arts, University of Wollongong, Australia.

Sano, M. (2006) *A Linguistic Exploration of Persuasion in Written Japanese Discourse: A Systemic Functional Interpretation,* PhD dissertation, Faculty of Arts, University of Wollongong, Australia.

Sano, M. (2008) The Rhetoric of Editorials: A Japanese case study. In E. Thomson and P.R.R. White (eds.) *Communicating Conflict: Multilingual Case Studies of the Rhetoric of the News Media.* London: Continuum.

Teruya, K. (1998) *An Exploration into the World of Experience: A Systemic-Functional Interpretation of the Grammar of Japanese*. PhD thesis, presented to Macquarie University, May. (Unpublished.)

Teruya, K. (2004) 'A metafunctional profile of Japanese'. In A. Caffarel, J. R. Martin and C. M. I. M. Mathiessen (eds) *Language Typology: a functional perspective*. Philadelphia: John Benjamins.

Thomson, E. A. (1996) *Complex Structures in Japanese: Clauses and Groups.* Presented at the Japan Association of Systemic Functional Linguistics Conference, November, Ritsumeikan University, Kyoto. (Unpublished.)

Thomson, E. A. (2001) *Exploring the Textual Metafunction in Japanese: A case study of selected written texts.* PhD thesis, presented to University of Wollongong, December. (Unpublished.)

Thomson, E. A. (2005) Theme unit analysis: A Systemic functional treatment of textual meanings in Japanese. *Functions of Language* 12(2): 151–179.

Thomson, E., Fukui, N. & White, P.R.R. (2008) Evaluating 'Reporter' Voice in Two Japanese Front-page Lead Stories. In E. Thomson and P.R.R. White (eds.) *Communicating Conflict: Multilingual Case Studies of the Rhetoric of the News Media*. London: Continuum.

Appendix A. Analysis of Text 1: the travel agent

Key notes: B; speaker B, the clerk, A; speaker A, customer.

RESIDUE	MOOD		Connective	Grp	Mood type	Con/ Inc	Sp/ funct
Other than Predicate	Predicate	NM					
B.	*Irasshaimase* welcome			V	Imp	Con	comm
May I help you?							
A.	Kondo desu This time	*ne*		N	Decl	Con	state
At the moment….							
ii [*shinkonryokoo de Oosutoraria ni* to Australia on honeymoon	*ikitai]- to* want to go *omou'n desu* thinking of		*keredomo* but,	V	Decl	con	state
I'm thinking that we want to go to Australia for our honeymoon but..							
iii *donna kanji no ga* what kind of (tours)	*aru'n deshoo* do (you) have?	*ka*		V	D-int	con	ques
what sort of options are there?							
B. i *Hai* Yes,	*kashikomarimashita* certainly			V	Decl	con	state
ii *Soo shimasu to kochira,* In that case, this is	*Oosutoraria no panfuretto nan desu* Australia brochure		*kedo* but	N	Decl	con	state

In that case, here is a brochure on Australia, if that's alright by you.							
iii *Hai shinkonryokoo daitai itsu gurai ni* yes, honeymoon roughly when about	*(ikaremasu*	*ka)*		(V)	D-int	con	ques
Ok, when do you plan to go on your honeymoon?							
A. *Aki gurai ni* autumn about	*(ikimasu)*			(V)	Decl	Con	state
some time in autumn							
B. i *Aki gurai ni* Autumn about	*(ikareru'n) desu*	*ka*		(V)	Inter	con	ques
About autumn ?							
ii *Hai, Oosutoraria wa* Well, Australia	*hiroin'n desu* big		*keredomo* but	Adj	Decl	con	state
Well..Australia is rather large so							
iii *Shidonii ni yahari* to Sydney as be expected	*(ikarerun'n desu*	*yone)*		(V)	inter	con	ques
..I guess you want to see Sydney							
A. i *[Shidonii to ato wa yahari Guretto Baria Riifu, ato wa Eaazu Rokku atari ni* Sydney, also the Great Barrier Reef and as well as the Ayers Rock	*ikitai* *-(to)]* want to go	*na*		Adj	Decl	con	state
	omotte iru'n desu thinking or		*kedo* but	V	Decl	con	state

As well as Sydney I have to see the Great barrier Reef and the area around Ayres rock							
B.	Eaazu Rokku desu Ayers Rock?	*ka*		N	Interr	con	ques
Ayers Rock?							
A. *Hai* Yes							
9. i *Hai* Well	*soo desu* let me see	*ne*			Decl	con	

Appendix B: Analysis of Text 2: the four women chatting

Key: S1, S2, S3, S4; speaker 1, 2, 3, 4

RESIDUE	MOOD		Grp	Mood type	Con/ Inco	Sp/ funct
Other than Predicate	Predicate	NM				
S1. *Shidonii yuni mo* at Sydney uni	*ooi* many	*no ne*	Adj	Decl	con	state
At Syd Uni, there are lots						
	S3. i. *Soo deshoo* You see		N	Decl	con	state
Yeah right.						
ii *dakara* so	*itta janai* I told you		V	Decl	con	state
See, I told you so						
S1. *Moo, ee moo, [yappari ano hito mo kashira] to* As you thought this person is also	< >					state
Yeah, yeah, he might as well be, you know						
	S3. i *Soo deshoo* You see		N	Decl	con	state
Yeah, right						

ii *betsuni* specially	*koko dake ja nai* not only here	*no yo*	N	Decl	con	state
You see, it's not just here						
saisho *at first*	S2. i *[Koko dake da] to* only here ii *omotta?* thought?		V	Decl	inco	ques
Did you think it was just here before?						
S1. *Iya iya iya, demo raiburarian no hitotte kekkoo* No, no, no, but librarians person quite	*ooi no* many	*ka na*	Adj	Inter	con	ques
No, no, no, but are there many who are librarians?						
S3. i *Raiburarian (mo* Librarians*?*	*ooi*	*no)*	Adj	Intter	con	ques
ii *A, raiburarian mo kekkoo* yeah librarians also quite	*ita deshoo ?* exist many		V	Decl	inco	ques
Yeah, there are also a lot who are librarians.						
S2.	Miteru watching		V	Decl	con	state
Good point						

S1. i *Josei ga moto moto* Women are originally	*domein* domain		Adj	Decl	con	state
Originally it was a woman's domain						
ii *ano* yeah	*ookatta* many		Adj	Decl	con	state
Yeah, there were lots of women						
S3. *soo* right	*ookatta* many	*no ne*	Adj	Decl	con	state
Yes, you're right, there were many.						
S1. *Ookatta tokoro tte* A place where many women were	*ooi* many	*no ne*	Adj	Decl	con	state
There are many (gays) in places where women work						
S3. *Un un,* Yes, yes	*ooi* many		Adj	Decl	con	state
Yeah, there are.						
S2. *Dakara sensei mo* That's why also teachers	*ooin'da* many	*yo ne*	Adj	Decl	con	state
So, that's why many of them are teachers, too.						

S3. *un, un dakara sensei mo* Yes, yes, that's why also teachers	*ooi* many	*no*	Adj	Decl	con	state
Ooh, that's why there's so many.						
S2. *Succhuwaadesu mo* Also flight attendant	*ooi (shi)* many (and)		Adj	Decl	con	state
There are lots of flight attendants, too.						
S3.	i *Succhuwaadesu deshoo* Flight attendant		N	Decl	con	state
There are flight attendants.						
	ii *Hosupitariti deshoo* Hospitality		N	Decl	con	state
Hospitality staff						
iii *sorekara biyooshi to ka* and hair dressers etc	*(soo deshoo)*		N	Decl	con	state
and there are hairdressers and so on.						
	iv *Soo deshoo* that's right		N	Decl	Inco	ques
Isn't it right?						
S2. i *Soo soo soo soo* Yes, yes, yes, yes						

ii *Yappari minna soo iu tokoro ni kanshin ga* As you can see their interests, these places	*iku'n da* go	*yo ne*	V	Decl	con	state
Yes, yes. They're interested in going to places like these, right?						
iii Nanaka *seikaku ga* their personality	*onna-poi kara deshoo* because feminine		N	Decl	Inco	ques
because they're feminine, aren't they?						
S1. *uuu n* well						
S3. *i onna poitte iu ka, [kime ga* feminine, rather	*Komakai tte* sensitive ii *itte agete* please say it for them	yo	V	Impe	con	comm
Yeah, but, rather than say that they're feminine, will you say that they are sensitive.						

Appendix C. Analysis of Text 3: *Momotaroo*

Key notes; N; narrator, J; the old man, B; the old woman,

RESIDUE	MOOD		Grp	Mood type	Con/ Inco	Sp/ funct
Other than Predicate	Predicate	NM				
N. *Mukashi mukashi, aru tokoro ni ojiisan to obaasan ga* Once upon a time, somewhere, an old man and an old woman	*sunde orimashita* were living		V	Decl	con	state
Once upon a time, somewhere, an old man and an old woman lived.						
N. i *Aru hi ojiisan wa yama e ki o* One day the old man to a mountain ii *obaasan wa kawa e sentaku ni* and the old woman to a river for washing	kiri ni to cut (trees) *ikimashita.* went		V	Decl	con	state
One day the old man went to the mountain to cut wood, the old woman went to the river to wash						
N. *Zabu zabu, goshi goshi, sabu.* *Scrub scrub scrub scrub*						
N. i. *Obaasan ga kawa de sentaku o* The old woman at the river washing ii [*kawakami kara nagarete kuru*] *mono ga* A thing which is floating in the river	*shite iru to,* was doing then, *arimashita.* existed.		V	Decl	con	state
While the old woman was at the river washing something floated down from upstream						
B *"Hate, are wa* "well that overthere	*nan jaroo?"* what is it?		N	D-intt	con	ques

"Goodness me, what is that?						
N. [*Yura yura, donbura, nagarete kita] no wa ookina* The one floating in the river	*momo deshita.* was a peach.		N	Decl	con	state
It was a big peach bobbing up and down.						
B. i "*Maa, nante ookikute oishi soo na* "What a big and looks delicious peach! Wow, that's a big, yummy looking peach	*momo < > !"*		N	Decl	con	state
ii iii *jiisan to* with the old man	*motte kaette,* taki it home *tabeyoo* shall we eat (it)?	*ka*	V	Obl	con	offer
I shall take it home and eat it with the old man						
N. i [*Yama kara kaetta] ojiisan mo* The old man who came back from the mountain ii	*bikkuri shitari,* (was) surprised and *yorokondari (shi-mashita)* (was) excited		V	Decl	con	state
The old man returning from the mountains was surprised and excited.						
J. i "*Konna ookina momo mita koto mo* Such a big peach, ever seen	*nai* (I) don't have	*noo*	V	Decl	con	state
I've never seen such a big peach						
ii	*Oishi soo ja* Looks delicious		Adi	Decl	con	sate
It looks yummy						

B.” *Dewa,* Well then	*itadaki mashoo* lets eat it	*ka*	V	Obl	con	offer
“Well then, let’s eat it”						
N.	*Sono toki desu* that time		N	Decl	con	state
At that moment						
N. *Momo ga hitori de ni pakan to* The peach by itself clap	waremashita broken		V	Decl	con	state
The peach burst open by itself						
B. *“Arya rya, kore wa nanto!”* “Oh my goodness,!”				M/cl		
N. *Wareta mono no naka kara otoko no ko ga* From the broken peach inside, a boy	*tobidashita dewa arimasen* as a surprise, appeared	*ka*	V	Inter	inco	state
and what do you know! A boy jumped out of the burst peach.						
B.i*”Maa nante kawaii genki na* What a cute, healthy	*ko deshoo”* child (he) is.		N	Decl	con	state
ii *Uchi no ko ni* As our child	*shimashoo”* let’s make (him)		V	Obl	con	Offer
“Let’s adopt him as our own”.						
N. *[Kodomo no inai] ojiisan to obaasan wa* The old man and the old woman who don’t have any children	*ooyorokobi (shima-sita)* very happy		V	Decl	con	state
The childless couple were very happy						

4 The system of THEME in Japanese

Elizabeth A. Thomson
UNSW, Canberra

This paper will describe one instance of the system of THEME in Japanese as it is realised in a set of selected written texts. The unit over which Theme/Rheme is mapped is the *Theme unit* which is defined grammatically as a co-referential unit in which the referent is the first constituent (Thomson, 2005:162), and semantically as one phase of continuous thematic progression (Thomson, 2005:165). The realisation of Theme is the constituent in first position of the Theme unit. The following description includes a treatment of single Themes, multiple Themes, implicit Themes and marked Themes.

The notion of THEME

By way of opening the discussion on the system of THEME in Japanese, let me begin with a discussion on whether or not the notion of Theme is useful in relation to Japanese. Halliday has defined the category of Theme within the theory as '... the element which serves as the point of departure of the message; it is that with which the clause is concerned.... the part in which the Theme is developed is called the Rheme' (Halliday, 1994:37).

Theme, as defined by Halliday, is a functional category. Inter alia, the category of Theme theoretically can be realised in different languages using different lexicogrammatical resources. For example, Theme in English is realised by first position in the clause (Halliday, 1994:38). Halliday illustrates this using the following examples in Table 1.

Table 1: Theme in English

Theme	Rheme
a. The duke	has given my aunt that teapot.
b. My aunt	has been given that teapot by the duke.
c. That teapot	the duke has given to my aunt.
d. Once upon a time	there were three bears.
e. Very carefully	she put him back on his feet again.
f. For want of a nail	the shoe was lost.
g. With sobs and tears	he sorted out those of the largest size

In each example, Theme is realised by the position of the elements, that is, first position, rather than by some other means such as *function, class* or *unit* on the rank scale. Each of these examples, due to their initial positioning, orient the message by establishing a point of departure for the ensuing ideational meaning.

Halliday postulates three kinds of Themes: the ideational, the interpersonal and the textual. Again, illustrating this using examples from English, the ideational Theme is the first element in the Transitivity structure of the clause (Halliday, 1994:53). It can be a Participant or a Circumstantial Adjunct of some kind, or, depending on the MOOD choice, a Process or an interrogative element. The interpersonal Theme, which precedes the ideational Theme, is an initial element that engages in attitudinal orientation (Matthiessen, 1995a:538) by the use of attitudinal adjuncts, vocatives and the presence of the Finite element. The textual Theme, which precedes the ideational Theme, is the first continuative, structural or conjunctive element fronting the clause (Halliday, 1994:53). In making his point, Halliday illustrates multiple Theme using the complex example in Table 2.

Table 2: Multiple Theme in English (Halliday, 1994:55)

well	**but**	**then**	**Ann**	**surely**	**wouldn't**	**the best idea**	**be to join the group?**
continuative	structural	conjunctive	vocative	modal	finite	topical	
textual			interpersonal			ideational	
THEME							Rheme

Halliday's discussion on Theme (1994) is illustrated descriptively by the operation of Theme in English. As stated, Theme in English is realised by first position. However, Theme as first position is one instantiation of the abstract concept of the system of THEME in the theory. It does not automatically follow that other languages will construe Theme as the initial element in the clause. This being the case, the intriguing questions for me were:

1. Is Theme a useful concept for languages other than English?
2. Does it exist in Japanese? and,
3. If so, how is it realised in the lexicogrammar of Japanese?

The first step in a discussion on whether or not Theme is a useful notion in relation to Japanese is to consider the nature of the clause in an authentic Japanese text environment, looking for clausal patterns which correlate with the organisation of text. If such clausal patterns exist, then this suggests that perhaps the system of Theme operates in Japanese to set up ideational constituents as points of expansion, that is, to give 'value to some term (node) in the instantial system as the current point of expansion or growth' (Matthiessen, 1995b:27). And further, it would be expected that these clausal patterns 'key into' the method of development of the text as it constructs an instantial system from a linear text (Matthiessen, 1995b:26). There is also an expectation to find clausal patterns which serve to link clauses to each other building up coherence and enabling single clauses to work together to build cohesion between them thereby constructing 'text' [1].

If, through an investigation of the clausal patterns, Theme can be identified, Fries and Francis (1992) have rightly pointed out that there are two critical steps in the development of the description of Theme in another language: 1) the description must be explicit, that is, have recognition criteria; and 2) it must be illustrated in context, linking thematic content to the interpretation of text (p.56). The treatment of Theme in this chapter attempts to provide explicit recognition criteria for Theme in Japanese, and to detail the choices of Theme within the texts of the corpus. These choices contribute, in part, to the overall social purpose of each text type.

Japanese clause patterning

There are two clausal patterns of organisation which suggest that a system of THEME operates in Japanese. The first pattern is the unmarked position of the process in a Japanese clause. Typically, the process is the clause-final constituent, all other constituents occurring before the process. The second pattern of organisation is the non-fixed order of the nuclear[2] and non-nuclear participants in the clause.

> Japanese is usually said to have a free word order with respect to the adjuncts. This means that so long as you put the predicate (the nuclear sentence) at the end, where it belongs in a well-planned sentence, you are free to present each of the build-up phrases early or late as you see fit ... thematisation, for example, will place an adjunct at the beginning of the sentence. (Martin, 1988:35)

An unfixed (preferable term to Martin's, 'free') order enables choice in what to position first, or second, or third and so on in the clause. What then motivates this choice of constituent order? One possible reason for the choice might depend on which constituent the writer wants to construe as a point of departure for the clause. By choosing a particular order, the writer might be allowing a particular constituent to act as a point of expansion from which the text may develop. The fact that the writer has a choice in constituent order suggests that first position may act as a salient site of textual organisation.

These two clausal patterns of Japanese suggest that the notion of Theme may be a useful notion in relation to the construal of textual meanings. Consequently, a pilot study was conducted to determine if indeed Theme in Japanese was realised by first position in the clause as the above reasoning suggests. This was a 'Theme scrambling' exercise similar to that conducted by Halliday (1977) on English. In the pilot study, it was hypothesised that 'if first position is salient for thematic organisation of a Japanese text, then changing the first element of the clause should disrupt the Theme, thereby making the message in the text difficult to retrieve' (Thomson, 1998:227). The expectation is that the text would be less cohesive internally with the co-text and less coherent externally with the context.

The study involved the manipulation of two newspaper articles by moving the first element in each clause to another position while maintaining grammaticality. The original and tampered versions of each text were then given to thirty Japanese speaking informants who were asked to read each version and decide which was easier to read and understand.

As anticipated, the readers preferred the original texts. 76 percent[3] of the informants preferred the original of text 1, *Setsubun,* and 96 percent preferred the original of text 2, *Ginkoo.* The informants gave a number of reasons for their preferences. These included:

1. the 'element + *wa*' was better positioned;
2. the 'word linking' method was better;
3. the subject was clearer and more straightforward;
4. you got lost in the tampered text;
5. the organisation of information in the tampered text was difficult to follow;
6. the SOV structure was clearer in the original texts;
7. the word order was wrong in the tampered texts.

(Thomson, 1998:228)

In brief, the readers found they got lost or else found it difficult to follow the point of the texts when they had their first position elements changed. In other words, the first position element functioned as an orienter (Fries, 1995a:318) for the unfolding of the message. It guided the reader/listener. Without this orientation the readers found the point of the information difficult to follow. This result suggests that Theme in Japanese is realised by first position and that first position plays a role in thematic development in Japanese.

However, it became apparent in the process of setting up the 'scrambling' exercise that first position needed to be further specified, that is, was it first position of the clause or first position of some other *unit* in the grammar? Within accepted SF theory, the *unit* of the clause is the segment of text over which the textual system of THEME operates (Halliday, 1994:36). This is despite the fact that the system of THEME is recognised as a fractal category – one which manifests in different ranking environments (Matthiessen, 1995a:90). Further, in relation to Japanese, Teruya (1998) also maps Theme/Rheme onto the *unit* clause.

However, conflating the span of operation of Theme to the clause ignores the effect of ellipsis and clause chaining[4] in Japanese – both of which are briefly described below. In order to account for the effect of these two grammatical features on the organisation of text, the theorisation of a unit larger than the clause is appropriate. Fries (1995b), in his work on Theme in English, has considered a unit larger than the clause and it was his work which was the motivation behind the pursuit of the notion that a unit larger than the clause may operate in Japanese. In accounting for the existence of a unit larger than the clause in Japanese, I have coined the term, Theme unit (Thomson, 2005), and have used it to understand how the system of THEME operates in Japanese.

Ellipsis and clause chaining

Before defining the Theme unit, I will give a brief description of how ellipsis and clause chaining act as forms of structural cohesion, linking clauses within clause complexes and between sentence boundaries in Japanese.

The first characteristic of Japanese which justifies the use of the Theme unit is that of co-referential ellipsis. While the system of ELLIPSIS operates in Japanese as one of the systems of the textual metafunction, it is the operation of co-referential ellipsis, specifically the presence of endophoric S (subject) ellipsis[5] (Hasan, 1996), which acts as a form of structural cohesion, linking items cohesively between clause complexes and across sentence boundaries. An example of this is provided in Table 3.

Table 3: Endophoric S ellipsis

'The old woman, being delighted, stretched out her hand and grabbed it'.

Obaasan wa	*ureshikute,*	***(zero)****	*sugu*	*te o*	*nobashite*	***(zero)****	*sore o*	*tsukamae-mashita.*
The old woman	being delighted,	**(she)**	immediately	hand	stretched out,	**(she)**	it	grabbed
Carrier	Attribute	Actor	Circ	Goal	Process: material	Actor	Goal	Process: material
Clause 1		Clause 2				Clause 3		

*the position of the elided constituent is located at the beginning of Clauses 2 and 3 because the quantitative result of this study indicates that the Actor is the unmarked Theme choice in a material process and as such is also available for selection as an implicit or elided element. Refer to the section on Implicit types.

In this example the Actor, *obaasan wa* (old woman) appears in first position of Clause 1, and even though *obaasan wa* continues to be the Actor in the following two clauses, *obaasan wa* is elided. The presupposed *obaasan wa* in clauses 2 and 3 is recoverable from the immediate cotext, that is, from Clause 1. It is an example of endophoric S ellipsis.

Endophoric S ellipsis occurs not only within clause complexes but, in written Japanese texts, across sentence boundaries as well. An example of this is presented in Table 4. Here, the couple, *hutari wa* operates as Actor in both sentences 1 and 2, although it is only explicitly stated following the connective element in Sentence 1.

Table 4: Endophoric S ellipsis across a sentence boundary

After that, the couple heated the water and **they** gave the baby its first bath. **They** also made the baby's first kimono and **they** dressed him.

1.1.Sore kara, **After that,**	*hutari wa* **the couple (they)**	*oyu o wakashite,* **heated the water and** *1.2 akanbo ni ubuyu o tsukawasemashita.* **gave the baby its first bath.**		**Sentence 1**
	(They) **(they)**	*2.1 Ubugi to iu kimono nan ka mo tsukutte* **also made (the baby's) first kimono and** *2.2 kisemashita.* **dressed (him) in (it).**		**Sentence 2**

Additional to endophoric ellipsis is the presence of formal, exophoric S ellipsis. 'A formal exophoric device is one whose interpretation is predetermined by the language system and permits no true variation in wording' (Hasan, 1996:207). This is a form of ellipsis which is based on our shared understanding of grammatical behaviour. These presupposed constituents are predicatable and implicit. In the example in Table 5, the reader knows that there is an elided Theme from their knowledge of the grammatical structure of the relational attributive process, *da/desu* (is). A clause ending in a relational process, typically begins with a 'participant+*wa*' constituent. The reader retrieves the elided Theme from their linguistic knowledge.

Table 5: Formal, exophoric ellipsis

(participant+wa) (The incident)	*sono ban no koto desu.* was that night.
Theme	Rheme

Another argument for justifying the presence of the Theme unit is the chaining effect of clauses in clause complexes in Japanese. Chaining structures are clause complexing structures involving a series of medial verbs followed by a final dominant verb which manifests a fuller structure than the preceding verbs (Longacre, 1985). In SF terms, these are hypotactic structures where the medial verbs, or beta clauses are dependent on the final, alpha clause for tense and mood type selection. Japanese tends to select chaining structures, that is, hypotaxis[6], more often that parataxis. A consequence of this is that chained clauses share nuclear and/ or non-nuclear participants which appear in first position in the first clause of the chain, but which are presupposed in the subsequent clauses. The clause complex in Table 3 is a hypotactic chain, co-referentially connected by the elided Actor, *obaasan wa* (the old woman).

The Theme unit in Japanese

Taking co-referential ellipsis and clause chaining into account, it seems reasonable to consider Theme in Japanese as being realised by first position in the Theme unit rather than by first position in the clause. The Theme unit can thus be defined both in grammatical and semantic terms. Grammatically, the Theme unit is realised by a segment of text that

> '…forms a co-referential unit in which the referent (that which is retrievable) is the first constituent in the unit. In other words, the segment of text forms of cohesive unit as a result of either the encoded presence of the referent; or the exophoric formal (S) ellipsis of the referent. Further, the operation of anaphoric subject (S) ellipsis ties subsequent clauses to the initial referent' (Thomson, 2005:162).

The semantic criterion for defining the Theme unit can be found in the thematic progression pattern which occurs as a result of the structural nature of the unit. Due to the combined effect of co-referential ellipsis and clause chaining, the Theme unit manifests a continuous thematic progression pattern (Daneš, 1974), in other words, the Theme unit is semantically defined as one phase of continuous thematic progression. This is illustrated in Table 6. The first constituent in the Theme unit, *obaasan* functions as Theme across the three clauses. The Theme is thus manifesting a continuous progression pattern.

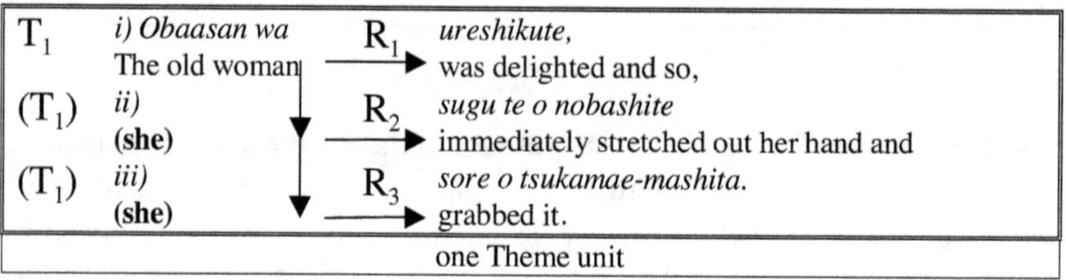

T_1	*i) Obaasan wa* The old woman	R_1 →	*ureshikute,* was delighted and so,
(T_1)	*ii)* **(she)**	R_2 →	*sugu te o nobashite* immediately stretched out her hand and
(T_1)	*iii)* **(she)**	R_3 →	*sore o tsukamae-mashita.* grabbed it.
			one Theme unit

Table 6: One phase of continuous thematic progression

Following on from the brief background discussion for the justification of the presence of the Theme unit in Japanese, this chapter will subsequently describe one instance of the system of THEME in Japanese. It will illustrate that Theme is realised by first position in the Theme unit and describe the various kinds of Themes in qualitative and quantitative terms, representing the full set of choices as a system network and indicating the unmarked and marked choices within the system.

The corpus

The corpus of this study consists of written texts which are taught in the Japanese language curriculum at the University of Wollongong. These texts fall into three common genres: news articles, nursery tales and narratives. There is an example of a hard news story, a soft news story, a news editorial, two nursery tales, two short stories and the opening section of a contemporary novel. This selection serves as a small but representative example of written genres found in Japanese and thus is useful to demonstrate possible generalisations in relation to textual meanings. The corpus is as follows:

1. Hard News story

   Ginkoo ni Tanjuu Gootoo: Sampatsu Hassha: 200 man-en ubatte toosoo (Armed Bank Robbery: 3 shots fired, robbers stole 2 million yen and fled), *Mainichi Shimbun* (The Mainichi Newspaper), 1 August, 1980. In Mizutani, O and Mizutani, N (1981) *An Introduction to Newspaper Japanese,* Tokyo, The Japan Times

2. Soft News story

   Samusa Yurunde Setsubun (The Cold Eases and it is the Bean-Throwing Festival), *Nihon Keizai Shimbun* (The Japan Economic Newspaper), 3 February, 1972. In Mizutani, O and Mizutani, N (1981) *An Introduction to Newspaper Japanese,* Tokyo, The Japan Times

3. News Editorial

   Keizai Kishoodai – Keisanki kara Zunoo e (Economic Forecast – From the Calculator to the Brain) *Asahi Shimbun* (The Asahi Newspaper), Evening Edition, 2 November, 1988. In Association for Japanese-Language Teaching (1991) *Reading Japanese Financial Newspapers,* Tokyo, Kodansha International

4. Long nursery tale

   Tsubota, J (1975) *Momotaroo* (The Peach Boy[7]), in Nihon Mukashi Banashi Shuu (A Collection of Folktales of Japan), Japan, Shincho Bunko. pp.24–38

5. Short nursery tale

   Tsubota, J (1975) *Urihimeko* (The Melon Princess[8]), in Nihon Mukashi Banashi Shuu (A Collection of Folktales of Japan), Tokyo, Shinchoo Bunko. pp.18–23.

6. Literary short story

   Miyazawa, K (1970). *Donguri to Yamaneko* (The Acorns and the Mountain Cat), in *Chuumon no Ooi Ryoori-ten* (The restaurant of many orders) Tokyo, Kadokawa Bunko pp.10–22.

7. Contemporary short story

   Atooda, T (1982) *Taberareta Otoko (The Man who was Eaten)* in Taberareta Otoko Japan, Kodansha. pp.249–256.

8. Opening section of a contemporary novel

   Murakami, H (1991), *Noruwei no Mori (Joo)* (Norwegian Wood), Tokyo, Kodansha. pp.7–12.

Methodology

The first step in the study was to parse each text in the corpus into clauses, which were then parsed into Theme units. The clause and Theme unit count is presented in Table 7. In total there were 647 Theme units consisting of 1,105 clauses.

Table 7: The clauses and Theme units in the corpus

Text type	Clauses	Theme units
The Newspaper articles		
Samusa Yurunde Setsubun	19	12
Ginkoo ni Tanjuu Gootoo	25	12
Keizai Kishoodai	36	23
The Nursery Tales		
Urihimeko	120	71
Momotaroo	335	190
The Narratives		
Noruwei no Mori	138	86
Donguri to Yamaneko	289	151
Taberareta Otoko	143	102
TOTAL	**1105**	**647**

The clauses in the corpus consisted of simplexes, complexes and clause fragments, consisting of single circumstances or onomatopoeia. The clause breakdown is presented in Table 8.

Table 8: Clause breakdown of the texts in the corpus

Texts	Total # clauses	Simplexes	Complexes		Sentence Fragments
			Parataxis	Hypotaxis	
News Stories					
Setsubun	19	6 (31.5%)	0	13 (68.5%)	0
Ginkoo	25	4 (16%)	2 (8%)	19 (76%)	0
Keizai	36	9 (25%)	2 (5.5%)	25 (69.5%)	0
Nursery Tales					
Urihimeko	120	37 (31%)	4 (3%)	68 (56%)	12 (10%)
Momotaroo	335	81 (24%)	18 (5.5%)	202 (60.5%)	34 (10%)
Narratives					
Taberareta	143	25 (17.5%)	25 (17.5%)	59 (41%)	34 (24%)
Noruwei	138	38 (27.5%)	10 (7%)	78 (56.5%)	12 (9%)
Donguri	289	46 (16%)	16 (5.5%)	179 (62%)	48 (16.5%)

The second step was to classify and count the constituents which appeared in first position in the Theme unit, taking into account two considerations: the possibility of multiple and single constituents in first position, and the possibility that first position constituents function to construe textual, interpersonal and ideational meanings. The categories of classification are illustrated in Table 9. Within the ideational domain there are the two categories of logical and experiential. For the experiential, Teruya's transitivity typology (1998), which is organised according to process type, was used. For the logical, it was assumed that if a clause complex was hypotactic, then the first clause would be a dependent, beta (ß) clause, functioning to construe the two logico semantic types of expansion and projection. Within expansion, meanings of enhancement, extension, and elaboration were anticipated, while within projection, locutions or ideas (see Halliday 1994 for a full description of logico semantic relations) were anticipated. Further, allowance was made for the possibility of multiple themes and no assumption was made in relation to the order or kind of metafunctional role played by the clause constituents, were they to cluster as a multiple theme sequence.

Table 9: Categories of classification of the constituents in first position in the Theme unit

Single	**Ideational**	**Experiential**	**Participant**	**Material**	**Actor**
					Goal
					Scope
					Beneficiary
				Mental	Sensor
					Phenomenon
				Relational	Carrier
					Attribute
					Grounds
					Carrier-domain
					Identified
					Identifier
					Existent
				Verbal	Sayer
					Receiver
					Verbiage
					Target
			Circumstance		Angle
					Matter
					Temporal Location
					Spatial Location
					Cause
					Manner
		Logical	Expansion		Elaborating
					Extending
					Enhancing
			Projection		Locution
					Idea
	Textual				Structural & non-structural connectives
	Interpersonal				Comment & Mood Adjuncts
Multiple					

Using these categories, the constituents in first position in the Theme units in each of the texts within the corpus were classified. The following section presents the qualitative and quantitative results.

Qualitative results

Single Themes

Single Themes in the corpus consist of textual, interpersonal and ideational Themes.

Textual Themes

Textual Themes are essentially connectives of various kinds, establishing cohesive relations of elaboration, extension and enhancement, and creating transitions in the text. There are examples of conjunctive particles (*setsuzokuji*), conjunctions (*setsuzokushi*), and also connective phrases. Examples of each taken from the corpus are in Tables 10, 11, 12 and 13. Note that despite the fact that these textual Themes are single Themes, there is a presupposed ideational Theme in each case. It could be argued that these are examples of multiple Themes. However, due to the operation of ellipsis, both endophoric S ellipsis and formal, exophoric ellipsis in the reality of the text, the ideational Theme is not stated. It is implicit, so these examples are treated as single textual Themes.

Table 10: Conjunctive Postposition as textual Theme

taken from *Taberareta Otoko*

	THEME		RHEME
Theme unit	Textual: **Conjunctive postposition**	elided ideational	
23.	*To,* And so,	(He)	*sutasuta arukidasu.* strode off briskly.

Table 11: Conjunction as textual Theme

taken from *Keizai Kishoodai – keisanki kara zunoo*

	THEME		RHEME
Theme unit	Textual: **conjunction**	elided ideational	
2	*Shikashi,* But,	(it)	*nakanaka fukyuu shinai.* has not spread much.

Table 12: Connective phrase as textual Theme

taken from *Taberareta Otoko*

	THEME		RHEME
Theme unit	Textual: **Connective phrase**	elided ideational	
13.	*ippoo de wa* on the one hand	(I)	*iv. kore wa kitto yoku nai dekigoto no zenchoo da to kigu o kanji,* felt that this was like a warning against a future, bad event, but
14.	*moo ippoo de wa* on the other hand	(I)	*v. nani ka yoku nai koto ga okotte hoshii to negau yoo na, sonna hukuzatsu na kangai o idaita mono datta.* had this kind of complicated, deep feeling which was wanting something bad to happen.

Table 13: Connective clause as textual Theme

taken from *Taberareta Otoko*

Theme unit	THEME		RHEME
	Textual: Connective Clause	elided ideational	
18.	*To itte mo,* By this I mean,	*(it)*	*ashi ga hutoku nattari, nagaku nattari shita wake de wa nai.* wasn't that his legs became fatter or longer.

Interpersonal Themes

Single interpersonal Themes occur in the corpus, but they are very rare. Their scarcity may relate to the fact that the lexicogrammar of the interpersonal metafunction of Mood and Modality tend to utilise the end of the clause where the process is most typically located rather than at the beginning of the Theme unit. When an interpersonal Theme occurs, it is the result of the writer wanting to foreground an interpersonal 'take' or 'spin' on the message. And so occasionally, single interpersonal Themes do occur and are most frequently realised by a comment adjunct. As is the case for the single textual Theme, the single interpersonal Theme is followed by a presupposed ideational Theme, as again, ellipsis is in operation. This is illustrated in the example in Table 14.

Table 14: Single Interpersonal Theme

taken from *Urihimeko*

Theme unit	THEME		RHEME
	Interpersonal: **Comment Adjunct**	elided ideational	
23.	*Hontoo ni* Truly,	 (it)	*tsume no kakaru hodo datta no desu.* was just a crack big enough for a finger nail.

Ideational Themes

Ideational Themes consist of experiential and logical types. Ideational Themes can either be explicitly or implicitly stated. If the choice is explicit, then the experiential set consists of participants and circumstances, while the logical set consists of beta expansion clauses and projections. Note that in this study, the term, 'ideational' Theme is used rather than 'topical' theme, to avoid any misunderstanding of the term 'topic'[9] in relational to Japanese.

Within the set of single experiential Themes, a restricted set of participants and circumstances occur. Similarly, within the set of single logical Themes, only enhancing, locution and idea beta clauses occur. Examples of each type taken from the corpus are in Tables 15, 16, 17 and 18.

Table 15: Participant

taken from *Taberareta Otoko*

Theme unit	THEME **Ideational: experiential participant (Medium)**	RHEME
1.	*Kore wa* This	*watashi no shitashii yuujin, S-kun ni okotta koto de aru* happened to my close friend, S-kun.

Table 16: Circumstance

taken from *Urihimeko*

Theme unit	THEME Ideational: experiential circumstance	RHEME
61.	*i.Ojiisan,obaasan no ie no soba no ki no ue ni,* In a tree beside the house of the old man and woman	*ichiwa no karasu ga tomatte,* one crow landed and *ii. 'Urihimeko no okago ni yo, Amanjaku me ga notte iku. Kaa kaa kaa kaa'.* *to nakimashita.* sang, 'In Urihimeko's carriage, the naughty Amanjaku is riding. Crow, crow, crow, crow'.

Table 17: Enhancing beta clause

taken from *Momotaroo*

	THEME Ideational: expansioin: enhancing beta clause	RHEME
1.24	*i. Mizu kara ue e sukoshi agatta to omou to,* When (she) thought (she) had lifted (it) from the water,	*ii. te ga subette,* her hands slipped and *iii. dobuun to, shita ni ochimashita.* (it) fell, 'KaBoom' back in.

Table 18: Projection

taken from *Noruwei no Mori*

	THEME Ideational: projection: locution	RHEME
26	*'Auf Wiedersehen!' to* 'Goodbye'	*Boku mo itta.* I also said.

Implicit Themes

As stated earlier, within the system of THEME as realised within in the corpus, the ideational Themes can either be explicitly or implicitly stated. The discussion above dealt with the kinds of explicit ideational choices. In this section, the implicit ideational choices are discussed.

The fact that implicit Themes occur can be explained by the presence of redundancy in the grammar of Japanese. According to Lemke (1995) redundancy is 'a formal way of describing what goes with what else.....the predictable relation or connection of two things'(p.169). Essentially, the implicit Themes are redundant in that they are predictable either from the grammar (formal exophoric ellipsis), from the surrounding text (endophoric ellipsis) or from the context. Table 19 presents an example of an implicit Theme due to redundancy in the grammar.

Table 19: Implicit Theme due to redundancy in the grammar

Theme unit	THEME	RHEME
	implicit Ideational:participant Identified	
2.1	(It)	*amanjaku no urihimeko ga oyome iri no asa no koto desu.* was on the morning of the wedding of Urihimeko's imposter

In this example, *amanjaku no urihimeko ga oyome iri no asa no koto desu* occurs at the beginning of the final stage of the nursery tale, *Urihimeko*. This is the narrator setting the scene for the final event which is about to unfold, that is, the murder of the imposter. This is an identifying, circumstantial, intensive relational process with only one participant, the Identifier, *amanjaku no urihimeko ga oyome iri no asa no koto* (on the morning of the wedding of Urihimeko's imposter) and the process, *desu* (to be). The Identified, if it were to have been explicitly stated, would have been either the noun group, *satsugai wa* (the murder) or the demonstrative pronominal, *sore* (it), and thus the clause could be glossed, 'The murder was on the morning of the wedding of Urihimeko's imposter'. However, the typical unmarked form of a scene-setting relational clause in Japanese grammar is Identifier plus Process only. Typically, the Identified, in this case, *sore* (it) is implied and only explicitly stated as a marked variation. This kind of grammatical redundancy, that is, a relational process without an Identified participant serves to 'set the scene', as it were, in the nursery tales and narratives, and occurs as a result of formal exophora, that is, from our shared knowledge of grammatical behaviour.

Table 20 illustrates an example of an implicit Theme due to redundancy in the co-text. In this example from *Momotaroo* (Theme unit 3.19), the presupposed participant Theme, 'he', refers co-referentially to the referent item, *Momotaroo,* in Theme unit 3.14. As the referent item is retrievable, there is no need in the text to refer again explicitly to *Momotaroo* while ever the referent item remains unchanged across the Theme units. The Theme is thus implicit as the referent item is unchanged. This is an example of redundancy in the surrounding co-text due to endophoric S ellipsis, as previously explained.

Table 20: Implicit Theme due to redundancy in the cotext

	THEME	RHEME
	implicit **Ideational: participant** **Actor**	
3.14	*Momotaroo wa* Momotaroo	*shuppatsu shimashita*... ... ... left... ... ...
3.19	(He)	*i. Uchi o deta,* left the house and, *ii. sukoshi iku to,* after going a little way, *iii. mura e demashita.* arrived at the village.

The final kind of redundancy which relates to the presence of implicit Themes is that of redundancy in the context of culture. Typically, nursery tales end in with the words, *medetashi, medetashi*. This translates figuratively as '... happily ever after', however literally it means, 'well done, well done'/ 'congratulations, congratulations'. This ending only makes sense if one knows what act 'well done' refers to, and that 'what' is implied by a presupposed beta clause which is left to the reader to construe. The construal of the beta clause however, is very predictable because the consumer of the text knows that the social purpose of a nursery tale is to teach a lesson or moral. Readers and listeners know to fill in the missing clause with something that relates to the lesson or moral of the story – something to do with the success of good over evil, or the fact that they understand the point of the story. This is supported by Tosu (1985) when he states that, '[t]he Japanese language tends to leave much room for the hearer to judge the implications'(p.179). Two possible versions of the presupposed beta clause are supplied in the example in Table 21. This predictability is a form of redundancy, but not in the grammar, or the co-text but in the reader's understanding of the function of the nursery tale within their culture. It is a form of cultural redundancy, which in this case, is realised by formal exophora not of the grammar, but of the culture.

Table 21: Implicit Theme due to redundancy in the culture

taken from *Momotaroo*

	THEME	RHEME
	implicit Ideational:beta clause	
5.49	*(i.Minna shiawase ni natte,)* (Because everyone was now happy,) or *(ojiisan, obaasan wa Momotaroo ga buji ni kaette kite ureshikute,)* (The old couple were happy because Momotaroo returned safely,)	*ii.medetashi, medetashi.* well done, well done.

Multiple Themes

In the corpus, there are two kinds of multiple Themes: univariate and multivariate. The univariate Themes are those that consist of two circumstantial Themes, that is, two constituents serving the same function. These Themes are found at the beginning of the hard and soft news stories and the nursery tales, and serve to set the scene of the action that is to follow.

The presence of a univariate Theme in the corpus signals that the text is either a news story or a nursery tale. It seems that single circumstances do not exhaust the thematic potential – they can stack up at the beginning of the Theme unit to foreground the circumstantial context of the event. The presence of univariate Themes in the news stories may be a feature of the genre as univariate Themes allow for a lot of information to be presented in a small amount of space. They allow for maximum impact in limited space. Consider the example in Table 22. The two circumstantial Themes, *Tsuitachi gozen juji gojuugo-hun goro* (on the first around 9:55am) and *Fukui-shi Kasuga-choo 238–1, Fukui Ginkoo Kasuga Shiten = Katoo Tomomasa Shiten–choo (44)= ni* (at the Kasuga branch of the Fukui Bank 238–1 Kasuga-choo = managed by Tomomasa Katoh (44)) supply all the circumstantial detail of the robbery – the date, time, place, address as well as details of the bank manager. Also as all this information is foregrounded, it is considered a multiple Theme, presented as two distinct nominal groups, both stacked up together and setting the scene for the detail of the actions of the robber, which are subsequently described in the Rheme.

Table 22: Univariate: circumstance ^ circumstance

taken from *Ginkoo ni Tanjuu Gootoo*

	THEME Univariate: (a) temporal circumstance ^ (b) spatial circumstance	RHEME
1.	*i. a. Tsuitachi gozen kuji gojuugo-hun goro,* *b. Hukui-shi Kasuga-choo 238–1, Hukui Ginkoo Kasuga Shiten =Katoo Tomomasa Shiten-choo (44) = ni,* a. On the first around 9:55am b. at the Kasuga branch of the Fukui bank 238–1 Kasuga-choo =managed by Katoo Tomomasa (44)=	*sanjussai kurai no kuro sangurasu o otoko ga kyaku o yosootte* a man about 30 years old wearing black sunglasses disguised as a customer, *ii.hairikomi,* entered the bank and *iii. raitenchuu o dooshi Itagaki-choo Shimonawate, shuhu, Sugaware Kimiyo-san (30) o ushiro kara ikinari hagai jime ni shita ue,* in addition to suddenly grabbing from behind Mrs. Kimiyo Sugawara, a house wife from Fukui City Itagaki-cho Shimonawate who was visiting the bank at the time, *iv. kauntaa chuo ni ita suitoo gakari no Yoshino Toshiyuki-san (29) ni pisutoru o muke,* (he) pointed a gun at Mr. Yoshino Toshiyuki (29) a bank clerk standing behind the counter, and v. '*Okane o dase, hayaku dase' to odoshita.* demanded, 'Take out the money quickly!'

The presence of circumstances functioning as univariate, multiple Themes in this corpus suggests that other kinds of univariate Themes may occur. While no tokens were present in the corpus, it is possible to envisage participants functioning as univariate, multiple Themes. Multiple participant Themes are often anecdotally presented when the function of particle *wa* is under discussion. However, in order to confirm their presence, examples need to be found in corpora and shown to be functioning thematically. There were no examples of univariate, multiple, participant Themes in the corpus.

The other kind of multiple Theme is the multivariate type. This is the more typical kind of multiple Theme in which different constituents serve different metafunctional roles at the beginning of the Theme unit. In the corpus, there are two kinds: a textual Theme followed by an ideational Theme; and an interpersonal Theme followed by an ideational Theme. The textual component of the multiple Themes have the same kinds of constituents as in the single textual examples. There are examples of conjunctive particles (*setsuzokuji*), conjunctions (*setsuzokushi*) and connective phrases. This is also true of the interpersonal and ideational components, that is, the same kinds of constituents which appear as single Themes appear as components of multiple Themes. 'The interpersonal Themes indicate to the reader that the ideational configurations that follow are to be taken from the writer's angle' (Matthiessen, 1995b:41). Examples are provided in Table 23 and 24. Note, that no examples of the multiple Theme type: textual followed by interpersonal followed by ideational, which is found in English, occurred.

Table 23: Multivariate: textual ^ ideational kind

taken from *Keizai Kishoodai – keisanki kara zunoo*

Theme unit	THEME		RHEME
	Textual: **connective clause**	Ideational: Agent	
24	*Kangaete mireba* When you think about it,	*i.ningen wa,* people	*aimai ni oomaka ni taishoo o torae,* take hold of phenomena broadly and ambiguously and, *ii. samazama ni shori shi,* deal with it is a variety of ways and, *iii. machigae nagara mo* while even making mistakes *iv. gakushuu shite* learn and *v. shidai ni kashikoku naru.* gradually become more intelligent.

Table 24: Multivariate: interpersonal ^ ideational kind

taken from *Urihimeko*

Theme unit	THEME		RHEME
	Interpersonal: **Comment adjunct**	Ideational: Medium	
19.	*Annojoo,* As expected,	*Amanjaku ga* Amanjaku	*yatte kimashita.* visited. *'Urihimeko, Urihimeko, ore to issho ni asobimashoo.'* 'Urihimeko, Urihimeko, let's play together'

Probabilities

The following section presents the probabilities or frequencies of the occurrences of the different Theme types as they appear in the corpus. The counts are used to justify the marked and unmarked choices of Theme. An unmarked choice is the most frequent choice and therefore the most probable constituent to be selected as Theme. Conversely, the marked choices are the least frequent and, thus, least probable.

Ideational themes

Table 25 sets out the total percentage of the participants, the circumstances and the clauses of expansion and projection in first position in the corpus. The participant is the most common first position element, occurring 72 percent of the time. Typically, the participant occurs most frequently as a single constituent (38.6 percent), but also features in multiple combinations, coupled with either textual or interpersonal elements, or as an implicit constituent.

Table 25: The percentage of participants, circumstances, beta clauses and projections in first position in the corpus

Text type	**Experiential**		**Logical**	
	participant	circumstance	enhancing clause	projection
The Newspaper articles				
Ginkoo ni Tanjuu Gootoo	4/12 33.5%	5/12 41.5%	3/12 25%	0
Samusa Yurunde Setsubun	5/12 41.5%	5/12 41.5%	2/12 17%	0
Keizai Kishoodai	20/23* 87%	2/23 9%	1/23 4%	0
The Nursery Tales				
Urihimeko	49/71* 69%	16/71 22.5%	5/71 7%	1/71 1.5%
Momotaroo	125/190* 66%	22/190 11.5%	25/190 13%	18/190 9.5%
The Narratives				
Taberareta Otoko	76/102* 75%	13/102 12.5%	12/102 11.5%	1/102 1%
Noruwei no Mori	62/86* 72%	10/86 12%	8/86 9%	6/86 7%
Donguri to Yamaneko	127/151* 84%	8/151 5.3%	11/151 7.3%	5/151 3.3%
TOTAL percent	468/647* 72%	81/647 12.5%	67/647 10.5%	31/647 5%

*includes implicit participants occurring singly or in combination with a textual or interpersonal element

On the other hand, if you look at the circumstances, they occur much less frequently in first position at only 12.5 percent of the time. Circumstances occur both as single constituents and as part of a multiple constituent comprising of textual or interpersonal elements. There are no circumstances in the implicit category, in other words, circumstances, if they are positioned initially, are always explicitly stated.

The frequency of enhancing beta clauses is also similar to that of circumstances, occurring in first position 10.5 percent of the time. However, unlike the circumstances, beta clauses occur across all three categories of single, multiple and implicit, even though the implicit beta clause that occurs appears in only one text type, that of the nursery tale, occurring in the final Theme unit of each tale. Further, the presence of a beta clause in a multiple combination only occurs in *Momotaroo*. There are no multiple tokens that include a beta clause in the newspaper articles or in the narratives.

The other constituent type which features in first position is the projection which is either a locution in a verbal process, or an idea in a mental process. These occur far less frequently at 5 percent and are only significant in *Momotaroo*. In *Momotaroo,* the fact that projections occur in first position and that multiple constituents include beta clauses points to a possible stylistic difference between *Momotaroo* and the other nursery tale, and also with the other texts in the corpus.

Participant types

Table 26 illustrates the choice of participant type within each text. Within the participant category, the kind of participant that is selected most frequently across the corpus is the Actor at 30 percent (193 tokens out of 647). This is followed by the Sayer at 20 percent (131 tokens out of 647). The constituent roles of Attribute, Grounds, Receiver and Target were not construed as Theme within the corpus. This raises the question of whether they are available to be selected as Theme at all.

Table 26: The probability of participant type within each text

	Ginkoo	*Setsubun*	*Keizai*	*Urihimeko*	*Momotaroo*	*Taberareta*	*Noruwei*	*Donguri*	**total**	**percent**
Actor	2	3	8	24	69	11	31	45	**193**	**41.2%**
Goal			3		2			2	7	1.5%
Beneficiary				1					1	0.3
Sensor				2		12	3	1	18	4
Phenomenon								3	3	0.7
Carrier			5	3	7	10	10	19	54	11
Attribute									0	0
Grounds									0	0
Carrier-domain							1	1	2	0.5
Identified	1	1	4	3	12	10	7	4	42	9
Identifier								2	2	0.5
Existent	1	1			2	1	7	2	14	3
Sayer				15	33	32	3	48	131	28
Receiver									0	0
Verbiage								1	1	0.3
Target									0	0
TOTAL									**468**	**100%**

Circumstance types

Table 27 illustrates the probability of circumstances within each text. The kinds of circumstances that are selected most frequently are the circumstances of spatial location at 5.5 percent (36 tokens out of 647) and of temporal location at 4.8 percent (31 tokens out of 647).

Table 27: The choice of circumstances within each text

	Ginkoo	*Setsubun*	*Keizai*	*Urihimeko*	*Momotaroo*	*Taberareta*	*Noruwei*	*Donguri*	**total**	**percent**
Angle	1					1			2	2.4
Matter						2			2	2.4
Temporal Location				8	8	6	5	4	31	37.3
Spatial Location	4	4		3	13	4	4	4	**36**	**43.3**
Cause			2	2	2				6	7.3
Manner		1		4			1		6	7.3
total	5	5	2	17*	23*	13	10	8	**83**	**100**

*includes the multiple univariate circumstantial constituents

Beta clause types

Table 28 illustrates the kinds of hypotactic clauses that appear in first position within each text. These hypotactic clauses are all enhancing in type. There are no examples of either elaborating or extending clauses. Within the enhancing type, the temporal kinds are selected most frequently across the corpus, with the successive temporal type being most common at 4 percent (27 tokens out of 647), followed by the simultaneous temporal type at 3 percent (19 tokens out of 647). Following this is the conditional enhancing beta clause, featuring at 2.3 percent (15 tokens).

Table 28: The kinds of beta clauses in first position

	Ginkoo	*Setsubun*	*Keizai*	*Uri*	*Mom*	*Taberareta*	*Noruwei*	*Donguri*	**Total**	**percent**
Enhancing										
simultaneous temporal		1		1	6	2	3	6	19	28.3
successive temporal	3	1		3	7	4	4	5	**27**	**40.3**
manner					4				4	6
causal				1	1				2	3
conditional			1		7	6	1		15	22.4
Total	3	2	1	5	25	12	8	11	**67**	**100 %**

Implicit types

Implicit Themes in the corpus typically consist of only ideational elements, with the most common constituent being participants. However, in the nursery tale texts there is the implicit beta clause at the end of each story serving to signal the story's ending (refer to Table 21 for an example). The implicit Themes present in the corpus are set out in Table 29.

Table 29: Statistical spread of implicit Themes

Text type	**Experiential**					**Logical**
	Actor	Carrier	Identified	**Sayer**	**Senser**	**ßclause**
The Newspaper articles						
Samusa Yurunde Setsubun	0	0	0	0	0	0
Ginkoo ni Tanjuu Gootoo	0	0	0	0	0	0
Keizai Kishoodai	0	2	1	0	0	0
The Nursery tales						

Urihimeko	1	0	2	7	0	1
Momotaroo	2	1	5	21	0	1
The Narratives						
Noruwei no Mori	3	0	0	3	2	0
Donguri to Yamaneko	0	0	1	16	0	0
Taberareta Otoko	1	0	0	30	2	0
Totals: 102	7	3	9	**77**	4	2
Percentage	6.8	2.9	8.8	**75.4**	3.9	1.9

The most common implicit Theme is overwhelmingly the Sayer and this is due to the fact that a Locution, of course, has a Sayer. It often does not need to be stated, particularly, if the turn-taking order of the direct speech in a story serves to indirectly identify who is speaking. The Sayer is, therefore, predictable and redundant. In the texts that include direct speech, that is, the nursery tales and the narratives, often only the Locution is explicitly stated. The Sayers are missing, thus the Theme is implicit. Predictably, the verbal processes are also missing from the Rhemes. Consider the example in Table 30. The Sayers, *Ichiroo* and *Yamaneko* and the process, *itta* (said) are elided. Only the locutions are explicit.

Table 30: Implicit Sayer Theme

taken from *Donguri to Yamaneko*

Theme unit	**THEME**	**RHEME**
	implicit Ideational: Sayer	
115	(Ichiroo)	*'Shoochi shimashita. Orei nanka irimasen yo.'* (said), 'You're welcome. You don't need to thank me.'
116	(Yamaneko)	*'Iie, orei wa doo ka totte kudasai. Watashi no jinkaku ni kakawarimasu kara. Soshite kore kara wa, hagaki ni kaneta Ichiroodono to kaite, kochira o saiban-sho to shimasu ga, yoo gozaimasu ka?'* (said), 'Please receive my 'thank-you' gift. Otherwise, I'll look bad. So, from now on, I'll address the postcard to 'Master Kaneta Ichiroo' from the 'Court House'. Is that OK?

Unmarked and Marked Themes

Given the probability frequencies of the various Theme types, it is possible to categorise them into Unmarked and Marked types.

Ideational themes

The quantitative analysis of ideational Themes clearly indicates the probability of selection of participant as Theme, as represented in Figure 1. At 72 percent, the participant is the most frequently selected ideational Theme. It is the unmarked choice. The choice of some other constituents such as a circumstance or a beta expansion clause is a marked choice, motivated by a desire to foreground as Theme something other than the participant for reasons which may relate to the overall textual organisation of the discourse, such as a scene setting function in terms of time, place or episodic order.

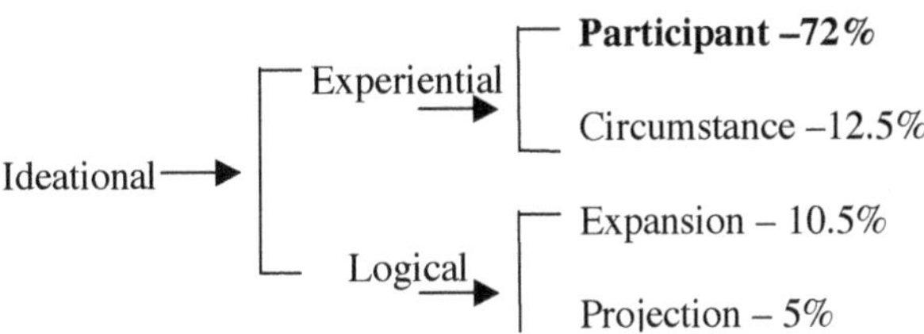

Figure 1: A taxonomy of the ideational probabilities

Another interesting marked choice is the explicit use of the demonstrative pronominal, *sore* (it), mentioned above in the discussion on implicit Themes. It appears far less frequently than the implicit alternative at 32.5 percent. It appears from the corpus that *sore* is the marked thematic choice in an identifying relational process. The unmarked choice is the formal, exophora of the identified or its referential substitute, *sore*. This occurred more frequently at 67.5 percent. This is due to redundancy in the grammar.

These kinds of marked choices are not, I believe, isolated to this corpus. Given the fact that the texts in the corpus are quite representative of Japanese texts in general, it is reasonable to suggest that this patterning is most likely to be a typical pattern of markedness in the language at large. However, in order to confirm this, a larger study of a wider variety of texts is necessary.

Having isolated the participant as the unmarked choice of Theme, it is interesting to consider which type of participant is most commonly selected as Theme. There is a clear pattern in the corpus, which relates to process type. Table 31 lists the participant types selected as Theme along with their selection probability. Significantly, there is a participant within each process type that is selected more frequently than any of the other participant roles associated with each process. For the material process, the Actor is the most frequently selected and therefore the unmarked option. For the mental process, it is the

Sensor; for the verbal process, the Sayer; for the existential, the Existent; for the attributive relational, the Carrier and for the identifying relational, it is the Identified.

Table 31: Unmarked and marked participant choices

Process	Participant		no. of tokens	% of total number	Marked (M) or Unmarked (U) choice
Material	Actor		193	96%	U
	Goal		7	3.4%	M
	Beneficiary		1	0.6%	M
	Scope		0	0	M
Mental	Sensor		18	86%	U
	Phenomenon		3	14%	M
Verbal	Sayer		131	99.2%	U
	Receiver		0	0	M
	Target		0	0	M
	Verbiage		1	0.8%	M
Relational:	Existential:	Existent	14	100%	U
	Ascriptive:	Carrier	54	96.4%	U
		Carrier-domain	2	0.6%	M
		Attribute	0	0	M
		Grounds	0	0	M
	Identifying:	Identified	42	95.4%	U
		Identifier	2	4.6%	M

The fact that these are the unmarked choices is further confirmed when you consider which participants can function as implicit Themes. It is only the unmarked choices which are available as implicit Themes. Referring back to Table 29, the implicit Themes in the corpus match up with the set of unmarked participants in each process type. This pattern serves to confirm the presence of the unmarked thematic options. The most probable choice is available for selection as an implicit option. The taxonomy of participant markedness is represented in Figure 2.

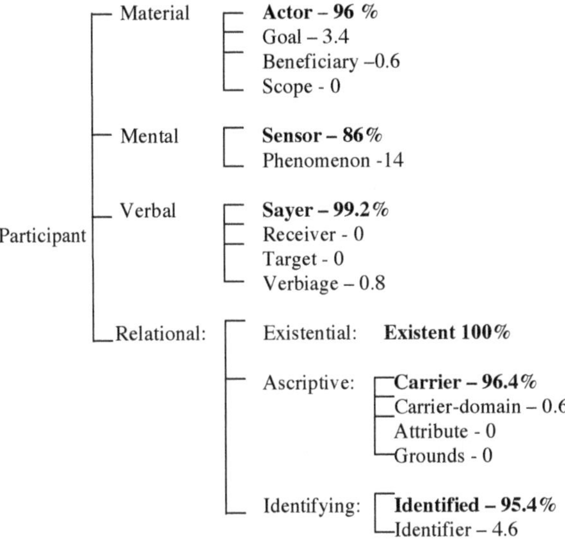

Figure 2: Marked and unmarked Themes taxonomy according to process type

Textual Themes

Table 32 illustrates the function and probability of the connectives in the corpus. The most common kind of connective was that of temporal enhancement, followed by those realizing causative enhancement and adversative extension. This pattern of probability suggests certain genres. Most of the texts in the corpus were narratives of various types. This being the case it is expected that the logico-semantic relations of the connectives would be in relation to time and place. Had there been more expository type texts in the corpus, one would have expected to find more causative and concessive connectives. The frequency pattern of the connectives reflects the kinds of genres of the corpus.

Table 32: The kinds of connectives in first position

	Ginkoo	*Setsubun*	*Keizai*	*Urihimeko*	*Momotaroo*	*Taberareta*	*Noruwei*	*Donguri*	**Total**
Enhancing									
manner	0	0	0	1	0	0	1	0	**2**
temporal	0	0	1	16	29	1	3	22	**72**
causative	0	0	0	6	11	2	7	0	**26**
concessive	0	0	0	0	1	0	0	0	**1**
Extending									
replacive	0	0	1	0	0	0	0	0	**1**

	Ginkoo	*Setsubun*	*Keizai*	*Urihimeko*	*Momotaroo*	*Taberareta*	*Noruwei*	*Donguri*	**Total**
adversative	0	0	2	3	5	2	4	2	**18**
additive	0	0	1	0	1	1	1	0	**4**
Elaborating									
apposition	0	0	2	0	2	1	0	0	**5**
clarification	0	0	0	0	0	1	1	0	**2**
Total									**131**

Interpersonal Themes

Table 33 illustrates the spread of interpersonal constituents in first position. The comment adjuncts feature the most frequently (86 percent). The modal adjuncts are infrequently selected (14 percent). This infrequency possibly relates to the fact that interpersonal meanings typically occur clause finally. Those that do appear in initial position are specifically versions of 'yes' and 'no'.

Table 33: The kinds of interpersonal constituents in first position

Interpersonal constituents	*Ginkoo*	*Setsubun*	*Keizai*	*Urihimeko*	*Momotaroo*	*Taberareta*	*Noruwei*	*Donguri*	**Total**
modal adjunct	0	0	0	0	0	2	1	0	**3**
comment adjunct	0	0	1	2	4	1	5	6	**19**
Total									**22**

The system network of Theme

Having described the kinds of Themes and their selection probability, the set of constituents which are available for selection as Theme is represented as a system network in Figure 3. The entry point is first position in the Theme unit. The first choice in the network relates to whether or not the Theme is single or multiple. If single, then the choice is between textual, interpersonal or ideational. If ideational, two simultaneous choices need to be made: one relating to explicitness and the other relating to the kind of ideational meaning, that is, logical or experiential. If experiential, then the choice is between participant and circumstance. If logical, the choice is between a limited set of beta clauses realizing meanings of enhancing expansion and projection.

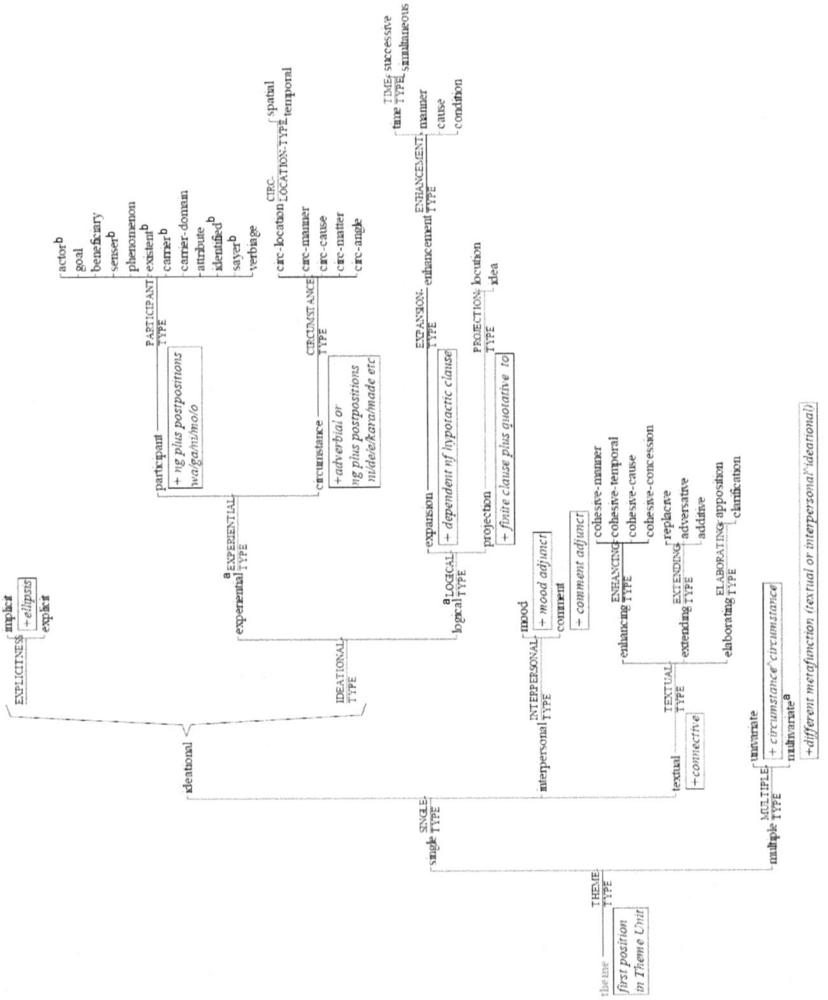

Figure 3: System network of THEME

If an implicit choice is made, then the kind of ideational options are very limited. As explained, only the unmarked participants relating to each process type or the causative beta clause can be selected as an implicit Theme. For example, only the Sayer in a verbal process can function as an implicit ideational Theme. This limited set of choices is indicated in the system network by the superscript letter, [b].

However, if a multiple Theme is construed, then the choice is between a univariate and a multivariate type. Note, that the multivariate Theme can only be either a textual^ideational or an interpersonal^ideational construal. The ideational component of both kinds of multivariate Themes requires a re-entry into the system between experiential and logical single Themes, in order to select the various kinds of ideational Themes. This re-entry is indicated by the superscript letter [a], meaning if [a], then select the 'single Theme' pathway [a].

Each of these Theme types are realised by different lexicogrammatical resources. The realisation statements appear in the boxes under each feature in the network. Participant Themes are typically realised by nominal groups marked by postpositions such as *wa, ga, ni, o*, while circumstances are typically realised by adverbial and nominal groups marked by postpositions such as *ni, de, e, kara, made* and so on.

Within the logical set of Theme types, the expansion set is realised by dependent clauses typically ending in hypotactic, non-finite inflections such as *–te, -tari,* stem only, *-eba, -tara, nara, de*, while the projection set is realised by a finite clause marked by the quotative postposition, *to*.

As previously mentioned, textual Themes are realised by connectives such as conjunctive particles, conjunctions and connective phrases, while interpersonal Themes are realised by either comment or modal adjuncts.

Conclusion

This chapter has addressed research questions which sought to determine the usefulness of the notion of Theme in Japanese; to test for the existence of Theme in Japanese; to describe how Theme is realised in the lexicogrammar and how it contributes to thematic development.

Before discussing the general issue of whether or not the notion of Theme is useful in relation to Japanese, the other, more specific questions are addressed. In relation to whether or not the system of Theme exists in Japanese, this chapter has demonstrated that it does, and that it is realised by first position in the Theme-unit. The Japanese language has a means of orienting the reader to a point of departure. This orientation occurs at the beginning of a Theme-unit and it sets up a potential point of expansion for subsequent messages. In other words, the selection of an ideational constituent in first position positions the constituent to be further developed. For example, by selecting Actor as Theme,

Actor becomes the point of departure and is available to be developed. Further, the analysis revealed the kinds of constituents within the lexicogrammar that are potentially available for selection as Theme. This is detailed in the system network. At the same time, it also identified those constituents which are not available for selection, such as Attribute, Receiver, Target and so on.

In addition, Theme has three metafunctional dimensions: the ideational, textual and interpersonal, which exist singularly or in multiple combinations. Within the set of possible multiple combinations, there are textual or interpersonal constituents followed by ideational ones. There is no evidence of a multiple Theme consisting of textual, interpersonal and ideational components, as there is in English.

The probability analysis revealed the constituents which are typically unmarked and those which are typically marked. Within the set of ideational Themes, the participant is the unmarked choice with circumstances and expanding clauses as marked options. Within the set of participant types, the unmarked choices are organised according to process type. To reiterate, they are Actor, Sayer, Sensor, Existent, Carrier and Identified. Further, the study demonstrated that implicit Themes are possible and that these conflate with the unmarked choices within the set of participants relating to the various process types.

While the above system network for Theme relates specifically to the texts in the corpus of this study, it is reasonable to generalise and suggest that this network of choices is not limited to the corpus but is representative of the system of THEME in Japanese at large. This relates, in part, to the general question of the usefulness of the notion of Theme in Japanese.

The usefulness of Theme lies in the fact that it plays an important role in textual organisation. Fries (1995c) postulated that, if thematic status was meaningful, then it is expected that thematic status in clause complexes would contribute to the interpretation of texts. By this he means that the choices of Theme order in particular ways which serve to contribute to the method of development of a text, either by setting up patterns which correlate with generic elements, or to genre as a whole. While this study did not set out to demonstrate the role of Theme in the method of development, it did indirectly offer some evidence to suggest that it does play an important part. For example, patterns of thematic progression (see Daneš, 1974) were identified, and different generic elements in different genres displayed different ideational Themes. In the narratives, the Complication stages only selected Actor and Sayer Themes, while the other stages selected from a wider range of participant types. Further, within the nursery tales and narratives, the unmarked implicit Theme, *sore* (it) always began a stage, and when this occurred, these stages were developed around scene setting information. Thus, it is evident that Theme is a useful notion in Japanese. However, this generalisation needs further investigation. Such an investigation would be based on a much larger corpus that includes a variety of genres. This is a task for the future.

Notes

1 'text' is defined as a semantic unit which is functional, in the sense that, it does a certain job in a certain context (Halliday and Hasan, 1985).

2 Nuclear participants are the central participants associated with each process type (Martin, Matthiessen et al., 1997:103).

3 The discrepancy between 76 percent in *Setsubun* and 90 percent in *Ginkoo* is due to the fact that the *Ginkoo* text is grammatically more intricate than the *Setsubun* text and so any manipulation of first position tended to have a greater effect on the meanings within the text. Respondents thus noticed the word order change more starkly in *Ginkoo.*

4 Clause chaining is a clause pattern where 'usually only one of the clauses is a nucleus containing the full range of verbal markers for tense, aspect, mood and so on. If the language is verb-final (OV), the fully marked verb is the last in the series' (Hopper and Traugott, 1993:174).

5 Endophoric S (subject) ellipsis (Hasan, 1996) is ellipsis which requires retrieval from the co-text. The interpretive source can be found either preceding or following the implicit device. When the interpretation for the ellipsis is found in the preceding co-text, it is called anaphoric.

6 Hypotaxis is a linking relation between clauses of unequal status. One is dominant, and it labelled the alpha clause, the other is dependant, and is labelled the beta clause (Halliday, 1994:221).

7 *Momotaroo* translates literally as Peach-*taroo*, – *Taroo* being a common boy's name in Japan. The story title is more commonly translated as The Peach Boy and thus I am using the common translation rather than the literal translation in this study.

8 I have chosen to translate *Uri* as 'melon' rather than as gourd or cucumber, both of which are acceptable translations of *uri* (Kenkyusha, 1974:1925). Melon, for me was the aesthetic option – Melon Princess being a much nicer image, to my mind, than either Gourd or Cucumber Princess.

9 The term, 'topic' is used very widely in Japanese linguistic descriptions and consequently has a number of disparate definitions. Within the Universal Grammar paradigm, Japanese has been typologised as a Subject prominent and Topic-prominent language (Li, 1976:460). Also, Givòn, in his typology work, uses the term 'topic' to mean 'the participant most crucially involved in the action sequence of the paragraph' (Givòn, 1983:9). In SF terms, this is a characterisation of a feature within the ideational metafunction, rather than within the textual metafunction, and it is the textual metafunction which is under investigation in this study. Further, the post-positional particle, *–wa* has been characterised as the 'topic' marker (Shibatani, 1990:262). Within the various descriptions of English as well, 'topic' is problematic in that it very often is used to refer to a

'given' Theme. This 'combining' approach was first proposed in 1939 by Mathesius which has been translated in Firbas (1964) and picked up van Dijk (1976) and Kuno (1972) thereby conflating the functionally distinct systems of THEME and INFORMATION STATUS. Therefore, given the disparate use of this term, 'topic', that is, the fact that it is used to describe a number of different linguistic phenomena within a range of different linguistic traditions, it is avoided. The term ideational Theme is sufficient for the purposes of this chapter as it identifies the Theme which relates to the ideational metafunction. It also allows for the range of ideational constituents which appear in first position within the corpus to be included under its banner. Further, it is not without precedent in the systemic context to use the term ideational Theme. Ghadessy (1995:131) uses the terms ideational Theme both as a marked and unmarked choice in his paper which compared the choice of Theme and Rheme across a range of registers including sports commentary, exposition, narrative and obituary.

References

Daneš, F. (1974) Functional Sentence Perspective and the Organisation of the Text. In F. Daneš (ed.) *Papers on Functional Sentence Perspective.* Prague, Academic.

Firbas, J. (1964) On defining the theme in functional sentence analysis. *Traveaux Linguistiques de Prague* 1: 267–289.

Fries, P. (1995b) A personal view of Theme. In M. Ghadessy (ed.) *Thematic Development in English Texts* 1–19. London: Pinter.

Fries, P. (1995c) Patterns of information in initial position in English. In P. Fries and M. Gregory (eds) *Discourse in Society: Systemic Functional Perspectives, Meaning and Choice in Language. Studies for Michael Halliday* 47–66. Norwood: Ablex Publishing Corporation.

Fries, P. and Francis, G. (1992) Exploring Theme: Problems for Research, *Occasional Papers in Systemic Linguistics* 6: 45–59.

Givon, T. (1983) Topic Continuity in discourse: an introduction. In T. Givon (ed.) *Topic Continuity in Discourse: a quantitative cross-language study.* Amsterdam: John Benjamins Publishing Company.

Ghadessy, M. (1995) Thematic development and its relationship to registers and genres. In M. Ghadessy (ed.) *Thematic Development in English Texts* 129–146. London: Pinter.

Halliday, M. A. K. (1977) Text as semantic choice in social contexts. In T. A. van Dijk and J. Petofi (eds) *Grammars and Descriptions*. Berlin: Mouton de Gruyter.

Halliday, M. A. K. (1994) *An Introduction to Functional Grammar*. London: Edward Arnold.

Halliday, M. A. K. and Hasan, R. (1985) *Language, Context, and Text: Aspects of language in a social-semiotic perspective*. Geelong: Deakin University Press.

Hasan, R. (1996) Ways of saying, Ways of meaning. In C. Cloran, D. Butt and G. Williams (eds) *Ways of Saying, Ways of Meaning* 191–242. London: Cassell.

Hopper, P. and Traugott, E. (1993) *Grammaticalisation*. Cambridge: Cambridge University Press.

Kenkyusha (1974) *Kenkyusha's New Japanese-English Dictionary.* Tokyo: Kuroshio.

Kuno, S. (1972) Functional Sentence Perspective. *Linguistic Inquiry* 3: 269–320

Lemke, J. (1995) *Textual Politics, Discourse and Social Dynamics*. London: Taylor and Francis.

Li, C. N. and Thompson, S. A. (1976) Subject and Topic: A new typology of language. In C. Li (ed.) *Subject and Topic* 457–490. New York: Academic Press.

Longacre, R. E. (1985) Sentences as combination of clauses. In T. Shopen (ed.) *Language Typology and Syntactic Description, Complex Constructions* 2: 235–287. Cambridge: Cambridge University Press.

Matthiessen, C. M. I. M. (1995a) *Lexicogrammatical Cartography: English Systems*. Tokyo: International Language Sciences Publishers.

Matthiessen, C. M. I. M. (1995b) THEME as an enabling resource in ideational 'knowledge' construction. In M. Ghadessy (ed.) *Thematic Development in English Texts* 20–54. London: Pinter.

Martin, J., Matthiessen, C. M. I. M. and Painter, C. (1997) *Working with Functional Grammar.* London: Edward Arnold.

Martin, S. E. (1988) *A Reference Grammar of Japanese*. Tokyo: Charles E. Tuttle Company.

Shibatani, M. (1990) *The Languages of Japan*. Cambridge: Cambridge University Press.

Teruya, K. (1998) *An Exploration into the World of Experience: A Systemic-functional interpretation of the grammar of Japanese*. Unpublished PhD dissertation. School of English, Linguistics and Media, Macquarie University, Sydney.

Thomson, E. (1998) Testing for Theme in Japanese. *Japanese Language Education around the Globe* 219–242. Tokyo: The Japan Foundation.

Thomson, E. (2001) *Exploring the Textual Metafunction in Japanese: A case study of selected written texts*. Unpublished PhD dissertation, Faculty of Education, University of Wollongong, Wollongong.

Thomson, E. (2005) Theme unit analysis: A systemic-functional treatment of textual meanings in Japanese. *Functions of Language* 12:2.

Tosu, N. (1985) *A Semiotic Analysis of an Aspect of Japanese Culture: Narrative structure of folktale*. Unpublished dissertation, New Haven, Yale University.

Van Dijk, T. A. (1976) Sentence topic and discourse topic. *Papers in Slavic Philology*. University of Amsterdam.

5 Classifying natural phenomena through language: lexicogrammatical resources for constructing taxonomies in Japanese biology textbooks

Chie Hayakawa
Nagoya University of Arts

This chapter aims to describe the linguistic resources deployed in science textbooks that are used in Japanese high schools. Textbooks are important resources for students in that they provide both models of written scientific discourse and the linguistic features typical of the genre of scientific discourse. This chapter takes a top-down view which treats grammatical devices as the resources for realising rhetorical purposes or functions. While the discourse of science has a variety of functions, this chapter focuses on the actual lexicogrammatical choices made to construct the aspect of science, which is the classification of phenomena into taxonomical orders. The relevant lexicogrammatical choices are those which contribute to micro-scale formation such as transitivity etc., and macro-scale organisation such as the thematic development of texts. The analysis will show that Japanese academic texts both provide a wide range of micro-scale linguistic resources necessary for constructing specialised taxonomies as well as effectively incorporating these resources into the macro-scale structure of texts in order to achieve the purpose of the text.

Introduction

Throughout our lives we continue to learn and most of what we learn, especially specialised and organised knowledge for higher education, we learn through language. Language plays a central role in education and could be referred to as a 'vehicle of learning' (Halliday, 1989:96). The description of educational language has been one of the major subjects of investigation in the theoretical framework of Systemic Functional Linguistics (SFL) (see for example Halliday and Martin, 1993; Martin and Veel, 1998; Painter, 1999 and Rose, 1997). Most of these works, however, focus on the English language; specifically explicating how it works to construct knowledge, what kinds of lexicogrammatical resources are used, and how these resources are incorporated into overall textual patterns.

While there are many studies which focus on the academic language of English, there are few which have explored Japanese academic language, as this chapter does. Specifically this chapter aims to investigate the Japanese linguistic resources for constructing knowledge, especially those deployed in science textbooks for Japanese high schools. Many scholars point out that textbooks are important resources for children because they introduce the distinctive language features of academic writing, providing them with the meaning making resources to construct knowledge through language. For example, Rose (1997) demonstrates that the literacy acquired through science textbooks of junior secondary school is the basis of the technical literacy required to read texts used in the industrial world (for example, procedures on how to operate a piece of machinery). Martin (1993a:167–168) argues that science textbooks play an important role in education by providing students with models of scientific discourse.

The purpose of this chapter is to investigate whether the textbooks used in Japanese schools provide enough linguistic resources to serve as models of scientific discourse, and how these linguistic resources are organised into the overall textual structure. To pursue this purpose, two biology textbooks used in Japanese high schools are analysed using the theoretical framework of SFL. The focus will be on the actual lexicogrammatical choices that are made in order to construct an aspect of science: the classification of natural phenomena into taxonomical orders. The relevant lexicogrammatical choices are those which contribute to micro-scale formation (transitivity etc.) and macro-scale organisation (thematic development) of texts. The first half of the chapter focuses on the description of micro-scale lexicogrammatical resources. The latter half of the chapter deals with the macro-scale resources and their interrelation with the choice of micro-scale resources. That is, I will investigate the actual use of micro-scale resources in the creation of text, and how they are organised into the overall structure of text.

The analysis will show that Japanese academic texts provide a wide range of micro-scale linguistic resources necessary for constructing specialised taxonomies, and that the distinctive language patterns in the macro-scale organisation of the texts can certainly be seen to reflect the purpose of those texts.

Data

The data are taken from two biology textbooks written for Japanese high schools, *Kaitei Seibutsu* (Revised Biology) and *Kootoogakkoo Kaitei Seibutsu IB* (High School Revised Biology IB). The selected parts are on the topic of heredity and amount to 36 pages in all and form the corpus for the study.

The reason for limiting the data to the biology texts related to heredity is that this investigation began as a comparative study of the lexicogrammatical resources deployed in Japanese and English science textbooks. In order to gain the most accurate comparison, texts dealing with the same subject matter (heredity) were selected from both English and Japanese textbooks. This chapter will discuss the finds from the Japanese texts only. However, it is extrapolated that the findings in this corpus might equally be applied to the texts of other topics and other subjects of natural science.

Model for analysis: three aspects of constructing geographical knowledge

Construction of specialised knowledge through language is a very broad issue as it is multifaceted, including such aspects as definition of terminologies and classification of phenomena into taxonomical orders. In order to separate the different aspects involved in knowledge construction, this chapter utilises the tripartite model proposed by Wignell, Martin and Eggins (1993) where a geography textbook used in an Australian secondary school was analysed. Their study classified three aspects of constructing geographical knowledge and also listed the English lexicogrammatical resources used to construct each of these aspects. This is summarised in Table 1:

Table 1: Knowledge construction in geography

Three aspects of constructing geographical knowledge	English lexicogrammatical resources constructing three aspects of geography
Defining: to label a geographical phenomenon with a technical term and define it.	Lexicogrammatical resources used for defining are (technical terms are **bold-faced**, and definitions are in *italics*): Verbal process[2] e.g. Thus *green plants* are called **producers**. Identifying relational process e.g. **Prevailing winds** are *winds which blow from one direction for long period during the year*. Embedded clause e.g. When water evaporates it changes into *an invisible gas* called **water vapor**. Expanded nominal groups e.g. **certain protozoa**, *single-celled animal*
Classifying: to categorise phenomena in an ordered, systematic taxonomy based on the principle of superordination (where something is a type of something else), or composition (where something is a part of something else).[1]	Lexicogrammatical resources used for classifying and constructing taxonomies are (classes are **bold-faced**, and subclasses are in *italics*): Intensive attributive relational process e.g. *Physical geography* is a **science**. Possessive attributive relational process e.g. **Desert landforms** consist mainly of *those due to erosion* and *those due to deposition*.

Three aspects of constructing geographical knowledge	**English lexicogrammatical resources constructing three aspects of geography**
Explaining: to explain the process or mechanism in which a geographical phenomenon occurs.	The lexicogrammatical resource used for explaining is an implication sequence which connects events logico-semantically and which indicates that an event occurs as the result of another event. e.g. When rain fails then carbon dioxide dissolves in rain, Event 1 Event 2 then water soaks into ground Event 3

What is interesting about this research is that the authors classify various linguistic resources in terms of the functions they fulfill regardless of their grammatical categories. Such perspective on language can be referred to as a *top-down* view (Martin, 1993a:167), as it views language from top level down, that is, firstly, through the meaning or function of language, and subsequently down to the grammar, in order to examine the linguistic resources which have fulfilled or realised the particular functions. One of the most typical examples of work based on this kind of generalised view is the logico-semantic relations analysis in the analytical framework of SFL. For example, Halliday (1994: Section 9.4) and Martin (1992: Chapter 4) deal with the realisational relations between the logico-semantic relations of events which exist at the level of semantics on the one hand, and various linguistic devices which are found at the level of lexicogrammar on the other hand. Martin treats these grammatical devices as variations on the same theme of relating two pieces of a text logically. Part of the variations, or options, that he has found on the theme of time relations are as follows:

Cohesive devices functioning between clause complexes

We walk the ring with our dogs. **Afterwards** we just wait. (cohesive devise)

Grammatical dependency inside a clause complex

We walk the ring with our dogs **and then** we just wait. (paratactic relation)
After we walk the ring with our dogs we just wait. (hypotactic relation; finite)
Subsequent to walking the ring with our dogs we just wait. (hypotactic relation; non-finite)

Grammatical metaphor

Our *tour* of the ring is **prior to** our *wait.* (as an Attribute in a clause)
Our *tour* of the ring **precedes** our *wait.* (as a Process in a clause)

(examples are taken from Martin, 1992:168–169)

All the devices listed above realise a temporal relation in which one event follows another. The grammar has various options for realising this relation: either realisation as a relationship *between* two processes (as in 1. and 2.) or as a relationship *within* a process (as in 3.) where grammatical metaphor nominalises the processes of walking and waiting into the nouns, *tour* and *wait*. Within each of these categories, the grammar has still more delicate choices as to how we represent the same relation of temporal succession. It can be realised by the use of cohesive devises, that is, either by the dependency of one clause to another, or within a clause, as an Attribute as well as a Process. These examples clearly illustrate the top-down view on language as there are a variety of lexico-grammatical resources listed which fulfill or realise the function of connecting events in time.

The complementary perspective is *bottom-up* or *grammar up,* which firstly views the forms of language, and then investigates their function in the discourse. This perspective tends to deal with various grammatical categories in isolation, whereas the top-down view aims to generalise them and to reveal how a language has evolved as the resource for serving particular functions. In this chapter, I will apply the top-down model to Japanese biology textbooks specifically focusing on the classificational function of the language of science.

Procedures

In order to investigate the linguistic features of Japanese science textbooks, the following research questions were formulated:

> What are the micro-scale lexicogrammatical resources found in the corpus for classifying phenomena?
>
> What are the macro-scale organisational resources appropriate for the classification of phenomena?
>
> How do the micro-scale resources collaborate with the macro-scale organisation?

Micro-scale resources for classifying phenomona

This section deals with the first research question of what micro-scale lexicogrammatical resources for classifying phenomena are found in the corpus.

The term 'micro' is used here to mean the resources which function to classify phenomena within grammatical units within a text, such as clause complexes, clauses and groups. The term 'macro', on the other hand, refers to the patterns which exist across a text and which contribute to the overall organisation of a text. The 'macro' organisation relates in part to the thematic development of text, which will be discussed subsequent to the following discussion on the micro-scale resources.

Table 2 contains the main micro-scale resources used to realise taxonomic relationships in the corpus. In total, 79 instances of classification were found. The table also shows the quantitative data in the right-hand column (the number of tokens / total instances of classification).

Table 2: Japanese lexicogrammatical resources for constructing taxonomies

logico-semantic relations between clauses (or clause complexes)	elaboration: exemplification	1/79	1.3%
	extension: addition	2/79	2.5%
process types	attributive relational process	17/79	21.5%
	existential process	11/79	13.9%
nominal group structures	hypotactic nominal group complex	10/79	12.7%
	pronouns	2/79	2.5%
	classifier within a nominal group	36/79	45.6%

Each of these resources is elaborated below with one or two examples taken from the corpus. Grammatical analysis of the examples basically follows that of Halliday (1994: Chapter 5). Yet, as his analysis is based on the English language, any application of his concepts and functional labels to Japanese require some modification. The modification will be discussed below as the need arises.

Classifying through logico-semantic relations

All the classifying resources listed in Wignell et al. (1993) are those which classify 'things' or nouns. They argue that 'in order to classify and organise with language, we need first of all to turn phenomena into things or nouns. The grammar has extensive resources within the clause and nominal group structure for organising things, but very limited resources for organising processes' (p.145). In the Japanese textbooks under consideration here, resources for organising processes are also rare. I found only three instances where processes or clauses, as opposed to things or nouns, were organised into taxonomical orders. This logico-semantic classifying function is fulfilled by the following linguistic resources.

The logico-semantic relation of elaboration: exemplification between clause complexes

The logico-semantic relation of exemplification is the relation in which a clause or clause complex is elaborated and exemplified by another clause or clause complex. The exemplifying relation is usually indicated explicitly by the conjunctive in the second clause which is realised by an adverbial element such as *tatoeba* (for example). This clause structure constructs a taxonomy by sub-classifying, or breaking down a class (exemplified clause) into subclasses (exemplifying clauses).

In Example 1, the class *senshokutai no koozoo no henka* (the change in chromosome structure) given in Clause 1 is sub-classified into three processes *aru senshokutai no ichibu ga kirete, sono dampen ga ushinawaretari* (a portion of a chromosome may be cut off and lost), [*aru senshokutai no ichibu ga*] *gyaku muki ni natte moto no ichi ni tsuitari* ([a portion of a chromosome] is turned the other way around and attached to the same chromosome), and [*aru senshokutai no ichibu ga*] *betsu no senshokutai ni kuttsuitari suru* ([a portion of a chromosome] is attached to another chromosome). These processes or clauses are paratactically combined into a clause complex through the enumerative form of a verb (*-tari*) and form a unit. The exemplifying relation is indicated by the conjunctive at the beginning of the unit which is realised by an adverbial element, *tatoeba* (for example) which is derived from a verb *tatoeru* (exemplify).

Example 1: Sub-classification of Phenomena through Elaboration

clause 1 / **unit 1** **class**	(i) *senshokutai no koozoo no henka ni wa, iroiro na rei ga* chromosome NO structure NO change NI WA various NA example GA *shir-are-te iru.* know-PAS-SUSP ASP
Conjunctive (elaboration: exemplification)	(ii) ***tatoe-ba,*** exemplify-CND
unit 2 **subclass**	*aru senshokutai no ichibu ga kire-te,* certain chromosome NO part GA cut-SUSP a portion of a chromosome is cut off and (iii) *sono dampen ga ushinaw-are-tari (kesshitsu),* that portion GA lose-PSV-ENU deletion (iv) *gyaku muki ni na-tte* opposite direction NI become-SUSP (v) *moto no ichi ni tsu-itari (gyakui),* former NO position NI stick-ENU inversion (vi) *aruiwa betsu no senshokutai ni kuttsu-itari (tenza) suru* CONJ different NO chromosome NI stick-ENU translocation do
As chromosome structures change, various examples are seen. For example, a portion of a chromosome is cut off and lost (deletion), turned the other way around and attached to the same position (inversion), or attached to another chromosome (translocation).	

The logico-semantic relation of extension: addition between clause complexes

The logico-semantic relation of addition is the relation in which two or more clauses or clause complexes are simply adjoined to each other without the implication of any causal or temporal relationships between them. The additional relation is sometimes indicated explicitly by a conjunction, such as *A bakari de naku B* (not only *A* **but** *B*). This structure constructs a taxonomy by listing sub-classes of a phenomenon. In Example 2, two clauses are related to each other through the conjunction *bakari de naku* (not only…but) representing the subclasses of the cause for which *totsuzenhen'i* (mutation) occurs. The class, cause for mutation, is not explicitly shown, but implicitly indicated as the common phenomenon to the two events described in the two clauses, that is, *totsuzenhen'i wa …ni yotte okoru / shoojiru* (mutation occurs / happens due to…).

Example 2: Sub-classification of Phenomena through Expansion

clause 1 / unit 1 **subclass 1**	*totsuzenhen'i wa [[idenshi de aru]] DNA no henka ni yotte okoru* mutation WA gene be DNA NO change NI YOTTE happen
conjunction (extension: addition)	***bakari de na-ku,*** only be-NEG-SUSP
clause 2 / unit 2 **subclass 2**	*[[idenshi o nina-tte iru]] senshokutai no koosei ya kazu no* gene O carry-SUSP ASP chromosome NO structure CONJ number NO *henka ni yotte mo shoojiru.* change NI YOTTE MO happen
Mutation occurs not only due to the changes in DNA which is a gene, but also due to the changes in the composition or numbers of chromosomes on which genes are located.	

Classifying through Process Types

The previous section dealt with the resources which classify processes, that is, clauses or clause complexes. The remaining resources, which will be discussed in this and the next sections, all classify things or nouns. The same resources, however, are used to classify processes which are semiotically constructed as 'things'. Consider the following example:

rimpakyuu ni wa B saiboo (B rimpakyuu, yaku 30 %) to,
lymphocyte NI WA B cell B lymphocyte about 30% CONJ
T saiboo (T rimpakyuu, yaku 70 %) ga ar-i, …
T cell T lymphocyte about 70% GA exist-SUSP

In lymphocytes, there are B cells (B lymphocyte, about 30 %) and T cells (T lymphocyte, about 70 %)

This is a typical example of the classification of 'things' or nouns. It constructs a taxonomy of things based on the superordinate principle which divides the class *rimpakyuu* (lymphocyte) into two subclasses, *B saiboo* (B cell) and *T saiboo* (T cell). The classifying function is realised by the existential process *ga ari* (or *aru*) (there are). Details of the experiential process as the classifying resource will be elaborated below.

In the discourse of science, the same resource is also deployable for organising processes. Consider the following example:

men'eki ni wa	*[[kore made*	*nobe-ta]]*	*yoo na*	*taiekisei men'eki*	*no hoka ni,*
immunity NI WA	this MADE	mention-PST	status NA	humoral immunity	NO other NI
saiboosei men'eki	*ga aru.*				
cellular immunity	GA exist				

In immunity, in addition to the aforementioned humoral immunity, there is also cellular immunity

This example classifies *men'eki* (immunity) into *taiekisei men'eki* (humoral immunity) and *saiboosei men'eki* (cellular immunity) through the use of the existential process *ga aru* (there are). What are classified here semiotically seem to be 'things', but semantically, immunity is a process where antibodies fight against viruses and protect a person from diseases. Before being classified into a taxonomy, immunity has been construed as a 'thing' through the process of reification.

hito wa kodomo no toki ni ichi do hashika ni kakaruto,
If a person catches measles,
ni do to hashika ni kakaranai ka,
(they) won't get measles again, or
kakatte mo
even if (they) do,
karukute sumu.
(it) will only be mild.
[[kono yoo ni [[ichi do kakatta]] byooki ni ni do to kakaranai]] koto wa, hoka no iroiro na saikin ya uirusu ni yoru byooki ni tsuite mo shirarete ite,
This phenomenon where you don't catch a disease that you have already had for a second time as explained is also known to occur for other diseases caused by various other microbes and viruses, and
kore o men'eki to yobu…
this is called immunity.
men'eki ni wa [[kore made nobeta]] yoo na taiekisei men'eki no hoka ni, saiboosei men'eki ga aru.
In immunity, in addition to the aforementioned humoral immunity, there is also cellular immunity.

The process of creating a semiotic 'thing', or *reification* (Halliday and Matthiessen, 1999:143), is schematically shown as Figure 1.

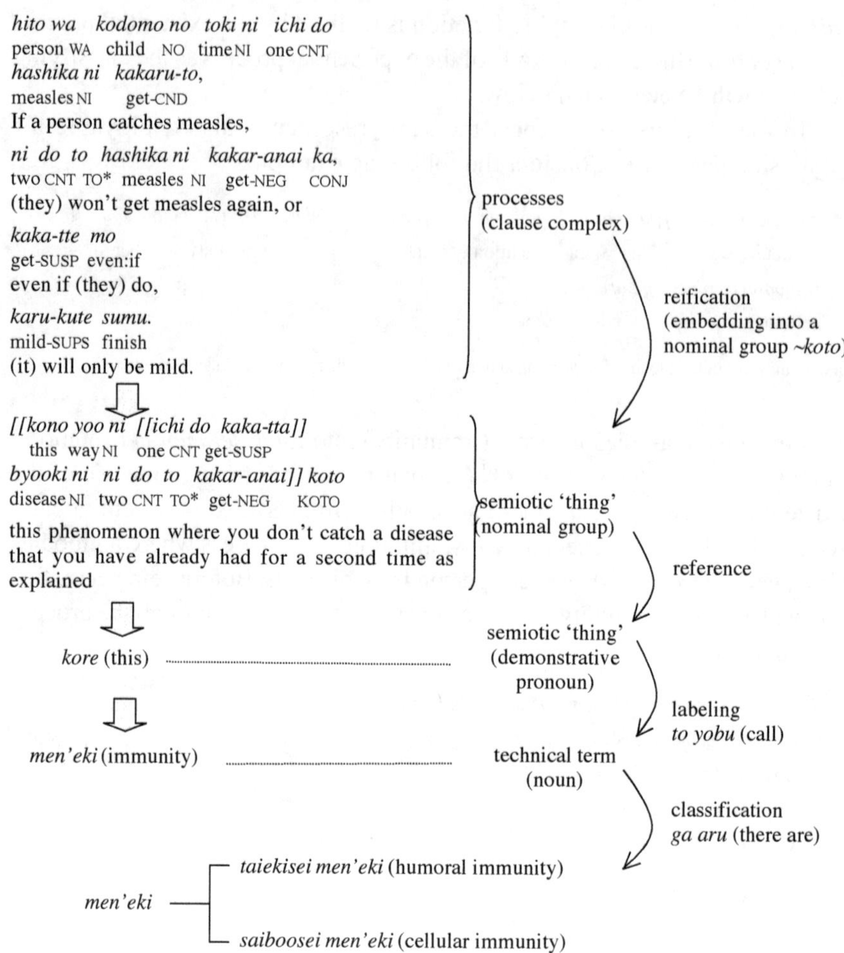

Figure 1: Reificational Process for Creating Semiotic 'Things'

Figure 1 shows how a sequence of processes is firstly reconstructed as a generalised 'thing', such as *[[kono yoo ni [[ichido kakatta]] byooki ni nido to kakaranai]] koto* (this phenomenon where you don't catch a disease that you have already had for a second time, as explained). Here, the process or clause, *kono yoo ni [[ichido kakatta]] byooki ni nido to kakaranai*, is nominalised by being embedded into a general noun *koto* (phenomena or fact). I will call such *koto* a 'rank-shifted nominal clause marker' following Teruya (2004:215).[3] The way the nominalising resource, *koto* effectively functions to organise Japanese text will become evident when I analyze the macro structure of the classifying text. The whole nominal group using the rank-shifted nominal clause marker, *koto* is maintained through the text by the use of a reference item *kore* (this), and then labeled with a technical term *men'eki* (immunity). The technical term is then organised into the taxonomy.

The reason why classification presupposes this kind of reification is that, by being construed as a noun, a process itself can act as the participant in another process, which functions to organise the semiotic 'thing' into a taxonomy. Wignell et al. (1993:153) refers to the importance of turning processes into technical labels in the classifying stage and states that 'it is only once phenomena have been named that the geographer's second task, grouping and classifying, can proceed.' This is the same for the discourse of science in Japanese. In the examples provided in both this and the next sections, nominalised technical terms such as *totsuzen hen'i* (mutation) and *men'eki* (immunity) enable an event or a sequence of events to act like a noun, which are then readily organised into a taxonomy.

In Japanese textbooks, two process types are used to classify phenomena at the clause rank. They are the attributive relational process and the existential process.

The attributive relational process

The Japanese attributive relational process used for classification takes the form of *a wa b de aru* (*a* is *b*), in which *a* is Carrier and *b* is Attribute. This clause structure constructs a taxonomy by classifying, or assigning a subclass (Carrier) to a class (Attribute). In Example 3, a subclass *[[shoojoobae no me ga boo joo ni naru]] boogan* (bar-eye by which the eyes of a fruit fly turn into the shape of a bar) is classified under the class of *totsuzen hen'i* (mutation) through the use of an attributive relational process *de aru* (be).

Example 3: Classification of Phenomena by a Relational Process

[[shoojoobae no me ga boo joo ni fruit:fly NO eye GA bar shape NI *naru]] boogan wa* become bar:eye WA	*...totsuzen hen'i* mutation	***de aru.*** be
Carrier **subclass**	Attribute **class**	Process: relational: attributive
Bar-eye by which the eyes of a fruit fly turn into the shape of a bar is a mutation.		

The existential process

The Japanese existential process used for classification takes the form of *a ni wa b, c...ga aru* (in *a* there are *b, c*...), in which *b, c* are Existents and *a* is a Circumstance indicating the location. This clause structure metaphorically constructs a taxonomy. In more everyday use (that is, not in the context of scientific texts), this structure constructs a taxonomy based on the principle of composition as opposed to superordination. For example, *kono heya ni wa piano to terebi ga aru* (in this room, there is a piano and a TV) constructs a compositional order in which *piano* and *terebi* are Existents or contents which exist in *kono heya* (this room), which functions as a Circumstance of location. In a scientific text, the same structure is used to divide classes into sub-classes. This means that scientists often talk about the relationship of existing objects and their location, with the meaning that the class is a location within a taxonomy where subclasses are located. In Example 4, two subclasses *B saiboo* (B cell) and *T saiboo* (T cell) are classified under the class of *rimpakyuu* (lymphocytes) through the use of an existential process *ari* (there are).

Example 4: Classification of Phenomena by an existential process

rimpakyuu ni wa lymphocyte NI WA	*B saiboo (B rimpakyuu,* B cell B lymphocyte, *yaku 30 %) to,* about 30 % CONJ	*T saiboo (T rimpakyuu,* T cell T lymphocyte, *yaku 70 %) ga* about 70 % GA	***ar-i,*** exist-SUSP
Circumstance: location **class**	Existent 1 **subclass 1**	Existent 2 **subclass 2**	Process: existential
Lymphocytes include B cells (B lymphocytes, about 30 %) and T cells (T lymphocytes, about 70 %), and...			

Existential processes are different from attributive relational processes, in that attributive processes classify (i.e. with the order of class unit following subclass unit) whereas existential processes sub-classify (i.e. with the order of class unit preceding subclass unit). The difference seems to have textual implications, and will be discussed again in the section on the macro organisation of the text.

The metaphoric use of an existential process in constructing a taxonomy based on the principle of superordination is not found in English science texts. The closest counterpart in English is an attributive relational process like '*a* consists of *b, c*...' and '*a* includes *b, c*...', which sub-classify classes into subclasses in terms of parts and wholes.

Classifying through nominal group structures

The classifying function of language is also carried out at group rank. According to Halliday (1994:180–196), a nominal group has a complex inner structure where a number of components like Deictic, Numerative, Epithet, Classifier, and Qualifier all modify the head word or Thing. The structure in English is shown in Figure 2.

Figure 2: English Nominal Group Structure

these	two	splendid	electric	trains	with pantographs
Deictic	Numerative	Epithet	Classifier	Thing	Qualifier
Premodifier				Head	Postmodifier

(adapted from Halliday, 1994:191)

Language utilises either the grammatical dependency of these components to the head or the interdependency between the nominal groups in a group complex for creating the taxonomic relationships between phenomena. These resources again involve not only things but also processes construed as 'things'. That is, a process is reified and treated as a semiotic 'thing', so that it can act as the head (functionally Thing) of a nominal group, which is ready to be classified.

The nominal group structure proposed by Halliday, however, is based on English nominal groups and requires some modification when applied to Japanese. The most significant difference is the order of components. Japanese nominal groups have the following characteristics (Thomson, 2000:331–333), which are relevant to the following discussion:

(i) The dominant element of a nominal group typically occurs at the final position in the group. Thus, in a nominal group, it is the head, or Thing, that always occurs in final position, and in a hypotactic group complex, the dominant group comes after the dependent groups.

(ii) Unlike in English, the order of the modifying components is relatively free. Thus in Japanese, we can say

subarashii	*ni dai*	*no*	*kamotsu yoo no*	*ressha*
splendid	two CNT	NO	freight use NO	train

splendid two freight trains

and

kamotsu yoo no	*subarashii*	*ni dai no*	*ressha*
freight use NO	splendid	two CNT NO	train

freight splendid two trains

as well as

ni dai	*no*	*subarashii*	*kamotsu yoo no*	*ressha*
two CNT	NO	splendid	freight use NO	train

two splendid freight trains

as long as the head *ressha* is placed at the group final position.

In Japanese textbooks, the following structures are used to classify phenomena.

The hypotactic nominal group complex

The Japanese hypotactic nominal group complex used for classification takes the form of *a ya b nado no c* (*c* such as *a* and *b*), in which *c* is the dominant group and *a, b* are the dependant groups which expand the dominant group. The hypotactic relation is usually realised by a postpositional particle complex *~nado no* (such as~). This structure constructs a taxonomy by classifying subclasses (dependant groups) to a class (dominant group). In Example 5, *saikinrui* (bacteria) and *gensei doobutsu* (protozoa) are related to each other through the paratactic conjunction *ya* (and) forming the subclass unit, and *tansaiboo seibutsu* (single-celled animal) forms the class unit.

The English corresponding nominal group complex might be '*a* such as *b* and *c*.' Notice the difference in the direction of classification. While the English nominal group complex sub-classifies (i.e. *a* is a class and *b* and *c* are subclasses), the Japanese one classifies (i.e. *a* and *b* are subclasses and *c* is a class). This is due to the characteristic Japanese word order discussed under point (i) above.

Example 5: Classification of Phenomena through Group Complexing

saikinrui ya *gensei doobutsu* bacteria CONJ protozoa	***nado no*** etc NO	*tansaiboo seibutsu* single:celled animal
dependent nominal group **subclass**	postpositional particle complex indicating exemplification	dominant nominal group **class**
single-celled animals such as bacteria and protozoa		

Pronouns

A class is sometimes sub-classified into two or more subclasses which are represented by the general pronouns *ippoo* (one) and *tahoo* (the other). In Example 6, the class *soodoo senshokutai* (homologous chromosomes) are sub-classified into *sono ippoo* (this one) and *tahoo* (that one). The Deictic *sono* in *sono ippoo* is a demonstrative referring back to the class *soodoo senshokutai*.

Example 6: Classification of Phenomena with Pronouns

<table>
<tr><td colspan="4">kono [[tsui ni na-tte iru]] senshokutai o soodoo senshokutai to i-i,
this pair NI become-SUSP ASP chromosome O homologous chromosome TO call-SUSP</td></tr>
<tr><td colspan="4"></td></tr>
<tr><td>sono
that</td><td>ippoo wa
one WA</td><td>[[haha kata kara, (uketsu-ida)]] (mono)
mother side KARA (inherit-PAST) (thing)</td><td>(de ar-i)
(be-SUSP)</td></tr>
<tr><td>Deictic
class</td><td>Thing</td><td rowspan="3">Attribute</td><td rowspan="3">Process: relational: attributive</td></tr>
<tr><td colspan="2">nominal group
subclass 1</td></tr>
<tr><td colspan="2">Carrier</td></tr>
<tr><td colspan="4"></td></tr>
<tr><td colspan="2">tahoo wa
other:one WA</td><td>[[chichi kata kara uketsu-ida]] mono
father side KARA inherit-PAST thing</td><td>de aru.
be</td></tr>
<tr><td colspan="2">Thing</td><td rowspan="3">Attribute</td><td rowspan="3">Process: relational: attributive</td></tr>
<tr><td colspan="2">nominal group
subclass 2</td></tr>
<tr><td colspan="2">Carrier</td></tr>
<tr><td colspan="4">These paired chromosomes are called homologous chromosomes, and one is inherited from the mother, and the other is from the father.</td></tr>
</table>

The Classifier within a nominal group

The internal structure of Classifier^Thing in a nominal group realises a sub-classification. That is, any phenomenon (which functions as Thing) is sub-classified through the addition of a classifying element (which functions as Classifier). In Example 7, by adding the Classifier *tansaiboo* (single-celled) to the Thing *seibutsu* (animal), you can have a subclass *tansaiboo seibutsu* (single-celled animal), which contrasts with, for example, *tasaiboo seibutsu* (multiple-celled animal).

Example 7: Classification of Phenomena with Classifier

<table>
<tr><td>tansaiboo
single:celled</td><td>seibutsu
animal</td></tr>
<tr><td>Classifier</td><td>Thing
class</td></tr>
<tr><td colspan="2">nominal group
subclass</td></tr>
<tr><td colspan="2">single-celled animal</td></tr>
</table>

In English, the Classifier is realised by the classes of noun, adjective or verb in the present or past participle form (V-*ing* or V-*en*). These elements all belong to the word rank. A (prepositional) phrase and a clause never realise the function of Classifier. When phrases and clauses modify the head, they are rank-shifted and function as the post-modifier, or Qualifier, of the nominal group, like *with pantographs* in *the trains with pantographs* and *he loves* in *the trains he loves*.

The difference between Classifier and Qualifier in English, then, seems to be a grammatical one; when a modification is realised by a word and placed before the head, it is a Classifier; and when a modification is realised by a phrase or a clause, it is placed after the head, becoming a Qualifier. The functions of these two elements are similar; they both categorise the Thing. That is, the train with pantographs is a kind of train which has pantographs. Actually, Halliday states that a Classifier realised by a participle is functionally agnate to a Qualifier. That is, *boiled water* is very close in meaning to '*water which has been boiled'* (Halliday, 1994:186).

In contrast to this, the distinction between Classifier and Qualifier is fuzzy in Japanese, because, as I discussed in point (i), all modifying elements in the Japanese nominal group precede the head, and as pointed out in (ii), there are no sequential rules in the Japanese nominal group which designate the kinds of elements by relevant order. Therefore, this chapter tentatively makes no distinction between Classifier and Qualifier in the Japanese nominal group, and presupposes that the Japanese Classifier can be realised by a group, a phrase or a clause as well as by a word. When functioning as Classifier, a group, a phrase and a clause are rank-shifted and embedded within a nominal group.

In Example 7 above, the Classifier of *seibutsu* (animal) was realised by a single noun, *tansaiboo* (single-celled). In Example 8, a clause complex, *shu to shite T saiboo ga chokusetsu ibutsu ni hataraite || hatsugensareru* (mainly affected by T cells directly working on alien substances) is rank-shifted and serves as Classifier which sub-classifies the class *men'eki* (immunity) into the subclass *[[shu to shite T saiboo ga chokusetsu ibutsu ni hataraite || hatsug-*

ensareru]] men'eki (immunity mainly effected by T cells directly working on alien substances).

Example 8: Classifier Realised by a Rank-shifted Clause

<table>
<tr><td>[[shu to shite T saiboo ga chokusetsu ibutsu ni hatara-ite ||
main TO* SHITE T cell GA directly alien:substance NI work-SUSP
hatsugen s-areru]]
effect do-PSV</td><td>men'eki
immunity</td></tr>
<tr><td>Classifier: rank-shifted clause</td><td>Thing
class</td></tr>
<tr><td colspan="2">nominal group
subclass</td></tr>
<tr><td colspan="2">immunity which is mainly effected by T cells directly working on alien substances</td></tr>
</table>

This nominal group structure is often used in an identifying relational process which functions to give a technical label to the subclass. Therefore, within the whole relational clause, classifying and defining occur simultaneously. In Example 9, the rank-shifted clause which functions as a Classifier sub-classifies the class *immunity* into its subclass, *the type of immunity which is effected by T cells directly working on alien substances*. The entire nominal group in turn functions as Identified in an identifying relational clause, and is given a technical term, *saiboosei men'eki* (cellular immunity) which functions as Identifier.

Example 9: Classifier^Thing Structure in an Identifying Relational Process

<table>
<tr><td>shu to shite T saiboo ga
main TO* SHITE T cell GA
chokusetsu ibutsu ni
directly alien:substance NI
hatara-ite || hatsugen s-areru
work-SUSP effect do-PSV</td><td>men'eki o
immunity O</td><td rowspan="4">(wareware wa)
(we WA)</td><td rowspan="2">saiboosei
cellular
men'eki
immunity</td><td>to iu
TO call</td></tr>
<tr><td>Qualifier: rank-shifted clause</td><td>Thing
class</td><td rowspan="3">Process:
relational:
identifying</td></tr>
<tr><td colspan="2">nominal group
subclass</td><td rowspan="2">Identifier
technical term</td></tr>
<tr><td colspan="2">Identified
definition</td></tr>
<tr><td colspan="5">Immunity which is mainly effected by T cells directly working on alien substances is called a cell-mediated response.</td></tr>
</table>

Sometimes the 'Deictic followed by Thing' structure such as *kono yoo na A* (things like this) or *sono yoo na B* (things like that) is used for classification. Here the function of Deictic is agnate to that of those Classifiers that are realised by an embedded clause. When the clause that is supposed to function as Classifier becomes too long to be embedded into a nominal group, that clause is presented as a ranking (i.e. not rank-shifted) clause or clause complex, and the demonstrative adjectives such as *kono yoo na* or *sono yoo na* referring back to the clause (complex) are used to classify the Thing.[4] Such a Deictic effectively functions to organise text. That is, a demonstrative *kono* (this) or *sono* (that) packages the referred piece of information and uses it as the departure point to introduce new information (in this case, a technical term).

In Example 10, the Deictic *kono yoo na*, which refers to the preceding clause *dookeisetsugootai wa...arawareru* (homozygous organisms produce...) sub-classifies the class *keitoo* (lineage) into a specific kind of lineage where homozygous organisms always produce the offspring of the same traits no matter how many times they are self-pollinated. The whole nominal group, then, is labeled with a technical term *junkei* (pure).

Example 10: Classification of Phenomena with Deictic

<table>
<tr><td colspan="6">dookeisetsugootai wa, jikajusei o nan dai kurikaes-hite mo,
homozygous:organism WA self:pollination O what generation repeat-SUSP even
onaji keishitsu no shison ga arawareru.
same trait NO offspring GA appear</td></tr>
<tr><td colspan="6"></td></tr>
<tr><td>kono yoo na
this state NA</td><td>kotai no
individual NO</td><td>keitoo o
lineage O</td><td>(wareware wa)
(we WA)</td><td>junkei
pure</td><td>to iu
TO call</td></tr>
<tr><td>Deictic</td><td>Classifier</td><td>Thing
class</td><td rowspan="3"></td><td rowspan="3">Identifier
technical term</td><td rowspan="3">Process: relational: identifying</td></tr>
<tr><td colspan="3">nominal group
subclass</td></tr>
<tr><td colspan="3">Identified
definition</td></tr>
<tr><td colspan="6">Homozygous organisms always produce the offspring of the same traits, no matter how many times they are self-pollinated. Lineages like this are called pure.'</td></tr>
</table>

The above 10 examples show that the Japanese language system possesses a wide range of lexicogrammatical choices for classifying. Some of them classify and others sub-classify. Some of them work at the clause rank, and others work above or below the clause rank. We can summarise these resources in the form of a matrix (see Table 3).

Table 3: Japanese Micro-scale Lexicogrammatical Resources for Classifying

	classifying	sub-classifying
between clauses (or clause complexes)		logico-semantic relation of elaboration: exemplification between clause complexes logico-semantic relation of extension: addition between clause complexes
within a clause	attributive relational process	existential process
between nominal groups	hypotactic nominal group complex	
within a nominal group		pronouns Classifier (or Deictic)^Thing structure

The fact that the Japanese language has diverse and abundant options in micro-scale resources does not necessarily mean that these options are always selected appropriately in the creation of actual texts so that they contribute to the rhetorical effectiveness of the overall structure of the texts. To investigate this issue, the next section will move on from micro-scale resources to the larger organisation of text.

Thematic organisation of text for classifying phenomena

This section deals with the second research question: What are the macro-scale organisational resources appropriate for the classification of phenomena?

In order to investigate the overall structure of a text, I need to introduce the concept of thematic development originally proposed by Daneš (1974) and its correlation with the three aspects of knowledge construction that were summarised earlier in this chapter.

Thematic development and the purpose of a text

One of the main ways in which information is organised in language is through the resource of Theme. Theme refers to 'the element which serves as the point of departure of the message; it is that with which the clause is concerned' (Halliday, 1994:37). It is realised by the first position of the clause which includes the first element carrying ideational meaning and all the elements that come before it. For instance, in *the duke has given my aunt that teapot*, the Theme is *the duke* (ibid.: 38). In *well but then Ann surely wouldn't the best idea be to join the group*, it is the whole stretch of words *well but then Ann surely wouldn't the best idea* (ibid.: 55). This is a multiple Theme consisting of interpersonal, textual and experiential elements. The remainder of the clause, the Rheme, is the part in which the initial departure point is developed.

The thematic choice does not have significant meaning in a single clause. In a whole text, however, the way in which Themes are chosen from clause to clause creates the flow of messages. The way Themes are organised in particular patterns in a whole text is the thematic development of the text. Daneš (1974) called such patterns in the choice of themes Thematic Progression (TP), and identifies three basic types of TP. These are: 1) continuous pattern, in which the same item is repeatedly chosen as Theme for a number of clauses; 2) linear pattern, in which the Rheme, or part of the Rheme of a previous clause is taken up as the Theme of the following clause and 3) derived pattern, in which the Theme of each clause is derived, or taken, from the hyper Theme, that is the introductory sentence of the text which identifies the overall Theme(s) of the text. The term hyper Theme indicates the fractal nature of Theme-Rheme structure. Daneš (1974:109) states that 'not only particular utterances but also sections of text, such as paragraphs, etc., and the whole text have 'themes' of their own ('hyperthemes').' These three types are schematically shown in Figure 3.

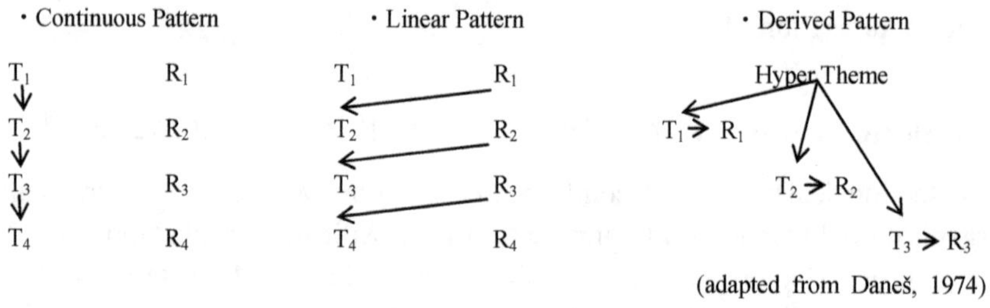

Figure 3: Three Patterns of Thematic Progression

Daneš (1974) found these three patterns in Czech, German, and English scientific and other professional texts. The analysis of Japanese scientific discourse undertaken in this chapter revealed that these three patterns are also found in the science text examples from Japanese.

The examples and their patterns in thematic development are shown below. For analysing the Japanese method of development, which seems to be organised by its distinctive linguistic units, I have adopted the concept of Theme unit as proposed by Thomson (2005). Based on several grammatical and semantic grounds, Thomson argues that Japanese does not map Theme onto the clause but onto the Theme unit, which may conflate or 'map onto clause simplexes, complexes, clauses within a complex and across sentences' (p.151).

Grammatically, the Japanese Theme unit is 'realised by a segment of text that forms a co-referential unit in which the referent (that which is retrievable in any non-initial clauses in the unit) is the first constituent in the unit' (p.162). Further, hypotactic enhancing clauses which precede the dominant clause serve as the Theme for the Theme unit, which includes both the dependent clause itself and the dominant clause, because these enhancing clauses function in a manner similar to that of circumstances (p.171).

Examples (numbers indicate Theme unit boundaries; ellipsis are indicated by double parentheses)

Continuous Pattern:

1. *tampakushitsu wa yaku 20 shurui no aminosan kara koosei s-are-te*
protein WA about 20 kind NO amino:acid KARA structure do-PSV-SUSP
iru…
ASP
Protein is composed of about 20 kinds of amino acids.

tampakushitsu wa [[tasuu no aminosan ga pepuchidoketsugoo ni yori
protein WA many no amino:acid GA peptide:bond NI YORI
renketsu s-hita]] nagai kusari (poripepuchido) kara deki-te iru…
connection do-PST long chain polypeptide KARA be:made-SUSP ASP
Protein is made of long chains of many amino acids connected to each other through peptide bonds (polypeptide).

2. *tampakushitsu no uchi ni wa, koraagen no yoo ni [[karada zentai no*
protein NO inside NI WA collagen NO state NI body whole NO
kokkaku ya ketsugoososhiki no seibun to na-tte iru]] mono mo
skeleton CONJ connective:tissue NO component TO* become-SUSP ASP thing MO
aru.
exist
Among proteins, there is one type, like collagen, which acts as the component of a skeleton and connective tissues of the body.

mata, ((tampakushitsu no uchi ni wa,)) [[hosoi sen'i joo no koozoo ni
further protein NO inside NI WA thin fiber state no structure ni
na-tte [[saibooshitsu chuu ni harimeguras-are-ta]] saiboo kokkaku
become-SUSP cytoplasm inside NI strech-PSV-PST cell framework
to shite hataraku]] mono mo aru.
TO* SHITE work thing MO exist
((Among proteins,)) there is another type which becomes a thin thread-like shape and functions as the cell framework stretched all over the inside of a cell.

3. *[[[[kono yoo ni seibutsu no katachi o tamotsu]] hataraki o suru]]*
this state NI organism NO shape O keep function O do
tampakushitsu o toku ni koozoo tampakushitsu to iu.
protein O special NI structural protein TO call
The protein which plays the role of retaining the shape of an organism, as explained, is specifically called structural protein.

(from *Kaitei Seibutsu*. p.18)

Figure 4: Continuous Thematic Pattern in the Japanese Text

Theme unit	Theme
1.	***tampakushitsu*** *wa* **Protein**
2.	***tampakushitsu*** *no uchi ni wa* Among **proteins**
3.	*[[[[kono yoo ni seibutsu no katachi o tamotsu]] hataraki o suru]]* ***tampakushitsu*** *o* The **protein** which plays the role of retaining the shape of an organism as explained

Linear Pattern:

1. *[[saiboo ga bunretsu suru]] sai ni wa, sore ni sakidat-te kaku no*
cell GA division do time NI WA that NI precede-SUSP nucleus NO
DNA ga fukusei s-areru.
DNA GA duplication do-PSV
At a time when a cell divides, prior to that, DNA in the nucleus is duplicated.

2. *sono sai kooso no hataraki ni yori nijuu no rasen ga bubunteki ni*
that time enzyme NO function NI YORI double NO helix GA partial NI
hodoke-te
come:loose-SUSP
At that time, by the function of enzymes, the double helix partially comes loose, and

((nijuu no rasen ga)) ippon zutsu no kusari ni naru.
double NO helix GA one each NO chain NI become
becomes (two) untwined chains.

3. *sorezore no kusari ga igata no yoo na sayoo o s-hite,*
each NO chain GA mold NO state NA function O do-SUSP
By each of the two chains acting like a mold,

[[enki no hairetsu ga choodo soohoteki ni naru]] yoo ni
base NO sequence GA just complemental NI become state NI

[[sozai to naru]] nukureochido ga narabu.
material TO* become nucleotide GA line:up
nucleotides, which are the material (of DNA), are sequenced in a way that the paired bases become mutually complementary.

4. *korera no nukureochido wa mae to wa betsu no kooso no*
these NO nucleotide WA before TO* WA different NO enzyme NO
hataraki ni yotte tagai ni ketsugoo s-hite
function NI YOTTE each:other NI connection do-SUSP
These nucleotides, by the function of other enzymes, are connected with each other, and

((korera no kooso wa)) nukureochido no kusari o tsukuru.
these NO enzyme WA nucleotide NO chain O form
form the chain of nucleotides.

5. *kono atarashii kusari to [[igata to na-tta]] kusari to kara*
this new chain CONJ mold TO* become-PST chain CONJ KARA
nijuu rasen ga tsukur-areru.
double helix GA form-PSV
From this new chain, and the chain which functioned as the mold, the (new) double helix is formed.

(from *Kaitei Seibutsu.* p.134)

Theme unit	Theme	Rheme
1.	*[[saiboo ga bunretsusuru]] sai ni wa* At a time when a cell divides	***…kaku no DNA ga fukusei sareru*** **DNA in the nucleus is duplicated**
2.	***sono sai*** At **that time**	***…ippon zutsu no kusari*** *ni naru* it becomes **(two) untwined chains**
3.	***sorezore no kusari*** *ga igata no yoo na sayoo o shite* By **each of the two chains** acting like a mold	***…[[sozai to naru]] nukureochido*** *ga narabu* **nucleotides, which is the material (of DNA)**, are sequenced
4.	***korera no nukureochido*** *wa* **These nucleotides**	***…nukureochido no kusari*** *o tsukuru* form **the chain of nucleotides**
5.	***kono atarashii kusari*** *to [[igata to natta]] kusari to kara* From **this new chain** and the chain which functioned as the mold	*nijuu rasen ga tsukurareru* the (new) double helix is formed

Figure 5: Linear Thematic Pattern in the Japanese Text

Derived Pattern:

1. *KAKUSAN [[shu to shite kaku ni fukum-areru]] deokishiribo kakusan*
   nucleic:acid main TO* SHITE nucleus NI contain-PSV deoxyribo nucleic:acid
   (DNA) to [[saibooshitsu oyobi kakushootai ni aru]] ribo kakusan
   DNA CONJ cytoplasm CONJ nucleoli NI exist ribo nucleic:acid
   (RNA) no ni shurui ga aru...
   RNA NO two type GA exist
   NUCLEIC ACIDS There are two types: deoxyribonucleic acid (DNA) which is contained mainly in the nucleus, and ribonucleic acid (RNA) which exists in cytoplasm and nucleoli.

2. *DNA no too wa deokishiriboosu de aru ga,*
   DNA NO sugar WA deoxyribose be CONJ
   While the sugar in DNA is deoxyribose,

3. *RNA no too wa riboosu de aru.*
   RNA NO sugar WA deoxyribose be
   the sugar in RNA is ribose.

4. *mata DNA de wa, adenin, guanin, shitoshin, chimin no 4 shurui no enki ga*
   further DNA DE WA adenine guanine cytosine thymine NO 4 type NO base GA
   aru ga,
   exist CONJ
   Further in DNA, there are four types of bases: adenine, guanine, cytosine, and thymine, whereas

5. *RNA de wa chimin no kawari ni urashiru ni na-tte iru.*
   RNA DE WA thymine NO substitute NI uracil NI become-SUSP ASP
   in RNA, the base thymine is replaced by uracil.

(from *Kaitei Seibutsu*. p.19)

These three types of organisation are not just accidental patterns in the grammar. They are motivated by the purpose of the text, and effectively function to organise the text appropriately for that purpose. Martin (1993b:244–247) discusses the correlation between the pattern of thematic development and the genre, that is, the general purpose of the text. From his analysis of report texts in science and history textbooks and explanation texts in science textbooks he argues that the Themes in these texts ‘can certainly be seen to pattern in specific ways, reflecting the different methods of development appropriate to Reports in science and history and to scientific Explanations’ (p.244).

Theme unit	Theme	Rheme
1. **Hyper Theme**	*kakusan* NUCLEIC ACIDS	*...deokishiribo kakusan (DNA) to..ribo kakusan (RNA) no ni shurui ga aru.* there are two types: neoxyribonucleic acid (DNA)..., and ribonucleic acid (RNA)...
2.	*DNA no too wa* The sugar in DNA	*deokishiriboosu de aru ga* is deoxyribose
3.	*RNA no too wa* the sugar in RNA	*riboosu de aru* is ribose
4.	*mata DNA de wa* Further in DNA	*...no 4 shurui no enki ga aru ga* there are four types of bases...
5.	*RNA de wa* in RNA	*chimin no kawari ni urashiru ni natte iru* the base thymine is replaced by uracil

Figure 6: Derived Thematic Pattern in the Japanese Text

In the Japanese science textbooks analysed in this study, the same correlation was found. That is, texts whose purpose is defining, classifying, and explaining show distinctive patterns in their thematic patterns to achieve their respective purposes. The interrelation between the purpose and thematic development of these texts is summarised as follows:

1. A defining text often shows a continuous pattern in its thematic development. Its purpose is to describe a particular event or thing and to define what it is. So the event or thing will be continuously in focus and appear in the thematic position for a number of Theme units. For example, the text analysed above as Figure 4 defines what *tampakushitsu* (protein) is. Figure 4 shows that the main topic *tampakushitsu* is repeatedly chosen as the Theme for a number of Theme units of the text.

2. An explanation text tends to show a linear pattern, as its purpose is to construct consecutive relations between events, showing that the previous event serves as the starting stage for the next event. Taking up the (part of a) Rheme of a previous Theme unit as the Theme of the following unit effectively realises such sequential relations between events. For example, the text analysed above as Figure 5 explains how DNA duplicates. Notice that the resulting products of the previous events (e.g. *ippon zutsu no kusari* (untwined chains) and *nukureochido no kusari* (the chain of nucleotides)), which appear in Rheme of Theme units, are chosen as the starting points (i.e. Themes) of the following Theme units. Such patterning effectively builds up the consecutive relations between events.

3. A classifying text is likely to show a derived pattern. Its purpose is to construct taxonomies by deconstructing phenomena into parts or subclasses.

> Thus the hyper Theme of the text, reflecting the purpose, decomposes, or sub-classifies classes into subclasses. These subclasses are taken up as the Themes of the following Theme units.
>
> For example, the text analysed above as Figure 6 classifies *kakusan* (nucleic acid) into *DNA* and *RNA*. The hyper Theme of the text is the first sentence, *kakusan [[shu to shite kaku ni hukumareru]] deokishiribo kakusan (DNA) to [[saibooshitsu oyobi kakushootai ni aru]] ribo kakusan (RNA) no ni shurui ga aru* (NUCLEIC ACIDS There are two types of nucleic acids: deoxyribonucleic acid (DNA) which is contained mainly in the nucleus, and ribonucleic acid (RNA) which exists in cytoplasm and nucleoli). The sub-heading attached to the sentence, *kakusan,* may be understood as the abbreviate form of *kakusan ni wa* (in kakusan). Thus, this sentence is agnate to the existential clause '*a ni wa b to c ga aru* (in *a* there are *b* and *c*)' which classifies phenomena at the clause rank.
>
> The hyper Theme introduces the class, *kakusan*, and its two subclasses, *DNA* and *RNA*, and indicates that the rest of the text is organised around the classification of phenomena. The Themes of the following Theme units maintain each one of the two subclasses. The Rhemes of the Theme units give us further information about the subclasses, that is, the differences between the two kinds of nucleic acids (i.e. in DNA, the sugar is deoxyribose, while in RNA, it is ribose; the bases contained in DNA are A, G, C, T, while RNA contains A, G, C, U). Such a pattern in the thematic development effectively constructs the taxonomical order of phenomena.

These three examples show that the thematic structure collaborate to construct the purpose of the text, and organises the text in an appropriate way to fulfill its purpose. The next section focuses on the collaboration between the micro- and macro- scale resources found in the corpus.

Thematic development of a Japanese classifying text

This section deals with the last step in the research project which was the investigation of the overall textual structures found in the corpus, and the noting of how the choice of micro-scale resources collaborated with the macro-scale organisation.

As seen in the last section, texts are easy to follow when they are organised according to the thematic pattern appropriate for the purpose of the text. Therefore, classifying texts often employ derived patterns of thematic development to effectively transmit the knowledge of taxonomical order of phenomena to students.

In the actual textbooks, however, the Japanese language tends to organise texts in more complicated ways than we have seen in the short examples in the previous section. This section will take one classifying text from the Japanese textbook, and carry out a case study on how this text organises and how the micro-scale resources are deployed carefully and appropriately in the creation of text.

The text is analysed and shown in Figure 7. It consists of four paragraphs and classifies the class *totsuzenhen'i* (mutation) into three subclasses, *senshokutai totsuzenhen'i* (chromosome mutation), *idenshi totsuzenhen'i* (gene mutation), and *jin'i totsuzenhen'i* (artificial mutation). Each of the latter three paragraphs describes one of these three types of mutation.

	Theme	Rheme
First paragraph		
1.	*[[onaji oya kara umare-ta]] kotai ni tsuite,* Regarding individual organisms born from the same parents,	*hitotsu hitotsu no keishitsu o shirabe-te-miru-to, iroiro na chigai ga mir-areru.* [...] if (we) investigate the traits of each one, (we) find a variety of differences. [...]
2.	*[[kotai kan ni mir-areru]] keishitsu no chigai o* The difference in traits found between individuals	*hen'i to iu.* is called variation.
3.	*hen'i ni wa,* In variation,	*[[iden suru]] mono to [[s-hinai]]mono to ga aru.* there is one which is inherited, and the other which is not inherited.
4.	**Hyper Theme** *[[iden suru]] hen'i ni wa,* In hereditary variation (=mutation),	*dono yoo na mono ga aru-daroo ka* what types are there?
Second paragraph		
5.	*do furiisu wa,* De Vries	[...] *koto ni kyoomi o moc-hi,* [...]. took interest in [...].
6.	*[[do furiisu ga miidas-hita]] oomatsuyoigusa no[[kawa-tta]] mono no ooku wa,* Most of the novel types of evening primroses De Vreis discovered,	*[[senshokutai no ijoo ni yoru mono de aru]] koto ga waka-tta.* turned out to be the result of abrupt changes in chromosomes.
7.	*[[kono yoo ni, senshokutai no koozoo ya kazu no henka ni yotte shoozuru]] totsuzenhen'i o* The mutation caused by the changes in the composition and number of chromosomes as explained	*senshokutai totsuzenhen'i to iu.* is called chromosome mutation.
Third paragraph		
8.	*[[idenshi no hontai de aru]]DNA ni henka ga okoru-to,* If changes occur to DNA, which itself is the gene,	*totsuzenhen'i o shoozuru.* (it) causes mutation.
9.	*kore o* This	*idenshi totsuzenhen'i to iu.* is called gene mutation.
Fourth paragraph		
10.	*[[totsuzenhen'i ga shizen ni okoru]] ritsu wa* The probability of mutation occurring spontaneously	*kiwamete hikui.* is extremely low.
11.	*1927 nen,* In 1927,	*maraa wa,* [...] *seikoo s-hita.* Muller succeeded in [...].
12.	*sono go,* After that,	*[[hooshasen, shigaisen ya* [...] *ni yotte mo, totsuzenhen'i ga okor-i yasu-ku naru]] koto ga waka-tta.* it turned out that mutations are also promoted by radiation, ultra-violet lays and [...].
13.	*[[kono yoo ni, jin'iteki ni yuuhatsu s-areru]] totsuzenhen'i o* The mutation brought about artificially as explained	*jin'i totsuzenhen'i to iu.* is called artificial mutation.

(From Seibutsu IB:168–176)

Figure 7: Thematic Development of a Classifying Text in a Japanese Textbook

The first paragraph is the introductory part where the terms *hen'i* (variation) and *totsuzen hen'i* (mutation) are introduced and then classified. Notice the reification process similar to the one we have seen in Figure 1 and its collaboration with the thematic development; the process given in Theme unit 1 is reified into a semiotic 'thing', *[[kotai kan ni mirareru]] keishitsu no chigai* (the difference in traits found between individuals) through the use of nominalisation (*chigai* (difference)). This is the nominalised form of *chigau* (to be different)), and is used as the departure point, or Theme, of Theme unit 2. The 'thing' is then labeled with the technical term *hen'i* (variation), and picked up as the Theme of the next Theme unit (Theme unit 3), which places the term into the taxonomical order. Theme units 3 and 4 consecutively sub-classify phenomena: Theme unit 3 sub-classifies the class *hen'i* (variation) into two different types of variations; and then Theme unit 4 sub-classifies the class *[[iden suru]] hen'i* (mutation) into the several different types of mutations. The final unit of the first paragraph, Theme unit 4, serves as the hyper Theme for the remainder of the text.

The most appropriate micro-scale resource for the hyper Theme of classifying texts is the existential process, as this is the only micro-scale resource which sub-classifies or decomposes phenomena into subclasses at the clause rank, so that the following clauses can pick up each one of the subclasses as Theme and add new information to it (see Table 1). This text uses the existential process which sub-classifies the mutation. However, the subclasses are not explicitly shown here. Instead, the existential process is used to ask a rhetorical question using a nominal group with an interrogative Classifier, *dono yoo na mono* (what types). This is used as a substitute of the subclasses, and indicates that the following paragraphs are devoted to the introduction and elaboration of each one of the subclasses of mutation.

The following three paragraphs are *about* these subclasses even though they do not select the subclasses as Theme of Theme units in a way the typical classifying text we have seen in the last section (see Figure 6) does. The units centre around the episodical description of science history, as they place a specific scientist (*Do furiisu* (De Vries)) and temporal circumstantial elements (*1927 nen* (in 1927) and *sono go* (after that)) in thematic position. These historical recounts are used as the introductory description needed to explain and define the technical terms, *senshokutai totsuzenhen'i* (chromosome mutation), *idenshi totsuzenhen'i* (gene mutation), and *jin'i totsuzenhen'i* (artificial mutation). These three subclasses of *totsuzenhen'i* (mutation) appear in the Rheme positions of the last Theme units of the paragraphs: Theme unit 7, 9 and 13, respectively. This is in keeping with 'new' information being typically introduced in the Rheme, where newsworthy information is located (Halliday, 1994:298–299).

Theme units 7, 9 and 13 select the appropriate micro-scale resource to serve as the defining statements. Two of these three select identifying clauses in which both classifying and defining occur simultaneously (see the section of the micro-scale resources which classify phenomena at the clause rank). By utilising this resource, these sentences (i) summarise the information given in the previous part of the paragraphs; (ii) place the summarised information in the taxonomical order of mutational phenomena; and (iii) close off the paragraph by giving a technical label to the phenomena. The structures of Theme units 7 and 13, which consist of single identifying clauses, are shown in Figure 8.

Figure 8: Identifying Clause with Rank-shifted Clause inside It

<Theme unit 7>

<table>
<tr><td>[[kono yoo ni, senshokutai
this status NI chromosome
no koozoo ya kazu no
NO structure CONJ number NO
henka ni yotte shoozuru]]
change NI YOTTE appear

Classifier:
rank-shifted clause</td><td>totsuzenhen'i o
mutation O

Thing
class</td><td rowspan="3">(wareware wa)
(we WA)</td><td rowspan="3">senshokutai
chromosome
totsuzenhen'i
mutation

Identifier
technical term</td><td rowspan="3">to iu
TO call

Process:
relational:
identifying</td></tr>
<tr><td colspan="2">nominal group
subclass</td></tr>
<tr><td colspan="2">Identified
definition</td></tr>
<tr><td colspan="5">The mutation caused by the changes in the composition and number of chromosomes as explained is called chromosome mutation.</td></tr>
</table>

<Theme unit 13>

<table>
<tr><td>[[kono yoo ni, jin'iteki ni
this state NI artificial NI*
yuuhatsu s-areru]]
inducement do-PSV</td><td>totsuzenhen'i o
mutation O</td><td>(wareware wa)
(we WA)</td><td>jin'i
artificial
totsuzenhen'i
mutation</td><td>to iu
TO call</td></tr>
<tr><td>Classifier: rank-shifted clause</td><td>Thing
class</td><td rowspan="3"></td><td rowspan="3">Identifier
technical term</td><td rowspan="3">Process:
relational:
identifying</td></tr>
<tr><td colspan="2">nominal group
subclass</td></tr>
<tr><td colspan="2">Identified
definition</td></tr>
<tr><td colspan="5">The mutation brought about artificially as explained is called artificial mutation</td></tr>
</table>

Notice how this text uses clause embedding or textual devices such as reference items in collaboration with the thematic development of the text to generalise and accumulate the specific historical descriptions into these summarising Theme units of paragraphs, so that the paragraphs as a whole focus on their respective token subclasses. Take for example the rank-shifted clauses in the Theme unit 7. In the second paragraph, the description of a number of varieties of the evening primroses listed in Theme unit 5 (which forms an unusually long unit consisting of four ranking clauses because of the successive ellipsis of the subject *do furiisu wa* (De Vries)) are generalised and summarised in the Theme of the next Theme unit as *[[do furiisu ga miidashita]] oomatsuyoigusa no [[kawatta]] mono* (the novel types of evening primroses De Vreis discovered). The Rheme of the unit then adds further information to it. The final unit of the paragraph, Theme unit 7, slightly expands that information, *senshokutai no ijoo ni yoru* (due to the abrupt changes in chromosomes), into *senshokutai no koozoo ya kazu no henka ni yotte hikiokosareru* (be caused by the changes in the composition and number of chromosomes), and generalise the information by embedding the clause into the superordinate term *totsuzen hen'i* (mutation). The embedded clause functions as Classifier,which sub-classifies the class *totsuzenhen'i* (mutation) into the subclass *senshokutai no koozoo ya kaku no henka ni yotte shoozuru totsuzenhen'i* (mutation caused by the changes in the composition and number of chromosomes). In this way, the clause gives the accumulated information its place in the taxonomical order. Finally, the subclass, which is placed at the departure point of the clause, is given the technical label *senshokutai totsuzenhen'i* (chromosome mutation), which is presented as the new information.

Similarly in the fourth paragraph, the information given in Theme unit 11 is accumulated in the next unit into the demonstrative *sono* (that), which refers back to the whole sequence of events described in Theme unit 11, and is used as the starting point for the next piece of information. The information given in the Rheme of Theme unit 12 (*hooshasen etc. ni yotte totsuzenhen'i ga okori yasuku naru* (mutations are promoted by radiation…etc.) is summarised into the rank-shifted clause *jin'iteki ni yuuhatsu sareru* (brought about artificially), and used as Classifier to produce a subclass of *totsuzenhen'i*: *jin'iteki ni yuuhatsu sareru totsuzenhen'i* (mutation brought about artificially). The technical label is then introduced.

Such accumulating and summarising functions of Theme units 7 and 13 is explicitly reflected by the demonstratives in the embedded clauses, *kono yoo ni* (in this way; as explained), which refer back to the previous parts of the paragraphs. The use of rank-shifted clauses as Classifier, then, is a very powerful device in the Japanese language in that it not only classifies phenomena at the micro-level, but also functions to organise the macro structure of the text. This may be one of the reasons why it is the most favoured micro-scale resource for classification in the corpus (it was used in 36 cases in the total 79 instances of classification; see Table 2).

We can observe the same pattern of accumulation in the third paragraph. The phenomenon described in the first Theme unit is packaged into a referential item *kore* (this), and used as the starting point to introduce the new information, that is, the technical term of the phenomenon.

Organised in this way, the text makes it quite explicit that it is organised around the classification of phenomena and that each paragraph gives additional information about one of the subclasses. That is, the whole text has a hyper Theme (Theme unit 4) which orients the text to the sub-classification of phenomena, and each of the following paragraphs centres around the description of one of these subclasses by giving a specific historical recount about the subclass, and gradually summarising it into a generalised technical term. The organisation of the text where the summarising information is placed at the end of a paragraph is a perfectly natural structure in Japanese text. This is something that has been pointed out by many scholars that Japanese is a language which characteristically tends to place important information at the end of the unit of discourse whether it is a clause, paragraph, or a whole text (see Kinoshita, 1994:194–206 for example).

In order to accumulate information toward the end of the paragraph, the Japanese language typically uses clause embedding or reference items as we have seen in the analysis. The Japanese rank-shifted nominal clause marker, *koto*, is also often utilised to introduce already generalised and accumulated phenomena as the shared information so that the authors can directly get to their point on the basis of the shared information. Examples are:

> *[[[[[[ryooshin to wa mattaku kotonaru]] keishitsu o motsu]] [[kawa-tta]] mono ga arawareru]] koto* (from Theme unit 1)
> the phenomenon where a novel type which has the trait completely different from its parents appears

> *[[[[oomatsuyoigusa ni [[kawa-tta]] keishitsu no kotai ga shibashiba hakken s-areru]]]] koto* (from Theme unit 5)
> the phenomenon where individuals with novel traits are sometimes found among evening primroses

> *[[[[korera no [[kawa-tta]] mono no keishitsu wa iden suru]]]] koto* (from Theme unit 5)
> that the traits of these novel type plants were passed along

Other languages, like English, have developed a linguistic device called nominalisation to package information so that it can be used as the departure point of the next piece of information. For example, through the analysis of text examples taken from various periods of history, Halliday (1993) illustrates how nominalisation has evolved in the English discourse of science in order to organise information. The analysis in this section has shown that the Japanese discourse of science depends more on textual devices than on nominalisation. Clause embedding, which is typical of the Japanese discourse of science, is the characteristic textual device of the 'pre-nominalised' discourse in the historical evolution of the English discourse of science (Halliday, 1993:66). In that sense, the analysis conducted in this chapter might suggest that the Japanese language is still on its way to developing more metaphorical ways of meaning making.

In any event, this analysis has illustrated that the Japanese language has its own distinctive resources for organising information and effectively uses these resources to construct appropriate patterns in the flow of information. It has also shown that the Japanese textbooks select appropriate micro-scale resources and fit them into the macro-scale structure of the text so that these two levels of resources effectively collaborate to fulfill the purpose of the text.

Conclusion

In this chapter, I aimed to describe how the Japanese language functions to construct one of the important aspects of science: classifying phenomena into systematic taxonomies. In this study, it was found that the resources from different subsystems of language collaborate with each other and construct distinctive patterns to fulfill the purpose of the text.

As for micro-scale formation, the Japanese language utilises the systems of transitivity and logico-semantic relations to produce a wide range of resources for constructing the classifying aspect of science. The resources range from those which operate at the clause rank to those which work above and below the clause rank. The options in the language system, however, are not all equally probable selections in the creation of text. The resource for classifying processes is rarely used in Japanese science texts; most processes are constructed as semiotic 'things' prior to their classification. In this process, it was found that a number of reifying devices (including nominalisation, the embedding of a clause into a nominal group, and the use of technical terms) were used to create semiotic 'things'.

As for macro-scale organisation, the study has shown that the analysed text can certainly be seen to reflect the methods of development appropriate for the classifying purpose of the text. That is, the analysed classifying text is basically organised in the derived pattern of thematic progression, which consists of the introductory part, which leads to the hyper Theme of the text and the following descriptive parts, which deals with the subclasses introduced in the hyper Theme. The hyper Theme utilises the existential process and sub-classifies the class to explicitly show that the whole text is oriented towards the decomposition of phenomena. The following part of the text selects the micro-scale resource of embedded clause as Classifier in order to summarise the previous parts of the text and introduce the token subclass.

This analysis has shown that Japanese scientific texts provide a wide range of micro-scale linguistic resources necessary for constructing specialised taxonomies and effectively incorporate these resources into the macro-scale structure of texts so that the structure fulfills the purpose of the text.

Notes

1 This chapter limits the scope of investigation to the taxonomies based on superordination for want of space.

2 This chapter categorises the clause with 'call (*to iu* or *to yobu* in Japanese)' as relational process rather than verbal process following Halliday (1994:171). According to Halliday, the clause in question is analysed as follows:

	we	call	green plants	producers
transitive	Assigner	Process: Identifying	Identified/Token	Identifier/Value
ergative	Agent		Medium	Range

	green plants	are called	producers
transitive	Identified/Token	Process: Identifying	Identifier/Value
ergative	Medium		Range

Based on this analysis, I analyze the Japanese clause with *to iu* and *to yobu*, such as *ryokushoku shokubutsu o seisansha to iu* as follows:

ryokushoku shokubutsu o green plant O	(*wareware wa*) (we WA)	*seisansha* producer	*to iu* TO call
Identified/Token	Assigner	Identifier/ Value	Process: Identifying
Green plants are called producers.			

3 The term rank-shift means that 'a unit may come to serve to realise an element of a unit of the same rank or of a lower rank' (Matthiessen, 1995:21).

4 Thomson (2000:315) calls such adjectives which require particle *na* to modify a noun 'nominal adjective.'

Interlinear notation key

ASP	aspect
ATP	attempt: [-*te*] *miru*
CJT	conjecture: V-*daroo*
CND	conditional: V-*to*
CNT	counter: [number] *ko, dai, do*
CONJ	conjunctive
COP	copula: da, aru
DE	nominal marker (Circumstance; 'in')
ENU	enumerative: [-*shi*] *tari*
GA	nominal marker (Participant; nominative)
INT	interrogative: V-ka
KARA	nominal marker (Circumstance; 'from')
KOTO	rankshifted nominal clause marker
MADE	nominal marker (Circumstance; 'from')
MO	nominal marker
NA	adnominal marker
NEG	negative: [-*shi*] *nai*
NI	nominal marker (Circumstance 'in / to', Participant)
NI*	adverbial marker
NO	nominal marker (Participant; possessive)
O	nominal marker (Participant; accusative)
PST	past
PSV	passive
SHITE	postposition ('as')
SUSP	non-finite, tactic verb form: -*shi*, -*shite*
TO	postpositional quotative clause marker
TO*	nominal marker (Circumstance 'in / to')
TSUITE	postposition ('about')
WA	nominal marker
YOTTE YORI YORU	} postposition ('by')

adapted from Teruya (1998: xxiii-xxiv)

References

Primary Sources

Takashi Fujii, Kooichi Akita, Nobuo Ekami, Takeo Mizuno, Hiroshi Kobayashi, Seiichiroo Kinoshita, Hitoshi Tazawa, Minoru Hara, Shigeo Takeuchi, Toshio Kanamaru, Yoshio Maruko, Tadamasa Momose, and Haruyoshi Moriya. (1993) *Kaitei Seibutsu* (Revised Biology). Tokyo: Tokyo Shoseki. pp18–19, 133–154.

Takamasa Tanaka, Kazuhiko Konishi, Tsuneyoshi Kuroiwa, Shoozoo Oosawa, Michio Tamura, Akio Tanaka, Akimichi Garai, Kooji Iiyama, Makoto Izawa, Hideo Ikeda, Shimpei Ono, Isao Kajikawa, Yuuji Kajino, Hiroki Kajiyama, Fujio Katoo, Tadashi Kubota, Mitsuo Hisaya, Shigehiro Kurizono, Tsuneo Tsukahira, Akinobu Tsujimoto, Kazutoshi Tomioka, Seishi Hiraoka, Takio Hirosawa, Hideyuki Fujimoto, Kazuhiro Matsuzawa, Hiromitsu Miyamoto, Hiroshi Yasui, Yoshihiko Yonezawa, and Masutomi Watabe. (2000) *Kootoogakkoo Kaitei Seibutsu IB* (High School Revised Biology IB). Tokyo: Daiichi Gakushu-sha. pp102–105, 138–145.

Secondary Sources

Daneš F. (1974) Functional sentence perspective and the organisation of the text. In F. Daneš (ed.) *Chapters on Functional Sentence Perspective* 106–128. The Hague: Mouton.

Halliday, M. A. K. (1989) *Spoken and Written Language*. London: Oxford University Press.

Halliday, M. A. K. (1993) On the language of physical science. In M. A. K. Halliday and J. R. Martin (eds) (1993) *Writing Science: Literacy and Discursive Power*. PA: University of Pittsburgh Press 54–68.

Halliday, M. A. K. (1994) *An Introduction to Functional Grammar*. 2nd ed. London: Edward Arnold.

Halliday, M. A. K. and Matthiessen, C. M. I. M. (1999) *Construing Experience through Meaning*. New York/London: Cassell.

Halliday, M. A. K. and Martin, J. R. (eds) (1993) *Writing Science: Literacy and Discursive Power*. PA: University of Pittsburgh Press.

Hayakawa, C. (2006) Construction and transmission of specialized knowledge: lexicogrammatical resources in Japanese and English science textbooks. Unpublished doctoral thesis, Graduate School of International Cultural Studies, Tohoku University.

Kinoshita, K. (1994) *Repooto no Kumitate Kata (How to Organise Reports)*. Tokyo: Chikuma Gakugei Bunko.

Martin, J. R. (1992) *English Text: System and Structure*. Philadelphia/ Amsterdam: John Benjamins.

Martin, J. R. (1993a) Literacy in science: learning to handle text as a technology. In M. A. K. Halliday and J. R. Martin (eds) (1993) *Writing Science: Literacy and Discursive Power*. PA: University of Pittsburgh Press 166–202.

Martin, J. R. (1993b) Life as a noun: arresting the universe in science and humanities. In M. A. K. Halliday and J. R. Martin (eds) (1993) *Writing Science: Literacy and Discursive Power*. PA: University of Pittsburgh Press 221–267.

Martin, J. R. and Veel, R. (eds) (1998) *Reading Science: Critical and Functional Perspectives on Discourses of Science*. London/New York: Routledge.

Matthiessen, C. M. I. M. (1995) *Lexicogrammatical Cartography: English Systems*. Tokyo: International Language Science Publishers.

Painter, C. (1999) *Learning through Language in Early Childhood.* London: Continuum.

Rose, D. (1997) Science, technology and technical literacies. In Francis Christie and J. R. Martin (eds) *Genre and Institutions: Social Processes in the Workplace and School* 40–72. London: Cassell.

Teruya, K. (1998) *An Exploration into the World of Experience: A Systemic-Functional Interpretation of the Grammar of Japanese*. Unpublished PhD dissertation. School of English, Linguistics and Media, Macquarie University, Sydney.

Teruya, K. (2004) Metafunctional profile of the grammar of Japanese. In A. Caffarel, J. R. Martin and C. M. I. M. Matthiessen (eds) *Language Typology: A Functional Perspective* 185–254. Amsterdam/Philadelphia: John Benjamins.

Thomson, E. (2000) Life as a noun in Japanese: a partial systemic functional description of the nominal group. In V. Mackie, A. Skoutarides, A. Tokita, P. Eckersall, S. Grant, C. Hayer, P. Jones, T. Savage and R. Spence-Brown (eds) *Japanese Studies: Communities, Cultures, Critiques. Volume four: New Directions in Japanese Linguistics* 311–337. Clayton: Monash Asia Institute.

Thomson, E. (2005) Theme unit analysis: a systemic functional treatment of textual meanings in Japanese. *Functions of Language* 12(2): 151–179. Amsterdam: John Benjamins.

Wignell, P., Martin, J. R. and Eggins, S. (1993) The discourse of geography: ordering and explaining the experiential world. In M. A. K. Halliday and J. R. Martin (eds) (1993) *Writing Science: Literacy and Discursive Power*. PA: University of Pittsburgh Press 136–165.

6 Nominalisation and nouniness as meaning strategies in Japanese political manifestos

Kinuko Sato (Suto) and Christopher Barnard
(Formerly) Tohoku University, Japan
Teikyo University, Japan

In this paper, we attempt to develop the traditional notion of nominalisation by constructing a cline of nominalisation. This cline comprises a range of expressions with various degrees of 'nouniness', showing that nominalisation arises when meanings are reconstrued by more noun-like or 'nounier' expressions. This cline is particularly useful when we analyse degrees of specificity or negotiability of information presented in texts. We will demonstrate the way to use this cline by analysing the Japanese general election manifestos of 2003 of the then incumbent party (the Liberal Democratic Party; ***Jimin-too***) and the largest opposition party (the Democratic Party of Japan; ***Minshu-too***). We will demonstrate that in these political manifestos a shift towards 'nounier' elements and nominalisation are used to construe the opponents' past/ongoing political failures in contrast with their own party's future political successes as having low negotiability and given information, as a strategy to implicitly persuade readers of the superiority of the party over other rival parties.

Introduction

Halliday (1994) states that nominalisation arises when 'any element or group of elements is made to function as a nominal group in the clause (p.41).' In the cline of nominalisation, which will be presented in the following section, elements other than a nominal group, such as a projected clause or a defining relative clause (restrictive clause) are also included, being ordered based on the recognition criteria of specificity and negotiability of information. In order to demonstrate the usefulness of the cline of nominalisation, we will subsequently analyse the political manifestos of the then ruling Liberal Democratic Party (*Jimin-too*; hereafter the LDP) and the largest opposition party, the Democratic Party of Japan (*Minshu-too*; hereafter the DPJ).

Firstly, it is useful to provide some background to the political manifestos that will be analysed. In the 2003 Japanese general election campaign, for the first time in Japanese history due to an amendment of the election laws, the distribution of itemised policy manifestos, in which political parties described the policies they would carry out upon winning an election was allowed. Prior to the publication of a manifesto, '*kooyaku* (political promises)' were considered to be a slogan-laced political 'wish list' of promises easily broken (The Japan Times 16 July, 2003). The Japanese manifesto is an import from Britain, where the birth of manifestos dates back to 1834 and manifestos are given practical significance, thus being closely examined by the nation regarding the feasibility and success of their implementation. The LDP and the DPJ manifestos are modelled after British manifestos (Kimura, 2003:19–23). In the 2003 election, the biggest issue at stake was whether Prime Minister Junichiro Koizumi's ruling LDP, which swept to power in April 2001, could maintain its hold on power, or whether the largest opposition party, the DPJ, led by Naoto Kan, could seize the reins. The DPJ was regarded as the first credible opposition in Japanese politics that could challenge the LDP, which has governed almost without interruption for the last 50 years (BBC News, 11 June 2003). While the DPJ made impressive gains, the LDP succeeded in winning the election. Taking this background into consideration, we will analyse the LDP and the DPJ manifestos in terms of the extent or degree of nominalisation deployed in these texts.

Methodology and data

The primary materials for analysis are the election manifestos circulated by the LDP and the DPJ in 2003. Secondary material is also used for the purpose of comparison with the primary texts. The secondary text is the British Labour Party manifesto published in 1997, by which the Labour Party led by Tony Blair defeated the Conservative Party, ending eighteen years of Conservative rule. The full text of the primary materials are reproduced in the appendix and their citations listed in the references list.

Due to extensive length, the analysis is restricted to the main policy section of each manifesto.[1] The information in these sections will be explained before proceeding with the analysis. The LDP advocates privatising the postal service and the four major highway-related public corporations under the main policy (Pledge 3), saying 'we will cut down waste in administration and strive for a simple and effective government [*gyoosei no muda o habuki kanso de kooritsuteki na seifu o mezashimasu.*].' On the other hand, the DPJ manifesto has as its main policy to 'abolish the Japan Public Highway Corporation and make motorways toll-free (within 3 years) [*dooro koodan o haishishi, koosoku dooro no ryookin o muryoonishimasu* (*3 nen inai*)]'. The British Labour Party's priority is on educational policies (Smith and Smith, 2000:465).

Using these texts as data, we will attempt to explore the following research questions:

1. To what extent and degree is nominalisation deployed in the manifesto texts? In other words, what kinds of nouny expressions are used and where do they fall on the nominalisation cline?
2. What kinds of Events tend to be nominalised and what elements of the transitivity configurations accompany the nominalised Events?
3. What effects does the use of nominalisation have on the meanings in the texts? Do they contribute to the social purpose of the texts, that of persuading the reader to vote for them?

The chapter will begin with an introduction of the analytical framework used for investigating these research questions, constructing a cline of nominalisation that comprises a range of expressions with various degrees of nouniness. Based on this cline, we will subsequently explore the research questions 1 and 2, analysing the LDP and the DPJ manifestos from the perspective of the extent or degree of nominalisation. Following this, we will attempt to answer research question 3, discussing the semantic effects stemming from the choices revealed in the nominalisation analysis, as well as presenting an alternative way of describing prospective policies by using the British Labour Party manifesto (1997) as an example. The overall theoretical framework is Systemic Functional Theory (hereafter SF Theory, cf. Halliday, 1994; Halliday and Matthiessen, 2004).

The construction of the cline of nominalisation (analytical framework)

In this section, we will construct a cline of nominalisation. In SF Theory, nominalisation is regarded as a kind of grammatical metaphor. In its traditional sense, a metaphor is a transfer of one word (lexical item) to another, as when *flood* is used to indicate 'a large number', rather than 'a moving mass of water' (Halliday, 1994:342). In SF Theory, the same mechanism is also applied to grammar – a transfer of one grammatical class to another. Any category in semantics has its typical or 'congruent' realisation pattern in lexicogrammar[2]:

people and things tend to be realised by nominal groups, actions by verbal groups, and logical relations by conjunctives. It is when one semantic category is realised by a non-typical or 'incongruent' pattern, as if it were another semantic category, that a grammatical metaphor arises. Nominalisation is an experiential metaphor which arises when an Event is lexicogrammatically expressed by a nominal group.

In this chapter, we expand the notion of nominalisation by introducing the term 'nouniness', assuming that nominalisation arises when meanings are reconstrued by more noun-like or 'nounier' expressions. In this cline, projected clauses and defining relative clauses (restrictive clauses), as well as nominal groups, can be regarded as a kind of nominalisation with differing degrees of nouniness. The linguist who advocated the concept of nouniness, Ross (1973) constructed a nouniness cline according to the syntactic behaviour of elements from the perspective of the Chomskyan paradigm. Ross determined the order of nouniness by degrees of the un/grammaticality of surface structures derived by transformational rules.[3] Since the discussion of un/grammaticality does not elucidate any meaningful point for our analytical purpose, we will reconstruct the cline using the framework of SF Theory, as well as altering the target language to Japanese.[4] Degrees of nominalisation are determined according to the following recognition criteria:

Recognition criteria for degrees of nominalisation

1. **Specificity**: the degree to which transitivity configurations 'why/when/where/how/ who does what to whom' at the semantic stratum are lexicogrammatically made explicit (Barnard, 2003:98–99, 105–106).
2. **Negotiability**: the degree to which expressions are readily negotiated, i.e., interrogated or negated, by addressees.

The cline of nominalisation is shown in Figure 1. The cline starts with a zero level of nouniness, wherein a semantic choice of an Event is realised by a congruent lexicogrammatical option of a clause with a finite process, followed by nouniness 1, wherein an Event is realised by a projected clause (nouniness 1–1), by a part of a nominal group such as a defining relative clause (a restrictive clause) or a rankshifted/embedded clause (nouniness 1–2), and by a nominal group (nouniness 1–3). The cline ends with nouniness 2, wherein a semantic choice of a Thing is realised by a congruent lexicogrammatical option in the nominal group. This final order includes common nouns or proper nouns. Various technical terms, which were originally referred to as an Event, but have established their status as a Thing after being repeatedly used as a Thing in numerous texts, are also categorised in this order.

	Order of Nouniness		Examples	Nominalisation
Decrease of Eventness & Increase of Thinginess 1. Transitivity configurations at the semantic stratum are lexicogrammatically made more implicit. (omission or implicit realisation of "why/when/where/ how/ who does what to whom") 2. Expressions are less likely to be negotiated (i.e., interrogated or negated) by addresses.	0	**Event realised as Clause** Semantically "Event" and Lexicogrammatically "Event" ☆ Congruent Realisation: lexical verbs used to realise Event in an independent clause	*Sono seijika wa, kookyoo jigyoo ukeoigyoosha* the politician WA public work contractor *kara fusei ni seiji kenkin o uketo-tta.* KARA illegal NI* political donation O accept-PST 'The politician illegally accepted political donations from public-works contractors.'	
	1-1	**Event realised as dependant projected Clause** Semantically "Event" and Lexicogrammatically "Event" • Metaphenomenon (Halliday 1994: 249)	*Shimbun wa, [sono seijika ga, kookyoo* newspaper WA the politician GA public *jigyoo ukeoigyoosha kara fusei ni seiji* work contractor KARA illegal NI* political *kenkin o uketo-tta] to hooji-ta.* donation O accept-PST TO report-PST 'The newspaper reported that [the politician illegally accepted political donations from public-works contractors].'	
	1-2	**Event realised as a rankshifted element in the Nominal Group (e.g. defining relative clause)** Semantically "Event" but Lexicogrammatically "Part of Thing"	*[sono seijika ga, kookyoo jigyoo ukeoigyoosha* the politician GA public work contractor *kara fusei ni seiji kenkin o uketo-tta] koto* KARA illegal NI* political donation O accept-PST NOMZ 'the fact that [the politician illegally accepted political donations from public-works contractors]'	
	1-3	**Event realised as Thing in Nominal Group & modified by constituents in the transitivity structure:** **- Thingisation** Semantically "Event" but Lexicogrammatically "Thing" • Macrophenomenon (Halliday 1994: 249)	*fusei na seiji kenkin no uketori* illegal NA political donation NO acceptance 'the illegal acceptance of political donations'	
	2	**Noun as Thing in Nominal Group** Semantically "Thing" and Lexicogrammatically "Thing" ☆ Congruent Realisation	*shuuwai* graft 'the graft'	

Figure 1: Cline of Nominalisation: from the perspective of Systemic Functional Theory

Notes: In Ross (1973), Nouniness 0 is absent, and Nouniness 1–1 and Nouniness 1–2 are treated as being within the same order.

Based on the recognition criteria of Specificity and Negotiability mentioned above, in nouniness 0 (Event realised as Clause), a transitivity configuration 'why/when/where/how/ who does what to whom' is explicitly realised by a clausal pattern of process, participants, and circumstances. Since a clause contains a finite process, readers are able to interrogate the content by adding an interrogative marker *-ka* in the forms of *Sono seijika wa, kookyoo jigyoo ukeoi gyoosha kara fusei ni seiji kenkin o uketotta **ka**?* 'Did the politician illegally accept donations from public-works contractors?' or negate the content by adding a negative marker *–nai*, saying *Sono seijika wa, kookyoo jigyoo ukeoi gyoosha kara fusei ni seiji kenkin o uketottei**nai*** 'The politician did not illegally accept donations from public-works contractors.'

Nouniness 1–1 (Event realised as Projected Clause) is more nounlike or nounier than nouniness 0, in that, despite the fact that the transitivity configuration is explicitly realised by a clausal pattern, the projected clause with a projection marker *–to* (*sono seijika ga, kookyoo jigyoo ukeoi gyoosha kara fusei ni seiji kenkin o uketotta* ***to*** 'that the politician illegally accepted donations from public-works contractors') is less likely to be interrogated or negated than the projecting clause (*shimbun wa...hoojita* 'The newspaper reported'). Nouniness 1–2 (Event realised as Part of Nominal Group) is even more difficult to negotiate since an Event 'the politician illegally accepted donations from public-works contractors' is rankshifted, being realised as a modifier of grammatical or lexical nominal heads *no/koto/tokoro* 'that', *jijitsu* 'the fact', or *heya* 'the room'. In nouniness 1–3 (Event realised as Nominal Group), transitivity configurations are often left implicit. For instance, in *sono seijika no kookyoo jigyoo ukeoi gyoosha kara no fusei na seiji kenkin no uketori* 'the politician's illegal acceptance of political donations from public-works contractors', the participant (e.g. 'the politician') and the circumstance (e.g. 'from public-works contractors'), as well as other components of the transitivity configuration, are deletable (e.g. *seiji kenkin no uketori* 'the acceptance of political donations'), lowering the specificity of the transitivity configuration. In other words, 'who' accepts or 'how' something is accepted, etc. need not be, and often are not, specified in this order. The tense of the Event is also unclear due to the lack of a finite process. In addition, negotiation becomes more difficult than nouniness 1–2 since the Event is 'thingised' by being realised as a nominal head rather than a modifier. We will refer to nouniness 1–2 and 1–3 as 'noun-like' or 'nouny' elements because they can function as participants or circumstances just like 'noun' elements of nouniness 2.

Moving on to the final and the highest order of nouniness, level 2 (Thing realised as Nominal Group), the transitivity configuration underlying this unit is completely omitted and cannot be interrogated or denied since a lexical item, say *shuuwai* 'the graft', has firmly established its status as a Thing in the course of phylogenesis.[5]

The introduction of nouniness makes it possible to consider the traditional notion of nominalisation from the perspective of a continuum, considering that nominalisation arises when meanings are reconstrued by more noun-like or 'nounier' expressions. Nominalisation is thus achieved by all the reconstruals in the following directions (as can be seen in Figure 1): nouniness 0 'Event realised as Clause' → 1 (1–1 'Event realised as Projected Clause' → 1–2 'Event realised as Part of Nominal Group' → 1–3 'Event realised as Nominal Group') → 2 'Thing realised as Nominal Group'. The next section examines the data in light of the cline of nominalisation.

Analysis of the LDP and the DPJ political manifestos

Results of the analysis

In this section, based on the nominalisation cline, we analyse the political manifestos of the incumbent party (the LDP) and the largest opposition party (the DPJ) for the purpose of investigating the research questions 1 and 2. The analysis will reveal that the LDP and the DPJ manifestos tend to condense most of the ideational content of their prospective policies into nominal groups by way of rankshifting (nouniness 1–2) or thingisation (nouniness 1–3). It will also reveal that the LDP and the DPJ both deploy the process of nominalisation, that is, a shift towards 'nounier' elements, in order to construe their opponents' political failures or their own political successes.

Beginning with the LDP manifesto, participants or circumstances are typically expressed by long nominal groups 'Premodifier (combination of 1–2 and 1–3) + Head (1–3 or 2)', wherein rankshifted Events (1–2) or thingised Events (1–3) that are given positive appraisal[6] modify thingised Events (1–3) or concrete things (2). The ideational contents of the policies are mostly condensed into nominal groups of this construction, and verbal groups consequently become semantically empty, simply meaning 'do' or 'promote' the nominalised processes. Example 1 represents the typical realisation of the LDP policy promise, wherein the participant (Y) and the circumstance (X) in a material clause 'from the perspective of X, we will promote Y' consist of nominal groups of this construction.

Example 1 The LDP: Premodifier (combination of 1–2 and 1–3) + Head (1–3 or 2)

Notes

[light box]	Elements of nouniness 1–2
[shaded box]	Elements of nouniness 1–3
in bold	elements with appraisals

Circumstance: Perspective

Kojin ***to*** ***kigyoo*** ***no katsuryoku o hikidas-hi, kokusai***
individual CONJ enterprise NO energy O imbue-SUSP international

kyoosooryoku o ***takame-te*** ***minkan keizai katsudoo o***
competitiveness O improve-SUSP private economic activity O

kasseika saseru *kanten* *kara*
activation do perspective KARA

'From the perspective of **imbuing energy into individuals and enterprises, as well as improving international competitiveness in order to activate private economic activity,**'

Participant: Goal

hoojin *kazei ya* *kin'yuu shotoku,* *tochi* *nado no shisan e no kazei no*
corporation taxing CONJ financial income land such: as NO asset E NO taxing NO
soogooteki, ***bapponteki*** *minaoshi*
overall fundamental reconsideration
too, *zeitaisei* *zentai no* ***kaikaku*** *o susume-ru.*
including tax: system overall NO reform O promote-INF

'(we will) promote **reform** of the overall tax system, including an **overall and fundamental** reconsideration of taxes on assets such as land, income and corporation.'

Circumstance: Perspective

Kojin to kigyoo no katsuryoku o	***hikidashi,***	***kokusai kyoosooryoku o***	***takamete***	***minkan keizai katsudoo o***	***kasseika saseru***	*kanten*	*kara*
energy of individuals and enterprises	imbue	international competitiveness	improve	private economic activity	activate	perspective	from
Qualifier 1(type 1–2)		Qualifier 2 (type 1–2)		Qualifier 3 (type 1–2)		Head / Thing (type 1–3)	
the LDP's future actions with positive appraisals							

Participant: Goal

hoojin kazei ya kin'yuu shotoku, tochi nado no shisan e no kazei no	***soogooteki, bapponteki***	*minaoshi too,*	*zeitaisei zentai no*	***kaikaku***	*o susumeru*
taxes on assets such as land, income and corporation	overall and fundamental	including reconsideration	overall tax system	reform	will promote
Qualifier (type 1–3)			Classifier (type 2)	Head / Thing (type 1–3)	
the LDP's future actions with positive appraisals					

As Example 1 shows, the LDP manifesto deploys nominalisation (i.e. rankshifting (1–2) or thingisation (1–3)) in order to construe the LDP's favourable future actions in the forms of nouny elements. Since elements of nouniness 1–2 or 1–3 all realise the semantic option of Event, the single clause in Example 1 realises as many as eleven Events that the LDP pledges to carry out after the election. Seven of the Events and the relations among them are packed into the circumstance, and four Events and their relations are condensed into the participant. To be specific, in the Circumstance of perspective, the nouniness 1–3 head *kanten* 'perspective' is modified by three rankshifted clauses of 1–2 *kojin to kigyoo no katsuryoku o hikidashi* 'imbue energy into individuals and enterprises', *kokusai kyoosooryoku o takame* 'improve international competitiveness', and *minkan keizai katsudoo o kasseika saseru* 'activate private economic activity'. These rankshifted clauses in turn contain participants of nouniness 1–3 such as *katsuryoku* 'energy', *kokusai kyoosooryoku* 'international competitiveness', and *minkan keizai katsudoo* 'private economic activity', which all represent thingised Events. These modifiers function to give positive attributes to the Circumstance, in that processes such as *katsuryoku* 'energy', *takame* 'improve' or *kasseika saseru* 'activate' implicate actions with positive appraisals. The Goal of the material clause has a similar structure, wherein the nominal head *kaikaku* 'reform' involves a future action of the LDP with positive appraisal in that 'reform' always means change for the better. The Goal also includes Events such as *kazei* 'taxation' (which occurs two times) or *minaoshi* 'reconsideration'. Similar examples are shown below.

The Liberal Democratic Party of Japan

Notes

[box] : Nominal Groups (with positive appraisals)

in bold elements with appraisals

A.

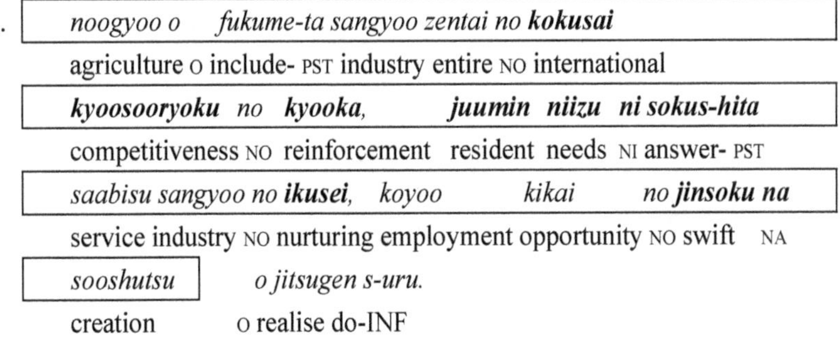

noogyoo o fukume-ta sangyoo zentai no ***kokusai***
agriculture O include- PST industry entire NO international
kyoosooryoku *no* ***kyooka,*** ***juumin niizu ni sokus-hita***
competitiveness NO reinforcement resident needs NI answer- PST
saabisu sangyoo no ***ikusei,*** *koyoo kikai no* ***jinsoku na***
service industry NO nurturing employment opportunity NO swift NA
sooshutsu o jitsugen s-uru.
creation O realise do-INF

'(we will) realise the **reinforcement** of **international competitiveness** of the entire industry including agriculture, the **nurturing** of service industries **that answer residents' needs**, and the **swift** creation of employment opportunities.'

B. *kessan shinsa no **sooki** jisshi to*
final: account examination NO early implementation CONJ
shinsa kekka no koonendo yosan e
examination result NO subsequent: year budget E
*no **tekikaku na** han'ei o susume-ru.*
NO appropriate NA reflection O promote-INF

'(we will) promote an **early** implementation of the final-account examination, and an **appropriate** reflection of the examination results into the budget of subsequent years.'

C. *zeizaisei shigen o,*
fiscal resource O
butsuryuu ya toshi saisei, arata na sangyoo
physical: distribution CONJ urban renaissance new NA industry
ya chiteki zaisan o soozoo s-hi,
CONJ intellectual property O create do-SUSP
koyoo o sooshutsu s-uru kenkyuu kaihatsu,
employment O create do- INF research development
gijutsu kaihatsu shien too, minkan tooshi o yuuhatsu s-uru
technology development including private investment O induce
bun'ya e daitan ni shuuchuu sase-ru.
do- INF field E bold NI* concentrate make- INF
'(we will) boldly concentrate tax and fiscal resources in fields **that induce private investments, such as physical distributions, urban renaissance, and the assistance of research development or technological development that can create new industries or intellectual properties, and that can produce employment, etc.**'

The DPJ manifesto also favours nominal groups 'Premodifier (combination of 1–2 and 1–3) + Head (1–3 or 2)'. As in the LDP manifesto, a great deal of the ideational content of policies are packaged into nominal groups, leaving the verbal groups to mean simply 'stop' or 'do' these nominalised processes. However, unlike the LDP manifesto, which tends to solely nominalise its own future actions with positive appraisals, the DPJ manifesto nominalises the opponent LDP's past or ongoing actions with negative appraisals (Y), as well as nominalising its own future actions with positive appraisals (Z). These are typically deployed side by side in a paratactic clause complex such as 'we will eradicate Y, and realise Z' or 'we will root out Y, and replace it with Z.' Using the terminology of the appraisal system from Martin and Rose (2003), the incumbent LDP's past or ongoing actions (Y) implicate inappropriateness or illegality, whereas the DPJ's future actions, if they were to take power from the LDP, involve appropriateness or ethicality. As an illustration, consider Example 2.

Example 2 The DPJ: Premodifier (combination of 1–2 and 1–3) + Head (1–3 or 2)

Participant: Goal
mudazukai no shoochoo de aru *kawabegawa damu jigyoo ya*
wasteful: use NO symbol be kawabegawa dam enterprise CONJ
yoshinogawa kadoozeki keikaku nado, daikibo na
yoshinogawa movable: dam plan including large: scale NA
chokkatsu kookyoo jigyoo no kensetsu ya keikaku o sutoppu s-hi,
government: ruled public project NO construction CONJ plan O stop do-SUSP

'(we will) stop construction or plans of large scale government-ruled projects including the Kawabegawa-dam enterprise and Yoshinogawa movable dam plan, **which symbolise the wasteful use of tax money**, '

Participant: Goal
shin ni chiiki shinkoo to naru *jigyoo ni furikae-masu.*
truly NI* region development become project NI replace-FML

'(and we will) carry out projects **that truly contribute to regional development**.'

Participant: Goal

mudazukai no shoochoo de aru	*kawabegawa damu jigyoo ya yoshinogawa kadoozeki keikaku nado,*	*daikibo na*	chokkatsu kookyoo jigyoo no	*kensetsu ya keikaku*	*o sutoppu shi,*
which symbolise the wasteful use of tax money	including the Kawabegawa-dam enterprise and Yoshinogawa movable dam plan	large scale	government-ruled projects	constructions or plans	will stop

mudazukai no shoochoo de aru	*kawabegawa damu jigyoo ya yoshinogawa kadoozeki keikaku nado,*	*daikibo na*	chokkatsu kookyoo jigyoo no	*kensetsu ya keikaku*	*o sutoppu shi,*
Qualifier (type 1–3)		Epithet	Classifier (type 2)	Head / Thing (type 1–3)	
the LDP's ongoing actions with negative appraisals					

Participant: Goal

shin ni chiiki shinkoo to naru	*jigyoo*	*ni furikaemasu*
that truly contribute to regional development	projects	will carry out
Qualifier (type 1–2)	Head / Thing (type 2)	
the DPJ's future actions with positive appraisals		

In Example 2, the first clause of the paratactic clause complex realises the LDP's ongoing actions with negative appraisals as a Goal, whereas the second clause realises the DPJ's future actions with positive appraisals as a Goal. To be specific, in the first clause, the Event that the LDP has been wasting tax payer's money is realised in a rankshifted clause (1–2) *mudazukai no shoochoo de aru* 'which symbolise the wasteful use of tax money', which functions as a modifier to the 1–3 head *jigyoo ya keikaku* 'enterprise and plan', which in turn functions as a modifier to the 1–3 head *kensetsu ya keikaku* 'constructions or plans'. On the other hand, in the second clause *shinni chiiki shinkoo to naru jigyoo ni furikaemasu* '(and we will) carry out projects that truly contribute to regional development', the DPJ's future solution is given positive appraisal in the form of a rankshifted clause (1–2) *shinni chiiki shinkoo to naru* 'that truly contribute to regional development'. The following are similar examples.

The Democratic Party of Japan

Notes

[box] Nominal Groups (with positive appraisals)

[double underline] Nominal Groups (with negative appraisals)

in bold elements with appraisals

A. *zeikin no* ***mudazukai*** o *yame, /*

tax: revenue NO wasteful: use O end-SUSP

koosei de toomeisei no aru *seiji*

fair COP: SUSP transparency NO be political: system

o jitsugen s-himasu.

O realise do-FML

'(we will) end **the wasteful use** of tax revenue and realise a **fair and transparent** political system.'

B. ***kenryoku ya yuchaku ni kakure-ta fusei***

power CONJ back: scratching NI hide-PST dishonesty

o konzetsu s-hi, / ***seikatsu no mesen*** *kara*

O root: out do-SUSP life NO perspective KARA

seiji to gyoosei no ***bappon kaikaku***

politics CONJ executive: branch NO radical reform

o susum-emasu.

O promote-FML

'(we will) root out **the dishonesty concealed by political power and back-scratching**, and promote **a radical reform** of politics and the executive branch from **the perspective of ordinary citizens' lives**.'

C. ***Tagaku no tooshi o shi-nagara yuukoo katsuyoo***

huge: amount NO* investment O do-CONCESSIVE effective use

s-are-tei-nai *koosoku dooro o* ***ikasu*** *koto*

do-PSV-ASP-NEG motorway O make: use: of NOMZ

de, chihoo o kasseika s-uru.

DE* region O stimulate do- INF

'By the fact of **making the best use** of motorways, **which in spite of the huge investment in them are not being used effectively**, (we will) stimulate the regions.'

Example C demonstrates that the same semantic pattern can be also realised in one clause, rather than a paratactic clause complex (Example 3 below). To be specific, the LDP's ill-management of motorways *tagaku no tooshi o shinagara yuukoo katsuyoo sarete inai koosoku dooro* 'motorways, which in spite of the huge investment in them are not being used effectively', and the DPJ's future solution towards it, *o ikasu* 'making the best use of', are realised in one rankshifted clause, which is followed by a nominaliser *koto*. The whole nominal group is followed by a postposition *–de* 'by', providing a Circumstance of means in a material clause.

Example 3 The DPJ

Circumstance: Means
Tagaku *no* ***tooshi*** *o* ***shi-nagara*** ***yuukoo*** ***katsuyoo***
huge: amount NO* investment O do-CONCESSIVE effective use
s-are-tei-nai *koosoku dooro o* ***ikasu*** *koto de,*
do-PSV-ASP-NEG motorway O make: use: of NOMZ DE*
'By the fact of making the best use of motorways, which in spite of the huge investment in them are not being used effectively,'

tagaku no tooshi o shinagara yuukoo katsuyoo sarete inai	*koosoku dooro*	*o* ***ikasu***	*koto*	*de,*
which in spite of the huge investment in them are not being used effectively	motorways	making the best use of	the fact of	by
Qualifier (type 1–2)			Head / Thing (nominaliser)	
the LDP's ongoing action with negative appraisal		the DPJ's future action with positive appraisal		

In this section, we have analysed the Japanese incumbent party LDP manifesto and the largest opposition party DPJ manifesto for the purpose of investigating research questions 1 and 2, namely the choices from the nominalisation cline, and the choices of Events that tend to be nominalised. To sum up the results, both the DPJ and the LDP deploy nominalisations, or shifts towards more noun-like elements, to condense the most ideational contents of prospective policies into nominal groups 'Premodifier (combination of 1–2 and 1–3) + Head (1–3 or 2)'. As a result, the verbal groups become semantically empty, simply meaning that they will 'do' or 'stop' the nominalised processes. These nominal groups construe their opponent's political failures (in the DPJ) or their own political successes (in the LDP and the DPJ). The discussion so far is summarised in Figure 2 below.

Figure 2: Summary: Answers to Research Questions 1 and 2

	Choices from the Nominalisation Cline	**Choices of Events that Tend to be Nominalised**
Liberal Democratic Party	Premodifier (Combination of 1–2 and 1–3) + Head (1–3 or 2) e.g., in '(from the perspective of X) we will carry out X'	the LDP's future actions with positive appraisals (=X)
Democratic Party of Japan	Premodifier (Combination of 1–2 and 1–3) + Head (1–3 or 2) e.g., in 'we will eradicate Y, and carry out Z' 'we will root out Y, and replace it with Z'	the LDP's past/ongoing actions with negative appraisals (=Y) the DPJ's future actions with positive appraisals (=Z)

Discussion of the results

In the previous section, we have observed two types of choices concerning nominalisation and nouniness that the Japanese incumbent party (the LDP) and the largest opposition party (the DPJ) tend to make in describing prospective policies: the choices from the nominalisation cline, and the choices of Events that tend to be nominalised. In order to answer research question 3, we will now consider the semantic effects of these two types of choices, particularly considering the effects stemming from the specificity or negotiability of policies.

To begin with, we will consider the kinds of nominalisation selected, which are typically rankshifting and thingisation. By condensing most of the experiential and logical meanings of the prospective policies into nominal groups which contain rankshifted or thingised Events, the 'why/when/where/how/ who does what to whom' configurations surrounding the Events become obscured (Specificity) and incontestable (Negotiability). As the name 'manifesto' suggests, the policies in election manifestos are regarded as pledges from the party to the nation, which are promised to be carried out upon winning the election and taking power. However, as a result of the nominalisation choices, the parties can escape from the examination of the feasibility, as well as the condemnation of not carrying out these policies after the election. As an illustration, consider an example of the LDP, the party that won the 2003 election and that was obliged to carry out their pledges.

Kessan shinsa no sooki jisshi to shinsa kekka no koonendo yosan e no tekikaku na han'ei o
final: account examination NO early implementation CONJ examination result NO subsequent: year budget E NO appropriate NA reflection O
susume-ru.
promote-INF

'(We will) promote [1-3][an early implementation of the final-account examination, and an appropriate reflection of the examination results into the budget of subsequent years].'

↓

Specificity Transitivity Configurations "why/when/where/how/ who does what to whom" are omitted.

1. **Participants** being responsible for the pledge

   e.g., X who { examine final-accounts, implement the examination early, produce results, appropriately reflect in the subsequent year's budget } are omitted.

2. **Circumstances** of the pledge

   e.g., { to what degree, by what means, for what reasons, in what year/date } X examine final-accounts; implement the examination early; produce results; appropriately reflect in the subsequent year's budget are omitted.

Negotiability feasibility (prior to the election) and success of implementation (after the election) cannot be negotiated, i.e., interrogated or negated.

Example 4 The LDP: Specificity and Negotiability

In Example 4, which is also a typical representation of the LDP pledge, some components of transitivity configurations that represent future actions of the party are ambiguous due to the semantic effect of nominalisation (Specificity). To be precise, participants responsible for the processes and circumstances of the pledge are not included in the nominal group. Temporal and causal relations of the processes are also difficult to uncover (in Example 4, we have tentatively assumed that the processes are supposed to be conducted in the order of 'examine final-accounts', 'implement the examination early', 'produce results', and 'appropriately reflect in the subsequent year's budget'). Without knowing this information, nobody can examine or negotiate, i.e., interrogate or negate, the feasibility and success of implementation of the pledge (Negotiability).[7]

Moving on to the second choices, namely those of Events or transitivity configurations that are rankshifted or thingised into nominal groups, once an Event is nominalised, it is available to be evaluated using the experiential structure of the nominal group. By condensing the opponents' past/ongoing actions with negative appraisals on the one hand, and their own future actions with positive appraisals on the other, it becomes possible to construe the unfavourability of the rival parties in contrast with the favourability of one's own party in a single clause complex. Since these actions are all packaged into nominal groups by way of rankshifting or thingisation, this evaluation is difficult to negotiate and might then be taken-for-granted as fact (Negotiability). At the same time, nominalisations function to avoid the blunt accusation of the opposing party or straightforward commendation of their own, since the agents or tenses of these actions do not have to be realised (Specificity). Referring to the LDP text, it was found that the policies are typically realised in the following clausal form:

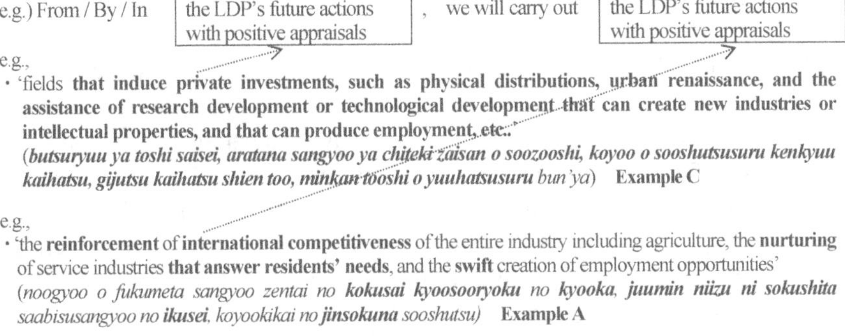

Figure 3: LDP Policies: Execution of Positive Actions

Past/ongoing actions with negative appraisals are not usually realised in the LDP manifesto, possibly because presenting them inherently means admitting their own political deficits. Consequently, the LDP realises their future policies as viable measures that will improve the existing successful situations that the Koizumi cabinet has created during the past two and a half years in power, thus implicitly conveying the message that the LDP is the best party to continue to be in power.

On the other hand, as the largest opposition party that has the biggest chance of defeating the LDP, the DPJ realises their future policies as solutions towards the ongoing problems they see as created by the incumbent LDP:

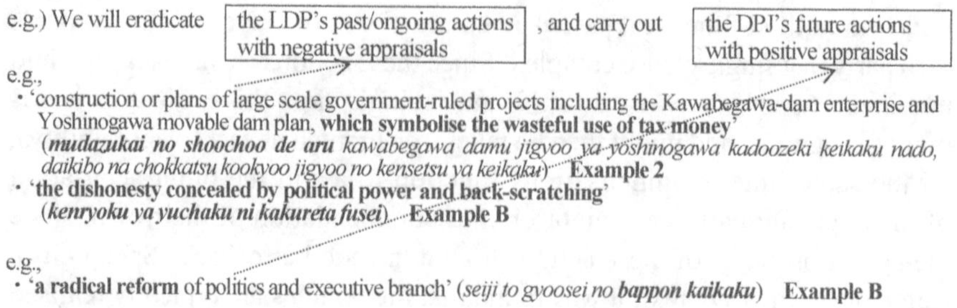

e.g.) We will eradicate [the LDP's past/ongoing actions with negative appraisals] , and carry out [the DPJ's future actions with positive appraisals]

e.g.,

- 'construction or plans of large scale government-ruled projects including the Kawabegawa-dam enterprise and Yoshinogawa movable dam plan, **which symbolise the wasteful use of tax money**'
  (***mudazukai no shoochoo de aru*** *kawabegawa damu jigyoo ya yoshinogawa kadoozeki keikaku nado, daikibo na chokkatsu kookyoo jigyoo no kensetsu ya keikaku*) **Example 2**
- **'the dishonesty concealed by political power and back-scratching'**
  (***kenryoku ya yuchaku ni kakureta fusei***) **Example B**

e.g.,

- '**a radical reform** of politics and executive branch' (*seiji to gyoosei no* ***bappon kaikaku***) **Example B**

Figure 4: DPJ Policies: Eradication of Negative Actions & Execution of Positive Actions

As is shown in the above examples, negative appraisals (e.g., unhappiness, insecurity, dissatisfaction) are frequently chosen when describing the status quo made by the incumbent LDP, whereas positive evaluations (e.g., happiness, security, satisfaction) are given to the DPJ's future actions. There is, however, no instance where the agent of the political faults, the LDP, is explicitly mentioned. Consequently, the DPJ's choices of nominalisation are convenient in order to implicitly persuade readers of the superiority of the DPJ over the rival incumbent party, without explicitly criticising the LDP.

It is important to notice that, on the surface, the LDP and the DPJ manifestos look like they just inform voters of their own future policies, with one or two clause complexes basically realising one policy. The nominalisation choices, however, make it possible to list many good points of the party in contrast with many political deficits of the rival party in the guise of description of prospective policies. By relying on nominal groups, the Japanese manifestos continually introduce new kinds of positive and negative evaluations, while obscuring 'participants + process + circumstances' configurations of the Events at any stage of the textual development. In this sense, these Events tend to appear in logico-semantic relations of 'extension' (i.e., addition), providing new and unrelated information to each other.

In contrast to these kinds of grammatical constructions, such as the logico semantic relation of extension, the manifesto of the British Labour Party is rather different. The British Labour Party manifesto (1997), which is widely recognised as being an effective manifesto and labelled as a 'vintage' manifesto by the experts (Kanai, 2003:12), uses the logico-semantic relation of elaboration. Further, the British Labour Party manifesto uses expressions along the full length of cline of nominalisation. In Example 5, the incumbent Tories' (Conservative Party's) political failure, which the Labour Party pledges to eradicate, is recursively construed in varying degrees of nouniness, thereby allowing varying degrees of specificity or negotiability. To be specific, the negative appraisal of the Tories' past action is firstly realised in the form of clause complexes, considered as examples of nouniness 0, as follows: '*Nearly half of 11 years-olds in England and Wales **fail to reach** expected standards in English and maths. Britain has a smaller share of 17 and 18 year-olds in full-time education than any major industrial nation*' and '*It **divides** children into successes and failures at far too early an age*.' However, the manifesto also uses thingisation, expressing the Event as the Thing in the nominal group, an example of 1–3 nominalisation, as follows: '*the Tories' biggest **failure***', '*education **divides***', *or* '*the public/private **divide***', and finally as a noun, an example of nominalisation 2 as follows: '*educational **apartheid***'. The experiential meanings of the Conservative's actions, as well as the interpersonal appraisals of unfavourability, have undergone logogenetic condensation, where specific or congruent Events underlying the abstract Thing, *'educational apartheid'* are specified in the course of logogenesis. In other words, these lexicogrammatical resources are in the logico-semantic relations of 'elaboration' (i.e., restatement, specification, exemplification), repeatedly construing similar kinds of Events by elaborating on each other.[8] In the Labour Party manifesto, this textual development, which starts with abstract things of type 1–3 or 2 that are unpacked in the following paragraphs by means of more congruent expressions of type 0, 1–1, or 1–2, and which concludes with a review containing abstract things 1–3 or 2 that re-pack the previous expressions, is persistent in all kinds of policies. In Figure 5, the textual developments we have discussed are diagrammatically represented.

Example 5 British Labour Party (1997), Opening Part of Educational Policies

Note

-Event/Thing	Rival party's past/ongoing actions with negative appraisals

We will make education our number one priority

- Cut class sizes to 30 or under for 5, 6 and 7 year-olds
- Nursery places for all four year-olds
- Attack low standards in schools
- Access to computer technology
- Lifelong learning through a new University for Industry
- More spending on education as the cost of unemployment falls

Education has been **the Tories' biggest failure.** It is Labour's number one priority.

It is not just good for the individual. It is an economic necessity for the nation. We will compete successfully on the basis of quality or not at all. And quality comes from developing the potential of all our people. It is the people who are our greatest natural asset. We will ensure they can fulfil their potential.

Nearly half of 11 year-olds in England and Wales fail to reach expected standards in English and maths. Britain has a smaller share of 17 and 18 year-olds in full-time education than any major industrial nation.

Nearly two thirds of the British workforce lack vocational qualifications.

There are excellent schools in Britain's state education system. But far too many children are denied the opportunity to succeed. Our task is to raise the standards of every school.

We will put behind us the old arguments that have bedevilled education in this country. We reject the Tories' obsession with school structures: all parents should be offered real choice through good quality schools, each with its own strengths and individual ethos. There should be no return to the 11-plus.

It divides children into successes and failures at far too early an age.

We must modernise comprehensive schools. Children are not all of the same ability, nor do they learn at the same speed. That means 'setting' children in classes to maximise progress, for the benefit of high-fliers and slower learners alike. The focus must be on levelling up, not levelling down.

With Labour, the Department for Education and Employment will become a leading office of state. It will give a strong and consistent lead to help raise standards in every school. Standards, more than structures, are the key to success. Labour will never put dogma before children's education. Our approach will be to intervene where there are problems, not where schools are succeeding.

Labour will never force the abolition of good schools whether in the private or state sector. Any changes in the admissions policies of grammar schools will be decided by local parents. Church schools will retain their distinctive religious ethos.

We wish to build bridges wherever we can across **education divides.** **The educational apartheid** created by **the public/private divide** diminishes the whole education system.

LDP and DPJ Manifestos: Realising Many Unfavourable Actions of the Rival Party in Contrast with Many Favourable Actions of Their Own in High Degrees of Nouniness
(→ Allowing Low Degrees of Specificity & Negotiability)

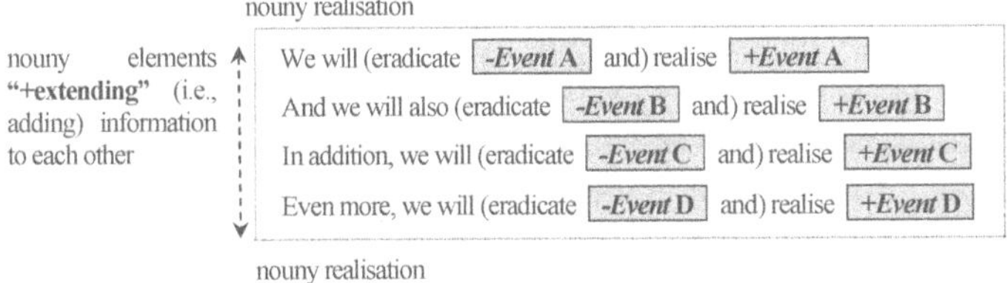

British Labour Party Manifesto: Realising One Unfavourable Action of the Rival Party in Varying Degrees of Nouniness (→ Allowing Varying Degrees of Specificity & Negotiability)

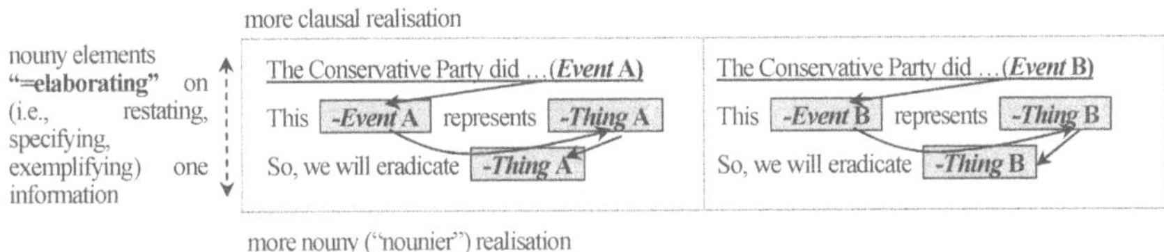

Figure 5: Textual Development

Notes

- Event/Thing	rival party's past/ongoing actions with negative appraisals
+ Event/Thing	it's own future actions with positive appraisals

Conclusion

In this paper, we have firstly attempted to add a dimension to the traditional SF notion of nominalisation by constructing a cline of nominalisation, explaining that nominalisation arises when meanings are reconstrued by more noun-like expressions (in Figure 1: 0 → 1 (1–1→1–2→1–3) →2). This cline is particularly useful when we analyse the extent and degree of nominalisation, and in particular, the extent and degree of specificity and negotiability of information, especially in a persuasive text.

Secondly, based on this cline of nominalisation, we have analysed the Japanese general election manifestos issued by the incumbent party (the LDP) and the largest opposition party (the DPJ), focusing on the choices from the nominalisation cline and the choices of Events that tend to be nominalised. Concerning the former choices, it has turned out that both the DPJ and the LDP deploy nominalisations, or shifts towards more noun-like elements, to condense the most ideational contents of prospective policies in nominal groups 'Premodifier (combination of 1–2 and 1–3) + Head (1–3 or 2)'. As a result, 'who does what to whom' configurations of Events relating to public policies are obscured and become non-negotiable, allowing the party to escape from the examination and condemnation of not carrying out these policies. As for the later choices, these nominal groups turned out to construe the opponent's ongoing political failures (in the DPJ) or their own political successes (in the LDP and the DPJ). Consequently, the groups of policies function to implicitly realise one party as superior to the rival parties in the guise of policy description, thus indirectly urging readers to chose and vote for that party. These strategies represent resources for persuasion in the political manifesto in Japanese.

Interlinear Notation Key

ASP	aspect
CJT	conjecture e.g. *–daroo*
CONCESSIVE	concessive e.g. *–nagara*
CONJ	conjunctive e.g. *–ya, -to*
COP	copula e.g. *-da, -aru*
DE	nominal marker (Circumstance 'in')
E NI	nominal marker (Participant, Circumstance 'in / to')
FML	formal form of the verb/adjective e.g. *-masu*
GA	nominal marker (Participant; nominative)
INF	informal form of the verb/adjective e.g. *-da, -ru,* adj-*i*
INT	interrogative e.g. *–ka*
KARA	nominal marker (Circumstance 'from')
NA NO*	adnominal marker
NEG	negative e.g. *-nai*
NI*	adverbial marker
NO	nominal marker (Participant; possessive)
NOMZ	nominaliser e.g. *–koto, -no, -tokoro*
O	nominal marker (Participant; accusative)
PST	past
PSV	passive e.g. *–sareru*
SUSP	non-finite, tactic verb form (*-te* form) e.g. *–shite,- shi*
TO	postpositional quotative clause marker
WA	nominal marker (Participant; nominative)
YORI DE*	postposition (Circumstance 'by')

Adapted from Teruya (1998: xxiii-xxiv) and Thomson (2005:28–29).

Appendix

The following translation of the original DPJ manifesto in Japanese is based on the Party's official English translation (http://www.dpj.or.jp/english/manifesto_eng/index.html). However, we have made changes that reflect more closely the original Japanese, especially when such changes are pertinent to the discussion and analysis of the data. The LDP's translation is our own.

Text 1: The Liberal Democratic Party (2003)

(pp.3–4)

kore ga, koizumi kaikaku.
This is the Koizumi Reform.

Sengen 1. nihon no akarui mirai o tsukurimasu.
Pledge 1. (We) will create a bright future of Japan

Sengen 2. kokumin no anzen o mamorimasu.
Pledge 2. (We) will ensure the safety of the people.

Sengen 3. gyoosei no muda o habuki, kanso de kooritsuteki na seifu o mezashimasu.
Pledge 3. (We) will cut down waste in administration and strive for a simple and effective government.

Sengen 4. omoikitte keizai o kasseikasasemasu.
Pledge 4. (We) will resolutely revitalise the economy.

Sengen 5. kuni no kihon o minaoshimasu.
Pledge 5. (We) will review the basics of the nation.

Sengen 6. kokueki ni sotta gaikoo o tenkaishimasu.
Pledge 6. (We) will pursue a diplomacy that serves Japan's national interests.

Sengen 7. jimintoo ga nihon o kaemasu.
Pledge 7. The LDP will change Japan.

(pp.16–19)

Sengen 3. gyoosei no muda o habuki, kanso de kooritsuteki na seifu o mezashimasu. Pledge 3. (We) will cut down waste in administration and strive for a simple and effective government.

1. *'kan kara min e' minkan ni dekiru koto wa minkan ni*

From the Government to the Private Sector: Whatever the Private Sector Can Do Should Be Left to the Private Sector

1. *'minkan ni dekiru koto wa minkan ni makaseru'–min shudoo, jiritsu gata no keizaishakai e*

'Whatever the Private Sector Can Do Should Be Left to the Private Sector': Towards a Private-Initiated, Autonomous Society

(1) *yuusei jigyoo kaikaku*
Postal Services Reform

- *yuusei jigyoo o 2007 nen 4 gatsu ni min'eika*
(We) will privatise postal services in April 2007

yuusei jigyoo o 2007 nen 4 gatsu kara min'eikasuru to no seifu no kihon hooshin o fumae, nihon yuuseikoosha no keiei kaikaku no jookyoo o mitsutsu, kokuminteki shingi o okonai, 2004 nen aki goro made ni ketsuron o eru.

Based on the basic stance of the government that it will privatise postal services from April 2007, (we) will conduct a public debate while observing the progress of management reforms of Japan Post, and will draw a conclusion by autumn 2004.

(2) *dooro kankei yon koodan kaikaku*
Reform of Four Highway-Related Public Corporations

- *doorokoodan o min'eikasuru hooan o 2004 nen no tsuujoo kokkai ni teishutsu*
(We) will submit a bill to privatise public highway corporations to the 2004 ordinary session of the Diet.

dooro kankei yon koodan min'eika suishin iinkai no iken o kihonteki ni sonchooshi, 2005 nendo kara yon koodan o min'eikasuru hooan o 2004 nen no tsuujoo kokkai ni teishutsusuru.

(We) will basically respect the opinions of the Promotion Committee for the Privatisation of the Four Highway-Related Public Corporations, and will submit a bill to privatise the four highway-related public corporations in fiscal 2005 to the 2004 ordinary session of the Diet.

(3) *kansei shijoo no minkan kaihoo*
Opening of Government-Led Market to the Private Sector

- *kuni to chihoo no gyoosei saabisu o minkan ni ijoo*
(We) will entrust national and local administrative services to the public sector.

nihon keizai no 4 wari o shimeru kansei shijoo o minkan ni kaihoosuru. Minkan kara no teian ni motozuku kyoodoo nyuusatsu too ni yori, kuni to chihoo no gyoosei saabisu o minkan ni ijoosuru.

(We) will open the government-led market that accounts for 40 % of the Japanese economy to the private sector. By means of a system such as a competitive bidding that is based on suggestions from the private sector, (we) will entrust national and local administrative services to the public sector.

(4) *koozoo kaikaku tokku no katsuyoo*
Utilisation of Designated Structural Reform District

koozoo kaikaku tokku o sekkyokukatsuyooshi, noogyoo o fukumeta sangyoo zentai no kokusai kyoosooryoku no kyooka, juumin niizu ni sokushita saabisu sangyoo no ikusei, koyoo kikai no jinsoku na sooshutsu o jitsugensuru.

(We) will make an active use of designated structural reform districts, and will realise the reinforcement of international competitiveness of the entire field of industry including agriculture, the nurturing of service industries that answer residents' needs, and the swift creation of new employment opportunities.

(5) *kan to min no fukoohei no zesei*
Correction of Inequalities between the Bureaucracy and the Private Sector

minkan to ruiji no kangyoo ni tsuite, zeiseijoo no toriatsukai nado, minkan to no ikoorufuttingu o susumeru. tokuni, kongo PFI o samazama na bun'ya de katsuyoosuru kanten kara, hoojin zei ya fudoosan shotoku zei, koteishisan zei nado no zeisei ya kisei men de kan to no baransu o kentoosuru.

Concerning government enterprises that are similar to those of the private sector, (we) will promote an equal footing with the private sector, in such areas as tax treatment. In particular, from the perspective of making use of PFI in various fields in the future, (we) will consider a balance with the government concerning taxation systems and regulations of a corporation tax, a real estate tax, and a fixed property tax, etc..

(6) *kisei kaikaku*
Regulatory Reform

- *soogoo kisei kaikaku kaigi dai 2 ji tooshin no chakujitsu na jisshi*
  Steady Implementation of Second Report of Overall Regulatory Reform Council
- *rainen 4 gatsu ni 'kisei kaikaku, min'eika too suishin iinkai (kashoo)' o secchi*
  (We) will establish 'a Promotion Committee of Regulatory Reform and Privatisation, etc. (provisional title)' next April.

jizen kisei no kanwa, teppai to jigo chekku taisei o kakujitsu na mono to suru tame, naikaku ni 'kisei kaikaku, min'eika too suishin iinkai (kashoo) o sec-chisuru.

In order to ensure the relaxation and repeal of ex-ante regulations, as well as to make sure an ex-post check system, (we) will establish 'Promotion Committee of Regulatory Reform and Privatisation, etc. (provisional title)'.

2. *minju o yuuhatsusuru saishutsu koozoo kaikaku*
Expenditure Structural Reform That Triggers Private Sector Demands

(1) *minkan keizai katsudoo o kasseikasuru zeisei kaikaku*
Tax Reform That Revitalises Private Economic Activities

kojin to kigyoo no katsuryoku o hikidashi, kokusai kyoosooryoku o takamete minkan keizai katsudoo o kasseikasaseru kanten kara, hoojin kazei ya kinyuu shotoku, tochi nado no shisan e no kazei no soogooteki, bapponteki minaoshi too, zeitaikei zentai no kaikaku o susumeru.

From the perspective of imbuing energy into individuals and enterprises, as well as improving international competitiveness in order to activate private economic activity, (we) will promote reform of the overall tax system, including an overall and fundamental reconsideration of taxes on assets such as land, income and corporation.

(2) *PFI no sekkyokuteki katsuyoo*
Active Utilisation of PFI

chihoo no seikatsu kiban seibi nado o kookyoo jigyoo to shite susumetsutsu, daitoshi ken too ni oite, jigyoo shuunyuu ga mikome, saisan ga toreru jigyoo ni tsuite wa, PFI o sekkyokutekini katsuyoosuru. tokuni, haneda kuukoo no saikakuchoo jigyoo wa, PFI shuhoo too ni yori seibi o okonau.

(We) will promote the improvement of the local infrastructure as public works projects, and will actively utilise PFI in businesses that can produce an operating revenue and turn a profit in metropolitan areas. In particular, as for the project of further expansion of Haneda Airport, (we) will make a preparation by means of a method such as PFI.

(3) *kookyoo jigyoo no kosuto kaikaku ni yoru saishutsu no kooritsuka*
Improvement of the Efficiency in Expenditures by Cost Reforms of Public Works Projects

minkan to kurabete takadomarishiteiru kookyoo jigyoo kosuto o, minkan no kosuto sakugen shuhoo too o sankoo ni minaoshi o tetteishi, muda o habuki kooritsukasuru.

(We) will make a thorough revision of the costs of public works projects that hover at a high price compared with the private sector by using cost-reduction measures deployed by the private sector, etc. as a guide, and will cut down on waste and improve efficiency.

(4) *2006 nendo ni meimoku GDP 2% ijoo no keizai seichoo o tassei*
(We) will achieve an economic growth of more than 2% nominal GDP growth in fiscal 2006.

(5) *2010 nendai shotoo no puraimarii baransu no kaifuku*
Recovery of Primary Balance in the Early 2010s.

kodomo ya mago no sedai ni futan o sakiokurisezu, shoorai no dai zoozei e no fuan o nakusutame, 2010 nendai shotoo ni puraimarii baransu (kokusaihi ya koosaikin shuunyuu o nozoita zaisei shuushi) no kurojika o jitsugensuru.

In order to avoid shifting burdens to the generations of children and grandchildren, and eliminate the people's anxiety for big tax hikes in the future, (we) will achieve a surplus of the primary balance (fiscal revenue and expenditure excluding revenues by national bonds and public loans) in the early 2010s.

(6) *tokubetsu kaikei, tokutei zaisan seido no bapponteki minaoshi*
Fundamental Review of Special Accounts and Earmarked Revenue Sources System

hikooritsu na tokubetsu kaikei ya tokutei zaigen seido ni tsuite, jigyoo no arikata ya keiei keitai no giron to awase, seiiki naku bapponteki ni minaosu.

(We) will drastically reconsider inefficient special accounts and earmarked revenue sources systems without allowing a sanctuary, as well as discuss modalities for businesses and managerial styles.

(7) *naikaku shudoo, mokuhyoo juushi no yosan hensei*
Cabinet-Led, Goal-Oriented Budged Compilation

- *fukusuunendoka (moderu jigyoo)*
  Multiple-Year Appropriation (Model Project)

ippan kaikei ni tsuite mo muda to hikooritsu o habuki juunan ni shikkoodekiru yoo ni surutame, yosan no fukusuunendoka o susume, saishutsu o goorikasuru. konotame, heisei 16 nendo yosan kara moderu jigyoo o jisshisuru.

As for a general account, in order to avoid waste and inefficiency and implement the account flexibly, (we) will promote a multiple-year appropriation of a budget and rationalise expenditures. For this purpose, (we) will carry out a model project from the fiscal 2004 budget.

- *jizen satei kara jigo hyooka e*
  From Ex-Ante Assessment to Ex-Post Evaluation

subete no yosan ni tsuite seisaku hyooka oyobi yosan shikkoo choosa o kakujuushi, yosan hensei sagyoo ni han'eisaseru shikumi o doonyuusuru.

For all kinds of budgets, (we) will introduce a mechanism in which policy evaluations and budget implementation surveys are expanded and reflected in the process of a budget compilation.

- *yosan no juuten haibun (seisaku gun)*
  Concentration of Budgets (Policies)

2004 nendo kara jisshisuru 'seisaku gun' nado, shoochoo kan no waku o koete juutenka, kooritsuka o jitsugensuru yosan hensei o susumeru.

Concerning 'Policies' that (we) will implement from fiscal 2004, (we) will bring forward a budget compilation that promotes concentration and efficiency beyond the bounds of ministries.

- *kessan shinsa no juujitsu*
  Improvement of Final-Accounts Examination

kessan shinsa no sooki jisshi to shinsa kekka no koo nendo yosan e no tekikaku na han'ei o susumeru.

(We) will promote an early implementation of the final-account examination, and an appropriate reflection of the examination results into the budget of subsequent years.

- *sukurappu ando birudo no ruuruka*
  Regularisation of Scrap-and-Build

kaku shoo ga ji nendo yosan ni oite shinki jigyoo shisaku o yookyuusuru baai ni wa, sukurappu ando birudo o ruurukasuru.

(We) will regularise scrap-and-build when a ministry requests measures of new public works projects in a budget of the following fiscal year.

(8) *minkan tooshi no yobimizu to naru bun'ya e no sentaku to shuuchuu*
Selection of and Concentration in the Field That Can Be a Prime for Private Investments

zeizaisei shigen o, butsuryuu ya toshi saisei, arata na sangyoo ya chiteki zaisan o soozooshi, koyoo o sooshutsusuru kenkyuu kaihatsu, gijutsu kaihatsu shien too, minkan tooshi o yuuhatsusuru bun'ya e daitan ni shuuchuusaseru.

(We) will boldly concentrate tax and fiscal resources in fields that induce private investments, such as physical distributions, urban renaissance, and the assistance of research development or technological development that can create new industries or intellectual properties, and that can produce employment, etc..

Text 2: The Democratic Party of Japan (2003)

(pp.0–2)

5 tsu no chikai

Five Promises

1. *shitsugyoo no nai, tsuyoi keizai o saiseishimasu.*
   (We) will rebuild a strong economy with no unemployment.
2. *zeikin no mudazukai o yame, koosei de toomeiseisei no aru seiji o jitsugenshimasu.*
   (We) will end the wasteful use of tax revenue, and realise a fair and transparent political system.
3. *'jiritsu ryoku' o motta, katsuryoku ni kagayaku chiiki o soozooshimasu.*
   (We) will create regions that have autonomy and are pulsing with vitality.
4. *kodomo ya kooreisha, josei ga anshinshite kuraseru shakai o tsukurimasu.*
   (We) will make a society in which children, the elderly, and women can live safely.
5. *kokumin no inochi to kenkoo o mamoru tsuyoi shakai o jitsugenshimasu.*
   (We) will realise a robust society that protects the lives and health of citizens.

5 tsu no yakusoku

Five Pledges

1\. *kasumigaseki kara no 'himotsuki hojokin' o zenpaishimasu. (4 nen inai)*
(We) will completely abolish the 'tied grants' from Kasumigaseki [the central government]. (within 4 years)

2\. *seiji shikin wa zenmenteki ni kookaishimasu.*
(We) will completely disclose political funds.

3\. *dooro koodan o haishishi, koosoku dooro no ryookin o muryoonishimasu. (3 nen inai)*
(We) will abolish the Japan Public Highway Corporation and make motorways toll-free. (within 3 years)

4\. *kokkai giin no teisuu to koomuin no jinken hi o, sorezore 1 wari sak*

ugenshimasu. (4 nen inai)
(We) will reduce the number of Diet members and the personnel costs of the civil service, both by 10%. (within 4 years)

5. *muda na kookyoo jigyoo o chuushishi, kawabegawa damu, isahayawan kantaku, yoshinogawa kadoozeki o tadachi ni tomemasu.*
(We) will halt useless public works projects, and immediately stop the Kawabegawa dam, the Isahaya Bay reclamation, and the Yoshinogawa moveable dam.

futatsu no teigen

Two Proposals

1. *kiso nenkin no zaigen ni wa shoohizei o ate, atarashii nenkin seido o soosetsushimasu.*
(We) will allocate consumption tax revenues to the funding of the basic pension, and create a new pension system.
2. *shoogakkoo no 30 nin gakkyuu o jitsugenshi, gakkoo no shuu itsukasei o minaoshimasu.*
(We) will realise a class size of 30 pupils in elementary school, and reconsider the five-day school week.

(p.16)
Keizai seisaku

Economic Policies

[…] *sono ue de, kokumin no minasan kara oazukarishiteiru zeikin no tsukaimichi o, seikatsu, kankyoo juushi ni tenkansuru no desu. sono shoochooteki na mokuhyoo ga, dooro koodan o haishishi, koosoku dooro o gensoku muryookasuru koto desu. oobei de wa koosoku dooro wa muryoo desu. sore ga futsuu desu. nihon toiu kuni wa, dooshite yoso no kuni de dekiru koto ga dekinai no deshoo ka. 'atarimae no koto' ga dekinai kuni, 'atarimae no koto' ga okinai kuni, nihon. sono gen'in ga zeikin no mudazukai no koozoo desu. watashitachi wa sono koozoo o kaikakushi, zeikin no tsukaimichi o daitan ni kaemasu. sore koso ga koozoo kaikaku desu.* […]

[…] Based on this, (we) will redirect the use of the tax revenues, which are received from all citizens, to a use which places emphasis on their daily lives and on the environment. An objective which symbolises this will be the abolishing of the Japan Public Highway Corporation and the making of most motorways toll-free in principle. In Europe and the Unites States motorways are free. Why is it that Japan cannot do what other countries can do? Japan–a country which cannot do what is natural, a country in which the natural does not occur. The reason is that it has a structure in which tax revenues are used wastefully. (We) will reform that structure and resolutely change the manner in which tax revenues are used.

That is exactly what structural reform is. [...]

(p.33)

2. *zeikin no mudazukai o yame, koosei de toomeisei no aru seiji o jitsugen-shimasu.* [...]
   (We) will end the wasteful use of tax money, and realise a fair and transparent political system. [...]

nihon o yowameteiru no wa, zeikin o mudazukaishiteiru 'obake' no yoona yuchaku no koozoo desu. seijika ya kanryoo no riken, soshite seikangyoo yuchaku o tetteishite haijoshimasu. sukoshi no zeikin mo mudanisezu, kenryoku ya yuchaku ni kakureta fusei o konzetsushi, seikatsu no mesen kara seiji to gyoosei no bappon kaikaku o susumemasu.

What is weakening Japan is the structure of collusion that is like a monster responsible for the wasting of tax revenues. (We) will totally eradicate the special interests of politicians and bureaucrats and also the collusion between politicians, business, and bureaucrats. (We) will root out the dishonesty concealed by political power to ensure that absolutely no tax revenues are wasted, and proceed with a radical reform of politics and the executive branch from the perspective of the ordinary citizen's life.

2–1. *zeikin no tsukai michi o daitan ni kaemasu.*
   (We) will resolutely change the manner in which tax revenues are used.

[1] *kookyoo jigyoo no muda o yame, seikatsu, kankyoo juushi ni tenkanshi-masu.*
   (We) will **halt wasteful public works, and switch emphasis to people's daily lives and the environment.**

kuni chokkatsu no oogata jigyoo o, heisei 18 nendo yosan an made ni, 3 wari, 9000 oku en o mokuhyoo ni sakugenshimasu. heisei 16 nendo yosan kara, muda-zukai no shoochoo de aru kawabegawa damu jigyoo (kumamoto ken, soo jigyoo hi 2650 oku en) ya yoshinogawa kadoozeki keikaku (tokushima ken, soo jigyoo hi 1040 oku en) nado, daikibo na chokkatsu kookyoo jigyoo no kensetsu ya keikaku o sutoppushi, shin ni chiiki shinkoo to naru jigyoo ni furikaemasu. Sarani, tokuyama damu (gifu ken) o hajime ta no kobetsu jigyoo ni tsuite mo seisashi, tooketsu, chuushi, minaoshi too ni bunruishite, dekiru mono kara tadachi ni chakushushimasu. kooji ga sootoo susundeiru isahaya kantaku jigyoo (2490 oku en chuu 2250 oku en ga shikkoozumi), kooji ga shuuryooshita nagaragawa kadoozeki nado ni tsuite mo, juumin, jichitai no iken o kikinagara kongo no arikata o minaoshimasu. jigyoo ryoo o herasu no de wa naku, denshi nyuusatsu no doonyuu sokushin nado o fukumeta nyuusatsu kaikaku de dangoo o booshishi, yori sukunai keihi de, yori ooku no jigyoo o kanoo ni shimasu.

Our target is to cut public works controlled directly by the government by 30%, or ¥900 billion, by the time of the budget bill for the 2006 fiscal year. From the budget for the 2004 fiscal year (we) will stop construction or plans of large scale government-ruled projects including the Kawabegawa-dam enterprise (Kumamoto Prefecture; total project cost ¥265 billion) and Yoshinogawa moveable dam plan (Tokushima Prefecture; total project cost ¥104 billion), which symbolize the wasteful use of tax money. For these we will substitute projects that genuinely aid regional development. In addition, we will closely examine other projects such as the Tokuyama dam (Gifu Prefecture) project. We will then divide them into categories according to how to deal with them, for example whether they should be frozen, terminated, or revised, and start immediately on the most feasible. With respect to projects such as the Isahaya Bay land reclamation project, on which work is well advanced (¥225 billion of the total cost of ¥249 billion already spent), and the Nagaragawa estuary dam project, which has been completed, we will review what is to be done with them after sounding out the view of local residents and local governments. Our aim is not to reduce the overall extent of projects but to make it possible to undertake more projects for less expense. We will achieve that by reforming tendering procedures so as to prevent collusion, including by expediting the introduction of electronic tendering.

[2] *dooro koodan o haishishi, koosoku dooro o gensoku muryookashimasu.*
(We) will abolish the Japan Public Highway Corporation and in principle make motorways toll-free.

chiiki de mo koosoku dooro o tsukaiyasukushi, butsuryuu kosuto no hikisage, seikatsu no riben koojoo o mezashite furiiwei to suru to tomoni, samazama na 'zoku obake' ga habikotteiru dooro o 'tsukuru, riyoosuru, kanrisuru' sorezore no men ni oite, chiiki to kokumin no te ni torimodoshimasu.

(We) intend to make motorways easy to use in the regions, to lower distribution costs, and to increase convenience in daily life by changing motorways into freeways, as well as putting back in to the hands of the regions and the citizens the different aspects of the making, using, and managing of roads, which have been in the thrall of various interest groups.

(1) *dooro koodan haishi to koosoku dooro gensoku muryooka*
The abolition of the Japan Public Highway Corporation and the making of motorways free in principle

tagaku no tooshi o shinagara, yuukoo katsuyoo sareteinai koosoku dooro o ikasu koto de, chihoo o kasseikasuru to tomoni, ryuutsuu kosuto no sakugen o hakaru tameni, koosoku dooro wa 3 nen inai ni, ichibu daitoshi o nozoki muryoo to shimasu. nihon dooro koodan, honshuu shikoku renrakubashi koodan wa haishishimasu. muryooka ni yotte, kosuto ga sakugensuru dake de naku, deiriguchi o oohaba ni zoosetsudekiru koto kara, chihoo no koosoku dooro ga kurashi ni ikaseru dooro to shite yomigaerimasu. koosoku dooro ni kakaru saimu hensai to dooro no iji kanri ni wa, nenkan 2 choo en ga hitsuyoo desu ga, genzai, kuni to chihoo o awasete 9 choo en ni tasshiteiru dooro yosan no ichibu furikae to, juutai, kankyoo taisaku no kanten kara reigaiteki ni chooshuusuru daitoshibu no tsuukooryoo de makanaimasu.

By the fact of making the best use of motorways, which in spite of the huge investment in them are not being used effectively, in order to stimulate the regions and to lower distribution costs, (we) will make all motorways free, except some in large cities. (We) will abolish the Japan Highway Public Corporation and the Honshu-Shikoku Bridge Authority. By making motorways free not only will costs be reduced, but by greatly increasing the number of exits and entrances [since toll booths will no longer have to be built and manned], regional motorways will be brought back to life as roads which people can use in their daily lives. Two trillion yen per year is necessary for motorway-related debt repayments and road maintenance and management, but a portion of the combined budgets for national and local roads, which currently total nine trillion yen, can be diverted to that, and other funding could be covered by exceptional tolls imposed as a measure to deal with congestion and environmental damage.

(2) *dooro tokutei zaigen haishi, jidoosha kankei shozei keigen, kankyoo zei soosetsu*
Abolition of earmarked funds for road construction, reduction of vehicle related taxes, establishment of an environmental tax.

jidoosha ni kakaru zeikin ga, doorokensetsu o yuusensuru tameni takaku setteisaretekita koto o fumaete, dooro tokutei zaigen o ippanzaigenkasuru to tomoni, zeikin o oohaba ni hikisagemasu. heisei 17 nendo chuu ni, dooro tokutei zaigen no haishi hooan to, jidoosha juuryoo zei hangen, jidoosha shutoku zei haishi no zeisei kaikaku hooan o kokkai teishutsushite, sono seiritsu o mezashimasu. dooji ni, shoorai no sedai ni ryookoo na chikyuu kankyoo o hikitsugi, mata kyooto giteisho no gichookoku toshite no kokusaiteki sekinin o hatasu tame, waga kuni sanngyoo kyoosooryoku no iji ni hairyoshita shochi o koojitsutsu, jikkooaru ondanka taisaku toshite nisankatanso no hasseigen ni, kankyoo fuka no teido ni oojite tanso gan'yuuryoo 1 ton atari 3000 en teido no zeikin o kakeru 'kankyoo zei' o soosetsushimasu.

Taking into account that taxes which are related to vehicles have been set high because of the priority given to road construction, (we) will, together with using funds earmarked for road construction for general use, reduce taxes substantially. During the 2005 fiscal year (we) will submit a bill for the abolishment of earmarked funds for road construction and a tax reform bill for halving of the vehicle tonnage tax and the abolition of the vehicle acquisition tax, and seek the enactment of these bills.

At the same time, in order to bequeath a pleasant global environment to future generations, and to carry out Japan's international responsibilities as chair country of the Kyoto Protocol, while formulating measures which take the maintenance of Japanese industrial competitiveness into consideration, (we) will establish an 'environment tax' on sources of carbon dioxide as an effective measure to deal with global warming, which will correspond to the extent of the environmental burden by imposing a tax of some 3000 yen per ton of carbon dioxide.

Notes

1 The main policies of the LDP and the DPJ have been identified based on *Asahi Shimbun*'s newspaper articles published during the election campaign.

2 The perception of language as a stratified system was originally developed by Hjelmslev (Hjelmslev, in Martin, 1992:493), who originally set up the hierarchy of content plane and expression plane. SF Theory further enriches the system by stratifying the content plane into semantics and lexicogrammar.

3 As one type of transformational rule, Ross (1973:161) provided negation. As elements become more noun-like they become more restricted in the types of negative items they can co-occur with.

Nouniness Squish and Negative Items (Adapted from Ross, 1973:162)

	Post-verbal seldom	Post-verbal never	Pre-verbal not	Pre-verbal never	no in subject	few in subject	not in subject
That S (that-clauses)	OK	OK	OK	OK	OK	OK	OK
for to (for NP to VX)	OK	OK	OK	OK	OK	?	?
Q (embedded questions)	OK	OK	OK	OK	OK	OK	?
Acc Ing (NP V + ing X) └+Acc┘	OK	?	OK	OK	??	??	??
Poss Ing (NP's V + ing X)	?	??	?	??	*	?*	?*

	Post-verbal <u>seldom</u>	Post-verbal <u>never</u>	Pre-verbal <u>not</u>	Pre-verbal_ <u>never</u>	<u>no</u> in subject	<u>few</u> in subject	<u>not</u> in subject
Action Nominal (Ing-of)	??	?*	*	*	**	**	**
Derived Nominal (Derived Nominal)	?*	*	**	**	**	**	**

Notes OK: grammatical *: ungrammatical ?: un/grammaticality is ambiguous

For example, co-occurrence with 'not' becomes more and more ungrammatical as elements become 'nounier':

<u>not</u> in Subject

a. OK [That <u>not</u> everyone will refuse our offer] is expected.
b. ? [For <u>not</u> everyone to refuse our offer] is expected.
c. ? [Under what circumstances <u>not</u> everyone will refuse our offer] is the subject of a heated debate.
d. ?? [<u>Not</u> everyone refusing our offer] was expected.
e. ?* [<u>Not</u> everyone's refusing our offer] was expected.
f. ** [<u>Not</u> everyone's refusing of our offer] was a surprise.
g. ** [<u>Not</u> everyone's refusal of offer] was a surprise.

Pre-verbal <u>not</u>

a. OK [That he does <u>not</u> prepare dinner] is good for her health.
b. OK [For him <u>not</u> to prepare dinner] is good for her health.
c. OK [Why he does <u>not</u> prepare dinner] is good for her health.
d. OK [Him <u>not</u> preparing dinner] is good for her health.
e. ? [His <u>not</u> preparing dinner] is good for her health.
f. * [His <u>not</u> preparing of dinner] is good for her health.
g. ** [His <u>not</u> preparation of dinner] is good for her health.

(Ross, 1973:161–163, brackets and underlining are ours)

4 The cline of nominalisation concerning English was developed in Suto (2003) using the framework of SF Theory. Our paper is based on the research.

5 In SF Theory, three types of semiotic time frames are assumed: logogenesis refers to the modification of the system in a text; ontogenesis indicates the development of the system in an individual; phylogenesis is the evolution of the system in a community (cf. Halliday, 1994; Matthiessen, 1995).

6 Appraisal is concerned with evaluation: the kinds of attitudes that are negotiated in a text, the strength of the feelings involved and the ways in which values are sourced and readers aligned (Martin and Rose, 2003:22). In our analysis, two kinds of realisations of appraisals, explicit and implicit realisations, are considered. Explicit realisations directly express the author's appraisals by attitudinal lexis such as an attitudinal epithet, whereas implicit realisations indirectly express the author's appraisals through experiential propositions depending on the textual context. For a full description of appraisal, refer to Martin and White (2005).

7 For reference purposes, in the following *Asahi Shimbun*'s newspaper article, the LDP's claim that they have fulfilled most of the 2003 manifesto pledges is reported, even though the reporter does not (or possibly is not able to) examine or verify the credibility of the claim.

Asahi Shimbun (9 April 2004; Our translation)

The Liberal Democratic Party released the spring campaign posters on the 8th. [...] Concerning the fulfilments of election pledges declared in the general election held last autumn, the posters claim that '93% of the pledges have began to be acted upon', emphasising the successful outcomes of 'Koizumi Reforms'. According to the chief of the public relations department who held a press conference, among the 130 political pledges, only 9 remain to be carried out, including the submission of a bill to the Diet that proposes amendments of the Antimonopoly Law, in which reinforcement of the authority of the Fair Trade Commission is the pivotal point, and the preparation of laws on the protection of rights of privacy. The remaining 121 pledges are in motion, in the form of introducing bills, deepening discussions in the LDP, etc..

8 Because the pledges are construed in varying degrees of nominalisations allowing varying degrees of specificity and negotiability, a violation of them will be obvious once it occurs. In fact, during the election campaign in 2001, various sections of the media, as well as opposition parties, blamed the Labour government for its incompletion of the promises presented in the 1997 manifesto (Kanai, 2003:24).

Works cited

Primary data

Text 1 Liberal Democratic Party (LDP) Manifesto 2003.

Koizumi Kaikaku Sengen: Jimintoo Seiken Kooyaku 2003. [Declaration of Koizumi Reforms: Pledges for an LDP Administration 2003] Jimintoo: Tokyo.

Text 2 Democratic Party of Japan (DPJ) Manifesto 2003.

Minshutoo no Seiken Seisaku: Manifesto. [Administrative Policies of DPJ: Manifesto] Minshutoo: Tokyo.

Secondary data

Text 3 British Labour Party Manifesto 1997.

New Labour: Because Britain Deserves Better. (Labour Party General Election Manifesto 1997) Labour Party: London.

References

Barnard, C. (2003) *Language, Ideology, and Japanese History Textbooks*. London and New York: RoutledgeCurzon.

Halliday, M. A. K. (1994) *An Introduction to Functional Grammar*. 2nd edition. London: Arnold.

Halliday, M. A. K. and Matthiessen, C. M. I. M. (2004) *An Introduction to Functional Grammar*. 3rd edition. London: Arnold.

Kanai, T. (2003) *Manifesuto: Atarashii Seiji no Chooryuu* [Manifesto: New Political Stream]. Tokyo: Kobunsha Shinsyo.

Kimura, G. (2003) *Manifesuto Ronsoo: Saisyuu Shinpan* [Manifesto Controversy: The Final Judgement]. Tokyo: Kobunsha.

Martin, J. R. (1992) *English Text: System and Structure*. Amsterdam: John Benjamins.

Martin, J. R. and Rose, D. (2003) Appraisal: Negotiating Attitudes. In J. R. Martin and D. Rose (eds) *Working with Discourse: Meaning beyond the Clause* 22–65. London and New York: Continuum.

Martin, J. R. and White, P. R. R. (2005) *The Language of Evaluation: Appraisal in English.* Basingstoke: Palgrave Macmillan.

Matthiessen, C. M. I. M. (1995) *Lexicogrammatical Cartography: English systems*. Tokyo: International Language Sciences Publishers.

Ross, J. R. (1973) Nouniness. In Fujimura Osamu, et al. (eds) *Three Dimensions of Linguistic Theory* 137–257. Tokyo: TEC Company, Ltd.

Smith, C. A. and Smith, K. B. (2000) A Rhetorical Perspective on the 1997 British Party Manifestos. In *Political Communication* 17, 457–473. London: Taylor and Francis.

Suto, K. (2003) *Seifu Bunsho to Sono Intaa-tekusuto no imi no shooryaku ni okeru meishika to meishisei* [Nominalisation and Nouniness as Meaning Strategies Seen in a US Government's Policy Document and its Intertexts]. JASFL (the Japan Association of Systemic Functional Linguistics) 11th Annual Conference. Tamagawa University, 4–5 October 2003.

Teruya, K. (1998) *An Exploration into the World of Experience: A Systemic-Functional Interpretation of the Grammar of Japanese.* Unpublished PhD dissertation. School of English, Linguistics and Media, Macquarie University, Sydney.

The Japan Times (2003) *'Manifesto' Replaces Slogans in Election Wordplay.* (http://www.japantimes.co.jp/cgi-bin/makeprfy.p15?nn20030716b3.htm) July 16, 2003.

Thomson, E. (2005) Theme Unit Analysis: a Systemic Functional Treatment of Textual Meanings in Japanese. In *Functions of Language* 12: 2: 151–179. Amsterdam: John Benjamins.

7 Learning how to mean in Japanese as an additional language[1]

William S. Armour and Reiko Furuya
UNSW, Australia
Nagoya University, Japan

Systemic-functional linguistic (SFL) theory has had little to say on learning languages other than the mother tongue. In this chapter the tape recorded conversations of five Japanese as an additional language learners are investigated. Issues regarding errors and the development of a Japanese meaning potential are raised. All five informants were audio taped while interacting in Japanese with a Japanese national as part of a larger project concerning their cross-cultural adaptation. They were asked to have three 'conversations' following a set of guidelines or prompts. Using these data, it may be possible to begin a discussion on how SFL theory can contribute to the socio-cultural theory of second language acquisition.

Background

Systemic-functional linguistic (SFL) theory has made almost no contribution to our understanding of second language development (SLD). In the early days of the formation of contemporary SFL theory (1960s through early 1970s), key thinkers such as Halliday were developing a theory of grammar or grammatics by investigating how children learn how to mean in the 'mother tongue'. Perrett (2000:92) notes that 'SFL has delivered hardly any research findings on the process of second language learning…this may seem surprising in view of the richness of the material on child language…'. In regards to the specific context of instructed foreign language learning, Byrnes (2009:2) notes that 'Published work using an SFL framework in order to inform non-English instructed foreign language learning is relatively rare'. The papers present in the special edition of Linguistics and Education 20 help fill the gap. So does Byrnes (2006) which also provides some papers that deal with advanced additional language learning, though not development.

The aim of this chapter, then, is to make a contribution to the debate regarding SLD using SFL as a theoretical springboard. The title of the chapter alludes to the seminal work done by M.A.K. Halliday in the 1970s, however, the contribution we are making here is relatively modest and by no means addresses the depth of insight that Halliday had when researching Nigel. The reason is simple. Perrett (2000) points out that the most appropriate method of longitudinal observation of changes in verbal behaviour of children developing their L1 is the continuous diary study which is easily employed by the researcher-caregiver. She suggests that to pursue an adult L2 learner using a similar technique, however, would be both impractical and an infringement on privacy (p.92). Rather than undertake such an elaborate longitudinal project to understand the processes involved in how an L2 learner might align the four strata of context-semantics-lexicogrammar-phonology/ graphology in their development of a meaning potential, we have decided to investigate certain samples of complete texts spoken by our informants at a single point in time.

While 'development' is privileged over 'acquisition' (see Halliday, 1978a:9 and Perrett, 2000:88), there are few specific SLD studies, however, there are many approaches to the study of second language acquisition (SLA) that should be considered. Since SFL prefers to study the social nature of language learning, we are interested in those approaches which cover a broad 'socio' range including the socio-linguistic, socio-cultural, and socio-historical. These are briefly addressed below.

Young (1999) notes that the socio-linguistic approach to SLA includes the areas of pragmatics, classroom second and foreign language learning (especially socialization issues), literacy, L2 influence on an individual's sense of identity, and multilingualism (p.105). One aspect of the socio-linguistic approach of interest to this study is the relation between the social context and the development and use of the L2.

Similarly the socio-cultural approach echoes much of the above. Ellis (1999:17) describes this approach as one that 'adopts a more holistic approach to discourse involving learners and their settings, and which, therefore, employs qualitative methods that are more sensitive to the ways in which interactions are constructed by participants as they dynamically negotiate not just meaning but also their role relationships and their cultural and social identities'. Drawing on the work of Lantolf, Ellis suggests that (semiotic) mediation, scaffolding, as well as Vygotsky's metaphor of the zone of proximal development are crucial elements in this approach. In our study, scaffolding[2] is a useful process to investigate the ways in which communication between each informant and the Japanese interlocutor unfold.

The socio-historical perspective is outlined in Hall (1995). She is interested in accounting for how one's knowledge of and ability to use the resources particular to any practice as well as the locally-situated conditions of the moment influences 'both the meanings residing in the linguistic resources we use to engage in face-to-face interaction and our ability to use them' (p.207). Hall draws on the work of Bakhtin. She claims that a socio-historical perspective has four implications for SLA: 1) the frame that it provides for 'understanding and explaining the findings from research on the development of language variation' (p.219); 2) the frame it provides for 'understanding issues concerned with language assessment and communicative development' (p.221); 3) Hall argues that such a perspective moves beyond the socio-cultural since it is insufficient for the development of an understanding of our and others' involvement in interaction (p.222); and 4) a socio-historical perspective 'allows us to see the inadequacy of such frequently used SLL/A [second language learning/acquisition] concepts as 'interlanguage', 'fossilization', and even 'second language acquisition' in explaining the ways we use and learn language' (p.223).

Theoretical underpinnings of the study

While these approaches are important, it is as equally as important to frame this study through the SFL lens. SFL theory privileges 'function' over 'form'. Lukin (2004:40) asserts that the most typical view of grammar is a set of rules with grammarians as metaphorical law enforcement agents giving out tickets for 'the most minor infringement'. Our interest in what Lukin is writing about is when 'grammar is more helpfully understood as a self-extending system[3] that, like matter and energy, changes according to the forces that act on it and through it' (p.40). For example, Lukin uses the example of SMS (short message service) claiming that it 'is not ungrammatical or grammatical, just as yet an uncharted exchange of meanings'.

At the outset, there seems to be a strong connection between making judgments about what learners say and write in their L2s and the so-called target language itself. For instance, Ross (1979) asks the question, 'Where's English ?' and answers by investigating 'a set of fully grammatical sentences, and a set of non-sentences' (p.128). While certain suggested hypotheses are dismissed such as 'English is that set of sentences which all speakers agree is grammatical' and that there is a *core* of English or 'a monolinear continuum of acceptability, shared by all speakers, leading away from the core' (pp.129–130), Ross settles on the following hypothesis to test: that the single continuum idea be replaced by 'an indeterminate number of continua, each leading away from the core in orthogonally different directions' (p.131). One conclusion is that each speaker's idiolect is 'as individual as his or her face – a linguistic fingerprint' (p.160). Halliday (1978b) makes the distinction between 'dialect' or variety according to the user and 'register' or variety according to the use (p.35). Moreover, he makes the point that dialects are 'different ways of saying the same thing and tend to differ in: phonetics, phonology, lexicogrammar (but not in semantics)' (Halliday, 1978b:35).

Hasan (2003:438) considers the 'ordinary' clause *Mona's husband is not a man*. She argues that 'when such a sentence is used in the living of life, listeners do not treat the speaker as in some way a-normal' due to the two part configuration of semantic features of 1) animate, homo sapiens, adult, male and 2) those inferentially related to each of the preceding features (p.438), that is, so-called denotative and connotative meanings. Hasan rejects the traditional view that connotative meanings 'are said to be based in an individual's experience, and so less stable across the community', preferring the view that 'languages possess a property I would refer to as *inherent elasticity of meaning*' (p. 439) and suggests that words that typically fall into group 1 type 'lie on the surface of our awareness; others [group 2] remain relatively submerged…they float into users' conscious awareness only when they become critical for making sense of some utterance…' (p.439). We will come back to this in the discussion section of the paper to consider some of the implications Hasan's ideas have for SLD.

Colombi and Schleppegrall (2002), who follow the SFL view that literacy is a social semiotic, argue that SFL offers a theory of language that is 'also needed for full understanding of the demands and challenges of advanced literacy' (pp.8– 9). They also consider the contribution that Basil Bernstein's social theory has made to SFL. Colombi and Schleppegrall note that

> Bernstein suggests that people have different ways of using language, or 'coding orientations', which are manifested in the ways that they participate in interaction. People are positioned differently, with different senses of what is significant and relevant, based on the social relations that are characteristic of their experiences in a particular social class and culture, which in turn are affected by the amount of power and control that people in that social group are able to exercise in their material lives, among other things. These different coding orientations mean that even when participating in the same contexts, such as schooling, students from different backgrounds will use language in different ways (p.9)

Bernstein's notion of differing coding orientations, we believe, has some significant implications for understanding how learners produce the L2.

Mohan and Beckett (2003) suggest that when 'focus on form' pedagogies are utilized, that is, pedagogies informed by the view that language is a code of (grammatical) rules, attitudes towards errors bring out the almost essential need to correct them purely on a syntactic level. Mohan and Beckett assert that they are 'not aware of any evidence or explicit and detailed claims that the correction of errors of grammatical form is a sufficient condition for the development of oral and written language as a medium of learning' (p.423). Mohan and Beckett explain that the SFL approach begins with the overall stand that 'learners are seen as expanding their resources for meaning, their meaning potential, rather than making a transition from errors in rules to the correct form of rules. *Supportive learning interactions help learners to expand their resources for meaning'* (pp. 423– 424, italics added for emphasis). They assert that 'the correction of errors is not seen as central to learning interactions, since its concept of language development is not based on language rules. This does not mean that SFL cannot recognize error, but it does mean that error is viewed in a much broader and different context than through 'focus on form' analysis' (p.424).

In light of these views, we can ask, 'Where's Japanese ?', especially for L2 learners. As Ramsey (2004) notes, in 2004 the *Kokugo Gakkai* (the Society of the Study of the National Language) changed its name to *Nihongo Gakkai* (the Society of the Study of Japanese). This emphasises the shift from what Japanese scholars study (*kokugo*) and what non-Japanese study (and learn) (*nihongo*). Ramsey traces this traditional bifurcated demarcation concluding that 'almost everywhere' *kokugo* is being replaced with *nihongo* 'to conform to newer, more international ways of thinking' (p.104). He finishes by asking how these changes will 'penetrate the Japanese educational system and Japanese life' (p. 104). We ask how non-Japanese have already contributed to the development of *nihongo* to mirror say the myriad of world Englishes that exist.

Following on from the discussion above, Schleppegrall (2002) considers the errors (mistakes and linguistic infelicities) made in her analysis of second-language writing. She shows how ESL students 'deploy the meaning-making resources of English in their science lab. reports in ways that differ from the choices made by a native speaker of English, with different results in terms of the overall shape and voice of the texts that they produce' (p.119). She claims that 'nonnative speakers are at a particular disadvantage, because they may have both limited resources in English and less experience with the genre and register expected in the assignments which they are given. That means that their attempts to tackle new genres with new register expectations may not only miss the mark in terms of genre and register choices, but also inevitably result in clause formations that depart from native speaker[4] norms ('errors')' (p.120). Schleppegrall also notes that 'identifying grammatical errors is an almost irresistible impulse for the academic reader of ESL writing, as they are typically salient and distracting' (p.136).

Schleppegrall notes that 'when we focus on only the surface errors…, we are accepting the overall structure and tone of the text and are attending only to *cleaning up* the grammatical forms. This takes our focus off the structure of the texts and whether the student has effectively presented the meanings that are most important for accomplishing [this] advanced literacy task. The problem with this approach is that, in many instances, correcting errors is not enough to make the text effective' (pp.138–139). Schleppegrall continues by suggesting that 'the student fails to meet the demands of the genre' when commenting on an example of text written by an informant (p.139). The student has failed to meet the demands of the reader or hearer as Schleppegrall has suggested before when commenting on that 'irresistible impulse' that many academics seem to have to correct. However, the important point that Schleppegrall makes in her paper is error correction on an item-to-item basis is not an effective appraisal strategy which often leads to making judgments about the person more than about the text[6]. Halliday (1978a) also attends briefly to the issue of errors in his discussion of the similarities and differences between L1 and L2 language learning. He boldly claims that 'many second language errors are actually the same as the errors made by mother tongue learners' (p.4).

Finally, a fundamental of SFL is register theory or 'the notion that all use of language, including the mother tongue, is to be explained by reference to the contexts in which language functions' (Halliday, 1978a:8). Given that the notion of meaning potential can be considered as all the choices one person can make and forever expanding in terms of delicacy, Halliday points out that there are different areas of meaning potential that are 'typically associated with different types of social context; hence the context will tend to determine which semantic systems are more readily 'accessed' by a speaker and listener' (p.8). Therefore there is considerable interest in the development of the L2 learner's different areas of his or her meaning potential in regard to learning a 'new reality…a reality in which people exchange different meanings' as well as the learner having to 'learn both the relevant contexts of situation, together with how to identify them, and the particular meanings that are likely to be exchanged in any type of encounter' (Halliday, 1978a:17).

Painter (2004:138) notes that 'Halliday has suggested that when first building a language, a child needs to find an initial entry point into new developments, and that this is typically an interpersonal one'. We claim that the L2 adult learner also needs an entry point and this appears also to be an interpersonal one. However, unlike the child learning his or her L1 in the context of the family or 'those with whom the child had the closest emotional bonds, making them not only key persons to be interacted with…, but also key aspects of experience to be reflected on and thus named' (Painter, 2004:140), the L2 learner gleans such emotional bonds (pseudo or otherwise) from the expert interlocutor for guidance and help (that is, they want to be scaffolded).

In traditional SLA research, *the nature of input* is often foregrounded as 'a necessary ingredient for successful language acquisition' (see Lee and VanPatten (2003) for a comprehensive treatment of *input* and *output*, pp.26–48). It seems to us that in discussing input, those actually producing such input appear to have been largely ignored, that is, the identities of the expert to whose input (language) novices are listening. Swain (2000) has also commented on this and suggests that the notion of the *collaborative dialogue* or a 'dialogue that constructs linguistic knowledge' (p.97) is much more useful. Swain stresses that it is 'how interaction provides opportunities for learners not only to negotiate the message of the input, but, in doing so, to focus on form as well' (p.98) and 'interaction also provides learners with the opportunity to use the target language, that is, to 'output'' (p.99). In SFL terms *input* and *output* really don't make much sense, neither does *linguistic knowledge*. However when *meaning potential* replaces *linguistic knowledge*, Swain's notion of the collaborative dialogue becomes useful in considering the SFL view of an interpersonal gateway into new language developments. How can a novice resolve a problem *in situ*, not in a classroom surrounded by a teacher, dictionaries and textbooks? The resources that novices appear to have are themselves, their (developing but limited) meaning potentials, and whoever is standing before them.

Research questions

There are three research questions that we wish to ask in this study.

Research question 1

Whenever anyone opens his or her mouth or writes or types a sentence, choices are made. The question is, to what extent are these choices both unlimited and acceptable? When choices are made, while there may be countless choices to be made, which makes the meaning potential vast, what constraints (contextual and/or systemic) are put onto the actual choice?

Research question 2

When L2 learners make errors, at what point does the expert interlocutor notice such errors? How does s/he 'correct' (through the process of scaffolding or semiotic mediation) the L2 learner as novice user to make the meaning clearer?

Research question 3

Do adult learners of an additional language require an entry point into initial (or new) stages of L2 development? Could this entry point be akin to Halliday's (1993) notion of the 'interpersonal gateway'?

Methodology

To answer these three questions, we have followed some of the suggestions made by Perrett (2000) regarding research into SLD. We undertook a cross-sectional study rather than a longitudinal study. As Perrett (2000:97) notes, in a cross-sectional study, texts are collected at a single point in time and compared to come to some conclusion about SLD. In establishing a focus and the selection of texts, we chose five adult informants and asked them to role play with an expert speaker of Japanese. The informants' biodata are found in Table 1. We were also careful in choosing informants with different Japanese proficiency levels (see Table 2).

Each informant was given three role-play situations to 'perform' with the Japanese co-author (referred to as the Japanese co-author or R). Perrett (2000: 93) insists that 'we can find out what learners actually do by collecting samples of learner language', that these samples 'need to be complete texts, complete instances of language-in-social-use', and that 'language development arises from general circumstances of use and communicative interaction'. They were video and audio taped while interacting in Japanese with R as part of a larger project concerning their cross-cultural adaptation. The Japanese co-author subsequently transcribed the audio tape and noted various errors in Japanese that occurred. She also reflected on her own choices throughout the interaction in a separate set of notes.

The data used below come from one of the role-plays[5]. Using a typical 'survival' type situation (at the bus centre), the interest here is detailing the types of choices the learners of Japanese as an additional language can make, how they negotiate meaning, the extent to which R scaffolds or semiotically mediates their Japanese language, and what each informant does with that in terms of extending their meaning potential.

Table 1 Biodata

Name[1]	Gender	Nationality	Age[3]	Length of time studying Japanese
Josh Franks	male	US	22yo	2yrs 5 mths
Lily Koh	female	Australia[2]	22yo	9yrs
Fred Baker	male	UK	22yo	2yrs 3 mths
Mike Carpenter	male	US	23yo	1yr
Kim Deal	female	UK	22yo	2yrs 3mths

Pseudonyms were chosen by each informant.

Lily Koh was Malaysian born, however, she has resided in Australia as a child.

since these data were collected in 2003, age of informant = age in 2003.

Table 2 Language ability[a]

	Speaking	Listening	Reading	Writing
Josh Franks	4	4	4	4
Lily Koh	2	2	2	3+
Fred Baker	3+	3	3	3
Mike Carpenter	1	1	1-	1
Kim Deal	1 ↙↘[b] 2	1 ↙↘ 2	2 ↙↘ 3	1 ↙↘ 2

a Informants indicated their Japanese language ability using a self-assessment scale based on the ASLPR[7]. The larger the number the better the L2 proficiency.

b ↙↘ = fluctuate between

In any role play, the identities of the participants are critical. The overall goal of the negotiation ('you want to take the bus to a small village in the mountains') presupposes that the participants already have some idea of what is happening in such a scenario and that they are ready to make certain choices to fulfill the task. The question, 'what is it to be a speaker?', implies that one has something to say. Having something to say in this case was directed by the task: 1) ask the ticket clerk at the bus centre when the bus leaves; 2) (ask) how long the trip takes; 3) (ask) how much a round-trip ticket costs; 4) ask what time the return bus leaves; and 5) (ask) what time it arrives back to Nagoya. This task appears to centre around each informant demanding information and R giving information. Therefore, the expected choices (instances of actual language) in the ensuing 'conversation' between learner and bus centre employee involve question-answer and statement-acknowledgment. In short, the learner is the one doing the demanding of information and therefore is required to choose questions whereas the bus centre employee gives the information. The situation can be summarised in terms of tenor with R as an enculturated Japanese adult (expert) and the informants as both cultural and linguistic novices, both on unfamiliar terms. The talk occurred in the context of a role play which attempted to mirror a specific situation in everyday life.

Data analysis

Transcriptions (wordings) of the informants' audio tapes are indicated in Data Sets 1 through 5. Pauses, either between interlocutors or within each interlocutor's talk, are not indicated. Observations are also given in each Data Set and should be read in tandem with what has been transcribed. These observations should also be viewed as part of the discussion that pertains to offering answers to the three research questions asked above. A translation into English of each Data Set appears in the Appendix.

Data set 1

FB = Fred Baker R = Japanese co-author

1FB: Eeto sumimasen ashita wa Takayama to iu mura ni ikitai n desu ga nanji gurai Nagoya kara aa basu ga ikimasu ka.

2R: Takusan dete'masu yo.

3FB: Soo desu ka. Eeto tabun 10-ji goro basu ga arimasu ka.

4R: 10-ji ni mukau ni tsukitai n desu ka, 10-ji ni Nagoya o shuppatsu shitai n desu ka.

5FB: Aa soo desu A, hai hai hai 10-ji gurai

6R: ni

7FB: detai desu.

8R: Nagoya o shuppatsu desu ne. Soo shimasu to, 10-ji 5-fun no basu ga arimasu.

9FB: A soo desu ka.

shift in topic of conversation

Eeto an n soo desu ka eeto nan-jikan kurai kakarimasu ka, Takayama made ?

10R: 5-jikanhan kakarimasu.

11FB: A sumimasen moo ichido itte kudasai.

12R: 5-jikan 30-pun kakarimasu.

13FB: 5-jikan 30-pun, soo desu ka.

14R: Hai.

shift in topic of conversation

15FB: Eeto oofuku wa ikura kurai desu ka.

16R: Oofuku wa 8,000-en desu.

17FB: 8,000-en desu ka. Eeto ne aa 5-jikan gurai soo desu ne eeto tabun aa asatte aan asatte Takayama kara aa basu ga tabun gogo de 2-ji gurai deru basu ga arimasu ka.

18R: Takayama o 2-ji ni shuppatsu shite Nagoya ni o-kaeri ni naritai desu ne.

19FB: Hai.

20R: Hai 2-jihan no basu ga arimasu.

21FB: Soo desu ka. Eeto sore mo 5-jikanhan gurai kakarimasu.

22R: Hai Nagoya ni 8-ji ni toochaku shimasu.

23FB: Aa soo desu ka eeto n fuu soo desu ne 8,000 -en desu 8,000-en desu ka.

24R: Hai.

shift in topic of conversation

25FB: Eeto aan seki wa aa chuumon chuumon desu ka.

26R: Yoyaku saremasu ka, seki o ?

27FB: Hai dekimasu ka.

28R: Hai dekimasu yo.

29FB: Ikura gurai desu ka, 8,000-en mo?

30R: Iya kore wa anoo 8,000-en ni fukumarete imasu.

31FB: marete imasu Sumimasen chotto

32R: A subete no basu subete no seki wa yoyaku-seki ni narimasu kara.

33FB: A soo desu ka.

34R: Hai

35FB: Eeto

shift in topic of conversation

36R: Kawaremasu ka.

37FB: Aan hai ashita no 10-ji no basu

38R: Soo suru to 1-gatsu 29-nichi 10-ji 5-fun Nagoya-hatsu de yoroshii desu ka.

39FB: Hai.

40R: Takayama o 1-gatsu 30-nichi 2-ji no basu de okaeri desu ne.

41FB: Hai.

42R: Wakarimashita.

43FB: Hai arigatoo.

Commentary on data set 1

1FB begins by initiating, then gives information (where he wants to go), then demands information (realised by sentence final question particle *ka*). The *kind* of information is important here. FB's choice of *~tai* (volitional) reveals a contextual misunderstanding, that is, he already wants to go to Takayama when asking for a bus schedule at this bus centre, therefore, it is reasonable to ask whether he would not normally ask for a bus schedule for a destination to which he has no interest in going?

6R scaffolds textually with *ni*. 7FB now uses *deru* (leave) as an uptake of the recast (2R), though 8R recasts again to *shuppatsu* (departure – nominalisation). In R's reflection, she notes that most of this negotiation could have been replaced with FB asking: *10-ji goro ni Nagoya o shuppatsu suru Takayama-yuki no basu wa arimasu ka.* (Is there a bus that departs Nagoya at about 10:00?). This suggestion is a major recast to support Mike Carpenter's discourse in Data Set 2 as well.

While *nan-jikan gurai kakarimasu ka* (About how many hours will it take? 9FB) is perfectly acceptable Japanese, R reflects that *Shoyô jikan wa dono gurai desu ka* (About how long is the required time ?) would be 'more adult like'. It is the transition from using 9FB's original *nan-jikan gurai kakarimasu ka* to R's recast based on nominalisation (*kakaru* [verb]➘shoyô jikan [noun]). Our suspicion is the FB is merely repeating a choice given to him from a Japanese (*nihongo*) language textbook. Note that R runs with FB's choice of *kakarimasu.*

15FB is asking for an approximate price here (*ikura kurai*), though R's answer supports FB's discourse by giving information.

17FB asks for the return bus schedule. He asks whether there is a bus leaving from Takayama at about (FB uses *gurai* rather than *goro*) 2pm. R's reflects that FB *successfully* asks her a question 'without my leading him to provide me with the necessary information'. That is, R doesn't feel it is necessary to scaffold FB, unlike in the first part of the role-play based on this judgment of 'successful asking'. Note 18R's answer: *Takayama o 2-ji ni shuppatsu shite* ➘ *deru* changes to *shuppatsu suru* and she adds some honorifics, an interpersonal choice, into the exchange: *Nagoya ni o-kaeri ni naritai desu ne.*

21FB should be asking R a question here. 23FB attempts back-channeling: *Aa soo desu ka eeto n fuu soo desu ne* that seem to function as hedges while he chooses what to say next.

25FB wants to know whether he has to make a reservation beforehand and chooses *chuumon* (order). 26R recasts with *yoyaku* (reservation), though R notes that *yoyaku wa hitsuyoo desu ka* (Is a reservation necessary ?) or *zenseki shitei desu ka* (Are all seats reserved ?) would be better choices. Note that R changes the word order in 26R to 'indirectly tell him that *yoyaku* not *chuumon* is appropriate here'. R emphasizes *yoyaku* by putting it first. While R scaffolded FB's vocabulary choice in her mind, there is no indication that FB got it. Is this an example of invisible semiotic mediation?

29FB wants to ask if there is a reservation fee included in the ¥8,000, however it is outside his meaning potential but he tries to express it with what is available. R understands: 'I think FB used *mo* to mean 'also' because he had no other way of checking with me whether the reservation fee was included in the ¥8000'. 30R scaffolds FB by saying *8,000-en ni fukumarete imasu* (It is included in the ¥8,000). This is new to FB who repeats *marete imasu* but elides the first part of the verb, and then admits he doesn't understand: *sumimasen chotto*. This is a plea for linguistic help and R recasts her own Japanese, however, she admits that it doesn't really answer his question. R reflects that 'I knew I was not successful when I heard *marete imasu*, so I decided to reword in 32R'. R's strategy here is that she tells FB that all seats (*subete no seki*) are reserved seats (*yoyaku-seki*): 'I thought he could indirectly understand that there is no need to pay extra for the reservation'. FB responds with a *soo desu ka* though it is unclear whether he knows if an extra fee is to be paid or not.

R asks FB if he will buy the ticket: *kawaremasu ka*. FB has no trouble comprehending honorific choices in Japanese. The conservation ends with confirmation of the information negotiated above. It could be appraised that FB successfully negotiated the meaning required to do the task despite the 'errors' indicated.

Data set 2

MC = Mike Carpenter R = Japanese co-author

1MC: Sumimasen.

2R: Hai.

3MC: Ano Fujieda e ikitai.

4R: Hai.

5MC: Ee uu basu wa itsu orimasu ka.

6R: Fujieda-yuki desu ne.

7MC: Un.

8R: Ima kara 20-pun ato ni shuppatsu shimasu yo.
Ima 2-ji desu kara 2-ji 20-pun no basu ga arimasu.

9MC: Aa sumimasen moo ichi-do itte kudasai.

10R: 2-ji 20-pun ni basu ga demasu yo.

11MC: ni-juu

12R: 20-pun

13MC: 20-pun

14R: Hai.

15MC: Un.

16R: 2-ji 20-pun

17MC: Aa hai wakatta arigatoo eeto nee un

shift in topic of conversation

jikan ga kakarimasu ka nanji kakarimasu ka.

18R: Jikan desu ka eeto Fujieda made wa 3-jikan kakarimasu.

19MC: 3-jikan.

20R: Hai.

21MC: Aa soo desu ka uun eeto nee

shift in topic of conversation

kippu raundo-torippu kippu ikura desu ka.

22R: Hai nan desu ka.

23MC: Ee Fujieda ni to aa Nagoya kaerimasu.

24R: Hai.

25MC: Ikura desu ka.

26R: Hai sumimasen moo ichido o-negai dekimasu ka.

27MC: Ee un sumimasen

28R: Hai hai.

29MC: Fujieda ni ikura desu ka.

30R: Fujieda made desu ka.

31MC: Fujieda made to Nagoya made

32R: Aa oofuku desu ne ryoohoo Nagoya kara
Fujieda made itte Fujieda kara Nagoya e kaette

kuru oofuku no kippu desu ne.

33MC: Aa hai hai hai

34R: Oofuku desu to 4,000-en desu.

35MC: 4,000-en desu. Hai arigatoo

shift in topic of conversation

eeto ne uun Fujieda no basu wa…

36R: hai

37MC: Itsu kaerimasu ka.

38R: Eeto Fujieda kara Nagoya ni kaeru basu no
jikan desu ka.

39MC: Hai soo soo

40R: Nanji goro mazu nan ano itsu ano Nagoya e modorareru yotei desu ka.

41MC: Uun moo ichi-do

42R: Itsu

43MC: Itsu

44R: Nagoya ni

45MC: Un

46R: kaette kuru n desu ka.

47MC: Hai.

48R: kaette kuru no wa ashita

49MC: Itsu

50R: Hai

51MC: Uun ee ashita

52R: Ashita desu ka eeto ashita wa suiyoobi desu
kara eeto wiikudei no sukejuuru ni narimasu.
Fujieda kara wa mai maifun 30-pun ni dete'masu.

53MC: Aa hai jaa arigatoo gozaimashita.

54R: Hai.

Commentary on data set 2

MC initiates. R reflects that the two utterances (3MC & 5MC) could be collapsed: *Fujieda-yuki no basu wa nanji ni demasu ka.* (What time does the bus for Fujieda leave ?). MC mixes his interpersonal codes slipping between so-called plain style *ikitai* (I want to go) and *~masu* style (*orimasu* = get off). 6R scaffolds with: *Fujieda-yuki desu ne* (You mean [the bus] for Fujieda, don't you). R has to do this collapsing for MC. The exchange has established that MC wants to go to Fujieda and 8R moves to give MC the information: *ima kara 20-pun ato ni shuppatsu shimasu yo. Ima 2-ji desu kara 2-ji 20-pun no basu ga arimasu.*([a bus] will leave in another 20 minutes. Now it's 2pm. There's a bus at 2:20pm.). R assumed that as a bus centre employee her responsibility was to be as informative as possible. R notes that 'If I were talking to a passenger who spoke Japanese as his/her mother tongue, my utterance in 8R was too redundant or even too impolite. Informative yet simple must be the key'. In 8R, she tells the passenger the time *ima 2-ji desu kara* and this made her feel that this <u>adult</u> passenger was in fact an idiot. R notes that if she had been speaking to a child, 8R would be suitable.

9MC doesn't understand: *Aa sumimasen moo ichi-do itte kudasai.*, so 10R recasts by unpacking the nominalised *shuppatsu suru* to *deru* and moves through the numbers with MC repeating after her. MC's choices are interesting in terms of mapping his development of the interpersonal: *hai wakatta* (plain) [I've understood] *arigatoo* [thanks] and *eeto nee* [uuum].

17MC asks: *jikan ga kakarimasu ka* (Does it take time ?) *Nanji kakarimasu ka.* This cannot be translated. He is trying to mean: *nanjikan kakarimasu ka.* (How many hours will it take ?). R needs to clarify this: *Jikan desu ka* (the time?) and scaffolds by answering with: *Fujieda made wa 3-jikan kakarimasu.* (It takes 3 hours to Fujieda). MC repeats the salient information: *3-jikan.* 18R is a reply to MC's question *nanji kakarimasu ka.* R realized that MC meant to say *nanjikan kakarimasu ka* so she decided to use as many words from MC's Japanese as possible to be clear for him.

Oofuku no kippu (a round trip ticket) is not in 21MC's vocabulary so he attempts to Japanise the English word without success: R: *nan desu ka* (what's that?). He attempts a rewording: *Fujieda ni aa Nagoya kaerimasu* (literally: to Fujieda, return to Nagoya) which makes perfect sense to him. He misunderstands R's *hai* by asking *ikura desu ka* (how much ?) as if he had solved the infelicity. R requires a recast: *sumimasen moo ichi-do o-negai dekimasu ka* (would you repeat that again?). 29MC asks, *Fujieda ni ikura desu ka* (how much to Fujieda ?) using *ni* not *made*, though R scaffolds by answering *Fujieda made desu ka.* 31MC uses the recast: *Fujieda made to Nagoya made* (to Fujieda and to Nagoya). R clicks and provides MC with the vocabulary:

32R *aa oofuku desu ne* (Oh you mean return, don't you). Then R provides the full explanation: *Nagoya kara Fujieda made itte Fujieda kara Nagoya e kaette kuru oofuku no kippu desu ne.* (You mean a return ticket that goes from Nagoya to Fujieda and return from Fujieda to Nagoya, don't you). 33MC is a response to R's explanation. 34R gives the answer (*4,000-en desu* [¥4,000]) to 25MC's question (*ikura desu ka*).

While R reflects that *Kaeri no basu no jikan o oshiete kudasai* (please tell me the time of the return bus) would have been the better choice (for 37MC), 38R asks for clarification: *Fujieda kara Nagoya ni kaeru basu no jikan desu ka.* ([You want to know] the time that bus returns to Nagoya from Fujieda ?). MC has no comprehension of her answer (40R-41MC). MC and R move slowly with MC repeating R's Japanese recasts. 40R: *Itsu Nagoya e modorareru yotei desu ka* (when do you plan to return to Nagoya?) being reworded as *Itsu Nagoya ni kaette kuru n desu ka.* (when will you return to Nagoya ?)

51MC replies: *ashita* (tomorrow). R explains firstly in private talk: *ashita wa suiyoobi desu kara eeto wiikudei no sukejuuru ni narimasu* (since tomorrow is Wednesday, it becomes the weekday schedule), then addresses MC: *Fujieda kara wa mai maifun 30-pun ni dete'masu* ([There's a bus] leaving every 30 minutes from Fujieda). Similar to 8R, 52R is an example of how the expert has to simplify the language to match the interlocutor's meaning potential. R is frank in her reflection and again notes that it sounds foolish talking like that to an adult.

Data set 3

JF = Josh Franks R = Japanese co-author

1JF: Sumimasen ga basu de Takayama e ikitai desu ga, kippu koko ni kaemasu ka.

2R: Hai kippu koko de kaemasu yo.

3JF: A, basu wa itsu shuppatsu shimasu ka.

4R: Ima kara sugu basu ni noraremasu ka.

5JF: Aa soo desu ka yokatta desu.

shift in topic of conversation

Ja Takayama made dono gurai kakarimasu ka.

6R: Katamichi sanzen-en desu.

7JF: Sanzen-en itte kaette ikura desu ka. Takayama made mata itte mata

Nagoya ni modottara ikura kakarimasu ka.

8R: Oofuku-ken desu ne.

9JF: Oofuku-ken desu. Soo deshita Ikura desu ka.

10R: Katamichi wa sanzen-en desu ga oofuku-ken o katte itadaku to gohyaku-en no waribiki ni natte gosen gohyaku-en ni narimasu.

11JF: Yokatta desu Dakara kore kaimasu.

shift in topic of conversation

Modoru basu wa itsu shuppatsu shimasu ka.

12R: Itsu modoraremasu ka.

13JF: Ato mikka-kan

14R: Etto kyoo ga nigatsu no yokka no kayoobi desu kara, mikka-go desu ka nanoka no hi desu ne.

15JF: Hai nanoka desu.

16R: Nagoya ni

17JF: Nanoka no o-hiru

18R: O-hiru ni mukoo o shuppatsu desu ka Nagoya ni o-hiru ni toochaku dochira desu ka.

19JF: A shuppatsu o-hiru no

20R: O-hiru ni

21JF: O-hiru ni shuppatsu

22R: Takayama shuppatsu desu ne.

23JF: Takayama shuppatsu desu hai

24R: 12-ji han no 12-ji han no basu ga arimasu.

25JF: 12-ji han ni shimasu.

shift in topic of conversation

26R: Hai yuki wa ima kara 10-pun go ni basu wa demasu ga, sore de yoroshii desu ka.

27JF: Hai 10-pun desu. arigatoo gozaimasu.

28R: Ima 1-ji 12-fun desu kara 1-ji 22-fun no basu de yoroshii desu ne.

29JF: Hai

30R: Hai okaeri ga nanoka no hi no Takayama o 12-ji han shuppatsu shite Nagoya ni 4-ji han 5-ji han chaku de yoroshii desu ka.

31JF: Hai

32R: Ja gosen gohyaku-en itadakimasu.

33JF: Hai

34R: Arigatoo gozaimasu.

Commentary on data set 3

JF initiates the conversation. 1JF: particle should be *de* not *ni* so note how R corrects this ('on purpose') in 2R. R reflects that JF must have misunderstood her last utterance (4R: demand for information) and thought there's a bus leaving very soon. This, she suggests, motivates his saying, *Aa soo desu ka yokatta desu* (oh really, good!).

In 5JF, R wonders whether he meant to ask, 1) *what's the cost* or 2) *how long does it take to Takayama?*, so R assumed that it was 1) because he asked her if he could buy a ticket here. In 7JF, he explains the word *oofuku* (return trip) in Japanese. R provides him with the Japanese word in 8R which he repeats in 9JF.

In 11JF *Dakara* is inappropriate here and needed to be either replaced with *de wa, sore de wa* or the more informal *jaa*. Moreover, JF's choice of *kore* would be okay if he were pointing at something to buy. Here it should be *sore*. R also notes that 11JF *modoru basu wa itsu shuppatsu shimasu ka.* is wrong and would be better as either, *Nagoya e/ni modoru basu wa itsu shuppatsu shimasu ka* or *Kaeri no basu wa itsu shuppatsu shimasu ka* (At what time does the return bus leave ?). Despite JF's 'error', she still understands his question and asks when he plans to return in 12R. 13JF makes a simple time expression error in which *ato* or a further (3 days) needed to be replaced with *~go* after (3 days).

20R corrects 19JF by preferring a particular word order here: *O-hiru ni* (as temporal Adjunct)^*shuppatsu*. 21JF uses the corrected utterance showing the JF has taken up R's recast.

In 26R, *10-pun go* (after 10 minutes [from now]) is used. Previously in 13JF, R points out that he cannot use this *~go* temporal suffix. R gives it to him, however, he doesn't uptake it into his own Japanese: *hai, 10-pun desu.* which doesn't make much sense in this context since it is simply a statement rather than a confirmation: *hai, 10-pun go desu ne.*

Data set 4

LK = Lily Koh R = Japanese co-author

1LK: Sumimasen.

2R: Hai

3LK: Ano Nozawa Onsen ni ikitai'n desu kedo ano Nozawa Onsen e iku basu wa itsu ano
shuppatsu shimasu ka.

4R: Itsu ikimasu ka.

5LK: Aa

6R: Ima sugu desu ka.

7LK: Aa hai

8R: Ima 11-ji 10-pun desu. Ano 11-ji 20-pun ano 10-pun go desu ne. Ano Nozawa Onsen-yuki no basu ga demasu yo.

shift in topic of conversation

9LK: Hai oofuku wa ikura desu ka.

10R: Katamichi desu to gosen-en oofuku desu to
kyuu sen-en ni narimasu.

11LK: kyuu sen-en

12R: Hai

shift in topic of conversation

13LK: Ano mata okaeri no basu wa itsu Nagoya ni tsukimasu ka.

14R: Itsu o-kaeri ni narimasu ka.

15LK: Aa konya de mo itsu de mo ii desu kedo Ano saigo no basu wa?

16R: Kaeri no basu desu ne.

17LK: Itsu desu hai hai

18R: O-kaeri wa heijitsu desu kara sore to mo do doyoobi desu ka.

19LK: Aa soo desu ka.

20R: Jikan ga chigaimasu kara doyoo to heijitsu de wa

21LK: Aa soo desu ka Dakara un ashita no

22R: Ashita Nagoya ni kaette kuru'n desu ka.

23LK: Asa

24R: Asu ga suiyoobi desu kara mokuyoobi heijitsu desu ne.
Nanji goro ni Nagoya ni toochaku yotei desu ka.

25LK: Etto aa tabun 12-ji 12-ji ano ohiru-gohan no mae ni Nagoya ni kaeritai desu kedo

26R: Asa ichiban no basu desu ne.

27LK: Aa

28R: Asa 6-ji no basu to 7-ji no basu ga arimasu ga, dochira ga yoroshii desu ka.

29LK: Aa 7-ji no basu

30R: Hai

31LK: Daijoobu desu.

shift in topic of conversation

32R: Oofuku kawaremasu ka.

33LK: Hai

34R: Ima 11-ji kyoo etto Nagoya wo shuppatsu 11-ji 20-pun desu ne. O-kaeri wa ashita no asa 7-ji

35LK: 7-ji

36R: Nozawa Onsen

37LK: Hai

38R: Shuppatsu de yoroshii desu ka.

39LK: Hai.

40R: Wakarimashita. Kyuu sen-en ni narimasu.

41LK: Hai.

42R: Arigatoo gozaimashita.

43LK: Arigatoo gozaimashita.

Commentary on data set 4

LK initiates. R suggests that LK omit this utterance (3LK: *Nozawa Onsen ni ikitai'n desu kedo* [I want to go to Nozawa Hot Spring and…]) and begin with her next line. LK has been scaffolded by a textbook variation of Japanese and therefore uses that here. It would be interesting to know whether the textbook has more scaffolding 'power' than the teacher or even the expert interlocutor, especially at the beginning stages of SLD.

R also notes that *itsu* (when) is too general a time word for this situation and she wanted to hear *nan-ji* (what time). This is reflected in the exchange 4R since R wasn't sure whether LK wanted to take the bus today, tomorrow etc. R needed to confirm with LK by asking *itsu ikimasu ka* (a demand for information [When are you going ?]). 5LK gives no adequate answer to 4R, so the scaffolding here required R to ask more questions, based on R's assumption that LK wanted to leave right away: *ima sugu desu ka* (right now ?). R notes that LK's discourse includes many *aa* and *hai* which presumably LK thinks are appropriate *aizuchi* or back channels. However R reflects that she was not sure whether LK got her message or not, hence the need for further input from R. The motivation here for this kind of scaffolding is that R requires that she knows that LK has got her message before she can move into the next part of the negotiation.

R notes that 'when you purchase a long distance bus ticket, the departure time is important. You need to buy a ticket that is assigned for the departure time of your choice. This customer just came in and said she wants to buy a ticket without telling me the departure time, so in 8R I was being too informative on purpose to let her know this'.

9LK uses the word *oofuku* (round trip), however, R has already made her own judgment about LK's Japanese (negatively appraised) by giving her both one way and round trip prices. Therefore, does this negative appraisal motivate the need in the expert to do more scaffolding, or better, more *invisible* semiotic mediation?

15LK: she would not have got on any bus if she had said this. Moreover, *saigo*（最後）*no basu* implies that there will be no more bus service and she needed to choose the word *saishuu* (最終) *no basu* R checked the difference between *saigo no basu* and *saishuu no basu* with her father: the expert asking another expert for help ! R's father commented that if you were in the bus centre talking to a bus driver or whoever works at the centre, and if a passenger says *saigo no basu*, it is taken for granted that s/he means *saishuu no basu* or the last bus of the day. However in another place or context, *saigo no basu* has the meaning of *aishuu* (sorrow, pity) and it's really the very last bus time. *Saishuu no basu* means that it may be the last bus for that day but you know there will be a bus service the next day.

16R responds with a confirmation: *kaeri no basu desu ne* because R wanted to ask LK if she wanted to know the time schedule for the bus returning to Nagoya. 17LK is an inappropriate answer, so R scaffolds by rewording her response: 18R: *okaeri wa heijitsu desu kara sore to mo do doyoobi desu ka* (because the return is a week day or is it a Saturday ?). 19LK is again inappropriate, since 18R is a demand for information. LK is overusing *aizuchi* to disguise her lack of comprehension. In the role play, R decides that the bus schedule for weekdays and for weekends were different, hence 20R.

R reflects in Japanese 「一応日本では１２時から１時が昼食時間ですが、実際にお昼を食べる時間はひとそれぞれでしょうから、『お昼ご飯の前』ではあまり何時ごろなのか具体的に伝えわっていません。」(Usually in Japan, lunch time is from 12~1, however, in reality since it's left up to the individual the time s/he eats lunch, the phrase ohirugohan no mae doesn't communicate what time very concretely.) R classifies it as 'non-native like Japanese' and suggests *shoogo made ni* (by midday) would be an alternative. LK has a finite meaning potential and at this time that's what she chose. That's her 'coding orientation' which reflects her L2 (Japanese) meaning potential.26R: *asa ichiban no basu desu ne* (the first bus of the day). R notes that this is a bit too colloquial for an *obasan* (middle aged woman) working at the bus centre. This is an interesting comment in light of the discussion above regarding goodness of fit between role play and actual situation. R wanted to try out this expression on LK who responded with *aa* (27LK). This then motivated the scaffolding utterance: *asa 6-ji no basu to 7-ji no basu ga arimasu ga,* which explains what she meant in her original 26R question.

31LK is described as unnatural and English language like, akin to 'OK'.

Utterances 32R, 34R, 36R and 38R (basically demands for information) were used to scaffold LK's comprehension to make her articulate that the bus centre worker indeed had the right tickets, destination and time.

40R: R reflects that her own Japanese was interpersonally flawed given that *wakarimashita* is rather rude and should have been *kashikomarimashita* (certainly madam). Again the goodness of fit between the tenor of the role play and the actual situation appears to have been compromised. R notes that she could not stop telling LK that she understood everything LK told her and this motivated *wakarimashita*. In R's experience as the expert, the sales clerk obtains all the necessary information from the customer so that the sale clerk can provide the service as accurately as possible. In this case, given the expert-novice (contact) situation, R seems to have been swayed by other influences that merely articulating the expected Japanese.

Data set 5

KD = Kim Deal R = Japanese co-author

1KD: Sumimasen.

2R: Hai.

3KD: Takayama ni ikitai'n desu kedo.

4R: Hai

5KD: Itsu Takayama no basu kimasu ka.

6R: Shuppatsu wa ?

7KD: Hai

8R: Sugu shuppatsu shitai desu ka.

9KD: Aa ichiban ann sugu desu.

10R: A hai etto ima 2-ji 23-fun desu kara 2-ji 40-pun no Takayama-yuki no basu ga arimasu.

11KD: 2-ji 40-pun

12R: Hai 2-ji 40-pun ni Nagoya ni shuppatsu

shift in topic of conversation

13KD: Dono gurai kakarimasu ka.

14R: Takayama made wa 5-jikan kakarimasu, basu de.

15KD: 5-jikan

16R: Hai.

17KD: Aan

shift in topic of conversation

18R: Kippu o kaimasu ka.

19KD: Hai etto watashi wa aan iku to kakaru mo kippu ga hoshii desu.

20R: A, oofuku desu ka. Takayama made itte soshite kondo Takayama kara Nagoya ni modorareru wake desu ne.

21KD: Hai.

22R: Oofuku no kippu desu ne oofuku desu to ano sen-en yasuku narimasu kara oofuku kawaremasu ka.

23KD: Gomen nasai moo ichi-do itte kudasai.

24R: Ano oofuku kippu o kau to sen-en yasuku narimasu waribiki ga arimasu no de

25KD: Aan ichiban yasui kippu kudasai.

26R: E anoo oofuku kau no hoo ga o-yasui desu yo.

27KD: Aa sumimasen chotto wakaranai

28R: Nagoya kara Takayama made no kippu to

29KD: Un

30R: Takayama kara Nagoya made ni-mai kau

31KD: Hai hai ryoohoo

32R: Ichiman-en nan desu ne.

33KD: Aa hai

34R: Dakedo Nagoya Takayama Takayama Nagoya to zenbu kaeri made kau to ichiman-en ja nakute kyuusen-en ni narimasu.

35KD: Sumimasen moo ichi-do itte kudasai.

36R: Ima kaeri no kippu mo kau to

37KD: Un

38R: ichiman-en de wa nakute

39KD: Hai

40R: kyuusen-en ni narimasu kara ima oofuku ga kaimasu ka.

41KD: Hai ryoohoo

shift in topic of conversation

42R: Hai ja o-kaeri wa itsu desu ka.

43KD: Aan ashita no gogo

44R: Ashita no gogo Takayama o shuppatsu saremasu ka.

45KD: nn yeah ashita gozen ni Takayama ni ikitai n desu.

46R: A

47KD: Aa

48R: Ima kara

49KD: Aa

50R: 2-ji 40-pun no basu ni noreru'n desu ka.

51KD: Ashita no gogo ni Nagoya ni kaeritai

52R: Nagoya toochaku wa nan-ji goro yoroshii desu ka.

53KD: Hai

54R: Nagoya ni wa nanji ni o-kaeri ni naritai desu ka.

55KD: Aan dotchi de mo ii kedo aan ichiban hayai

56R: Nagoya ni ichiban hayaku toochaku suru ni wa etto Nagoya ni 10-ji hatsu 10-ji chaku no basu ga arimasu no de Takayama wo 5-ji ni yuugata no 5-ji ni shuppatsu shimasu.

57KD: 5-ji

58R: Hai sore de yoroshii desu ka.

59KD: Hai

60R: Ja yuki wa 2-ji 40-pun ato 15-fun de shuppatsu shimasu kyoo no 2-ji 40-pun desu ne.

61KD: aamu

62R: Kaeri wa ashita no yuugata no 5-ji Takayama shuppatsu Nagoya ni yoruno 10-ji toochaku de yoroshii desu ka.

63KD: Aan nanji Nagoya ni kaeru ?

64R: Toochaku desu ne. 10-ji ni toochaku shimasu yo. Yoru no 10-ji desu.

65KD: Yoru no 10-ji.

66R: tte Takayama o 5-ji ni shuppatsu shimasu.

67KD: Hai wakarimashita.

68R: Kore de yoroshii desu ka.

69KD: Hai

70R: Hai

71KD: Zenbu daijoobu desu.

72R: Hai 9sen-en itadakimasu.

73KD: Hai

74R: O-tsuri sen-en desu.

75KD: Arigatoo gozaimasu.

Commentary on data set 5

KD initiates. R notes that 3KD uses the same way of initiating as FB and LK. This coding orientation is most likely due to the choices set out in their Japanese language textbooks. Since *Takayama no basu* is somewhat ambiguous: the bus leaving for Takayama or the bus leaving from Takayama, R scaffolds with 6R hoping KD would be clearer. The issue is the material process *kimasu* which implies movement to where R and KD are. Furthermore, *itsu* is inappropriate here and has been discussed above. R's scaffold (6R) does not work since KD answers *hai* which R notes is inappropriate. So another scaffolding attempt is made in 8R (a demand for information) since R had to assume that KD wanted information on the bus leaving for Takayama.

9KD was trying to express something like 'the bus that leaves the soonest' which over-generalises this specific structure. R remarks that it sounds strange, however, R understands KD (10R). 11KD is a confirmation of the time so R assumed that KD had understood the time, yet R checks with *Nagoya ni shuppatsu* (leaving Nagoya) 'hoping' that KD understood that's the time a bus leaves Nagoya for Takayama.

17KD: *aan* stops the flow of the conversation, so to restart it R asks *kippu o kaimasu ka* (Are you going to buy a ticket ?). R reflects that 17KD could have been *aizuchi* to the reply *5-jikan* (5 hours) but KD needed to continue the conversation here. R remarks that 18R could be interpreted as sarcasm but this was not her intention. It was actually a scaffolding device to help keep the talk going. R notes that had she been talking to a Japanese she would have said *kippu o kawaremasu ka* using the honorific form for *kau* to buy or *kippu o koonyuu saremasu ka koonyuu* + suru (in honorific form) to purchase. But R dismissed these choices as new to this speaker and avoided both.

19KD does not know the word *oofuku* (return ticket) nor could she explain what she meant, so R had to give her the vocabulary (20R: demands information then explains) and then scaffolded her by rephrasing what *oofuku* means: *Takayama made itte soshite kondo Takayama kara Nagoya ni modorareru wake desu ne* (You mean go to Takayama and then return to Nagoya from Takayama, right ?).

22R~26R: perhaps this is another example of *invisible* semiotic mediation since R as the bus centre clerk wants KD to buy the right tickets as well as getting the best deal. R 'did her best' to inform KD that it's cheaper buying the round trip ticket as well as asking her if that's the type of ticket KD wanted. However 23KD and 27KD reveal that KD doesn't understand so R goes through it a second and third time 24R, 26R, 28R, 30R, 32R and 34R.

35KD: KD still needs more scaffolding, so she asks R to repeat it again. 36R, 38R, 40R are the scaffolds with R asking *oofuku ga kaimasu ka* (Are you going to buy a round trip ticket ?) which is a kind of comprehension check for KD and is reminiscent of 18R.

R is surprised at reading her transcription: 'Did I really say this ?' 40R: *oofuku ga kaimasu ka* should be *oofuku o kaimasu ka.*

45KD : *ikitai* = (I) want to go (to). KD should have said *Takayama kara kaeritai* (I want to return from Takayama). KD gets the process choice correct here (51KD).

In 52R, *nan-ji goro* (approximately what time ?) is answered with *hai.* R asks again in 54R with KD responding with *ichiban hayai* (the earliest [bus]). This is KD's coding orientation to which R responds in 56R using the word *toochaku* (arrival: nominalisation) plus *suru* making it into a material process.

58R continues to scaffold KD's comprehension through her constant checking of in this case making sure KD was actually leaving for Takayama *today.*

63KD reveals that she does not understand *toochaku* (arrival). Note R is intent on getting KD to learn the word *toochaku* (a learning through language type of scenario) by repeating it twice in 64R.

R remarks that a Japanese national would not say this (71KD could be glossed as 'everything's okay [or fine]). However R notes that this is a 'very good indication' that KD has understood everything that R had said. Although KD's response is technically an error, R notes that it made her feel that she did sell her the tickets of her choice.

Discussion

In relation to the first research question, all five novices drew upon their Japanese language meaning potentials to fulfil the task. Each was more or less successful (Mike Carpenter was the least successful case). Choices for these L2 learners are not unlimited and there are several examples throughout each data set that indicate how each novice approaches the limits of his or her own meaning potential, that is, at a certain point in the conversation, to use an ecological metaphor, their resources simply ran out and at this point what comes out of their mouths has been judged less acceptable by the expert.

Constraints can be understood in terms of how novices misalign context-semantics-lexicogrammar-phonology strata to their meaning potentials. Constraints of context didn't seem to appear due to the familiarity with such a context, though having said this, there are examples of minor contextual infelicities. Therefore the bulk of the constraints lay within the semantics-lexicogrammar strata. There may have also been phonological constraints, though these were not considered. It is unsurprising that novice language users (/learners) are constrained at the level of these strata.

For example, in Data Set 1 (1FB) and Data Set 2 (3MC), both novices choose a common formula that often appears in Japanese language textbooks which provides the suggested choice for this context. R suggests some completely different choice, a replacement of the volitional *–tai* with a more directed question that, for R, would have been the more *acceptable expert-like* way of asking the bus clerk when the bus leaves such as *Fujieda-yuki no basu wa nanji ni demasu ka* [At what time does the bus for Fujieda leave ?] (taken from Data Set 2).

Lexicon choice problems or constraints were also revealed in all the data sets. Given that the lexicon and the grammar are conflated in SFL, there needs to be a way of describing such constraints however this is beyond the scope of this chapter. The word *oofuku kippu* 'return ticket' stands out in all data sets as one of the more necessary words to 'know' in this context and it has been interesting to see how each informant dealt with the problem of not 'knowing' it.

In the observation section of Data Set 4 we asked whether the Japanese language textbook has more scaffolding power than the teacher or even expert interlocutor at the beginning stages of SLD. Armour (1998) has suggested that textbooks provide all the choices the novice must make in contexts chosen by the textbook authors. The influence of model dialogues can be seen in the examples above, especially at the initiation stage of the talk. Unlike model dialogues, the novice *in situ* can become totally lost (like Mike Carpenter and Kim Deal) when the language choices do not conform to those of the model. The expert has theoretically unlimited choices, the novice at the beginning stages of SLD has rules which need applying *in situ*, hence the case of badness of fit arises.

In terms of coding orientation, each speaker has demonstrated his or her own particular and peculiar coding orientation. However, in this case the expert has attempted to assert her own particular and peculiar coding orientation onto the novices during the talk. There's no judgement whether this is good or bad, useful or disruptive, it just seems to happen. Whether it happens as a general rule in conversation between experts and novices in the L2 context is beyond the scope of this study to offer any clear answer. R's own reflections are valuable in understanding how and when she code orients each of the novice users during the role play. We hasten to add that it is actually unclear whether her motivation or, better, *investment* (Peirce, 1995) to code orient comes from R's position as the bus clerk (a pretend role) or her 'real' role as an international student advisor at her university, a role which implies caring about the interlocutor.

We also come back to Hasan's notion of the *inherent elasticity of meaning*. What strikes us about each data set is that meaning making was achieved albeit for some such as Mike Carpenter and Kim Deal rather awkwardly. This is what it means to be a novice or, as Wells (1999) called it, a 'semiotic apprentice'. R reflected much on the contextual and semantic differences between *saishuu no basu* and *saigo no basu* (the last bus) so much so she had to defer to her father (an *older* [= more expert ?] Japanese national) for his opinion. This is an example of the inherent elasticity of meaning. While the novice may not have been consciously aware of the semantic issues being raised in her choice, it struck a chord with the expert R who responded the way she did in her talk as per the transcription. We feel that such inherent elasticity needs to be further researched in SLD.

Research Question 2 mentions the act of 'noticing'. Schmidt (1990, 1994, 1995) alerts researchers to how L2 learners 'notice' language (as Ellis (1999:35) notes in terms of L2 items and rules) in interaction. However, we are interested in how the expert notices when a novice requires help to make their meanings clearer. There are several examples of R noticing each novice getting 'stuck' (examples include Data Set 1 25FB-26R, Data Set 2 9MC-17MC, Data Set 3 6R-11JF, Data Set 4 25LK-31LK, and Data Set 5 9KD-10R plus more).

Noticing seems to occur before the processes of scaffolding or semiotic meditation. This is unsurprising. The expert however must make a choice whether to scaffold or not, especially when s/he is in a role other than teacher (or caregiver) in a classroom. Since we couldn't get these five novices to perform the role play *in situ*, we will never know if a 'real' bus clerk would notice, then scaffold. In this case, it may be that R's real educator role 'kicked in' when the novices needed her assistance and she willingly scaffolded (linguistically intervened) to assist in making their meanings clearer.

R corrected in a number of ways: contextually, semantically and lexico-grammatically. Unlike Schleppegrall's (2002) study, these corrections were made as a part of the unfolding spoken talk. Corrections in writing are somewhat different given the semiotic tools and purposes at the disposal of the corrector. For example, R didn't use a *red* pen to point out to each novice his or her error. Instead, there were recasts and rewordings but never a rebuke or a flat out period of tense silence – a refusal to take part in any dialogue with any of the novices. There is also a time factor which needs to be accounted for in speech. Given that in a real situation, there could have been others (experts) waiting in line to get bus tickets too, in this context – a contact situation – how much time the expert allows the novice to have to actually produce the talk could be a crucial trigger in determining the expert's need to correct or scaffold. Mike Carpenter and Kim Deal were the weakest of the five novices in producing the language necessary for the 'successful' (implying acceptable) production of this task.

And finally in relation to research question 3, the issue of whether adult learners of an additional language require an entry point into initial stages of L2 development seems to have been answered above. We believe that yes there is such a requirement. Each expert literally becomes or is positioned *in loco parentis* whether she or he likes it or not. The five novices each required a varying degree of scaffolding to do this task. Mike Carpenter and Kim Deal needed quite a lot of support. In Data Set 2 9MC-17MC, the way that R would respond to his requests for her to repeat is perhaps more an example of a listen-and-repeat drill of a L2 teaching methodology of a previous era. However Mike Carpenter desperately required R to act as she did for the sake of his own comprehension. In Data Set 5 Kim Deal had to ask for repeats several times throughout her attempt at negotiation. The nature of the *input* is important though as Swain has suggested, it is the collaboration between interlocutors that is most likely crucial to how the novice actually develops his meaning potential. The novice cannot simply resolve a meaning making problem *in situ* without the help of the expert. Thus this expert is positioned as caregiver even for the slightest moment when the novice's choices run out.

Conclusion

The purpose of this study has been to understand how meaning is made collaboratively in a SLD context. In each data set, errors made by these L2 learners have been foregrounded, however, this acted as an aside to understanding what actually happened in the talk. R scaffolded all the informants' Japanese discourse by asking questions (demanding information, for instance she did this four times with FB, five times with MC, six times with JF, nine times with LK, and fourteen times with KD who needed the most scaffolding of all); recasting; providing vocabulary; and confirmation. Two questions sprung to mind: 1) did R do this because she is an educator ?; and 2) would a 'real' bus centre clerk scaffold the L2 in the same way ? Definitive answers are elusive.

It was stated in the beginning part of this chapter that choices are made based on one's vast meaning potential. However, in the L2 learner's case, their meaning potential is somewhat more restricted, not in the Bernsteinian sense of restricted code but their coding orientations are limited through certain constraints such as vocabulary or more broadly linguistic knowledge (a restriction in field).

In this study we privileged an exchange of meanings to give some insight into how these L2 learners have aligned the four strata of context-semantics-lexicogrammar-phonology. What this allowed us to do in our observations was to make comments on each of the learner's (L2) linguistic fingerprints as examples of language variety in Japanese. Where's Japanese? This rests with the expert, in this case R, who highlighted the infelicities made in interactions with her. However, she did this after the fact not during the talk. R held each of the L2 learner's proverbial hands through what could be described metaphorically as a mind field of potential choices. R held everyone's hands regardless of their proficiency level. This is one way she was socialising them into a discourse community. R simply wanted to do her job as the bus centre clerk and make sure that each individual got to their destination and back to Nagoya on the buses and times of their choosing.

In the interactions above, R did not actually focus on form during the actual talk. She was much more concerned with focus on both the interpersonal and the semantic. It is unsurprising that all five informants did the same task in basically a similar manner. Yet there were varying lengths of talk to achieve a positive outcome (though we are not sure whether Mike Carpenter actually got on the bus to Fujieda or not). Kim Deal did the most talking and needed the most scaffolding. Josh Franks did the least talking however despite his superior Japanese language proficiency, still required assistance.

R as the bus centre clerk provided a supportive environment in which all the learners could attempt to express themselves in their variety of Japanese language. Through both her visible and invisible semiotic mediation, R was able to influence the coding orientations of all L2 interlocutors and by the end of the set task appeared to have expanded their resources for meaning making.

Notes

1 We would like to acknowledge the generous assistance provided by Nagoya University, the University of New South Wales, and Dr. S. Goto and Mrs. H. Goto. This study would not have been possible with this assistance. The term 'additional language' is used interchangeably with L2 or foreign language.

2 In a plenary paper presented at the International Systemic Functional Linguistics Congress 32, Geoff Williams challenged the scaffolding metaphor by suggesting that, following Hasan (2004), *explicit* and *invisible* semiotic mediation could be viable alternatives. We take up the challenge and attempt to use Hasan's terms in this study.

3 See Larsen-Freeman's (1997) discussion of chaos/complexity science and second language acquisition for comparison.

4 We find the term 'native speaker' problematic. We adopt Rampton's (2003) view that when the communicative aspects of language are investigated, the terms should be accomplished users or *experts* rather than native speakers since expertise differs from identification; it is learned, relative, and partial; and the achievement of expertise can be reviewed and disputed (p.109). We refer to the Japanese national interlocutor as the 'expert' and the five L2 learners with whom she interacts as 'novices'.

5 'You want to take the bus to a small village in the mountains. Ask the ticket clerk at the bus centre when the bus leaves, how long the trip takes, and how much a round-trip ticket costs. Ask what time the return bus leaves, and what time it arrives back to Nagoya'.

6 This study concerns 'oral' literacy, that is, not written down (apart from the transcriptions). 'Errors' may actually be more obvious in writing since it may be the case that when listening to spoken language, the listener may simply ignore or not have enough time to attend to the infelicities. On reflection, when listening to music and errors are made by the musician, there can be a slight jarring effect. Is listening to spoken language any different? One limitation of this study is that the phonology stratum of the informants' meaning potentials has not been considered.

7 See a detailed explanation of how the self-assessment scale is constructed and its validity in Armour (2004).

Appendix

Translations into English of Informants' Conversations

Note: it was found to be difficult to 'translate' the errors that each informant made into the English gloss, so the following translations are merely a guide for non-Japanese language readers to what each informant has attempted to say.

Fred Baker

1FB: Um excuse me, I'd like to go to the village called Takayama tomorrow.

About what time do buses go from Nagoya ?

2R: There are lots.

3FB: I see. Um, is there a bus at about 10 perhaps ?.

4R: Do you want one that arrives there at 10 or leaves Nagoya at 10 ?

5FB: Um I mean

6R: at

7FB: leaves

8R: Departing from Nagoya right. Therefore, there's the 10:05 bus

9FB: Oh really? Um about how long does it take to Takayama ?

10R: It takes 5 and half hours.

11FB: Um excuse me could you say that again.

12R: It takes 5 hours 30 minutes.

13FB: 5 hours 30 minutes, really ?

14R: Yes.

15FB: Um about how much does a return trip cost ?

16R: Return is ¥8000.

17FB: ¥8000? And it takes about 5 hours. Is there a bus that leaves Takayama at about 2pm the day after tomorrow ?

18R: You want to return to Nagoya departing Takayama at 2pm, right.

19FB: Yes.

20R: Okay, there a bus at 2:30.

21FB: Really. Um and that takes about 5 and a half hours too.

22R: Yes. It arrives into Nagoya at 8.

23FB: Um I see. ¥8000. Is it ¥8000 ?

24R: Yes.

25FB: I'd like to order a seat.

26R: Book a seat ?

27FB: Yes, is that possible ?

28R: Yes.

29FB: How much is it ? ¥8000 too ?

30R: No, it is included in the ¥8000.

31FB: 'marete imasu' sorry can you say that again.

32R: Oh, all bus seats are reserved seats.

33FB: Really ?

34R: Yes.

35FB: Um

36R: Are you going to buy (a ticket) ?

37FB: Um yes for the 10am bus tomorrow.

38R: So it's the 10:05 bus leaving Nagoya on January 29th ?

39FB: Yes

40R: And you are returning on the 2pm bus from Takayama on January 30th, right?

41FB: Yes

42R: Fine.

43FB: Thank you.

Mike Carpenter

1MC: Excuse me.

2R: Yes.

3MC: Um I'd like to go to Fujieda.

4R: Yes.

5MC: Um when do I get off the bus ?

6R: Leaving for Fujieda, right ?

7MC: Yes.

8R: One leaves 20 minutes from now. It's 2pm, so there's a bus at 2:20.

9MC: Oh sorry please say it again.

10R: The bus leaves at 2:20!

11MC: 20…

12R: 20 minutes

13MC: 20 minutes

14R: Right.

15MC: Un.

16R: 2:20

17MC: Oh right got it, thanks. Um how many hours does it take ?

18R: The hours ? Well, to Fujieda it takes 3 hours.

19MC: 3 hours.

20R: Yes.

21MC: Really, um…how much for a *round trip* ticket ? (MC says this in English indicated in italics)

22R: What's that ?

23MC: To Fujieda and return to Nagoya.

24R: I see.

25MC: How much ?

26R: Okay, sorry could you say that again please ?

27MC: Sorry

28R: That's okay.

29MC: How much to Fujieda ?

30R: To Fujieda ?

31MC: To Fujieda and to Nagoya.

32R: Oh you mean return ticket, don't you ? A return ticket that goes both from Nagoya to Fujieda and from Fujieda to Nagoya, right ?

33MC: Um yes, yes yes.

34R: A return is ¥4000.

35MC: ¥4000. Thank you. Um the Fujieda bus…

36R: Yes ?

37MC: When does it return ?

38R: Well, the time of the bus that returns from Fujieda to Nagoya ?

39MC: Right !

40R: Firstly when you plan to return to Nagoya ?

41MC: No…once again

42R: When

43MC: When

44R: to Nagoya

45MC: yes

46R: will you return ?

47MC: yes

48R: returning tomorrow ?

49MC: When ?

50R: yes

51MC: no…yes, tomorrow

52R: Tomorrow ? Well since tomorrow is Wednesday, it becomes the week day schedule. There's a bus that departs Fujieda every 30 minutes.

53MC: Thank you very much

54R: Yes.

Josh Franks

1JF: Excuse me. I'd like to go to Takayama by bus. Can I buy the tickets here ?

2R: Yes, you can.

3JF: Um, when doe the bus depart ?

4R: You can take the bus soon from now.

5JF: Really ? That's good. So, about how much to Takayama ?

6R: One way is ¥3000.

7JF: ¥3000 to go and to return, how much ? How much to Takayama and when I return to Nagoya ?

8R: You mean a return ticket ?

9JF: A return ticket. Yes, how much ?

10R: One way is ¥3000 and when you buy a return ticket you get a ¥500 discount so ¥5500.

11JF: Good. So I will buy this. When will the return bus depart ?

12R: When will you return ?

13JF: In 3 days.

14R: So, today is Tuesday February 4th and after 3 days it'll be the 7th, right.

15JF: Yes the 7th.

16R: To Nagoya…

17JF: lunch time on the 7th.

18R: Departing there at lunch time or arriving in Nagoya at lunch time…which one?

19JF: Departing at lunch

20R: At lunch time

21JF: departing at lunch time

22R: Departing Takayama, right ?

23JF: Yes.

24R: 12:30…there's a 12:30 bus.

25JF: I'll take the 12:30.

26R: Yes, the bus going there will leave in 10 more minutes, is that okay ?

27JF: Yes in 10 minutes. Thank you.

28R: So it's 1:12 now. The 1:22 bus is okay with you, right ?

29JF: Yes

30R: And returning on the 7th, departing Takayama at 12:30 and arriving Nagoya at 4:30 5:30, right ?

31JF: Yes.

32R: That's ¥5500.

33JF: Here you are.

34R: Thank you.

Lily Koh

1LK: Excuse me.

2R: Yes

3LK: Um, I'd like to go to Nozawa hot spring. When um does the bus that goes to Nozawa hot spring depart ?

4R: When are you going to go ?

5LK: Well…

6R: Right now ?

7LK: Um yes…

8R: It's 11:10 now. Um, at 11:20…in another 10 minutes..the um bus to Nozawa hot spring will leave.

9LK: Okay, how much does a return cost ?

10R: One way is ¥5000 and return is ¥9000.

11LK: ¥9000.

12R: Yes.

13LK: Um when will the return bus arrive in Nagoya.

14R: When will you return ?

15LK: Oh anytime this evening…the last bus is...

16R: The return bus right ?

17LK: When is it…yes yes

18R: Since the return is on a weekday…there's also Saturday.

19LK: Really

20R: The times on Saturday and week days are different

21LK: Really ? and tomorrow ?

22R: Will you return to Nagoya tomorrow ?

23LK: In the morning…

24R: Since the morning is a Wednesday, and Thursday is a week day, right? About what time do you plan to arrive into Nagoya ?

25LK: Um perhaps at 12…um I'd like to return to Nagoya before lunchtime.

26R: The first bus in the morning, right ?

27LK: Hmmm

28R: There's a 6am and a 7am, which one is good for you ?

29LK: Um the 7am bus.

30R: Okay

31LK: Fine.

32R: Will you buy a return ticket ?

33LK: Yes.

34R: Now it's 11…you will depart Nagoya today at 11:20. The return is tomorrow at 7am.

35LK: 7am

36R: Nozawa hot spring…

37LK: Yes

38R: Is that the departure then ?

39LK: Yes.

40R: Fine. That'll be ¥9000.

41LK: Here you are.

42R: Thank you.

43LK: Thank you.

Kim Deal

1KD: I'd like to go to Takayama.

2R: Yes

3KD: When does the Takayama bus go ?

4R: Depart ?

5KD: Yes

6R: Do you wish to depart immediately ?

7KD: Um immediately

8R: I see..well it's 2:23 now. There's a bus at 2:40.

9KD: 2:40

10R: Yes it departs Nagoya at 2:40.

11KD: About how long does it take ?

12R: To Takayama ? by bus, 5 hours.

13KD: 5 hours.

14R: Yes.

15KD: Hmmm

16R: Are you going to buy a ticket ?

17KD: Yes. Um I want a ticket to go and to come back

18R: Return ? You mean that you'll go to Takayama and then from Takayama you will return to Nagoya, right.

19KD: Yes.

20R: That's a return. With a return you get it ¥1000 cheaper. Will you buy a return ?

21KD: Excuse me. Please say that again.

22R: Um when you buy a return ticket, there is a discount and it's a ¥1000 cheaper.

23KD: Um give me the cheapest ticket.

24R: Well the return is the cheaper way to buy.

25KD: Oh I'm sorry I cannot understand you.

26R: Buying two tickets from Nagoya to Takayama

27KD: Yes

28R: and from Takayama to Nagoya

29KD: Yes yes both

30R: This is ¥10000.

31KD: Yes.

32R: But Nagoya Takayama Takayama Nagoya, when you buy the return it isn't ¥10000 but it becomes ¥9000.

33KD: Sorry can you say that again.

34R: If you buy the return ticket now

35KD: yes

36R: it's not ¥10000

37KD: yes

38R: it'll be ¥9000. Will you buy a return now ?

39KD: Yes both.

40R: Yes, when is the return ?

41KD: Um tomorrow afternoon.

42R: Will you depart Takayama tomorrow afternoon ?

43KD: Um yeah I want to go to Takayama tomorrow morning.

44R: Oh

45KD: um

46R: from now

47KD: um

48R: will you take the 2:40 bus ?

49KD: I want to return to Nagoya tomorrow afternoon.

50R: About what time would you like to arrive into Nagoya?

51KD: Yes…

52R: What time will you return to Nagoya ?

53KD: Um any is fine…um the earliest.

54R: For the fastest arrival into Nagoya there's a 10:00 departure 10:00 arrival, so that departs Takayama at 5, 5pm.

55KD: 5

56R: Yes, is that alright ?

57KD: Yes.

58R: Okay, going there is 2:40, departing in another 15 minutes…today at 2:40, right.

59KD: Um

60R: The return is departing Takayama at 5pm tomorrow, arriving into Nagoya at 10pm. Okay

61KD: Um what time will it return to Nagoya ?

62R: You mean arrive, don't you. It will arrive at10pm ! 10pm

63KD: 10pm.

64R: and it will depart Takayama at 5:00.

65KD: Yes I got it.

66R: Is that all okay ?

67KD: Yes.

68R: Good.

69KD: Everything is fine.

70R: ¥9000 please.

71KD: Yes

72R: Your change is ¥1000.

73KD: Thank you.

References

Armour, W. (1998) Putting more than words in their mouths: using model dialogues to construct social reality in the Japanese language classroom. *Japanese Studies* 18(2): 181–197.

Armour, W. (2004) Becoming a Japanese Language Learner, User, and Teacher: Revelations from Life History Research. *Journal of Language, Identity, and Education* 3(2): 101–125.

Byrnes, H. (ed) (2006) Advanced Language Learning: The Contribution of Halliday and Vygotsky. London and New York: Continuum.

Byrnes, H. (2009) Systemic-functional reflections on instructed foreign language acquisition as meaning-making: An introduction. *Linguistics and Education* 20: 1–9.

Colombi, M. C. and Schleppegrell, M. J. (2002) Theory and Practice in the Development of Advanced Literacy. In M. J. Schleppegrell and M. C. Colombi (eds) *Developing Advanced Literacy in First and Second Languages: Meaning With Power* 1–19. Mahwah, New Jersey: Lawrence Erlbaum Associates.

Ellis, R. (1999) *Learning a Second Language Through Interaction.* Amsterdam and Philadelphia: John Benjamins Publishing Company.

Ellis, R. (1999) Factors in the Incidental Acquisition of Second Language Vocabulary from Oral Input. In R. Ellis (ed.) *Learning a Second Language Through Interaction* 35–61. Amsterdam and Philadelphia: John Benjamins Publishing Company.

Hall, J. K. (1995) (Re)creating our Worlds with Words: A Sociohistorical Perspective of Face-to-Face Interaction. *Applied Linguistics* 16(2): 206–232.

Halliday, M. A. K. (1978a) 'Is Learning a Second Language like Learning a First Language All Over Again?' In D. E. Ingram and T. J. Quinn (eds) *Language Learning in Australian Society: Proceedings of the 1976 Congress of the Applied Linguistics Association of Australia* 3–19. Melbourne: Australia International Press & Publications Pty. Ltd.

Halliday, M. A. K. (1978b*) Language as social semiotic: The social interpretation of language and meaning.* London: Edward Arnold.

Halliday, M. A. K. (1993) 'Towards a language based theory of learning'. *Linguistics and Education* 5: 93–116.

Hasan, R. (2003) Globalisation, literacy and ideology. *World Englishes* 22(4): 433–468.

Hasan, R. (2004) The world in words: Semiotic mediation, tenor and ideology. In G. Williams and A. Lukin (eds*) The Development of Language: Functional perspectives on species and individuals* 158–181. London and New York: Continuum.

Larsen-Freeman, D. (1997) Chaos/Complexity Science and Second Language Acquisition. *Applied Linguistics* 18(2): 141–165.

Lee, J.F. and VanPatten, B. (2003) *Making Communicative Language Teaching Happen*, 2nd edition. Boston: McGraw Hill.

Lukin, A. (2004) We'd sat it better with a theme effort. *The Australian Higher Education Supplement* 23 June: 40.

Mohan, B. and Beckett, G. H. (2003) A Functional Approach to Research on Content-Based Language Learning Recasts in Causal Explanations. *The Modern Language Journal* 87(iii): 421–432.

Painter, C. (2004) The 'Interpersonal First' Principle in Child Language Development. In G. Williams and A. Lukin (eds*) The Development of Language: Functional Perspectives on Species and Individuals* 137–157. London and New York: Continuum.

Peirce, B. N. (1995) Social Identity. Investment, and Language Learning. *TESOL Quarterly* 29(1): 9–31.

Perrett, G. (2000) Researching second and foreign language development. In L. Unsworth (ed.) *Researching Language in Schools and Communities: Functional Linguistic Perspectives* 87–119. London and Washington: Cassell.

Rampton, B. (2003) Displacing the 'Native Speaker': Expertise, affiliation and inheritance. In R. Harris and B. Rampton (eds) *The Language, Ethnicity and Race Reader* 107–111. London and New York: Routledge.

Ramsey, S. R. (2004) The Japanese Language and the Making of Tradition. *Japanese Language and Literature* 38: 81–110.

Ross, J. R. (1979) Where's English? In C. J. Fillmore, D. Kempler and W. S-Y. Wang (eds) *Individual Differences in Language Ability and Language Behavior* 127–163. New York: Academic Press.

Schleppegrell, M. J. (2002) Challenges of the Science Register for ESL Students: Errors and Meaning-Making. In M. J. Schleppegrell and M. C. Colombi (eds) *Developing Advanced Literacy in First and Second Languages: Meaning With Power* 119–142. Mahwah, New Jersey: Lawrence Erlbaum Associates.

Schmidt, R. (1990) The Role of Consciousness in Second Language Learning. *Applied Linguistics* 11: 129–158.

Schmidt, R. (1994) Deconstructing Consciousness in Search of Useful Definitions for Applied Linguistics. *AILA Review* 11: 11–26.

Schmidt, R. (1995) Consciousness and Foreign Language Learning: A Tutorial on the Role of Attention and Awareness in Learning. In R. Schmidt (ed.) *Attention, Awareness in Foreign Language Learning*. Honolulu: University of Hawaii Press.

Swain, M. (2000) The output hypothesis and beyond: Mediating acquisition through collaborative dialogue. In J. P. Lantolf (ed.) *Sociocultural Theory and Second Language Learning* 97–114. Oxford: Oxford University Press.

Wells, G. (1999) *Dialogic Inquiry: Toward a Sociocultural Practice and Theory of Education*. Cambridge: Cambridge University Press.

Williams, G. (2005) *Memory, Literacy and the Ontogenesis of Vertical Discourse*. Plenary Paper presented at ISFC32, University of Sydney, July 17–22.

Young, R. (1999) Sociolinguistic Approaches to SLA. *Annual Review of Applied Linguistics* 19:105–132.

8 Modelling writing: using the genre approach in the Japanese as a foreign language classroom

Yuko Ramzan and Elizabeth A. Thomson
Ritsumeikan University, Japan
UNSW, Canberra

Over the last 15 to 20 years, the teaching of Japanese as a Foreign Language (JFL) in the Australian education context has been based on a communicative approach. This approach establishes an 'information gap' between speaker and listener, thereby setting up a 'real' need to communicate, introducing and practicing language patterns in a social context. However, while this approach has been popular with teachers, particularly at a beginners level in the teaching of speaking and listening, the same cannot be said in relation to the teaching of writing to more advanced students. Constructing 'information gaps' in social situations without reference to the bi-directional effect[1] of the context on the text is inadequate. Another approach which foregrounds the social purpose, the genre and the context of a text that is based on linguistic analysis of the characteristic lexico-grammatical features is needed. One such approach that has been successful in the ESL classroom is the Genre Approach based on Systemic Functional Linguistics as developed by the Sydney School (Johns, 2003). This paper presents an argument for the adoption of the Genre Approach in the JFL classroom. The approach in demonstrated in two parts. Firstly, a model text of the type that students are expected to write is analysed in terms of its context, social purpose and lexico-grammatical features. This, in turn, is incorporated into a proposed lesson plan based around the framework of the Genre Approach, which embeds writing in a lesson module extending over 7 weeks, for two hours per week. This kind of description provides JFL teachers with an example of a writing pedagogy that locates learning in the cultural context of the target language, highlighting not just the lexicogrammatical features of the text but also the social purpose and registerial characteristics which serve to identify the text as one instance of the genre to which it belongs.

Background

As teachers of Japanese as a Foreign Language (JFL) we have been involved in the ongoing process of the development of learning/teaching resources. While resources for listening and speaking are readily available, varied and interesting, the same cannot be said about resources for reading and writing. Typically, the resources that are available for reading and writing tend to concentrate students' attention on the development of *kana* and *kanji* (Kano, 2010; Suzuki, Hajikano and Kataoka, 1999) and clause level grammar (AOTS 1993). Some textbooks do deal with whole texts (Banno, Ikeda, Ohno, 2011; Hagiwara, 2008; Tohsaku, 2005) but in doing so they make no connection between the text example in the textbook and the kind of text or family of text types, that is, the genre, to which the example may belong. In other words, each text is dealt with in isolation, with no attempt made to relate linguistic features to meaning and subsequently, to genre. This lack of connection suggests that all text examples are unrelated to each other, which, from our point of view, is not an efficient or motivating way to present whole texts to students of Japanese language. It does not offer a systematic approach to learning how to read and write.

But how do teachers introduce whole texts into the classroom, and in so doing, locate them in the context of their genre? And how do learners know what linguistic features within a text correlate to the purpose of the text and its genre? These two questions form the motivation behind the ongoing task of mapping genres in Japanese with the intention of developing effective resources for the teaching of reading and writing. However, the task is not limited to resource development, but rather it also requires attention to L2 pedagogy. What pedagogical approach should teachers take when teaching reading and writing whole texts and how does one implement it in the classroom?

This chapter will describe the process of understanding the linguistic features of a model text and offer a description of how the model text could be taught in the JFL classroom using the Genre Approach, an L1 pedagogy that has been adapted to the L2 context (see Feez, 2002). We will show how Systemic Functional (SF) Theory can be used to underpin the reading and writing of whole texts in the JFL context.

The following section will briefly introduce how SF Theory has been used to deconstruct Japanese texts using the notion of genre. It will then illustrate the linguistic features of a model text, describing the text in terms of generic elements and related language features. We suggest that this model text could then be used in the classroom using an adapted Genre Approach pedagogy. The final section of the chapter will discuss writing pedagogy in a second language (L2) and describe how the Genre Approach could be successfully adapted to the

Japanese L2 context, using a suggested lesson plan, concluding with an example of student writing, which resulted from a piloting of the suggested lesson plan.

The notion of genre

The notion of genre is the subject of considerable debate. This arises from the fact that it has a number of conceptualisations based on different linguistic traditions. Discussion on the full set of different conceptualisations within different traditions detracts from the purpose of this chapter and thus will not be entered into here, however, it is useful to define the conceptualisation which is used in this study and the justifications for its use.

The conceptualisation of genre in this study is that which arises out of SF Theory. There is, however, a range of understandings of genre within SF circles. Despite this debate about the nature of genre, the fact remains that genre has the following general characteristics. It is a functional model of context based on social purpose, which can be represented typologically as a system network. Essentially, a genre is a population[2] of texts. Variations exist within that population, but the probability of the features of each genre serve to define the population as one kind of population (refer to Nesbitt and Plum (1988) for a discussion on systemic probabilities). For example, there is a population of narrative texts, of nursery tale texts, or of newspaper texts. A useful way of describing these probabilities and the relationship between genre, register (contextual variables) and the grammar is through the modal concept of usuality. The most usual features would topologically place a particular text centrally within the text type, while texts with less than the usual features would exist indeterminately on the boundary of a genre. Further, the application of the notion of genre lends itself to teaching contexts, a feature that interests us greatly, as analyses of different genres directly informs the teaching of Japanese as a Foreign Language.

While there are two notions of genre within SFL, one based on Halliday and Hasan (1985) and the other on Martin (1999), this chapter uses Martin's conceptualisation, which is sketched below. Martin's conceptualisation of genre is based on Gregory's category of functional tenor (Gregory, 1967; Gregory and Carroll, 1978). Martin (1999) found the category of functional tenor to have a practical utility in that it introduced the notion of global purpose, that is, a text as a whole has a specific, social purpose. Martin developed the notion of genre from this idea and defines genre as 'staged goal-oriented social process[es]' (Martin, 1986:246); this is a model of context which is viewed as a connotative or secondary social semiotic system which allows exploration of the functionality of language in relation to how it is used (Martin, 1999:31).

Martin (1999) organises genres both typologically and topologically. That is to say, he clusters genres according to types in a typological system network, however he also describes genres from a complementary topological perspective which serves to capture the issue of gradience – the degree of proximity between categories within similar genre types or families. A topological perspective also accommodates the issue of mixed genres, whereby one text may move through a number of social purposes, combining the features of two different genres in one text as a mixed genre. Topological perspectives have been especially useful in the education work undertaken by Martin and his colleagues in curriculum design, as his primary aim was to map culture as a system of genres (Martin, 1999) in order to identify the lexicogrammatical features of different genres with the aim of finding ways to reveal, compare and teach the different kinds of valued texts within primary and secondary schools in NSW.

Martin (1984) emphasized that genres are not innate, but learned through social interaction and thus can be taught by using a variety of teaching techniques. In a more recent article, Martin (2002) explains that early in the 1980s, he and his colleagues planned to begin mapping culture as a network of social practices, one set of genres in relation to another. Their efforts gave clear direction to language teachers on what to teach and how to teach a language by directing them to build a bridge between text and context.

The following description of the model text draws on the SF notions of genre in the sense that the model text is viewed as one instantiation of a genre serving a particular culturally valued social purpose. The model text is situated within a context which realizes particular meanings which are consequently realised by particular lexicogrammatical choices. Matthiessen, Slade and Macken explain that:

> .... the relationship between context (of culture and of communicative use) and language (as system and as process) can be interpreted as one of realisation – language realizes context. But this does not mean that the relationship is one-way. On the contrary, while context influences language, it is also constructed by language. In terms of the history of language, of an individual, and of a text, context and language develop together, in constant exchange – we can say that they co-evolve (1993:139).

Further, as this study describes only one text, it is not our intention to make any statements on the nature of the genre to which it belongs. In other words, we make no general claims about the genre, nor about the kinds of generic elements and whether or not they are obligatory or optional. That being said, we do however make statements about the nature of the model text in relation to its social purpose and context. This is discussed below.

The model text

Selection of the model text:

The selection of the model text is determined by the needs of the target students. The target students were in their first semester of a second year of the Japanese major in Australia. Essentially, these students have already had about 230 class contact hours. During these class hours, their language learning class experience had been around everyday activities such as commuting, studying, shopping, outdoor activities and entertainment. While they were comfortable with reading and writing both *hiragana* and *katakana*, their level of *kanji* was limited to about 180 characters. Predominantly they were young adults with an interest in contemporary Japanese culture. Thus the model text needed to be, in the first instance, of interest to the students, and in the second instance to be a text that the students would more than likely read in an authentic immersion context. Further, it needed to be short in length and grammatically familiar to them. After some searching we chose a short article on a young, male, soccer player, *Teruyoshi Ito*. The article was published in the Japan Airlines in-flight magazine, *JAL Club* (Cabin Services Planning Section, Japan Airlines 1996). It was felt that this text was appropriate as our students would more than likely be travelling to Japan and would therefore, more than likely, come across similar texts during their travels. The original text is reproduced here.

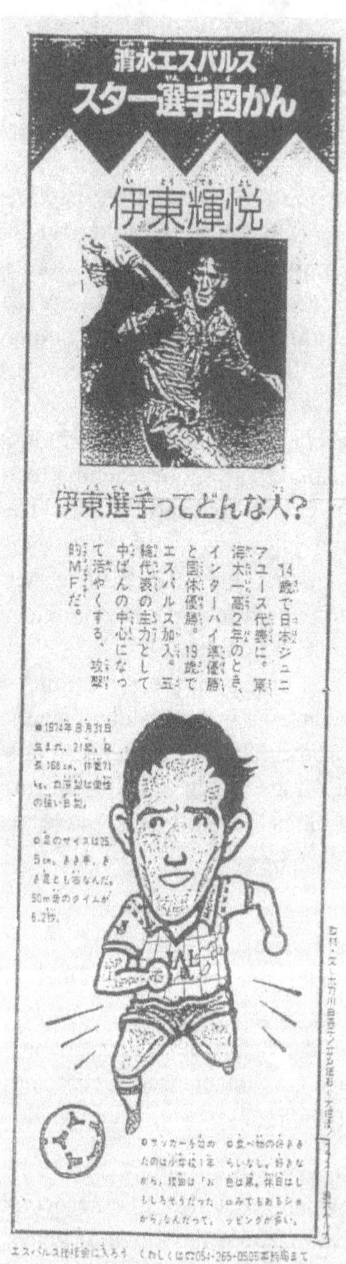

清水エスパルス
スター選手図かん

伊東輝悦

伊東選手ってどんな人?

14歳で日本ジュニアユース代表に。東海大一高2年のとき、インターハイ準優勝と国体優勝。19歳でエスパルス加入。五輪代表の主力として中ばんの中心になって活やくする、攻撃的MFだ。

●1974年8月31日生まれ、21歳、身長168cm、体重71kg。血液型は個性の強いB型。

●足のサイズは25.5cm。きき手、きき足とも右なんだ。50m走のタイムが6.2秒。

●サッカーを始めたのは小学校1年から。理由は「おもしろそうだったから」なんだって。

●食べ物の好ききらいなし。好きな色は黒。休日はしゅみでもあるショッピングが多い。

エスパルス後援会に入ろう くわしくは☎054-265-0505事務局まで

Picture 1: The original article

The context of the text

Before investigating the nature of the model text, it is helpful to consider the context of the text itself. To begin with, in SF Theory, context is divided into two components, that is, there is a *context of culture* which comprises the full set of possible *contexts of situation*. And importantly, the context of situation is an instantiation of the context of culture (Halliday, 1991:8). Further, the context of situation is made up of three variables. These are *Field*, *Tenor* and *Mode*. The field is what a text is about, that is, the 'what' of the text; the tenor is the nature of the social relationships in relation to the text, that is, the 'who' of the text; and the mode is the channel of transmission of the text, that is, the 'how' of the text. The following section will discuss the context of culture before proceeding to describe the context of situation of the text.

Despite that fact that the model text is relatively short and grammatically uncomplicated, it contains some interesting cultural values that are perhaps unusual for a non-Japanese reader and therefore need explanation. For example, the blood type of the player appears to be a salient attribute, as does the fact that the young man likes shopping as a hobby. The Japanese interest in blood type is a similar cultural phenomenon to that of star signs in western contemporary culture. In the same way that one's star sign may suggest certain personality types, one's blood type may also point to certain personality traits. And in the case of this young man, Ito, his B blood type represents individual strength, a quality that is being selected as salient for someone who is a champion soccer player. Similarly, shopping is construed as prominent, as it is a pastime of the cashed-up shopping youth known as Generation Y, who, whilst they originated in the US (Armour, 2005), are considered part of Japanese culture as well. Thus the young player's interest in shopping is foregrounded and worthy of mention as it identifies him as a member of Generation Y. Yet, another interesting attribute which is selected by the writer to describe *Ito* is his favourite colour. This seems a rather unexpected aspect to be described in relation to a world class soccer player. Again though, this is representative of his generation and it is an attribute which the young audience is keen to know about.

Context of situation

Turning now to the context of situation, the Field of the model text is that of a talented soccer player, *Teruyoshi Ito*, who has been in the Japanese media spotlight since he was 14 years old. The model text gives a brief recount of his soccer career as well as a description of his personal attributes.

The Tenor of the model text is determined by the identity of the target readers and the writer. In this case, the writer is a reporter and the target readers are the magazine audience, specifically airline passengers and in particular, teenagers and Generation Y. This is evidenced by the choice of the sport, soccer. Soccer is perceived as a young person's sport in Japan, in contrast to *sumo* which is a more traditional sport. Further, the article focuses on a handsome, young, single, attractive soccer player, rather than focusing on the sport of soccer itself.

The Mode of the text, while it is in written form, has an informal and conversational style. This is achieved through particular language choices, which are discussed below. Even though the writer is socially distant from the readership, it is clear that the writer uses casual and informal language in an attempt to connect to the reader.

The biographical recount genre

In terms of text type or genre, this text functions to introduce a 'star' soccer player to a young audience, in order to pass the time while they are in the aircraft. The title of the article uses the word, *zukan* (profile) which suggests that the article 'introduces' a significant person. The kind of text that introduces significant people is the biographical recount genre.

> A Biographical Recount is a text that retells the events of a person's life. Often this person will be regarded as having played a significant role in history. The events focused on in a Biographical Recount tend to be the most important ones in the person's life – either those that led up to the events that make the person significant or the significant events themselves...Typically a Biographical Recount also *evaluates* the person, and draws out the historical significance of their life (DSP, 1996:54).

Typically, a Biographical Recount, at least in English, has two obligatory elements and one optional one: the obligatory elements are Background and Record of Events; the optional element is the Evaluation of Person (DSP, 1996: 54). While this chapter is not suggesting that a biographical recount in Japanese necessarily has the same kinds of elements as one in English, research on the genre in English can act as a starting point to think about how a biographical recount might be structured in Japanese. Thus, by way of considering the structure of the genre in Japanese, the following section will describe the genre in English as a starting point before analysing the model text in Japanese.

In English, the Background stage introduces information relating to the 'vital statistics' of the significant person. For example, who they are; where and when they were born; why they are significant etc. This is then typically followed by the Record of Events stage, which records the significant events of the person's life in chronological order. The final element, the Evaluation of

Person stage functions to express the significance of the person's contribution to society. In this element, the writer appraises either the person, their life, their contribution or behaviour etc.

In order to express the meanings of each stage or element, particular language features are selected. In other words, the language features of each stage have a particular configuration which expresses the function of the structural element. For example, in English, the Background element typically uses circumstances of time and place; the Record of Events uses material processes in the past tense with specific, human participants combined with expressions of time, which are typically construed as Theme; and finally the Evaluation of Person is realised by relational processes expressing the attributes of the person and the judgements of the writer (DSP, 1996:64).

Analysing the model text

Taking the above description as our starting point, the model text was thus investigated. The analysis is reproduced in Table 1. However, prior to attending to the text's structure, the overall layout will be briefly examined. The first thing to notice about this is the presence of two illustrations: one is a photograph of *Ito* in action on the soccer field and the other is a flattering caricature of him kicking a soccer ball. The photograph is placed within the title, which immediately aids in the identification of the 'field' of the text, while the caricature is placed towards the end and is surrounded by the latter half of the body of the text. This caricature is very informal, reminiscent even of a cartoon, thereby serving to support the informal, casual tenor of the article. Further, at a glance, the text seems to be divided into three parts: the title (clauses 1–3), a recount of the player's soccer history (clauses 4–6) and a description of the attributes of the player (clauses 7–23).

On closer investigation, the lexico-grammatical features of the text can be organised into two types: those which are evident throughout the text and those which are limited to each of the generic elements. The following description will begin with the 'global' lexicogrammatical features which 'colour' the text as a whole and serve to realise the interpersonal meanings related to the tenor of the article, followed by the lexicogrammatical features specific to each generic element.

Table 1 Text analysis

Stages of the Biography	Text (with numbered clauses) and English translation	Language Features
Title	1. *Shimizu esu-parusu sutaa senshu zukan.* Shimizu S-Pulse Star player profiles	-The 'who', *Shimizu S-Pulse*
	2. ***Ito Teruyoshi*** Ito, Teruyoshi	*Teruyoshi Ito* and his affiliation –
Subtitle	3. *Ito senshu tte donna hito (da)?* What kind of person (is) Ito?	-A rhetorical question which orients the reader.
Record of events Clauses 4, 5 & 6	4. *14-sai de Nihon junia yuusu daihyou ni (natta).* At 14 years of age, (he) became a representative (of a team that participated in) the Japan Junior Youth Soccer Competition.	-Circs. of time as Theme -using elided or partially elided relational and material processes.
	5. *Tookaidai ichiko 2nen no toki, intaahai junyuushou to kokutai* yuushou (shita). (At the) time (when he was in his) 2nd year of Tookaidai High School, (he came) second (in an) inter-high school athletic competition and (he came) first (at the) National Athletics Meet.	-the past tense is elided.
	6. *19-sai de Esu-parusu* kanyuu (shita). At 19 years of age, (he) entered S-Pulse.	-time is expressed by Circumstances
Attributes of the Player (implicit evaluation) via facts about various aspects of *Ito* Clauses 7 to 23	7. *Gorin daihyou no shuryoku toshite<<8>>katsuyaku suru.* As a core player of (Japan's) Olympic team, <<8>> (he) actively participates. 8. << *chuuban no chuushin ni natte* >> (by) becoming a key midfielder.	-*Ito's* characteristics realised by the use of elided relational processes.
	9. *Koogekiteki MF* da. (He) is an attack midfield player.	-the present tense is elided.
	10. *1974-nen 8-gatsu 31-nichi umare,* (He was) born on 31/8/74 and, 11. *21-sai (da).* (He is) 21 yrs old. 12. *Shinchou 168cm (de),* (He is) 168cm tall (and), 13. *taijuu* 71kg (da). (he is) 71 kgs. 14. *Ketsuekigata wa kosei no tsuyoi* B-gata (da). (His) blood group (is) B-type which shows (his) individual strength. 15. *Ashi no saizu wa* 25.5cm (da). (His) feet (are) 25.5cm.	*-clauses consist of 'new' rhemes.*

Stages of the Biography	Text (with numbered clauses) and English translation	Language Features
	16. *Kiki-te, kiki-ashi tomo migi nan da.* He (is) right handed as well as right footed. *17. 50m soo no taimu ga* 6.5byou (da). (His) 50m sprint time (is) 6.5 seconds. *18. Sakkaa o hajimeta no wa shoogakkoo 1-nen kara (da).* (The) start of his soccer (career) was Year 1 of Primary School. 19. *Riyuu wa 'omoshirosou datta kara' nan da* 20. *tte.* (He) said that the reason was because it looked like fun. 21. *Tabemono no suki-kirai nashi (da).* (He does)n't (have) food likes or dislikes. 22. *Sukina iro wa kuro (da).* (His) favourite colour (is) black. 23. *Kyuujitsu wa shumi de mo aru shoppingu ga ooi.* On (his) days off, (he) does a lot of shopping as a hobby.	

Global lexico-grammatical features

As previously mentioned, the language of the whole article is very casual, informal spoken language. This casual, informal style is achieved through a number of lexico-grammatical features, in particular, (i) the choice of verbal groups expressed in the 'plain' form, (ii) the use of contracted clausal forms typical of speech, (iii) the ellipsis of the specific, human participant, *Ito*, as well as the ellipsis of the tense and redundant components of the verbal group such as the relational copula, *da* and iv) clauses consisting of new (N-)Rhemes only. Each of these features is explained below.

1.Verbal groups expressed in the 'plain' form:

Within the interpersonal grammar of Japanese there is the system of POLITENESS (refer to Teruya (1998) and Fukui in this volume) which requires a choice between formal or informal verb morphology. The formal choice selects the *masu* form of the verb, while the informal choice selects the plain form (the *–u/-ru* form). Most newspaper articles are written in the 'plain' form. Therefore, it is not surprising to find that the *Ito* text also uses the plain form. However, in conversation, plain forms are selected when the social distance between the interlocutors is close, that is to say, when there is a degree of familiarity and/or intimacy. The verbs in the article are **all** expressed in the plain form, evoking a familiar relationship between reader and writer. Clearly though, the writer does not know the readers intimately, and may have selected the plain form purely to comply with the conventions of newspaper articles. Yet, in addition to another feature of spoken language (see point 2 below) the plain form functions together with this second form to set up a friendly, casual prosody throughout the text. This is one of the grammatical resources used by the writer to realise the tenor of the text. Examples of this include the plain form of the copula verb 'to be', *da* (Clause 16) and the plain form of the compound verb 'to participate', *katsuyaku suru* (Clause 7).

2. Contracted clausal forms typical of speech

Another global feature of the text is the use of contracted forms, which again express the spoken-like, casual tenor between writer and readers. For example, in clauses 3 and 13, the constituent, *tte* is a contraction of the expression *to iu* (is called) which is typically used in speech and not in writing. The use of the contracted form construes a very chatty style.

3. Ellipsis of the specific, human participant, of tense and of predictable verbs

In Japanese, ellipsis is used as an implicit device (refer to Hasan (1996) for a description of the full set of implicit devices)which is 'an encoding unit which involves a semantic dependence for its precise interpretation' (Hasan, 1996:196). This means that the interpretation of an implicit device is not available from within the text itself, but requires the reader to retrieve the meaning from elsewhere. There are a number of different kinds of implicit devices, but the kind which interests us here is that of formal exophoric ellipsis. Formal exophoric ellipsis is 'one whose interpretation is predetermined by the language system and permits no true variation in wording' (Hasan, 1996:207). In Japanese, formal exophoric ellipsis of both the participant and the process occur. It occurs when the participant and or the process is interpreted from one's knowledge of the tendency of the language to leave it out (refer to Thomson (2005a) for a description of ellipsis in Japanese). Typically, this kind of ellipsis is prevalent in spoken Japanese, as speech is more ancillary than constitutive (refer to Hasan and Halliday (1985)) and therefore more context dependent. For example, apart from Clause 3 which is part of the title, every clause in the model text is without the specific, human participant, *Ito*. This is despite the fact that the participant in every clause **is** *Ito*. This is an example of formal, exophoric ellipsis.

Similarly, another kind of formal, exophoric ellipsis occurs within the verbal group in Japanese. Either all or part of the Process in the verbal group is elided. This occurs when the process is predictable from the grammar. For example, the Attributive relational clause, 'Carrier *wa* Attribute *da'*, drops the relational process *da* as it is entirely predictable from the interlocutors' knowledge of the pattern of the attributive relational process in Japanese. This characteristic features in the text no less than 10 times, representing 43% of the clauses. A consequence of the formal exophoric ellipsis of the process is that the tense is also elided. Time, particularly past time, is thus realised not through the morphology of the verb but through circumstances of time (Clauses 4, 5 & 6).

4. Presence of n-rheme clauses:

A further consequence of the prevalence of formal exophoric ellipsis is that many of the clauses are left with only explicitly stated new information in the Rhemes. These have been identified and named N-Rhemes (where N refers to New information) by Fries (1993) in English. Similarly, N-Rhemes occur in Japanese. The ellipsis of the participants results in implicit Themes, and the ellipsis of all or part of the process results in Rhemes consisting of New constituents only, that is, of N-Rhemes. The analysis in Table 2 below illustrates the phenomenon. Consequently, the text consists of many N-Rheme clauses (Clauses 4, 11, 12, 13 & 21).

Table 2: An example of an N-Rheme

11	*(Ito wa)*	*21-sai*	*(da)*
	(Ito WA)	21-age	to be-pres
	ellipsis	**N-Rheme**	ellipsis
	Theme	Rheme	
	(He is) 21 years old.		

Lexico-grammatical features specific to each generic element

As suggested earlier, the text appears to have three generic elements. These are the Title (clauses 1–3), a Record of Events of the player's soccer history (clauses 4–6) and a description of the Attributes of the Player (clauses 7–23). This section will describe the lexico-grammatical features of each of these elements, suggesting that these features in fact serve as the evidence for the justification of the delineation of these generic elements.

Title

In the Title element of this article, clauses 1 & 2 are nominal groups. Clause 1 is an expanded noun group with *zukan* (profiles) as Thing, while Clause 2 is a proper noun, the name of the player, written with the surname first. These two clauses are essentially clause constituents rather than complete clauses. Clause 3, however, is a complete clause: an informal question inviting the reader to consider *Ito*, the person. This question sets up an expectation in the reader that the rest of the article will describe the kind of person that *Ito* is. The use of the question in the title is motivated to draw the audience in.

Record of events

The Record of Events element recounts the early soccer experience of the player. These clauses (4–6) are expressed in the past tense and have circumstances of time as Theme. The processes are mostly material, related to *Ito*'s participation in various sports events. Additionally, the global features of participant and process ellipsis are also evident.

Attributes of the player

The Attributes of the Player element begins at Clause 7 when the tense changes from past to present and continues to the end of the text. This section describes the kind of person *Ito* is. However, before his attributes are listed, Clauses 7 and 8 explicitly evaluate *Ito*'s soccer value using the following epithets, *shuryoku* (core) and *chuuban* (key). This positive evaluation sets up a justification for the rest of the description. In other words, because he is a valuable and significant soccer player, the reader will want to know what kind of person he is. The description which follows Clauses 7 and 8 is expressed primarily through the use of attributive relational processes, as in Clauses 9, 11, 12, 13, 14, 15, 16, 17, 21, & 22. Exceptions to this include Clauses 19 and 20, which are a projection by *Ito* himself commenting on his reason for playing soccer. An interesting feature of this section of the article is that there is only a small amount of explicit evaluation. Most of the attributes are factual rather than evaluative, however, it is the choice of facts that is in itself an implicit evaluation of *Ito*'s significance. For example, his height, weight and feet size relate to his soccer skill; and his interests, such as his shopping hobby and his food preferences identify him as a member of Generation Y, thereby enabling the reader to identify with him despite him being a 'famous' person. Though this section does not use overtly evaluative language, it still evaluates the player, his skill and his worth via the strategic choice of 'facts'.

This section has described the features of the model text both in terms of context and lexicogrammatical features. From a teaching perspective, this information can be used to formulate a lesson plan as this text serves as the model of a biographical recount which can be used to teach both reading and writing, and speaking and listening. As our interest is particularly in writing, the following sections will firstly discuss writing pedagogy in second/foreign language learning, focussing particularly on the Genre Approach and then secondly offer a lesson plan based around the *Ito* text to illustrate how the Genre Approach can be used to teach writing in the Japanese as a Foreign language classroom. This is all embedded in a lesson which integrates speaking, listening, reading, interculturality and writing. This section concludes with an example of a student's text written independently at the end of the learning cycle.

Writing pedagogy

Over the last 20–25 years, research on second language writing has been progressing enthusiastically (Polio, 2003). Polio has developed a useful taxonomy of writing research which provides a framework for locating our research. Firstly, the body of research is divided into topics of research: namely, research that focuses on writers' *texts*; writers' *processes*; the *participants* in the learning and teaching process; and the *context* of L2 writing (Polio, 2003:37). Further, the research is divided into five methodological approaches: quantitative studies which are experimental, correlational, causal-comparative; or which survey a group of identified stakeholders, and qualitative studies which describe an L2 writing phenomenon. Our research falls under the topic of the *social context* of L2 writing, in the sense that we are attempting to describe the nature of an authentic text in its native social context, a text that is similar to the texts the learners are expected to write. However, in addition to this, our research is also about the *participant*, specifically the teacher, and their views and approaches to writing. In both topic areas our approach is qualitative, as we have described the model text and will also describe an appropriate writing pedagogy.

What is important to note is that, according to Polio (2003), little research has been done on what actually happens in writing classes, particularly in the context of writing in a foreign language. For example, questions like the kinds of techniques and materials used in the teaching of writing as well the nature of the syllabi have not been addressed (p.59). Further, in the context of writing in a foreign language, Matsuda (2003) points out that there is an increasing number of studies on L2 writing that draw on L1 and ELS composition research from the United States. While this is an innovative response to the need for developing L2 writing pedagogies, Matsuda cautions that this is problematic if L2 pedagogy is 'derived only from one language or one context…..for second language writing instruction to be most effective in various disciplinary and institutional contexts, it needs to reflect the findings of studies conducted in a wide variety of instructional contexts as well as disciplinary perspectives' (2003:28). This papers attempts to redress the dearth of research into L2 writing in a foreign language context and offers itself as one contribution to the field, providing an Australian institutional context from the disciplinary tradition of systemic functional linguistics to the teaching of Japanese as a Foreign Language.

When describing the Genre Approach, it is important to firstly locate it in the overall field of L2 writing research. The Genre Approach is one pedagogical methodology within the larger field a genre theory and research (Johns, 2003). Johns has identified three 'schools': the English for Specific Purposes school, an international movement based around the basic ESP principles of 'needs assessment, situational analysis, and discourse analysis' (p.205); the New Rhetoric school, whose 'values, concepts, arguments, and conclusion stem from rhetorical, social, ideological stances rather than from detailed analyses of language and text organisation' (p.209) and the Sydney School, whose proponents 'envision perpetual interaction between the culture and social context, and the purposes, organisation and language of texts' (p.201). The Sydney School bases their research on the model of language from the tradition of Systemic Functional Linguistics.

The genre approach

The name, the Genre Approach has been given to the theoretical scholarship and practical learning/teaching materials arising from the research conducted by the NSW Board of Education in collaboration with Jim Martin and colleagues during the 1980s and 1990s at the University of Sydney. The research project was based on the notion of genre from Martin's (1999) perspective and was motivated by an interest in developing a model of context that could be used to inform literacy teaching in schools. This led to the 'development of Australia's distinctive genre-based literacy programs in primary and secondary schools' (Martin, 1999:25). In the first instance, the Genre Approach was developed for application in L1 classrooms where a needs-based assessment of disadvantaged school children indicated a need to know and teach the highly valued written genres of school education. The *Write it Right* Project, as it came to be known, produced learning/teaching materials designed to examine the teaching of factual writing in Years 5–6 in primary school and in Years 6–8 in secondary school in the discipline areas of English, History, Geography and Science (DSP, 1991). This was later followed by literacy work on the genres of industry, specifically media, business administration and science (DSP, 1992–1995). This body of work has been labelled the Sydney School (Johns, 2003) by researchers in the field of second language writing and has been described by Johns as the 'most sophisticated and mature genre pedagog[y] (2003:200). She explains:

> Sydney School research and pedagogies have been designed, at least initially, for younger students and for ESL/EFL immigrants whose cultural norms and valued genres are most distant from the norms of the mainstream cultures. These populations benefit from a pedagogical focus that provides explicit instruction in developing 'cultural capital' (2003: 201).

This explicit instruction involves 'a genre-based cycle of teaching and learning' based on the work of Vygotsky (1934/1978). The cycle supports, or 'scaffolds', the learner through an interactive process of analysis, discussion and joint and individual construction texts (Feez, 2002, in Johns, 2003). As a result, students no longer have to guess what is expected of them when they write. The cycle has been especially helpful for disadvantaged students who suffer most when they are expected to write things but are not shown how. The learning/teaching cycle is briefly described below.

Learning cycles

The application of the Genre Approach is exemplified in Hammond *et al.* (1992) and Feez (2002), and is shown as a four stage teaching and learning model. The first stage, *Building the context,* helps learners build knowledge of a specific field. This is a process of understanding the context in which the text is produced. During this stage, students engage in discussion on context of culture and context of situation, often structured in staged activities and guided by the teacher. The second stage, *Modelling and deconstructing the text,* facilitates the learners' examination of the model text. The teacher provides students with a model of the genre under investigation and guides them to explore the social purpose of the text. During this process, they examine the specific elements of structure and the distinctive linguistic features of the genre. In the third stage, *Joint construction of the text,* the learners and the teacher jointly construct a text relevant to the field, tenor and mode of the context, selecting the appropriate lexico-grammatical features in preparation for the independent writing of a text of the genre under study. Both the teacher and the students share their knowledge of the structures and features of the focus genre. In the final stage, *Independent construction of the text,* students construct a text independently and evaluate their work, which helps them understand the social purpose and context of the genre. The processes of drafting, conferencing, editing, and publishing are encouraged by the teacher during this stage.

An adapted genre approach

As previously mentioned, the Genre Approach, while developed originally in an L1 context, has also been used in the ESL/EFL context, particularly in the context of migrant education in Australia. Despite the fact that to our knowledge it has not been used in a Japanese L2 writing context, it is our contention that this approach could be an effective pedagogy. This relates to the fact that the Genre Approach provides both the students and teacher with explicit assistance in learning the sorts of language needed for successful social interaction (Hammond, 2001; Feez, 2002). Our students study in a 'foreign' language context, in other words, they don't have the benefit of immersion in the culture as they would if they were studying Japanese in Japan. Using the Genre Approach mitigates this to a certain degree in the sense that they at least have the opportunity to discuss the social and cultural influences on language and meaning. Students need an L2 context in which to learn a genre, which enables them to understand the social purpose of the genre in its natural context. Halliday, who explicated the connection between social context and meanings, articulates,

> ...language comes to life only when functioning in some environment. We do not experience language in isolation....but always in relation to a scenario, some background of persons and actions and events from which the things which are said derive their meaning. This is referred to as the 'situation', so language is said to function in 'contexts of situation' and any account of language which fails to **build in** [our emphasis] the situation as an essential ingredient is likely to be artificial and unrewarding. (Halliday, 1978:117)

Equally, it could be argued that any pedagogy of language which fails to 'build in' the situation as an essential ingredient is likely to result in the production of unnatural and socially inappropriate language. Building in the situation gives teachers and students clear direction to explore the social and cultural context of a genre, the content of the genre, and the role of the speaker or writer of the genre within the Japanese language speaking community. This pedagogical approach also provides a way for teachers and students to consider the intended audience of the genre and the relationship between participants in the genre within Japanese society.

From our teaching experience, we have found that our students' difficulties lie in the meaning making process rather than in the production of syntactically correct clauses. Developing an understanding of the contextual variables and how this affects the lexicogrammatical choices is the key to the successful exchange of meanings in a particular context of situation. The initial stage of the learning/teaching cycle, *Building the context*, facilitates this understanding.

Feez summarises in the following way:

> Using Halliday's theory, which systematically links context with language use, systemic functional linguists investigate the way language varies from context to context. They are also interested, within that variation, in the relatively stable underlying patterns or 'shapes' that organize texts so they are culturally and socially functional. The exploration and description of these patterns and their relationship to language variation has been the focus of genre theory and the resource which genre pedagogy exploits. (Feez, 2002:53)

Working on examining and identifying different genres in Japanese means that students are investigating many aspects of the meaning making practices of Japanese people, such as what they write about, how they express themselves, how they choose their words, what meanings lie behind the words, and how they think, amongst other things. In the process of this investigation, the students find similarities and differences between their mother tongue and Japanese. While understanding the differences, they learn how to communicate with the Japanese language speaking community in a manner that is accepted by that community. Paltridge (2001) together with such writers as Johns (1997), Swales (1990), Prior (1995), (in Paltridge, 2001:59) argues that there is a need for having students carry out ethnographic investigations of the genres and the contexts in which these genres occurs. It is certainly important that the students investigate how Japanese language constructs Japanese culture and vice a versa. Thus, it is crucial that teachers scaffold (refer to Hammond & Gibbons, 2001 for a description) the students in their investigation of genres, their social purpose and their context.

To conclude, from our point of view, the Genre Approach is an appropriate L2 writing pedagogy and, with some adaptation, can be applied to the L2 writing classes in Japanese. The most significant adaptation, we believe, relates to the language of instruction. In beginners and low intermediate Japanese language classes, the language of instruction is usually a combination of English and Japanese which slowly transitions into Japanese only. Typically, the language of instruction in an L1 context is the L1. As the majority of our students speak English, we would therefore need to introduce Japanese metalanguage in a graded and sequenced manner while at the same time developing students' L2 writing with a view to eventually weaning them off English as the language of instruction. However, despite this, the utility of the Genre Approach should be tested in the

Japanese L2 writing context. The following section will outline a proposal for the adoption of the Genre Approach in a Japanese L2 writing context.

A description of a lesson

The following description applies the learning cycle of the Genre Approach to the *Ito* biographical recount with a view to working towards students writing a similar text using the generic elements and lexicogrammatical features as presented in the model text. This learning cycle helps the teacher and the students set up a contextual framework as well as guiding them to examine the meaning making processes of the biographical recount. This is an actual opportunity to examine the system of culture in Japanese society. Following this learning cycle, we expect that the students will gradually connect more comfortably with the social context of the genre in Japanese.

Using the Genre Approach to teach writing involves immersing the students in a learning context that addresses the macro-skills of speaking, listening, reading writing and interculturality[3], which are all simultaneously immersed in a cultural context. This is illustrated in Figure 1. The outer circle represents the cultural influences on the macroskills, which include both generic and specific skills. The lesson will have specific skills objectives but at the same time, generic skills[4] are integrated and taught. These skills comprise the students' language development, which in turn enables the production of an instance of a genre. Thus the central circle represents the production of an instance of genre, which is the output of their language development.

Figure 1: Modelling the teaching context

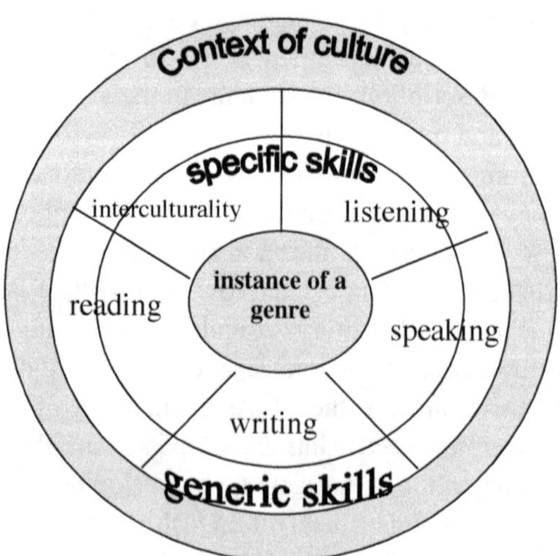

The full set of specific learning objectives of the proposed lesson is outlined in Table 3. Each objective is numbered and referred to in the description of the four stages of the learning cycle in Table 4. Each stage of the learning cycle addresses a number of the learning objectives.

Table 3: Specific learning objectives according to the macroskills.

READING	
1	Recognises that texts are constructed for particular purposes and appeal to certain groups.
2	Evaluates effects of different patterns in written texts.
3	Systematically finds and records information
4	Draws on the knowledge of linguistic structures and features to explain how texts are.
SPEAKING	
5	Identifies the effect of context, audience and purpose
6	Evaluates the effects of different patterns in spoken texts.
7	Discusses and experiments with some linguistic structures and features that enable speakers to influence audiences.
WRITING	
8	Identifies the specific effect of context, audience and purpose on written texts.
9	Draws on planning and review strategies that assist in effectively completing a biographical recount.
10	Uses *Kana* and *Kanji* appropriately for the text.
11	Controls the linguistic structures and features to communicate ideas and information clearly in a report genre.
LISTENING	
12	Listens strategically and systematically records spoken information.
13	Interacts with peers in structured situations, using a variety of text types to discuss familiar or accessible subjects involving challenging ideas and issues.
INTERCULTURALITY	
14	Recognises the interdependence of language and culture manifested in the context of the text.
15	Articulates and resolves the conflicts the student will encounter in trying to reconcile the sometimes opposite values between their native language and culture, and Japanese language and culture by exploring the differences, particularly those identified in the text.
	[adapted from Lo Bianco (2004)].

Rationale

This learning cycle, as illustrated in Table 4, can be implemented in a 2hr class once a week for 7 weeks. The first stage, *Building knowledge of the field* enables students to explore cultural similarities and differences that they are going to be experiencing when reading this particular genre. They examine Japanese society as the background to the text they are going to study.

Table 4: The proposed learning cycle for teaching the writing of the biographical recount in Japanese

Weekly distribution

Wk1: activities 1–7, Wk2: 8–11, Wk3: 12–16, Wk4: 17–20, Wk5: 21–24, Wk6: Start independent construction in class time, Wk7: Complete the text independently in class time.

Theme genre **Biographical recount**	**Model Text: SHIMIZU S-Pulse Star player profile**	
Learning cycle	Objectives **(Ref. Table 3)**	Sequence of the activities
Stage 1 *Building knowledge of the field*	1, 7, 8, 13, 14, 15	1. Group discussion about 'sports magazines' in Japan, Australia and other countries. *Who are the readers of sports magazines?* *What do you expect to know from sports magazines?* *Why do you buy the magazine rather than just reading the newspaper?* *What are the most popular sports in Japan recently?* *And the reason for the popularity is?* The questions are asked in 'simple' Japanese, the students are encouraged to answer in Japanese as much as possible.
	1, 7, 8, 13	2. Class discussion about the above. Analysis and synthesis of the results from each group. This section is also in Japanese. However English is allowed if needed for the discussion.
Stage 2 *Modelling the Ito text*	1, 8, 14	3. Introducing the conventions of the text: Reading the heading, subheading and photograph: Key questions: *What is the text about? Who is the audience for this text? Why do you think so? Why are such texts written?* -Taught in English to ensure understanding-
	3, 12	4. An oral reading of the text by a teacher.
	1, 2, 4, 14, 15	5. Deconstruction of context and text: Key questions: *What are the generic elements of structure?* *What are the major grammatical patterns? Both global and specific.* As a class, students label each generic element with teacher guidance
	1, 2, 3, 4, 14, 15	6. Shared reading by the student in pairs. The students are encouraged to identify new words and structures, predict unknown words by considering the *kanji/kana* used in the text, purpose of the text, register, and structure of the text.

Theme genre **Biographical recount**	**Model Text: SHIMIZU S-Pulse Star player profile**	
		7. Word meaning discovery. As a whole class, students write all unknown words on the board, and sharing their knowledge rather than use the dictionary.
	1, 2, 3,4, 8	8. A similar short article on another member of the *Shimizu* S-Pulse team taken from the same magazine is given to the students to analyse. The students work in pairs to identify the grammatical patterns and generic elements of structure, which are similar to those found in the model text. All the pairs are given the same text.
	1, 2, 4, 8, 14, 15	9. Students draw a diagrammatic representation of the text of a biographical recount about a particular sports player as a group on butcher's paper, which is put on the wall for discussion – metalanguage in English. In the discussion, attention is drawn to the purpose, context, structure, and language features of genre.
	1, 2, 4	10. Teacher models the generic stages and language features of the above text.
	1	11. As the final part of the Modelling, go back to the main text (*Ito* text), and discuss if the text fulfils the social purpose of the text.
Stage 3 *Joint construction/ Preparation for Independent construction*	1, 2, 4, 14, 15	12. Starting the Joint construction. Revision The teacher, together with input from the whole class, draws the generic elements of structure of the biographical recount on the board as a revision. Together they discuss the field information and tenor that the students want to include in the text together with the specific information relevant to each element of structure. A discussion follows on the lexicogrammatical choices needed to construe the specific meanings within each element and the global meanings within the text. *–Prior to the Joint Construction stage, the students are asked to find information about a local soccer club. This information will be written up as a jointly constructed biographical recount on the goalie-* Group project (a group of 3–4 students) - Expected to: jointly construct a written biographical recount on the goalkeeper of a local team in Japanese. Step 1: choose one particular player from the local team, and present the biographical recount of the player of the local team orally to the whole class in Japanese (The class members are to take notes from the speech, and find out which player the group is talking about). (Outlined below in activities no.13 – 20).

		Step 2: write a short reflection on their oral recount in English noting the social purpose, the target audience, the elements of structure and the lexicogrammatical choices of the text in order to compare the differences between spoken and written language. (Outlined below in activities no.21 – 22).
		Step 3: jointly write a biographical recount on the goalie. (Outlined below in activities no.23 and 24.
		13. As a group, discuss contents of the text that they are going to write, and the reasons for that.
	8, 9, 10, 11	14. Information gathering about the team players and note taking. The students are encouraged not to translate from English to Japanese, when gathering the information but to write it down in Japanese, then distribute the information to the group members and organize the information appropriately.
	8, 9, 10, 11	15. The students independently write a draft of their talk about their assigned player.
	1, 2, 3, 4, 8, 9, 10, 11, 14, 15	16. Conferencing among the group members, and then, with the teacher
	8,9,10,11	17. Editing according to the conferencing.
	8,9,10,11	18. Re-draft the text. Attention should be paid to *kanji/kana* use, use of punctuation marks, and grammatically distinctive feature that the students identified from the model text.
	5, 6, 7	19. The students prepare for oral presentation - write a draft speech text, then conference with the teacher. Finalise the speech text.
	5, 6, 14, 15	20. The class discussion on what might be the differences between oral and written presentation.
	5, 6, 7, 12	21. Oral presentation. The class will take notes in Japanese when their peers present the report, and submit the notes to the teacher. The notes should be corrected by the teacher to check that students are using the target language features.
	5, 6, 7, 8	22. The class discussions on the students' oral presentation. Discuss with some linguistic structures and features that differ from the written text.
		23. Group project presentation. Students repeat the process but this time they draft a written biographical recount on the goalie.
	1, 2, 4, 8, 9, 10, 11, 14, 15	24. Class peer evaluation of the group report. Each text is put up on the walls in the classroom and critiqued by the students and teacher.
Independent construction	1, 2, 3, 4, 8, 9, 10, 11, 15	25. The students produce their own Biographical recount text on any sport player. This done in class with the teacher available over two lessons, however, students can work on it at home between the two lessons.

The questions of 'why', 'what', 'who', 'how' provide the students with a clear framework of the learning context in this stage. This preparation leads the students into reading this genre. As Macken-Horarik explains (2002:24), 'why' points to the purposefulness of genres; 'what' to the 'aboutness' of a text's subject matter, *field*; 'who' to those involved in the act of communication, *tenor*; and 'how' to the means by which the communication is achieved, *mode*. The students are encouraged to investigate the social context of this text in detail. This part of the lesson is crucial in order to better understand the different social context of Japan.

In the second stage, *Modelling the text*, students explore the social purpose of the text. The focus is directed to the linguistic features of the text and its connection to the social context. The development from the first stage to the second stage is important as the students are provided opportunities to link Japanese society and language. In this stage the teacher helps students explore the Japanese social purpose of the text, the characteristic generic elements of structure and the language features, both globally and those specific to each element of structure. In other words, understanding genre explains the reason why the various lexicogrammatical choices are made.

Only after discussion of the genre and social purpose is the model text presented to the students. The oral reading of the text by the teacher is important to ensure practice in listening to natural pronunciation, intonation, and the accent of the language. While the model text is not written to be read, this step in the learning cycle affords an opportunity for the students to listen to native pronunciation and intonation patterns.

Following the model reading, the students are then guided through a deconstruction of the text. The purpose of the deconstruction of the text is to look at the generic elements of structure and grammatical patterns of the text. Both the global and specific language features, as outlined earlier in the chapter, are introduced and explained.

Once the text deconstruction is complete, the students then participate in a shared reading activity. In this activity, the students read the text intensively, and they are encouraged to read without the dictionary. In our experience, if the students use the dictionary habitually, they do not learn to look at the text as a whole. They become unable to read the text if they do not know every word. They have to learn that the meaning is predictable by looking at the whole text and its context. The teacher encourages the students to be 'meaning' detectives by using all the clues available, including their new understanding of the genre and register together with clues housed in the choices in *hiragana, katakana* and *kanji*.

In the next stage, *Joint construction*, the purpose is for the students to review the special features of the genre that they examined in the first and second stages, and to try and see if they can apply their new knowledge of the genre. A jointly constructed biographical report of the goalkeeper of a local soccer team is to be written as group work. The students revise what they have been discussing by drawing a diagrammatical representation of the genre, clarifying the social purpose, the elements of structure, and the register of the report genre.

The purpose of the written reflection is to ensure their understanding of the particular stages and features of the text.

In the final stage, *Independent construction*, the students write a one page long biographical recount independently on their favourite sports player. In this phase, the students are involved in the activities of information gathering, draft writing, conferencing with peers and the teacher, editing and re-drafting, and publishing. The text is submitted and marked by the teacher.

An example of a student text is reproduced in Picture 2. This text is about the English soccer team during the World Cup in 1998. Thus, the *field* is the English national soccer team: the team members, their uniforms, their past results and their expectations. The *tenor* is similar to the model text in that the global lexico-grammatical features of i) verbal groups expressed in the plain form, and ii) ellipsis of human participants, tense and redundant verbs are evident. The *mode* is of course written, but unlike the model text, it is presented as a poster for public discussion and display in class.

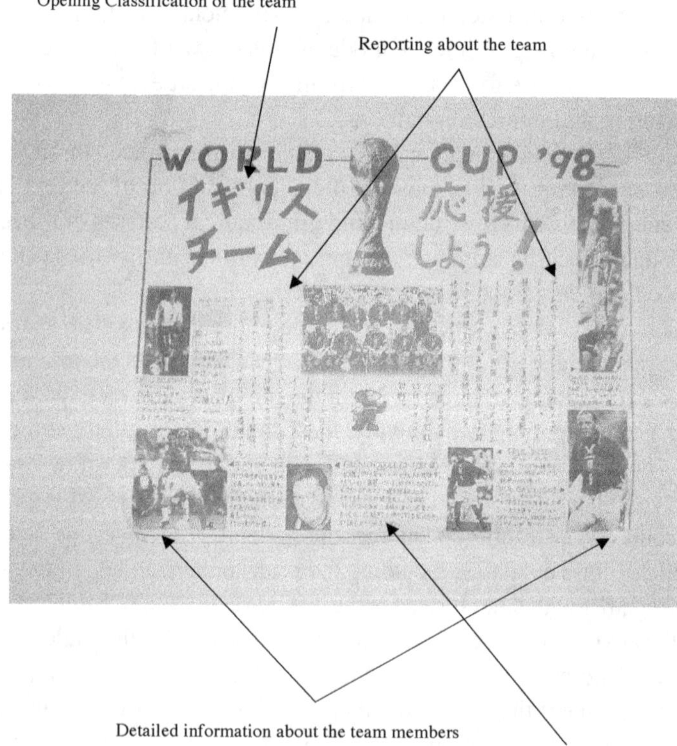

Picture 2: student writing sample

Generally, the student text follows the model text in terms of stages and language features. An extract of the student text is reproduced in Table 5. The extract includes all the stages of the model, although not in the same order. The first stage is the Title stage, telling the reader that the text is about the World Cup, specifically the team from England. This is followed by the Attribute stage, which describes the characteristics of the team. However, this is in contrast with the model, which places the Record of Events before the Attribute stage. The student text includes a recount of the team's past World Cup achievements and their position in the current competition. In addition, the student text includes further descriptions of the team members, using additional Attribute stages. These Attribute stages are presented as secondary information in terms of the layout of the text, in the sense that the team biographical recount is bordered by the descriptions of the team players.

Table 5: extract from student text

		elided
Record of Events	*6. waarudo koppu de 1966nen, chanpion (datta).* At 1966 World Cup, (they were) the champions. *7. 1990 nen, 4-banme (datta).* In 1990, (they were) 4th. *8. kotoshi, igirisu-chiimu FIFAchii ga 5-ban.* This year, the English team (was) 5th in the FIFA grade. *9. shikaku kekka wa igirisu tai marudoba yuushoo(shita).* The result of the heat, England won against Maldives. *10. tai joojia, yuushoo (shita).* Against the Georgian team, (they) won. *11. tai itaria, dooten (shita).* Against Italy, (they) tied. *12. odorokubeki nyuusu wa Pooru Gasugoin ga shooryaku (shita).* Surprising news was that Paul Gascoigne was omitted from the team.	-Past tense elided -human participant elided -time is expressed as circumstances and selected as Theme -using elided relational and material processes.

The choice of language features in the extract is in accordance with the model. In the Record of Events stage, the past tense, human participants, relational and material processes are elided. Time is expressed as circumstances and foregrounded in the clause as Theme. However, unlike the model, the student chose to include some evaluation in this stage in the use of the term *odorokubeki nyuusu wa* (surprising news). Explicit evaluation such as this was used in the Attributes stage of the model text, rather than in the Record of Events stage. Within the Attributes stages, the student appropriately uses existential and relational processes, most of which are elided as is the present tense. Further, the 'attributes' are typically factual in nature. In short, the student has successfully appropriated the features of the model text in their own original piece of writing.

Conclusion

This chapter set out to argue the case for the adoption of the Genre Approach in the teaching of writing in the Japanese as a Foreign Language classroom. In brief, it described the features of a model text from the genre of biographical recount, analysing the context of culture, the context of situation, the social purpose, the generic elements of structure and the requisite global language features and specific features of each generic element within the text. These features were then incorporated into a sample lesson plan demonstrating how the Genre Approach could be applied to the JFL context. The approach introduces students to the art of writing using a four stage learning cycle, beginning with the stage, *Building knowledge of the field* in which the social purpose and cultural context is introduced and explored. This is followed by the *Modelling the text* stage in which the lexico-grammatical features are taught, embedded within the context of culture and situation. The final two stages, *Joint construction* and *Independent construction,* concentrate on the process of writing firstly in a group format and finally as independent writers. Throughout the stages of the lesson, specific learning objectives are addressed which are designed to build towards independent writing. During all stages, the language of instruction is both English and Japanese.

As we see it, the Genre Approach offers three advantages, in the teaching of L2 writing. Firstly, the approach scaffolds the students, step by step, through the process of learning 'writing' as a cultural practice. This process of language development includes the development of intercultural knowledge, speaking, listening and reading, which culminates in the valued practice of writing socially motivated texts.

Secondly, the Genre Approach moves the learner beyond superficial, clause level, 'textbook' formulations of Japanese (see Armour and Furuya in this volume) to the more realistic activity of expressing one's experiences, thoughts, and ideas in the form of a coherent whole text. And finally, by using this method, preoccupation with grammatical correctness on the part of the teacher is removed. The production of an independent piece of writing is not about the production of perfect clauses. Rather, it is about the student needing to communicate and knowing which lexicogrammatical resources to select in what social context to achieve successful communication. This is achievable even with lexico-grammatical infelicities. Essentially, the Genre Approach constructs the students as writing apprentices in an ongoing process of language development, motivated by specific communication needs. This apprenticeship is clearly demonstrated by the student extract. While it is not a perfect, mistake-free piece of writing, it does however, achieve the social purpose of 'evaluating and drawing out the historical significance' of the subject, in this case, the

English World Cup team. Importantly, it conforms to the genre and uses the appropriate lexicogrammar of the genre to realise the expected meanings.

Notes

1 Refer to Hasan and Halliday (1985) for a description of bi-directionality, that is, 'the notions of text and context are inseparable; text is language operative in a context of situation and contexts are ultimately construed by the range of texts produced within a community' (Halliday and Hasan, 1985:117).

2 This term has been borrowed from Chris Cléirigh who, modestly, is not prepared to claim it as his own, but who, nonetheless, is not able to say who coined it first. Thus, in the absence of information to the contrary, the term, 'population of texts' is attributed to Cléirigh (2001).

3 Interculturality was initially described by Claire Kramsch (1993) in foreign language education. Traditional thought in foreign language education has limited the teaching of culture to the transmission of information about the people of the target country, and about their general attitudes and world views. However, understanding a foreign culture requires understanding the 'target' culture in relation to one's own. Thus, an intercultural approach to the teaching of culture is radically different from a transfer of information between cultures. It includes a reflection both on the target and on the native culture. Interculturality is a created sphere to understand the other culture in relation to one's own. Crozet, Liddicoat and Lo Bianco (1999:13) refer to this as *'a meeting place'*, where an understanding of how different worldviews operate frees the mind to explore and at the same time to create interculturality. It is the 'meeting place' where unity and diversity can be reconciled.

4 Some examples of generic skills for listening and reading (receptive skills) recognize the context of a conversation, and the roles and relationships of the participants; discern the attitude of the writer or speaker. Generic skills for speaking and writing (productive skills) include: react appropriately to an interlocutor's talk, thus creating coherent discourse; recognise and use an appropriate register in a particular context.

References

Association for Overseas Technical Scholarship (AOTS) (1993) Shin Nihongo no Kiso, 3A Corporation, Tokyo.

Armour, S. (2005) Generation Y: They've arrived at work with a new attitude, *USA Today* 6th November, 2005, viewed July 6, 2006, http://www.usatoday.com/money/workplace/2005–11–06-gen-y_x.htm).

Armour, W. and Furuya, R. (in this volume) 'Learning how to mean in Japanese as an additional language'. In Thomson, E. and Armour, W. (eds) *Systemic functional perspectives of Japanese: descriptions and applications,* Equinox Publishing, London.

Banno, E., Ikeda,Y., Ohno,Y, Sakane,Y, et al. (2011) *Genki: An Integrated course in Elementary Japanese I[Second Edition]*, The Japan Times, Tokyo.
Cléirigh, C. (2001) personal communication, 23 March.
Cole, M. (ed.) (1978) *Mind in society: the development of higher psychological processes / L.S. Vygotsky*. Harvard University Press, Cambridge (Mass.)
Crozer, C., Liddicoat, J.A. and Lo Bianco, J. (1999) Intercultural Competence: From Language Policy to Language Education. In Crozer, C., Liddicoat, J.A. and Lo Bianco, J. (eds) *Striving for the third place, Intercultural Competence through language Education*, Language Australia, Melbourne, (pp1–20)
Feez, S. (2002) Heritage and Innovation in Second Language Education. In A. Johns (ed.) *Genre in the Classroom*. NJ: Lawrence Erlbaum Associates.
Fries, P. H (1993) 'Information Flow in written advertising'. In J. E. Alatis (ed.) *Georgetown University Round Table on Languages and Linguistics 1992*. Washington D.C.: Georgetown University Press.
Fukui, N. (this volume) 'A Description of Mood in Japanese'. In E. Thomson and W. Armour (eds) *Systemic Functional Perspectives of Japanese: descriptions and applications*. London: Equinox Publishing.
Gregory, M. and Carrol, C. (1978) *Language and Situation: language varieties and their social context*. London: Edward Arnold Publishing.
Gregory, M. (1967) 'Aspects of varieties differentiation'. *Journal of Linguistics* 3: 177–198.
Hagiwara, K.,(2008) *Itsukadokokade*, 3A Corporation, Tokyo.
Halliday, M. A. K. and Hasan, R. (1985) Language, context and text: Aspects of language in a social-semiotic perspective. Victoria: Deakin University Press.
Halliday, M. A. K. (1978) *Language as Social Semiotic*. London: Edward Arnold.
Halliday, M. A. K. (1991) 'The Notion of Context in Language Education'. In T. Le (ed) *Language Education: interaction and development* 1–26. Launceston: University of Tasmania.
Hammond, J. and Gibbons, P. (2001) What is Scaffolding? In J. Hammond (ed.) *Scaffolding*. Newtown: Primary English Teaching Association.
Hammond, J. (1992) *English for Social Purposes*. Sydney: National Centre for English Language Teaching and Research, Macquarie University.
Hasan, R. (1996) 'Ways of Saying, Ways of Meaning'. In C. Cloran, D. Butt and G. Williams (eds) *Ways of Saying, Ways of Meaning: selected papers of Ruqaiya Hasan*. London: Cassell.
Johns, AM (2003) Genre and ESL/EFL composition instruction. In B. Kroll (ed.) *Exploring the Dynamics of Second Language Writing*. Cambridge: Cambridge University Press.
Kano, C. [et al.] (2010) *Basic kanji book: kihon kanji 500(revised edition)*. Bonjinsha, Tokyo.
Kramsch, C. (1993) *Context and Culture in Language Teaching*. Oxford: Oxford University Press.
Lo Bianco, J. (2004) *Resources for Cultural Language Learning*. Melbourne: CAE Press, Language Australia.

Macken-Horarik, M. (2001) "Something to Soot For': A Systemic Functional Approach to Teaching Genre in Secondary School Science'. In A. Johns (ed.) *Genre in the Classroom*. NJ: Lawrence Erlbaum Associates, Inc.

Makino, S., Hatasa, Y. and Hatasa, K. (1998) *Nakama 1*. Boston: Houghton Mifflin Company.

Martin, J. (1984) Types of Writing in Infants and Primary School in *Working with Genre*. Papers from the LERN Conference, UTS, Sydney, Nov. 1989.

Martin, J. R. (2002) 'A Universe of Meaning – How Many Practices?' In A. Johns (ed.) *Genre in the Classroom*. NJ: Lawrence Erlbaum Associates, Inc.

Martin, J. R. (1986) Grammaticalising ecology: the politics of baby seals and kangaroos. *Language, Semiotics, Ideology*. Sydney: Sydney Association for Studies in Society and Culture.

Martin, J. R. (1999) Modelling context: the crooked pather of progress in contextual linguistics (Sydney SFL). In M. Ghadessy (ed.) *Text and Context in Functional Linguistics* 25–61. Amsterdam: John Benjamins Publishing Company.

Matsuda, P. K. (2003) Second language writing in the twentieth century: A situated historical perspective. In B. Kroll (ed.) *Exploring the Dynamics of Second Language Writing*. Cambridge: Cambridge University Press.

Matthiessen, C., Slade, D. and Macken, M. (1993) Language in Context: A New Model for Evaluating Student Writing. In *Genre Approaches to Literacy*. proceedings of LERN Conference.

Metropolitan East Disadvantaged Schools' Program [DSP] (1991) *The Report Genre*. Sydney: NSW Department of School Education.

Metropolitan East Disadvantaged Schools' Program [DSP] (1992–1995) *Literacy in Industry Research Project Write-it-Right Project*. Sydney: NSW Department of School Education.

Metropolitan East Disadvantaged Schools Program [DSP] (1996) *Exploring literacy in school history*. NSW Department of School Education, Sydney

Nesbitt, C. and Plum, G. (1988) Probabilities in a systemic-functional grammar: the clause complex in English. In R. Fawcett and D. Young (eds) *New Developments in Systemic Linguistics*. London: Pinter Publishers.

Paltridge, B. (2001) *Genre and the Language Learning Classroom*. Michigan: The University of Michigan Press.

Polio, C. (2003) Research on second language writing: An overview of what we investigate and how. In B. Kroll (ed.) *Exploring the Dynamics of Second Language Writing*. Cambridge: Cambridge University Press.

Suzuki, R., Hajikao, A. and Kataoka, S. (1999) *Business Kanji*. North Clarendon: Charles E. Tuttle Company.

Tohsaku, Y. (2005) *Yookoso! An invitation to contemporary Japanese* 3rd ed., New York: McGraw Hill.

Teruya. K. (1998) *An Exploration into the World of Experience: a systemic-functional interpretation of the grammar of Japanese*. Sydney: Macquarie University.

Thomson, E. (2005a) Theme unit analysis: A systemic functional treatment of textual meanings in Japanese. *Functions of Language* 12(2): 151–179.

Thomson, E. (2005b) Informing curriculum design using genre analysis: A study of three genres in Japanese. In B. Bourke (ed.) *Innovative Practice in Japanese Language Education* 17–41. Queensland: Queensland University of Technology Press.

9 A computational model of language in context and its application to the understanding of Japanese text

Noriko Ito and Toru Sugimoto
Doshisha University, Japan
Shibaura Institute of Technology, Japan

This chapter describes the development of a computational model for a language system, in this case, Japanese which includes context as well as an algorithm for text understanding. This algorithm is based on the WAG systemic parser (O'Donnell, 1994), but is significantly extended to incorporate the results of an existing (non-systemic) parser and machine readable dictionary. This paper is concerned with computational methods for constructing a linguistic database, based on both the Systemic Functional model of language and an algorithm for Japanese text understanding based on the database. By way of explaining the lexicogrammatical and semantic dimensions, the results of analyses of sample texts and relevant system networks in the Wording Base and the Meaning Base are shown.

Introduction

The purpose of this chapter is to describe the development of a computational model of a Japanese language system which includes context based on the theoretical model of Systemic Functional Linguistics (henceforth, SFL) and its application to the understanding of Japanese text. This research is a core part of the Everyday Language Computing (ELC) Project, a project which was headed by Michio Sugeno, at the RIKEN Brain Science Institute, which aimed to provide computers with language abilities to allow all types of computing operations to be performed through everyday language, thus closing the digital divide[1] (Sugeno, 2002). To achieve this goal, the project aimed to realise a language-based computing environment which enables us to manage and execute all kinds of computing by using everyday language (Sugeno & Kobayashi, 2003). For demonstration purposes, the project has developed applications, which are driven by language, such as a language-based word processor (Iwazume, Kobayashi & Sugeno, 2004), a language-based programming system (Sugimoto, Ito, Iwashita & Sugeno, 2004), and a smart help system (Iwashita, Ito, Kobayashi, Sugimoto & Sugeno, 2004). They have a common interface, which is a speech recognition system named Julius (Lee, Kawahara & Shikano, 1992), and an animated secretary agent. Julius's language model is customised to suit our situation types.

Each application can analyse a user's inputted request through a program which includes a text understanding algorithm and which performs some operations as a result of the understanding. Table 1 shows a scenario between the secretary agent and the user, where the language-based word processor understands what the user says and manipulates an existing word processor to help the user create an invitation letter to a Christmas party.

	Speaker	Utterance
1	Secretary	*Konnichiwa. Hisho no Pinoko desu. Nani wo shi-mashoo ka?* hello secretary NO Pinoko COP=FOR what O do-FOR=CIT Q (Hello, I am the Client secretary, Pinoko. Can I help you?)
2	User	*Kurisumasu-kai no shootai-joo wo kaki-tai.* christmas-party NO invitation-card O write-OPT=INF (I want to create an invitation to a Christmas party.)
3	Secretary	*Shootai-joo no tenpureeto wo hiraki-masu.* invitation-card NO template O open-FOR (I will open the template for invitation cards.)
4	Secretary	*Hiraki-mashi-ta.* open-FOR-PST (I have opened the template.)
5	Secretary	*Shootai-joo no taitoru wa nan desu ka?* invitation-card NO title WA what COP=FOR Q (What is the title of the invitation card?)
6	User	*Taitoru wa "kurisumasu-kai no osasoi" de onegaishi-masu.* title WA christmas-party NO invitation DE ask-FOR (The title is "Invitation to Christmas Party.")
7	Secretary	*Taitoru wo nyuuryokushi-mashi-ta.* title O input-FOR-PST (I have entered the title.)
8	User	*Moji wo moosukoshi kyoochooshi-tai.* characters O a-bit-more emphasize-OPT=INF (I want to emphasize the characters of the title a bit more.)
9	Secretary	*Taitoru no moji wo moosukoshi ookikushi-te futoji ni shi-mashoo ka?* title NO character O a-bit-more enlarge-SUSP bold NI make-FOR=CIT Q (Shall I enlarge the characters of the title and change them to bold?)
10	User	*Hai, onegaishi-masu.* yes ask-FOR (Yes, please.)
11	Secretary	*Konna moji wa ikaga desu ka?* this character WA how-about COP=FOR Q (How about this?)
12	User	*Ii desu ne.* nice COP=FOR N (Looks nice.)
13	User	*Nichi-ji wa 12 gatsu 24 ka 14 ji desu.* date-time WA 12 month 24 day 14 o'clock COP=FOR (The date and time are Dec. 24th, 16:00.)
14	User	*Basho wa Hirosawa kurabu desu.* place WA Hirosawa Club COP=FOR (The place is Club *Hirosawa*.)
15	User	*Koko ni kurusumasu no e wo ire-tai.* here NI christmas NO picture O insert-OPT=INF (I want to insert a Christmas picture here.)
16	Secretary	*Kore wa ikaga desu ka?* this WA how-about COP=FOR Q (How about this?)

The research questions out of which the system was developed were as follows:

1. How can context and its influences on language use be modeled? and
2. How can these influences be represented systematically in a computational form?

To answer these two questions, SFL was employed, as it provides the most powerful framework among the existing theories of language for incorporating context into a model of language. Its strength lies in the fact that it describes language comprehensively in terms of function rather than form, whereby the functions are organised into three kinds: ideational (reflecting the world of experience), interpersonal (enacting our social relationships) and textual (enabling coherence across combinations of meaning). These meanings are embedded in a context and are realised by wordings, that is, lexicogrammar. Consequently, the model has three strata: context, semantics and lexicogrammar. Further, SFL provides a unified way of modeling language use in context by means of system networks with realisation statements. These networks are the sets of choices available in the meaning making process whereby each choice in terms of function is realised by a particular grammatical form. The stratal organisation and systemic sets of choices of the SF model lend themselves to computational application and have thus been applied in the modeling of a language-based computer system in the ELC project.

Adopting SFL as the theoretical basis, a computational model of language in context was constructed called the Semiotic Base, a database consisting of four strata: context, semantics, lexicogrammar, and graphology.[2] Along with the Semiotic Base, computational algorithms for text understanding and generation were developed. Part of this process included the design of the following data structures: *the Context Base, the Meaning Base, the Wording Base, the Expression Base, the General Dictionary, the Situation-Specific Dictionary*, and *the Concept Repository*, and compilation of the entries in these databases with appropriate values providing details sufficient for text understanding and generation in the scenarios that we assume.[3]

This chapter will firstly describe the structure of the Semiotic Base and the linguistic resources stored in it, referring to the perspectives proposed in SFL that have been incorporated into the design of the resource. The chapter will secondly depict the text understanding algorithm using the Semiotic Base and the outputs of the process. The final section of this chapter will explore the distinctive features of the model, comparing it with previous SFL based text understanding systems.

Linguistic resource: the semiotic base

The Semiotic Base is a computational linguistic database based on SFL. The main components of the Semiotic Base are the Context Base, the Meaning Base, the Wording Base and the Expression Base. Each base describes the contextual or linguistic features that characterise the relevant part of the system of language, as well as the relations among the features within the base and their relations with other bases. Table 2 summarizes the structure of the Semiotic Base.[4]

Table 2: Structure of the Semiotic Base

<table>
<tr><td rowspan="5">Main components</td><td rowspan="2">Context Base</td><td>FIELD, TENOR and MODE system networks</td></tr>
<tr><td>Stage Base</td></tr>
<tr><td colspan="2">Meaning Base (MB)</td></tr>
<tr><td colspan="2">Wording Base (WB)</td></tr>
<tr><td colspan="2">Expression Base (EB)</td></tr>
<tr><td rowspan="4">Subsidiary components</td><td rowspan="3">Machine readable dictionary</td><td>General Dictionary (GD)</td></tr>
<tr><td>Situation-Specific Dictionary</td></tr>
<tr><td>Concept Repository (CR)</td></tr>
<tr><td colspan="2">Corpus Base (texts with annotations)</td></tr>
</table>

The Context Base stores those features that characterise the situation of a dialogue, namely the system networks of FIELD ('what is happening'), TENOR ('who is taking part') and MODE ('what part the language is playing') (Halliday & Hasan, 1989). In addition, the Context Base contains the Stage Base. The Stage Base stores generic structure potentials, which encode models of dialogue structures. A dialogue structure consists of stages, which specify a linguistic action, a material action or another stage.

The Meaning Base accommodates both those features which describe meanings relative to a situation type, as well as the constraints on lexicogrammar such as which lexicogrammatical features are available for realising particular meaning features in a situation type. Within the Meaning Base, the model of ideational semantics is based on the Ideation Base (Halliday & Matthiessen, 1999), while the model of interpersonal semantics is based on SPEECH FUNCTION (Matthiessen, 1995), and the model of textual semantics, on Rhetorical Structure Theory (Mann & Thompson, 1988), appropriately adjusted to a model of Japanese lexicogrammar.

The Wording Base accommodates features that describe texts in terms of Japanese lexicogrammar and the constraints in relation to which graphological features are available for realising particular lexicogrammatical features in a situation type. Within the Wording Base, Teruya's (2004) description of Japanese grammar at clause and group ranks is used, while the grammar at word and morphological ranks is based on the well-known Japanese morphological and dependency structure parsers, *ChaSen* and *CaboCha* (Matsumoto, Kitauchi, Yamashita & Hirano, 1999; Kudo & Matsumoto, 2002). For processing convenience, the system networks of WORD CLASS are constructed, based on the part of speech classification assumed in *ChaSen,* and the definitions of group, phrase, and clause based on *bunsetsu* (that is, group or phrase) segment boundary recognised by *CaboCha.*

The Expression Base is currently designed to deal with written texts. It accommodates graphological features associated with punctuation and the rules to lay out a word list using a conventional publication language, for example, HTML.

In the Semiotic Base, contextual, semantic, lexicogrammatical and graphological features and the constraints in relation to how to relate them are expressed as system networks and realisation statements, respectively. Figure 1 shows part of the lexicogrammatical **system network** and its associated **realisation statements** in the Wording Base.

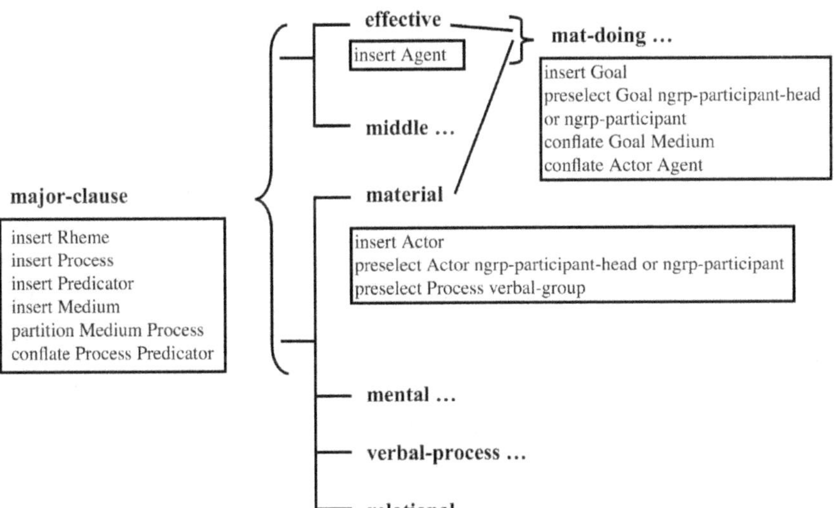

Figure 1: A part of lexicogrammatical system network and associated realisation statements

A system network is a directed graph that consists of sub-systems whose specifications are represented by contextual or linguistic features. In each system, only one feature can be selected. The selected feature may be an entry condition for other systems. In Figure 1, 'major-clause' is the entry condition for two systems. If this feature is selected, either 'effective' or 'middle' must be chosen for the first system and either 'material', 'mental', 'verbal' or 'relational' must be selected for the second. If 'effective' and 'material' are selected, 'mat-doing' is selected. More than one feature can be assigned to a given text segment.

Some features are associated with realisation statements that specify the effects of a feature selection on the resulting structure, on the choice of features in other units in the structure and on the relation between the units generated within and across the strata and the ranks. For instance, 'insert Agent,' which is associated with the feature 'effective,' indicates that a unit containing 'effective' should have a child unit whose role is 'Agent.'[5] The 'Preselect Process verbal-group,' associated with the feature 'material,' requires that if a unit containing 'material' has a child unit whose role is 'Process,' this child unit should contain a feature 'verbal-group' which is located on a system network at a lower rank.

In addition to the main bases, the Semiotic Base accommodates the Corpus Base and a machine-readable dictionary. The Corpus Base stores texts that have been already analysed by means of the resources in the Context Base, the Meaning Base, the Wording Base and the Expression Base. As the corpus grows, it is expected to be populated with texts with the same or similar features to ones to be processed, allowing the text understanding and generation systems to use case-based inference.

Three types of machine-readable dictionaries are provided: a General Dictionary, a Situation-Specific Dictionary and a Concept Repository. The General Dictionary contains standard dictionary information. In addition to information on pronunciation and parts of speech, the appropriate electronic dictionary (EDR) (Japan Electronic Dictionary Research Institute 2003) concept identifier and concept relation label are listed for each lexical item, as well as the SFL-based linguistic features and roles.[6] Table 3 shows an example of the General Dictionary record.

The records in the Situation-Specific Dictionary are sorted according to a situation type, like those in the Concept Repository. The lexicogrammatical and semantic features and EDR concept identifiers are limited to those which are appropriate when a head word is used in a given situation type. In processing, the General Dictionary is used when a situation of an inputted text has not been identified or is not found in the Context Base. The Situation-Specific Dictionary is used when the situation is successfully identified.

Table 3: Example of General Dictionary record

Headword		*writing*
Kana		kaku
EDR Part of Speech		verb
EDR Concept Identifier		0fe07c
MB Features		fg-creative
WB Features		creative&lg-concrete or creative&lg-abstract
SFL Roles for Headword		Event
	EDR Concept Relation Label	*SFL Roles*
1	agent	Actor&Agent
2	object	Goal&Medium
3	instrument	Means

In the Concept Repository, concepts are listed in the form of frame representation, associated systemic features and roles, along with the EDR concept identifiers. Table 4 shows an example of a Concept Repository record.

Table 4: Example of Concept Repository record

Head Concept Name		*writing*	
Concept Type		class	
EDR Concept Identifier		0fe07c	
MB Features		fg-creative	
WB Features		creative	
Upper Concept Name		domain-action	
	Slot Name	*Slot Value Type*	*SFL Role*
1	agent	agent	Actor
2	object	document	Goal
3	instrument	word-processor	Means

The records in the Concept Repository are sorted according to a situation type to which a given concept is relevant. In this sense, the Concept Repository is different from the EDR concept dictionary, which is designed to encode a general taxonomy.

A computational model of language in context based on SFL

The Semiotic Base is characterised as 'a computational language model based on SFL.' This means that in the design of the Semiotic Base the dimensions in language and their ordering principles suggested in Halliday & Matthiessen (2004:20) are adhered to. These are summarised in Table 5.

Table 5: The dimensions (forms of order) in language and their ordering principles (cf. Table 1(3), Halliday & Matthiessen, 2004:20)

	Dimension	*Principle*	*Orders*
1	structure (syntagmatic order)	rank	clause – group or phrase – word – morpheme [lexicogrammar]
2	system (paradigmatic order)	delicacy	grammar – lexis [lexicogrammar]
3	stratification	realisation	semantics – lexicogrammar – phonology – phonetics
4	instantiation	instantiation	potential – subpotential or instance type – instance
5	metafunction	metafunction	ideational [logical – experiential] – interpersonal – textual

In what follows, the discussion will recapitulate the basic architecture of the Semiotic Base with reference to each dimension and principle.

Structure (syntagmatic order)

According to Halliday & Matthiessen (2004:20), structure is 'the compositional aspect of language. ... The ordering principle...is that of **rank**: compositional layers, organised by the relationship 'is a part of'.' It can be assumed such compositional hierarchies exist not only in writing and grammar as shown in Halliday & Matthiessen (2004:20), but also in semantics and context (Table 6).

Table 6: Compositional hierarchies in Japanese (cf. Table 1(4), Halliday & Matthiessen, 2004:20)

	Domain	*Compositional hierarchy*
a	in writing:	text – paragraph – line break unit – sentence – comma unit – letter
b	in grammar:	clause – group or phrase – word –morpheme
c	in semantics [ideational]:	figure – element
d	[interpersonal]:	move
e	[textual]:	rhetorical unit
f	in context [generic structure]:	stage

A given text is represented by a tree whose nodes are called units. A unit consists of a feature selection path. The path of SFL feature selection follows from the root feature of the system network, and a set of (SFL) roles that this unit is considered to play within the parent unit. The Semiotic Base and the text understanding algorithm are designed to construct the units of a text arranged in a rank-scale at each stratum.

System (paradigmatic order)

Following the SFL convention, language and context are represented in the form of **system networks**. The relationship between a system and its subordinate systems are described in terms of **delicacy**: 'the second one is more delicate than the first' or 'A is a kind of B' (Halliday & Matthiessen, 2004:22). Along with the idea of 'lexis as most delicate grammar' suggested by Hasan (1996), the lexicogrammatical system network in the Wording Base starts with grammatical features and ends with lexical features associated with lexical items stored in the General Dictionary.[7] Accordingly, semantics can be divided into two parts, grammatical semantics and lexical semantics. Grammatical semantics is concerned in a congruent manner with those meanings that are realised by grammatical construction while lexical semantics is concerned with those which are realised by lexical items. The semantic system network in the Meaning Base starts with grammatical-semantic features and ends with lexical-semantic features associated with the concepts in the Concept Repository.

Stratification

In SFL theory, a language is regarded as 'a complex semiotic system, having various levels, or **strata**' (Halliday & Matthiessen, 1999:4). There are four levels: context, semantics, lexicogrammar and graphology (or phonology). The main components of the Semiotic Base are drawn from this kind of stratificational organisation of language within context.

'The process of linking one level of organisation with another is called **realisation**,' according to Halliday and Matthiessen (2004:26). More specifically this term refers to the relationship between the strata and the one between the ranks within the same stratum.

These relationships are specified in realisation statements (or realisation rules). In the Meaning Base, there are realisation statements specifying not only associations among semantic features, but also associations between semantic and lexicogrammatical features. Figure 2 shows part of the semantic system network and the associated realisation statements. For instance, 'preselect effective,' which is associated with 'agentive,' indicates that a lexicogrammatical unit corresponding to a semantic unit that contains the semantic feature 'agentive' should have the lexicogrammatical feature 'effective.'

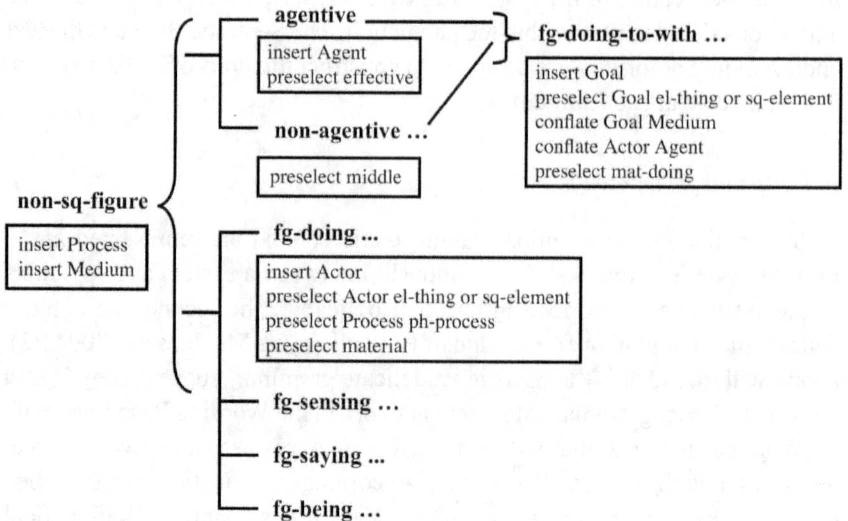

Figure 2: A part of semantic system network and associated realisation statements

Instantiation

There are two perspectives for language: language as system and language as text. The concept of **instantiation** is a dimension and relationship covering these two in such a way that '[t]he system of a language is 'instantiated' in the form of text' (Halliday & Matthiessen, 2004:26). 'The relationship is a cline... between these two poles (that is, potential and instance), there are intermediate patterns… A **register** is a functional variety of language – the patterns of instantiation of the overall system associated with a given type of context (a **situation type**)' (Halliday & Matthiessen, 2004:27).

In this light, the FIELD, TENOR and MODE system networks in the Context Base and the content in the Meaning Base, Wording Base and Expression Base can be considered as potentials located at one end in the cline of instantiation.[8] On the other hand, the content in the Corpus Base is considered to consist of instances, while a sum of those instances that share certain patterns makes up an instance type. The rest of the resources, namely the Stage Base, the Concept Repository and the Situation-Specific Dictionary, are provided with reference to a situation type located in the middle of the cline. Thus, they can be considered as instance types. Table 7 locates the characteristics of the components in the Semiotic Base along the cline of instantiation and across the hierarchy of stratification.

Table 7: The intersection of the cline of instantiation and the hierarchy of stratification

		← *INSTANTIATION*		→
		Potential	*Subpotential/ Instance type*	*Instance*
STRATA ↕	*Context*	FTM system networks	Stage Base	Corpus Base
	Semantics	Meaning Base	Concept Repository	
	Lexicogrammar	Wording Base, General Dictionary	Situation- specific Dictionary	
	Expression	Expression Base	-	

By intersecting the cline of instantiation with the degree of delicacy, the components of the lexicogrammatical and semantic resources can be classified into four as indicated in Table 8.

Table 8: The intersection of the cline of instantiation and the degree of delicacy (cf. Table 0–2 Butt, Halliday, Matthiessen, Teruya & Wu, 2005:114)

		← *INSTANTIATION*		→
		Potential	*Subpotential/ Instance type*	*Instance*
DELICACY ↕	*Less delicate (grammatical)*	Meaning Base, Wording Base	(Concept Repository)	Corpus Base
	More delicate (lexical)	General Dictionary	Concept Repository, Situation-Specific Dictionary	

Most of the constituents in the Meaning Base and the Wording Base represent general (or situation insensitive) models of grammatical (-semantic) systems, while some also involve lexical (-semantic) systems. In this light, the Meaning Base can be considered as an equivalent to the Upper Model in the Penman system (Matthiessen & Bateman, 1991). The General Dictionary is an inventory of general lexical items. The Concept Repository provides an inventory of situation specific meanings. The Situation-Specific Dictionary is an inventory of situation specific lexical items. The texts in the Corpus Base are annotated with both grammatical (-semantic) and lexical (-semantic) features.

Returning to realisation, inter-stratal mapping in the Semiotic Base is represented by realisation statements. This is the case with the relation between the Meaning Base and the Wording Base. In order to represent the link between context and language, register-specific files are provided, each of which is composed of a set of system networks with reference to each situation type. This is instead of using realisation statements in the Context Base, in order to avoid the (logical) complexity of the statements.

This situation type/linguistic register link ensures that all the relevant resources for text understanding and generation are provided in accordance with the situation. It also helps to infer a situation from the linguistic features of a text.

Metafunction

Halliday & Matthiessen (2004:29) define the basic functions of language in relation to our ecological and social environment as 'making sense of our experience' and 'acting out our social relationships,' which they call the **ideational** and **interpersonal** metafunctions, respectively. In addition, there is a third metafunction, the **textual** one, which is concerned with 'organising ideational and interpersonal meaning as discourse' (Halliday & Matthiessen, 1999:8). Table 9 summarizes the major systems stored in the Semiotic Base in terms of metafunction and stratification.

Table 9: Language system in context

		METAFUNCTION		
		Ideational	*Interpersonal*	*Textual*
STRATA	*Context*	Field	Tenor	Mode
	Semantics	Phenomenon	Speech Function	Rhetorical Structure
	Lexicogrammar	Transitivity, Complexing	Mood, Modality	Theme

While it is pointed out that the favoured type of structure may vary for each metafunction, a constituent type modeling of structure (tree structure) is applied to all the metafunctions in this study, as adopted in many SFL based descriptions (see Halliday & Matthiessen, 2004:33, 61).

Size and coverage

The construction of the contents of the Semiotic Base started in 2002. To deal with three sentences (see 2, 8, and 15 in Table 1), we provided 600 systems, 1200 features, 1000 realisation statements, 100 records in the Concept Repository and 40 records in the General Dictionary. With these resources, the text understanding system of the Semiotic Base is able to analyse a material clause simplex with a nominal group that consists of more than one noun combined by particle '*no*' (NO), like '*kurisumasu-kai no shootai-joo wo*' (an invitation to a Christmas party); the ellipsis of the subject '*watashi wa*' (I) as in '*[watashi wa] koko ni kurisumasu no e o ire-tai*' (I want to insert a Christmas picture here); and a non-obligatory unit such as a circumstance '*moosukoshi*' (a bit more) in '*moji o moosukoshi kyoochooshi-tai*' (I want to emphasize the characters a bit more).

The Semiotic Base was extended to 700 systems, 1600 features, 1100 realisation statements, 130 records in the Concept Repository and 70 records in the General Dictionary in order to process three coherent sentences each of which constitute a clause complex (see three sentences shown in Figure 17). The text understanding system can perform rhetorical structure analysis of these sentences. By the end of the project, the Semiotic Base has grown sufficiently to process more than 100 sentences, including relational clauses and rankshifted clauses. Table 10 shows itemised figures of the latest Semiotic Base.

Table 10: Size of the Semiotic Base

	Context Base	*Meaning Base*	*Wording Base*	*Expression Base*	*TOTAL*
System	124	286	481	4	895
Feature	246	708	1144	19	2117
Realisation statement	0	432	899	23	1354

	Concept Repository	*General Dictionary*	*Situation-Specific Dictionary*
Record	401	291	128

Construction of the resources

To construct the resources of the Semiotic Base, we developed computational tools that help perform and record systemic functional analyses in machine-readable forms as demonstrated in Table 11.[9]

Table 11: Developer tools for systemic resource construction

Tool Type	*Tool Name*	*Description*
Converter	cd3 file builder (Java)	We can • convert KPML '.systems' files to Systemic Coder '.cd3' files. • load Systemic Coder '.cd3' files and draw partial system networks from the loaded system networks by specifying (a) feature(s) as a root (starting point) or leaves (end points) of the networks.
Editor	Coding tool (Java)	We can • load Systemic Coder '.cd3' files, and annotate an inputted text by specifying the features and roles associated with a given text segment by referring to the loaded system networks and realisation statements.
Viewer	Annotated text browser (Java)	We can • view an annotated text '.xml' file, which represents the result of the text understanding process.
Viewer	KWIC concordance (Java)	We can • search a corpus (a set of annotated texts) with complex query specified with systemic features and roles as well as part of speech and EDR information • display the context of the keyword • sort the results.

Regarding the systemic potential (that is, system networks and realisation statements), we developed a tool called cd3 File Builder to convert Bateman's (1997) KPML[10] '.systems' files to O'Donnell's (2002) Systemic Coder '.cd3' files, so that the system networks which were originally in different formats can be compared easily. See Figure 3. cd3 files can be loaded and partial system networks can be drawn from the loaded system networks by specifying features as a root (starting point) or leaves (end points) of the networks.

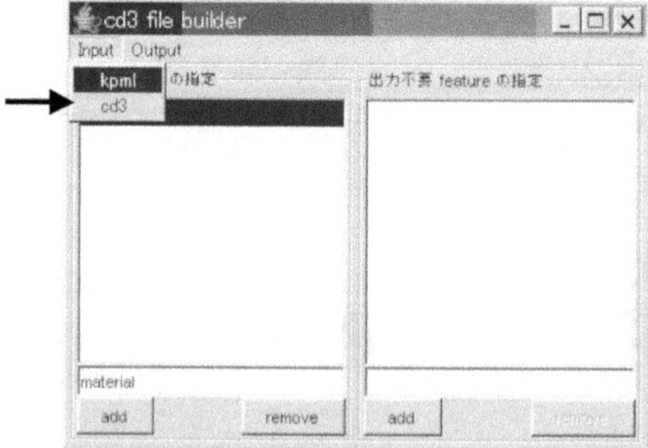

Figure 3: Screenshot of cd3 file builder

For the annotated texts, including the preprocessing and concept analysis results, three tools were developed. To record manual systemic functional analyses in machine-readable forms, we first used O'Donnell's Systemic Coder but found that, while coding an inputted text, it was difficult to recall the constraints (for example, those on role insertion and feature selection) specified in the realisation statements. Consequently, a coding tool that can check consistency of the coding results by referring to the realisation statements contained in the loaded cd3 file was developed. This is illustrated in Figure 4.

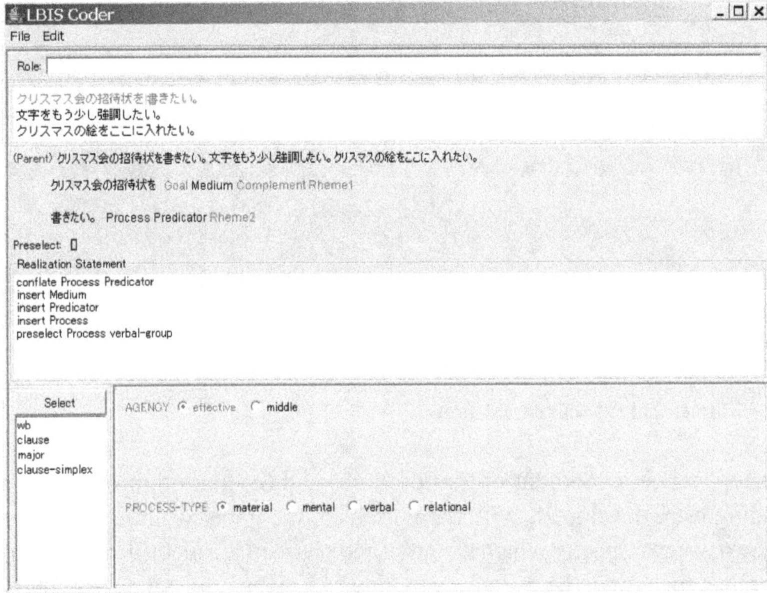

Figure 4: Screenshot of coding tool

To review the results of the text understanding process, we developed a browser and extended it by adding the concordance function. This KWIC[11] Concordancer can process Japanese text, performing searches on a corpus (a set of annotated texts) with complex queries specified with systemic features and roles as well as parts of speech and EDR information, displaying the context of the keyword and sorting the results. Figure 5 shows the result of the search for a key unit that is a group rank unit, which contains the strings '*moji*' ('character') and whose role is Goal or Qualifier.

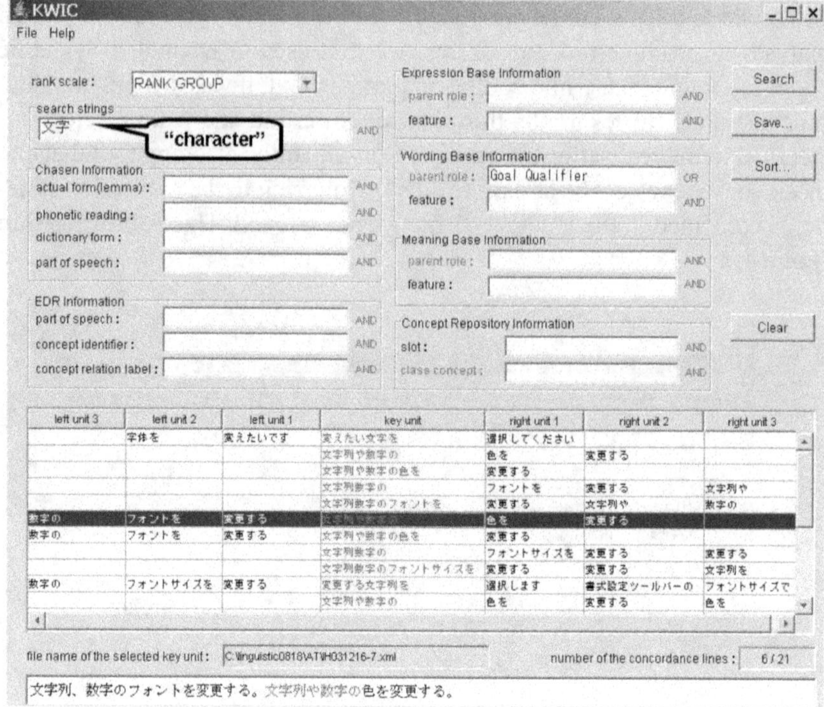

Figure 5: Screenshot of KWIC concordancer

Finally, a test environment of the resources and the algorithm of text understanding were developed. With the buttons in the upper window as shown in Figure 6, we can specify which resource and phase of the algorithm to examine. After the processing, the instance structure of a given unit in the annotated text browser interface mentioned above can be checked.

Linguistic process: text understanding algorithms

The Everyday Language Computing Project has produced a prototype computational system of Japanese text understanding in Java, combining an existing parser and dictionary with the linguistic resources in the Semiotic Base. This prototype can perform preprocessing, graphological analysis, lexicogrammatical analysis, semantic analysis and conceptual analysis. Figure 7 shows the flow of the text understanding.

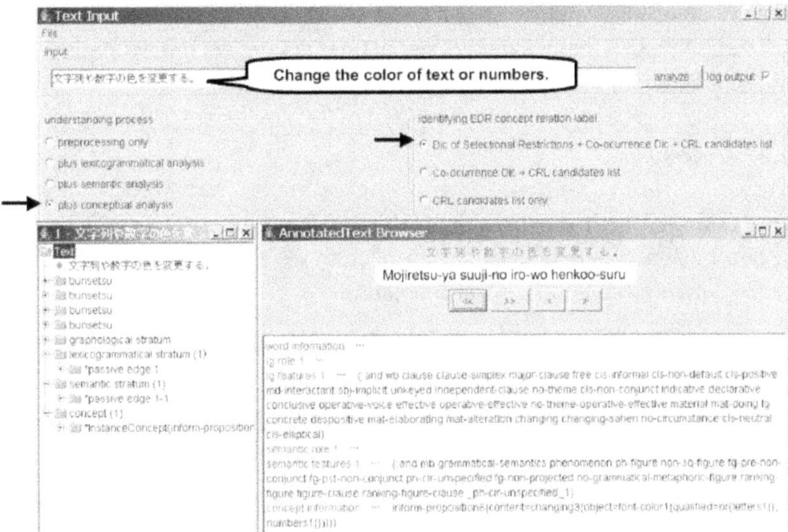

Figure 6: Screenshot of test interface

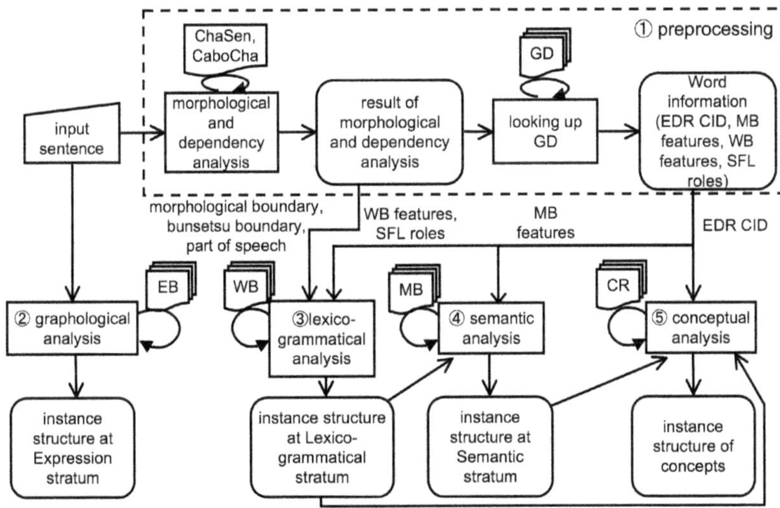

Figure 7: Overview of text understanding process

The purpose of each step is to construct an instance (that is, text) structure associated with SFL features and roles. In this section, we briefly explain each step in this diagram using an example output of the system.

Step 1: Preprocessing

Preprocessing is the first step in the understanding process and starts with the morphological and dependency structure analyses by *ChaSen* and *CaboCha.* Take the Japanese sentence (1) as an example.

(1) *watashi wa kurisumasu-kai no shootai-joo wo kaki-tai.*
I WA Christmas-party NO invitation-card O write-OPT=INF
I want to write an invitation card to a Christmas party.

The results are shown in Table 12.[12]

Table 12: Results of morphological and dependency structure analysis

*Morpheme (Dependency relation in the rows with *)*	*Part of speech*
*0 3D	
watashi	pronoun
wa	thematic particle
*1 2D	
kurisumasu	noun
kai	noun
no	nominalisation particle
*2 3D	
shootai	noun
joo	nominal suffix
wo	case particle
*3 -1O	
kaki	lexical verb
tai	auxiliary verb
.	full stop
EOS	

This table shows what the part of speech is for each morpheme and which segment is dependent on which. For instance, the first segment '*watashi wa*' is dependent on the fourth segment '*kaki-tai*,' and the second segment '*kurisumasu-kai no*' on the third segment '*shootai-joo wo*.' Such a dependency structure which includes parts of speech reveals the group simplex/complex unit boundary and class (for example, nominal group simplex) and whether a verbal group is rankshifted or not (note, it is rankshifted if a verbal group unit is dependent on a nominal group unit).

These results are important but not sufficient to traverse the entire system network. Thus, the system refers to the General Dictionary and enriches the input features in preparation for the SFL-based analyses. After a General Dictionary lookup, EDR concept identifiers are assigned to each word segment and EDR concept relation labels are assigned to each dependency pair of *bunsetsu* segments by looking up the EDR dictionary for selectional restrictions of Japanese verbs, the Japanese co-occurrence dictionary and the concept dictionary. Some word sense ambiguities are also resolved in this phase. For instance, there are four records whose headword is '*kaku*' in the General Dictionary. Each record has a different concept identifier. After looking up the EDR dictionary for the selectional restrictions of the Japanese verbs with reference to the concept identifier given to the verb record, a selectional restriction specification is obtained. By checking the consistency of the selectional restriction with the concept identifiers assigned to each word in the input sentence, the system can reduce the four choices to one. Following this, candidates of the SFL roles of each segment are obtained from the concept relation labels by referring to the mapping table in the General Dictionary record. For instance, by looking up the EDR dictionary for the selectional restrictions of Japanese verbs, the system assigns the EDR concept relation label 'object' to the third segment of this sentence '*shootai-joo wo.*' Then by referring to the General Dictionary record for '*kaku*, ' the system maps 'object' onto the SFL role 'Goal & Medium.'

The results of the preprocessing are summarised in Table 13.

Table 13: Results of the preprocessing

GD headword	*EDR CID*	*MB features*	*WB features*	*SFL roles*
watashi	0e7e95	mb-conscious	-	Actor & Agent
wa	2621d5	-	kakari-wa	
kurisumasukai	3ceda8	macro-thing	ngrp-abstract	-
no	2621d5	sq-el-attribution-qualifier	ngrp-attribution	
shootaijoo	0e3e07	mb-material-object	ngrp-concrete	Goal & Medium
o	2621d5	-	case-o	
kaku	0fe07c	fg-creative	lg-concrete creative	-
tai	2621c8	mb-demanding & ph-modal	aux-tai	

Step 2: Graphological analysis

In the graphological analysis, the graphological instance structure of the inputted text is constructed with reference to the Expression Base. All that the current system does is to recognise sentence boundaries based on punctuation. This process is independent of all the other processes.

Step 3: Lexicogrammatical analysis

In the lexicogrammatical analysis, the lexicogrammatical instance structure of the inputted text is constructed by referring to the Wording Base resources, that is, the system network and the realisation statements. The method is based on O'Donnell's (1994) idea realised in his WAG [13] systemic parser, which uses data structures called partial-structures and a bottom-up chart parsing strategy. The phase can be divided into five phases as indicated in Figure 8.

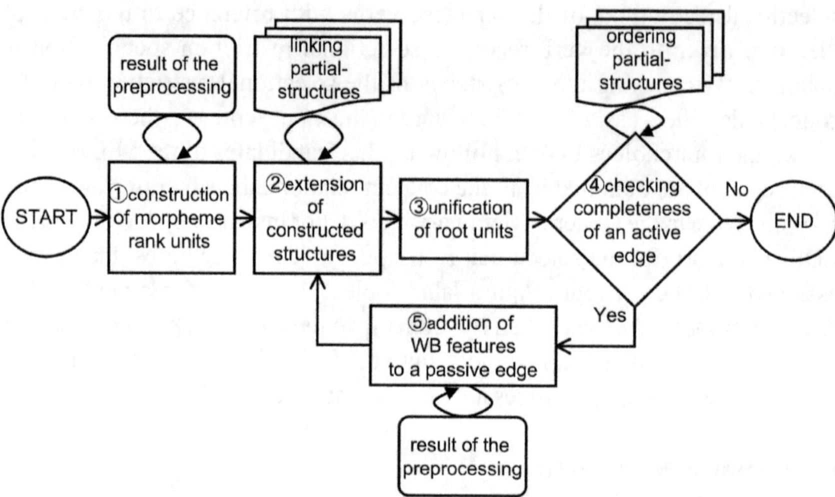

Figure 8: Flow of lexicogrammatical analysis

Each phase is explained in the following subsections, using the Japanese sentence (1), which consists of ten morphemes. Before illustrating the process, the *partial-structures* and a *chart parsing* strategy are explained.

Partial-structures

Partial-structures (O'Donnell, 1994) are data structures that represent linguistic constraints derived from combinations of realisation statements. They are compiled beforehand from realisation statements in the Semiotic Base, and are used in the construction of instance structures in lexicogrammatical and semantic analyses as explained below. Figure 9 represents the partial-structures converted from the realisation statements shown in Figure 1. [14]

```
link_Actor_1

(and wb clause clause-simplex major-clause
 effective material mat-doing)
                     | Actor/Agent
(and wb group-phrase groups nominal-group
  (or (and ngrp-simplex nominal-head
        ngrp-participant-head)
      (and ngrp-complex ngrp-hypotactic
        ngrp-participant)))

link_Actor_2

(and wb clause clause-simplex major-clause material)
                     | Actor
(and wb group-phrase groups nominal-group
  (or (and ngrp-simplex nominal-head
        ngrp-participant-head)
      (and ngrp-complex ngrp-hypotactic
        ngrp-participant)))
```

Figure 9: Examples of partial-structures

There are two kinds of partial-structures: a *linking partial-structure* and an *ordering partial-structure*. A linking partial-structure represents a possible pattern of parent/child unit pairs and is compiled from a combination of insert, conflate and preselect realisation statements in the Wording Base and Meaning Base networks. 'link_Actor_1,' for instance, is a linking partial-structure and represents a unit whose features are 'wb clause clause-simplex major-clause effective material mat-doing' may have a child unit whose roles are Actor and Agent and features are 'wb group-phrase groups nominal-group ngrp-simplex nominal-head ngrp-participant-head' or 'wb group-phrase groups nominal-group ngrp-complex ngrp-hypotactic ngrp-participant.' This linking partial-structure is derived from a combination of the four realisation statements in Figure 1, 'insert Agent, insert Actor, preselect Actor ngrp-participant-head or ngrp-participant, conflate Actor Agent,' and the feature selection path from the given features to a root feature, that is 'wb' in the case of lexicogrammatical system network.

An ordering partial-structure specifies a constraint on the ordering of child units in a parent/child unit pair, and is compiled from insert, conflate, order and partition statements. 'order_Medium#Process'[14] is an ordering partial-structure and represents a unit whose features are 'wb clause clause-simplex major-clause' may have two child units whose roles are Medium and Process, conflating Predicator, respectively, and the unit with Medium is followed by the one with Process/Predicator. This ordering partial-structure is derived from a combination of the five realisation statements in Figure 1, 'insert Process, insert Predicator, insert Medium, partition Medium Process, conflate Process Predicator,' and the feature selection path from the given feature, that is 'major-clause' in this case, to a root feature.

Parse-chart

This method is based on a chart parsing strategy, which uses a data structure called a parse-chart to prevent recomputing fragments of an instance structure which have already been obtained during the parsing. A parse-chart is a graph structure which keeps intermediate results along the parsing process as edges. There are two types of edge. One is called a passive edge, which represents a completed result, such as a completed nominal group 'my car' in 'My car is black.' The other is called an active edge, which represents an incomplete result, which does not have all the required units, such as a possessive pronoun in a nominal group 'my' in 'My car is black.' As the parsing advances, such edges are incorporated into the parse-chart.

Construction of morpheme rank units

The first phase in the lexicogrammatical analysis is to generate morphological units based on the results of preprocessing. Of the lexicogrammatical features drawn from preprocessing, the features that are located at the morpheme rank system network are assigned to each morpheme unit. For example, the sixth morpheme unit '*shootai*' and the seventh '*joo*' are given the Wording Base features 'base' and 'suffix' respectively, as shown in Figure 10.

Figure 10: Morpheme rank instance structures

The morpheme units thus generated are incorporated into the parse-chart as passive edges.

Extension of the constructed instance structure

The second phase involves looking up the precompiled linking partial-structures to pick out those partial-structures that have selection paths compatible with the root unit of the constructed structures, that is, passive edges. The partial-structures whose child unit contains 'base' or 'suffix' are found as shown in the figure below.

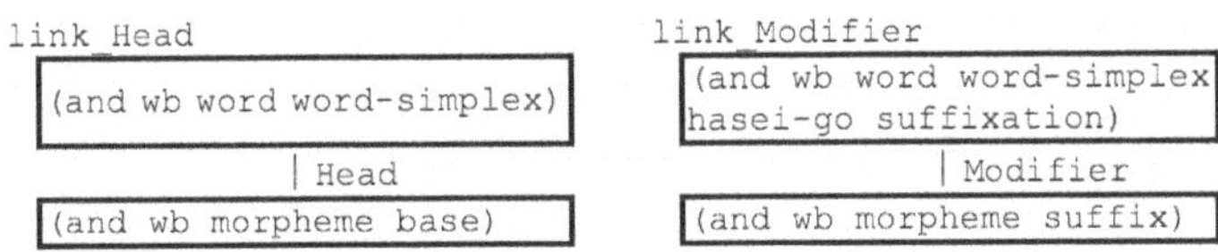

Figure 11: Linking partial-structures for base and suffix

Figure 12 shows the result of unification of the morpheme units into each of these linking partial-structures.

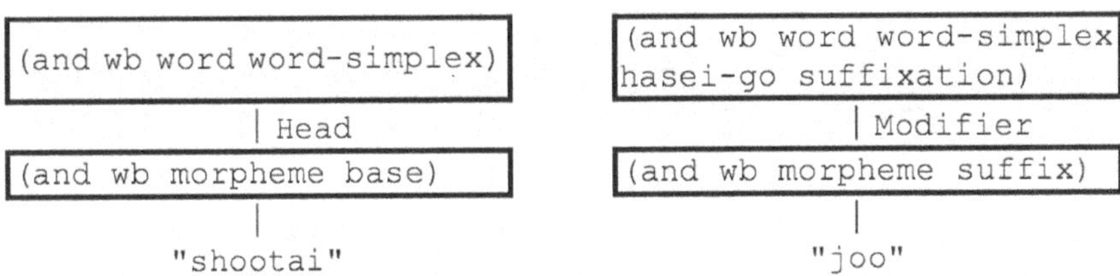

Figure 12: Two morpheme and word rank instance structures

The instance structures thus extended are incorporated into the chart as active edges.

Unification of the root units of the constructed instance structures

The third phase is to attempt to unify the root unit of the extended instance structure with the root unit of an active edge in the chart. As indicated in Figure 12, the parent units of '*shootai*' and '*joo*' have compatible selection paths. Thus, the system can unify these units, resulting in a new unit that corresponds to the word '*shootai-joo*.' The units that have been successfully unified are then incorporated into the parse-chart as an active edge.

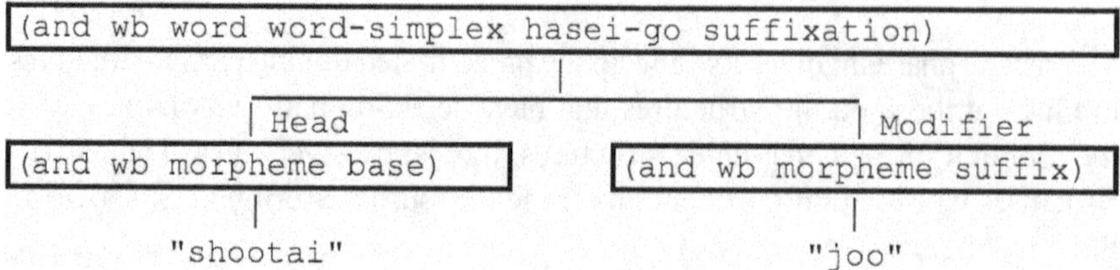

Figure 13: One unified morpheme and word rank instance structure

Checking completeness of an active edge

The fourth phase involves looking up the precompiled ordering partial-structures to pick out those partial-structures which contain the same features as the root unit of an active edge. Suppose the instance structure shown in Figure 13 is currently in the chart as an active edge. In order to see whether this edge is to be completed or not, the following ordering partial-structure, which has the same selection path as the '*shootai-joo*' unit, is invoked.

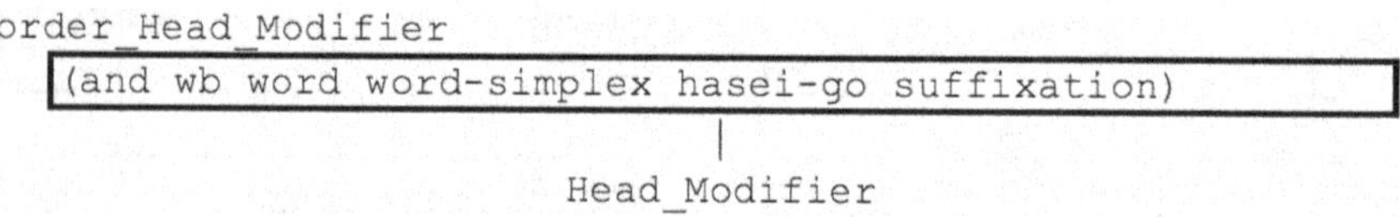

Figure 14: Ordering partial-structure

This indicates that a given unit can have two child units, the one with the role Head and the other with the role Modifier, and that the Head unit precedes the Modifier. As shown in Figure 13, the '*shootai-joo*' unit has two child units that meet such role constraints. If the ordering partial structure in Figure 14 is the only match found, it is warranted that there is no partial structure in which a given parent unit is required to have a child unit whose role is something else than Head or Modifier. Therefore, the active edge in question can be regarded as completed. Then, this is incorporated into the chart as a passive edge, ready for the fifth phase.

If a given active edge is not completed, unification with other units will be necessary. This process starts with identifying the next morpheme boundary and constructing a new morpheme unit. As each morpheme unit is incorporated into the parse-chart, the parser then moves on to incorporate the next morpheme unit. This process continues until all morpheme units have been checked.

Addition of lexicogrammatical features to a passive edge

The fifth phase is to add lexicogrammatical features to the root unit of a passive edge by referring to the results of preprocessing. Suppose the instance structure shown in Figure 13 is currently in the chart as a passive edge, by referring to the result of the General Dictionary lookup, word rank features such as 'common-noun' are added to the root unit '*shootai-joo*.' Then, the process returns to the second step, searching for linking partial-structures whose child unit has selection paths compatible with the root of the passive edge, in order to unify the edge with appropriate linking partial-structures.

Using these data structures, the preprocessing results and a unification algorithm for units, an instance structure is constructed from morpheme rank units in a bottom-up manner. Figure 15 shows the result of the lexicogrammatical analysis of (1).

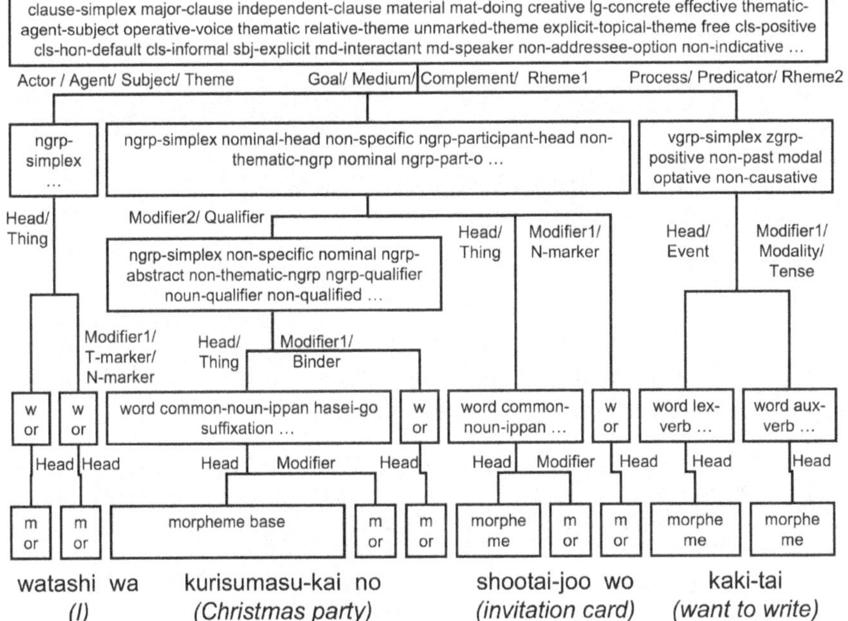

Figure 15: Instance structure at lexicogrammatical stratum

Step 4: Semantic analysis

In the semantic analysis, a semantic instance structure of the inputted text is constructed using the corresponding lexicogrammatical instance structure and semantic features of the words in the text. The parent/child relation of the semantic units is augmented and the consistency among them is checked in a similar way to the lexicogrammatical analysis. Semantic features incorporated in the current version of implementation include ideational semantic features that characterise propositions, interpersonal semantic features that characterise speech acts and textual semantic features that characterise the rhetorical structure of a text. Figure 16 shows the result of the semantic analysis for (1).

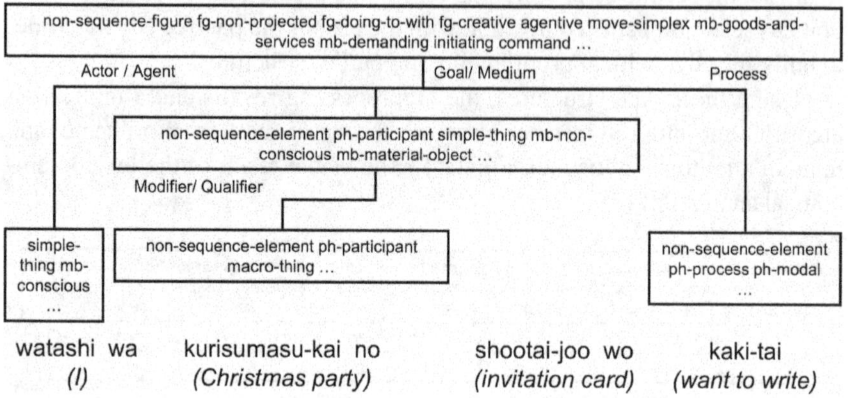

Figure 16: Instance structure of single sentence at semantic stratum

When an inputted text consists of more than one sentence, the units that constitute a rhetorical structure are constructed over and above the element-figure/move unit structure. The rhetorical relations and roles between such units are assigned basically according to the conjunctions in the sentence.[15] Figure 17 shows the rhetorical structure of three sentences below.

(2) *RIKEN no hito kara no meeru wa 'RIKEN' foruda ni ireru.*
RIKEN NO people KARA NO mail WA RIKEN folder NI move=INF
Move mail from people in RIKEN to 'RIKEN' folder.

(3) ***Tadasi**, kenkyuu-shitsu no hito kara no meeru wa 'kenkyuu-shitsu' foruda ni ire-te,*
however lab NO people KARA NO mail WA lab folder NI move-SUSP
jitaku ni tensoosuru.
home NI forward=INF
However, move mail from people in the lab to «lab» folder, and forward them home.

(4) ***Mata**, 'oshirase' toiu daimei no meeru wa, i-sshuukan ta-ttara, sakujosuru.*
and notice QUO title NO mail WA one-week pass-PST=CND delete=INF
And, delete mail with the title 'Notice', if one week has passed since their reception.

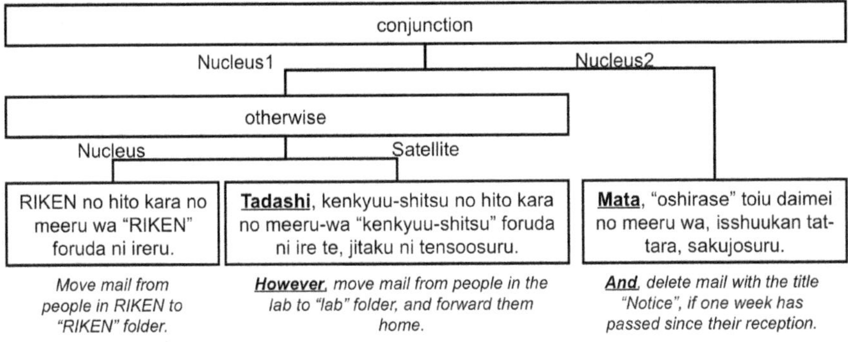

Figure 17: Instance structure of multiple sentences at semantic stratum

Step 5: conceptual analysis

In the conceptual analysis, a conceptual frame instance corresponding to the conceptual content of the inputted text is constructed by referring to the semantic instance structure, the EDR concept identifier for each word in the text, and information in the Concept Repository which is relevant to the current situation type. Slots for concepts are filled recursively by concept instances that correspond to child segments of the text. Checks are carried out as to whether type constraints correspond to the slot fillers with respect to both the class hierarchy of the Concept Repository and the EDR concept classification hierarchy, which has richer content than the Concept Repository. Figure 18 shows the result of the conceptual analysis.

Figure 18: Instance structure of concepts

In summary, Table 14 shows the results of the whole understanding process.

Table 14: Results of understanding

Level	Layer											
translation		I want to write an invitation card to the Christmas party.										
gloss		I	WA	Christmas	party	NO	invitation	card	O	write	OPT=INF	-
Pre-processing	morphological &dependency analyses	watashi	wa	kurisumasu	kai	no	shootai	joo	wo	kaki	tai	-
Pre-processing	morphological &dependency analyses	0 3D		1 3D			2 3D			3 -10		-
Pre-processing	GD search CID	0e7e95, 2dc301	2621d5	3ceda8		2621d5	0e3e07		2621d5	0e910d, 0e910f	2621c8	-
Pre-processing	GD search CRL	agent		scene			object			-		-
Graphological analysis	sentence	eb-graphology-base sentence										
Graphological analysis	comma-unit	Head										Tail
Graphological analysis	comma-unit	eb-graphology-base comma-unit										full-stop
Graphological analysis	letter	Head	2	3-7	8	9	10-11	12	13	14-15	Tail	-
Graphological analysis	letter	j-characters...	j-characters...	j-characters ...	j-characters...	j-characters...	j-characters ...	j-characters...	j-characters...	j-characters...	j-characters ...	-
Lexicogrammatical analysis	clause simplex rank	clause-simplex major-clause independent-clause non-conjunct cls-neutral no-circumstance material mat-doing creative lg-concrete effective thematic-agent-subject operative-voice thematic relative-theme unmarked-theme explicit-topical-theme free cls-positive cls-hon-default cls-informal sbj-explicit md-interactant md-non-addressee md-speaker non-addressee-option non-indicative cls-optative unkeyed ...										-
Lexicogrammatical analysis	group simplex rank	Actor/ Agent/ Subject/ TopicalTheme		Goal/ Medium/ Complement/ Rheme1						Process/ Predicator/ Rheme2		-
Lexicogrammatical analysis	group simplex rank	specific determinative nominal-head thematic-ngrp personal pronominal general-theme-marker speaker non-qualified ...		ngrp-simplex non-thematic-ngrp nominal-head non-specific ngrp-participant-head nominal ngrp-part-o ngrp-concrete qualified ...						vgrp-simplex zgrp-positive temporal non-past modal modulation rediness-inclination optative option-tai non-causative active-voice ...		-
Lexicogrammatical analysis	rankshifted group simplex rank			Qualifier/ Modifier1								-
Lexicogrammatical analysis	rankshifted group simplex rank			ngrp-simplex non-specific nominal ngrp-abstract non-thematic-ngrp ngrp-qualifier noun-qualifier non-qualified ...								-
Lexicogrammatical analysis	word simplex rank	Thing/ Head1	Thematic-marker/ Nominal-marker/ Modifier1	Thing/ Head1		Binder/ Modifier1	Thing/ Head1		Nominal-marker/ Modifier1	Event/ Head1	Tense/ Modality/ Modifier1	-
Lexicogrammatical analysis	word simplex rank	pronoun-ippan ...	j-kakari-zyoshi kakari-wa ...	common-noun-ippan hasei-go suffixation ...		j-zyoshi-rentai-ka ...	common-noun-ippan hasei-go suffixation ...		j-case-marker case-o ...	lexical-verb	auxiliary-verb aux-tai ...	-
Lexicogrammatical analysis	morpheme rank	Head	Head	Head1	Modifier1	Head	Head1	Modifier1	Head	Head	Head	-
Lexicogrammatical analysis	morpheme rank	base ...	base ...	base ...	suffix ...	base ...	base ...	suffix ...	base ...	base ...	base ...	-
semantic analysis	figure/ move	ph-figure fg-non-projected fg-doing-to-with fg-creative agentive move-simplex mb-goods-and-services command mb-demanding initiating ...										-
semantic analysis	element	Actor/ Agent		Goal/ Medium						Process		-
semantic analysis	element	simple-thing mb-conscious ...		non-sequence-element ph-participant simple-thing mb-non-conscious mb-material-object...						ph-process...		-
semantic analysis	element			Qualifier/ Modifier1								-
semantic analysis	element			non-sequence-element ph-participant macro-thing ...								-
conceptual analysis		want-action{speaker = user, hearer = system, content = writing{agent = user, object = invitation-card{purpose=Christmas-party{}}}										-

The Semiotic Base and the text understanding algorithm illustrated so far have been implemented in Java. The results of the analyses are output as XML annotations on the inputted texts.

Bypassing through reference to the Corpus Base

Alternative algorithms for text understanding have been developed: for instance, the system can shortcut the in-depth analysis of an inputted text by using the results already obtained in a preceding analysis if the Corpus Base already includes an analysed text with identical words. Before performing lexicogrammatical, semantic and conceptual analyses of a text, an algorithm searches for similarities in texts in the corpus and if found, copies the analyses given there.

Contextual analysis

The contextual analysis is a process of inferring a situational configuration of the inputted text from the linguistic features of the text and the history of the dialogue, by referring to the Context Base. In our design, the contextual analysis is conducted between the preprocessing and the SFL-based lexicogrammatical analysis in order to set up situation-specific resources so that the rest of the procedure of text understanding proceeds in an efficient manner.

Methods for inferring the current situation from the preprocessing results of the inputted text are being finalised. Three paths to reach the identification are proposed. One is to check the results of the General Dictionary lookup of the inputted text against the words in the Corpus Base texts for matching. A second method is to search the results of the General Dictionary lookup for matches with the heading in the Situation-Specific Dictionary. The third way is to search for matches between the concepts of the lexical items contained in the inputted text and those contained in the Concept Repository.

For each route, the overall matching value is calculated and the situation type with the highest value in the Corpus Base texts, Situation-Specific Dictionary records, or Concept Repository records is specifically chosen for the inputted text. Depending on what has been chosen, the current situation type is either confirmed to stay in place or a new type is identified. If a new type is identified, a set of system networks and the Concept Repository records associated with the identified situation type are activated for the SFL-based analysis.

The above explanation of the text understanding model that has been developed as part of the Everyday Language Computing Project outlined the following features: firstly, the model exploits the contextual and linguistic features of texts. Via the Semiotic Base, the situation type of a user's inputted text is identified and its linguistic features are extracted. Secondly, the features serve to help the system in identifying the stage in a dialogue and selecting moves that the system is expected to carry out.[16]

Discussion

Related works on SFL-based text processing system

SFL has been used as the basis for many natural language generation systems (for example, Mann & Matthiessen, 1985; Fawcett, Gordon & Lin, 1993; Bateman, 1997; Teich, 1999). Less work has been done for natural language understanding systems. The main reason is that the SFL-based text understanding process is likely to be complicated and take enormous computation time due to the strong descriptive power of the theoretical representation using system networks and realisation statements, in particular, disjunctive entry conditions and role conflations, which involve massive cross-classification. Because of this, most of the previous studies deal with small fragments of the whole theory, for example, dealing with only one metafunction, or translating the grammar into non-systemic formalisms such as functional unification grammar (Winograd, 1972; Kasper, 1988; Bateman, Emele & Momma, 1992; O'Donoghue, 1994). Such studies reduce the generality of the linguistic model that SFL provides and the descriptive framework where grammatical contrasts and constraints are represented declaratively in system networks and realisation statements. One exception is the WAG system, which uses precompiled partial-structures, bottom-up chart parsing, and indexation to improve the efficiency problem of the parsing process mentioned above. Therefore, we have adopted this parsing method. Table 15 shows a comparison of the systems illustrated in this chapter and other major SFL-based text processing systems, Penman, KPML and WAG, in terms of linguistic resources and processes.

Table 15: Coverage of semiotic dimensions in theoretical design of the Semiotic Base (cf. Table 0–2, Butt et al. 2005:114–115)

		Penman, KPML	*WAG*	***our system***
strata	*context*	-	-	+
	semantics	partial	partial	+
	lexicogrammar	+	+	+
	expression	-	-	+
process	*generation*	+	+	+
	understanding	-	+	+
metafunction	*indeational*	+	+	+
	interpersonal	semantics: - lexicogrammar: +	+	+
	textual	semantics: - lexicogrammar: +	sematics: partial lexicogrammar: +	+

Our text understanding system is equipped with far more functions than would be expected for a standard parser. It conducts conceptual analyses in order to ground linguistic (semiotic) objects to material objects in the real (material) world, a necessity for any application system to 'understand' linguistic texts. We have started implementing the methods of contextual analysis that proceed with the rest of the procedure of text understanding in an efficient manner. We have managed to shortcut the procedure with our implementation of a corpus-based method.

Innovations made to the WAG parser

We extended the WAG system in several significant ways. Firstly, a method for unifying the results of non-SFL-based natural language processing (NLP) tools was added. In particular, the results of the preprocessing phase incorporated instance structures to add information so that our system can filter out implausible interpretations. When a new passive edge is added to the chart, an attempt is made to import word information into the root unit of the edge. When an attempt is made to create a larger active edge by unifying the root unit of a passive edge with a unit contained in a partial-structure or an active edge, unifications of feature/role information and verification of consistency between the current instance structure and the dependency structure identified in the preprocessing phase are performed, as well as the standard unification of feature selection paths (Kasper, 1987). For example, as for nominal groups with a case particle '*de*,' four linking partial-structures with role 'Means', 'Quality', 'Temporal Location' and 'Spatial Location' are compiled from the current Wording Base network. However, when the input sentence is (5), only 'Means' is consistent with the preprocessing result and hence is used to construct the instance structure for this sentence.

(5)	*shootai-joo*	*wo*	*emuesuwaado*	*de*	*kaki-tai.*
	invitation-card	O	MS Word	DE	write-OPT=INF

I want to write an invitation card by MS Word.

The second way that the WAG system has been extended is through the introduction of *inter-stratal linking partial-structures* that explicitly represent the relationship between lexicogrammatical units and semantic ones. These are used to map instance structures taken from the lexicogrammatical stratum onto the semantic stratum. Figure 19 represents an example of these inter-stratal linking partial-structures.

```
wblink_1
 (and mb grammatical-semantics non-rhetorical-unit
  exchange move-simplex role-assigning initiating
  mb-demanding mb-goods-and-services command)
                          |
 (and wb clause clause-simplex major-clause free
  non-indicative cls-optative md-interactant
  md-non-addressee non-addressee-option)
```

Figure 19: Example of inter-stratal linking partial-structures

To put it plainly, this indicates that a clause unit at a lexicogrammatical stratum corresponds to a figure/move unit at a semantic stratum. It assures that if a unit in the lexicogrammatical instance structure has the features listed in the lower box, a semantic unit which contains the features listed in the upper box is constructed in the process of a semantic analysis.

Moreover, a forward chaining style of inferences was incorporated to deal with *co-selection constraints* (Matthiessen & Bateman, 1991), with a *gate* having only one feature and default feature selections. We also provided a mechanism for lower rank units to inherit features from upper rank units in order to sustain a chain of the necessary conditions for a structure to be morphosyntactically well-formed. In general, a realisation statement does not specify constraints on units more than one rank below. For instance, consider a feature selection for VOICE (that is, operative or receptive) made at the clause rank. This affects the feature selection at the morphological rank (for example, a passive suffix '*-(a)reru*' is added to a verb root in Japanese, as in English). In such a case, one might want to express morphological constraints directly in the clausal realisation statement, but this kind of rough specification is not executable. Therefore, system networks and realisation statements that are apparently redundant but are in fact computationally necessary were added, so that selections at group rank and word rank are not skipped.

Conclusion

This chapter has illustrated a computational model for a language system which includes context and a semiotically-based text understanding algorithm. The model has both advantages and limitations. One of the most important advantages of the model, which is mainly due to SFL, is the richness of the contextual and linguistic features that the system can invoke. The model is also equipped with a mechanism for incremental specification of such features by means of system networks. This becomes a computational advantage as the project attempts to build a robust system. Furthermore, we expect the organisation of the Semiotic Base to have strong enough connections inside its constituent system networks as well as with the data outside of it to do knowledge management and acquisition through texts. By combining the existing parser and dictionary with our systemic resources, we aim to reduce the required resources involved in the system development while maintaining the standard accuracy of the analysis.

The limitations of the current work relate to the lexicogrammatical and semantic analyses. In particular, the resources for grammatical metaphor are under construction, so the system is not able to construct appropriate instance structures of an inputted text with nominalisation. As for the contextual analysis, an algorithm needs to be implemented for inferring situational configurations from a distribution of linguistic features which are realised in a text with reference to the entire Semiotic Base. At the moment inferences are not processable.

Despite the size of system networks, the number of the acceptable sentences is still relatively small (130 patterns). We assume that the limited performance of the understanding system derives from two sources. One is the current scarcity of the General Dictionary. If an inputted text contains lexical items which are not found in the General Dictionary, the system cannot obtain the results of the lexicogrammatical, semantic and conceptual analyses. In many cases, this is because there is no trigger, unless some bridge is devised between non-systemic and systemic features within the General Dictionary. To resolve this problem, we are designing a default assignment of SFL features to lexical items by means of a mapping table of EDR concept identifiers that are located at the relatively higher nodes in the taxonomy and SFL features. The second problem is the size of the partial-structures. Since it is difficult to design methods for precompiling the partial-structures automatically and organising them effectively, the precompilation is done by hand-coding. As a result there are still many realisation statements which are not utilised in the lexicogrammatical and semantic analyses. Recently, another algorithm which does not require (precompilation of) partial structures and can refer to system networks and realisation statements more straightforwardly was developed. Now the system is ready to fully evaluate how many and what types of clauses (or texts) it can analyse with the resources in the Semiotic Base. We believe these problems, currently being actively tackled, will see successful resolution in the near future.

As mentioned in the introduction, the development of the Semiotic Base and the text understanding system is part of the Everyday Language Computing project. The project is interdisciplinary and it has been reviewed by different fields of research. From the (systemic functional) linguistic point of view, the Semiotic Base and the text understanding and generation algorithms are evaluated by Butt et al. (2005) as follows:

> The system is the first major systemic functional computational system handling Japanese text generation and analysis;
>
> The system is the first major systemic functional computational system handling generation and analysis using the same resources and relating these processes to other (semiotic) processes; and
>
> The system is the first major systemic functional computational system involving the control of software application in addition to generation / analysis.
>
> (Butt et al., 2005:112–113)

From the computer science point of view, the attitude towards our project can be summed up as positive. We know this because our research team successfully participated in a five year competitive challenge with other intelligent software development projects. The Challenge entitled, *Challenge for Realizing Early Profits* was initiated and sponsored by the Japan Society for Artificial Intelligence. The purpose of the challenge was to support and promote promising ideas in artificial intelligence technologies. The participating challengers proposed their ideas which were then evaluated by conference participants. The challengers who placed in the top-five in the competition each year earned the right to organise a workshop featuring their project at the next annual conference. This continued over a five year period. The Everyday Language computing project was proposed in 2001 and remained in competition until 2005. In other words, each year our project remained competitive and has therefore been recognised in the artificial intelligence community as valuable and contributing to society. From this challenge, it is evident that the approach of language-based computing is being recognised in the artificial intelligence community.[17]

However, the likelihood of the commercialisation of our research achievement is quite low at the current moment. To motivate the industry to commercialisation, it is important to provide 'non-academic' prototype systems, which would cost millions of dollars, and to provide estimates of the cost and time to develop practical systems. By using our experience as a steppingstone, we encourage more linguists and computer scientists to get involved in this kind of computational project.

Acknowledgements

We would like to thank Prof. Michio Sugeno of European Centre for Soft Computing and the former members of the Laboratory for Language-Based Intelligent Systems for their invaluable support throughout all the phases of this research.

We are also indebted to Dr. Elizabeth A. Thomson for her helpful comments in the preparation of this article.

Notes

1 The digital divide refers to the gaps in treatment, opportunity and wealth between groups in relation to their ability to use information technologies such as personal computers and the internet effectively. It has been an issue since the late 1990s.

2 The idea of the Semiotic Base is inspired by the meaning base suggested by Halliday (1995).

3 See Table 1.

4 In the table, the dotted cell indicates the contents that are not relevant to the text understanding process. For the details of these contents, see Takahashi, Kobayashi and Iwazume (in this volume).

5 If Unit A is one of the elements that immediately constitute Unit B, then Unit A is a child unit of Unit B and Unit B is the parent unit of Unit A.

6 EDR stands for Japan Electronic Dictionary Research Institute. The EDR dictionary is the largest existing machine readable dictionary of Japanese. Its Japanese Word Dictionary stores approximately 270,000 records, and Japanese Concept Dictionary stores 410,000 records.

7 The main reason that we provide grammatical (-semantic) and lexical (-semantic) resources separately in the Semiotic Base, though questionable this treatment may appear from a theoretical viewpoint, is to make it easier to maintain and expand these resources. Although it is very difficult for theorists without systemic functional linguistic background to write system networks and realisation statements, it should be straightforward even for such non-systemic theorists to compile dictionary entries that are linked with major systemic features. It is essential to ensure the sharing and reusability of the resources in the information engineering community.

8 At present, however, we must admit that they consist of registers located in the middle of the cline of instantiation, rather than a system that covers the full potential of Japanese language.

9 The tools presented here are basically for Japanese texts and only the coding tool is currently available for sample use with English texts. All of them operate on Windows with Java. However, the coding tool operates on Mac OS X, though it is not thoroughly tested.

10 KPML stands for Komet-Penman multilingual development environment.

11 KWIC stands for keyword in context.

12 Every *bunsetsu* segment is assigned a number from 0. *0 3D indicates that a segment in question is segment 0 and it is dependent on segment 3. *3 -1O indicates that a segment in question is segment 3 and it is dependent on nothing. EOS stands for end of sentence.

13 WAG stands for workbench for analysis and generation.

14 The hash # symbol means 'followed by.'

15 Since we cannot expect that every sentence has a conjunction, we refer to other linguistic information, such as, process type of a clause. For the details of the rhetorical structure analysis, see Ito, Sugimoto, Iwashita, Kobayashi and Sugeno (2004).

16 For the details of identification of the stage and selection of the move, see Sugimoto, Ito, Fujishiro and Sugeno (2002) and Takahashi et al. (in this volume).

17 For details on the program of the *Challenge for Realizing Early Profits* and the evaluations, see Laboratory for Language-Based Intelligent Systems (2005).

Interlinear notation key

CJT	conjecture. For eg. *-daroo, -mashoo*
CND	conditional. For eg. *-tara*
COP	copula. For eg. *da*
DE	nominal group marker
FOR	formal form of the verb. For eg. *-masu* form
INF	informal form of the verb/adjective. For eg. *da, -ru*, adj-*i*
KARA	nominal group marker
N	negotiator. For eg. *ne*
NI	nominal group marker
NO	nominal marker
O	nominal group marker
OPT	optative auxiliary. For eg. *-tai*
PST	past
Q	question marker. For eg. *ka*
SUSP	non-finite, tactic verb form. For eg. *-te* form
QUO	quotative marker. For eg. *toiu*
WA	thematic marker

References

Bateman, J. A. (1997) Enabling technology for multilingual natural language generation: the KPML development environment. *Journal of Natural Language Engineering* 3 (1): 15–55.

Bateman, J. A., Emele, M. and Momma, S. (1992) The nondirectional representation of systemic functional grammars and semantics as typed feature structures. *Proceedings of the 10th International Conference on Computational Linguistics* 916–920.

Butt, D., Halliday, M. A. K., Matthiessen, C. M. I. M., Teruya, T. and Wu, C. (2005) Review report on the research results of the Laboratory for Language-Based Intelligent Systems, BSI, RIKEN. In *Research Report* 112–125. Wako: Laboratory for Language-Based Intelligent Systems, Brain Science Institute, RIKEN.

Fawcett, R. P., Gordon, T. H. and Lin, Y. Q. (1993) How systemic functional grammar works: the role of realization in realization. In H. Horacek and M. Zock (eds) *New Concepts in Natural Language Generation: Planning, Realization and Systems* 114–186. London: Pinter.

Halliday, M. A. K. (1995/ 2000) Computing meanings: some reflections on past experience and present prospect. *Proceedings of the 2nd Conference of the Pacific Association for Computational Linguistics* 19–22. Translated by Kazuhiro Teruya, *Journal of Japan Society for Fuzzy Theory and Systems* 12(5): 615–634

Halliday, M. A. K. and Hasan, R. (1989) *Language, Context, and Text: Aspects of Language in a Social-semiotic Perspective*. London: Oxford University Press.

Halliday, M. A. K. and Matthiessen, C. M. I. M. (1999) *Construing Experience Through Meaning: A Language-based Approach to Cognition*. London: Cassell.

Halliday, M. A. K. and Matthiessen, C. M. I. M. (2004) *An Introduction to Functional Grammar* (3rd edition). London: Arnold.

Hasan, R. (1996) The grammarian dream: lexis as most delicate grammar. In C. Cloran, D. Butt, and G. Williams (eds) *Ways of Saying, Ways of Meaning: Selected Papers by Ruquiya Hasan* 73–103. London: Cassell.

Ito, N., Sugimoto, T., Iwashita, S., Kobayashi, I. and Sugeno, M. (2004) A model of rhetorical structure analysis of Japanese instructional texts and its applications to a smart help system. In W. Thissen, P. Wieringa, M. Pantic and M. Ludema (eds) *Proceedings of the 2004 IEEE International Conference on Systems, Man & Cybernetics* 3641–3646.

Iwashita, S., Ito, N., Kobayashi, I., Sugimoto, T. and Sugeno, M. (2004) Everyday language help system based on software manual. In W. Thissen, P. Wieringa, M. Pantic and M. Ludema (eds) *Proceedings of the 2004 IEEE International Conference on Systems, Man & Cybernetics* 3635–3640.

Iwazume, M., Kobayashi, I. and Sugeno, M. (2004) Natural language mediated software control. In W. Thissen, P. Wieringa, M. Pantic and M. Ludema (eds) *Proceedings of the 2004 IEEE International Conference on Systems, Man & Cybernetics* 5560–5566.

Japan Electronic Dictionary Research Institute, L. (2003) *EDR Dictionary* (3rd edition). Tokyo: Japan Electronic Dictionary Research Institute, Limited.

Kasper, R. T. (1987) A unification method for disjunctive feature descriptions. *Proceedings of the 25th annual meeting of Association for Computational Linguistics* 235–242.

Kasper, R. T. (1988) An experimental parser for systemic grammars. *Proceedings of the 6th International Conference on Computational Linguistics* 309–312.

Kudo, T. and Matsumoto, Y. (2002) Japanese dependency analysis using cascaded chunking. In D. Roth and A. van den Bosch (eds) *Proceedings of the 6th Conference on Natural Language Learning* 63–69. Retrieved on 20 October 2004 from http://chasen.org/~taku/software/cabocha/

Laboratory for Language-Based Intelligent Systems. (2005) *Research Report*. Wako: Laboratory for Language-Based Intelligent Systems, Brain Science Institute, RIKEN.

Lee, A., Kawahara, T. and Shikano, K. (2001) Julius: an open source real-time large vocabulary recognition engine. *Proceedings of European Conference on Speech Communication and Technology* 1691–1694. Retrieved on 20 October 2004 from http://julius.sourceforge.jp/en/julius.html

Mann, W. C. and Thompson, S. A. (1988) Rhetorical structure theory: toward a functional theory of text organization. *Text* 8 (3): 243–281.

Matsumoto, Y., Kitauchi, A., Yamashita, T., Hirano, Y., Matsuda, H. and Asahara, M. (1999) Japanese morphological analysis system: ChaSen version 2.0 manual (2nd edition). *NAIST Technical Report*: NAIST-IS-TR99009. Nara: Nara Institute of Science and Technology. Retrieved on 20 October 2004 from http://chasen.naist.jp/hiki/ChaSen/

Matthiessen, C. M. I. M. (1995) *Lexicogrammatical Cartography: English Systems*. Tokyo: International Language Science Publishers.

Matthiessen, C. M. I. M. and Bateman, J. A. (1991) *Text Generation and Systemic-functional Linguistics: Experiences from English and Japanese*. London: Pinter.

Mann, W. C., Matthiessen, C. M. I. M. (1985) Demonstration of the Nigel text generation computer program. In J. D. Benson and W. S. Greaves (eds) *Systemic Perspectives on Discourse*, 1: 50–83. Norwood: Ablex.

O'Donnell, M. (1994) *Sentence Analysis and Generation: a Systemic Perspective*. PhD Dissertation, University of Sydney, Sydney. Retrieved on 20 October 2004 from http://www.wagsoft.com/Papers/Thesis/index.html

O'Donnell, M. (2002) *Systemic Coder: a Text Markup Tool* (version 4.6). Retrieved on 20 October 2004 from http://www.wagsoft.com/Coder/index.html

O'Donoghue, T. F. (1994) Semantic interpretation in a systemic functional grammar. In T. Strzalkowski (ed.) *Reversible Grammar in Natural Language Processing* 415–447. Boston: Kluwer Academic Publishers.

Sugeno, M. (2002) Verbalizing computers: a way to everyday language computing. In N. R. Pal and M. Sugeno (eds) *Advances in Soft Computing* 117–120. Heidelberg: Springer-Verlag.

Sugeno, M. and Kobayashi, I. (2003) Nichijoo-gengo-konpyuutingu he no syootai. *Gengo* 32 (4): 86–93. Tokyo: Taishuukan.

Sugimoto, T., Ito, N., Fujishiro, H. and Sugeno, M. (2002) Dialogue management with the Semiotic Base: a systemic functional linguistic approach. *Proceedings of the 1st International Conference on Soft Computing and Intelligent Systems* 24B1–3.

Sugimoto, T., Ito, N., Iwashita, S. and Sugeno, M. (2004) Script generation using rhetorical information in a task specification text. In W. Thissen, P. Wieringa, M. Pantic and M. Ludema (eds) *Proceedings of the 2004 IEEE International Conference on Systems, Man & Cybernetics* 2687–2692.

Takahashi, Y., Kobayashi, I. and Iwazume, M. (2013) The components and structure of the context base, a database for computer text generation. In this volume.

Teich, E. (1999) *Systemic Functional Grammar in Natural Language Generation: Linguistic Description and Computational Representation.* London: Cassell.

Teruya, K. (2004) Metafunctional profile of the grammar of Japanese. In A. Caffarel, J. R. Martin and C. M. I. M. Matthiessen (eds) *Language Typology: a Functional Perspective* 185–254. Amsterdam: Benjamins.

Winograd, T. (1972) *Understanding Natural Language*. Massachusetts: Academic Press.

10 The components and structure of the context base, a database for computer text generation

Yusuke Takahashi*, Ichiro Kobayashi and Michiaki Iwazume
Justsystem Corporation
Ochanomizu University, Japan
National Institute of Information and Communications Technology

This paper describes the construction of a prototype computer system which operates using everyday or commonsense language. It is part of a larger project, the Everyday Language Computing (ELC) project (Kobayashi and Sugeno, 1997; Iwazume et al., 2003; Ito and Sugimoto, 2006) which was conducted at the Institute of Physical and Chemical Research (RIKEN ; RIkagaku KENkyujo) in Japan.

For a computer system to operate using everyday language, the context which surrounds language use must be considered. This prototype uses a model of language for text processing which contains a model of context called the Context Base. In this paper, we describe the content and the data structure of the Context Base and the correlations which exist between them. We also describe the relationship between the Context Base and the other two bases in the system: the Meaning Base and the Wording Base. Further, we present an example of text processing which uses the Context Base in text generation.

Introduction

As a part of the ELC project, we have developed a database for text processing based on Systemic Functional Linguistics (SFL). This database is known as the Semiotic Base. Since context critically affects our everyday use of language, this project regards as important the role of the context within which language is used. Consequently, the Semiotic Base contains the Context Base, which deals with contextual information in terms of SFL. When using this database, we can generate text strings taking context into consideration.

The main components of the Context Base are a sub-database of context and a sub-database of text development. There are also the following subsidiary components: a Concept Repository (CR), a Text Corpus, Verbalised Knowledge and a Situation Specific Dictionary (SSD). The Concept Repository registers all the concepts used within a given situation. The Text Corpus stores the texts and discourses which are divided according to the contexts in which they are produced as well as which are annotated conceptually and linguistically with the resources within the Semiotic Base. The Verbalised Knowledge is the knowledge used in a given situation. It is described with natural language and tagged with the Semiotic Base resource, that is, annotated with the information of concepts, context, semantics and lexicogrammar. The Situation Specific Dictionary (SSD) describes the linguistic features of the concepts registered in the CR.

Using the Semiotic Base with the incorporated Context Base, the computer can generate text strings as a response to a user's inquiry or request. Text generation is generally divided into two phases. First, there is the content specification phase or, text planning ('what to say') and, second, there is the phase of the linguistic representation of the specified content or string generation ('how to say it'). Text planning is executed mainly within a section of the Context Base known as the Stage Base by specifying the content for generation using the transition information therein. String generation is executed using the entire Semiotic Base by firstly determining the rough clause structure and subsequently the detailed group structure and then specifying the lexical items for the text string.

This chapter is divided into sections: the first section introduces the background of our work, where we give a brief sketch of the ELC project and SFL, which is deployed as the language model in this project. This is followed by a short explanation of the Semiotic Base and a text example used as an illustration. The third section explains the overall content of the Context Base and the data structures concerned with it. The fourth section presents an explanation of the process of text generation using the Semiotic Base, followed by an explanation of text planning and subsequently string generation. The fifth section presents other text processing systems in order to illustrate the characteristics of the Semiotic Base. The sixth section identifies future work and the final section provides a summary of this chapter.

Background

This section gives a brief sketch of our project 'Everyday Language Computing' and addresses some related issues. We adopted SFL (Halliday and Matthiessen, 1999, 2004) initiated by M.A.K. Halliday as the basic theory for modelling the desired language and for working with language in context, a fundamental underpinning of SFL theory.

The notion of Everyday Language Computing and SFL

This section provides an outline of the project 'Everyday Language Computing', which has as its aim the verbalisation of the computer. Typically, computational information processing uses numbers and formal symbolic logic as its computer language. However, the RIKEN team proposed a paradigm shift away from numbers and symbolic logic to that of everyday language. In other words, it was hypothesised that a computer could be made to understand and generate information via natural language. To test this hypothesis, a five-year (2000–2005) project called 'Everyday Language Computing' was launched at the Brain Science Institute (BSI) of RIKEN in Japan. The project's goal was to realise language-based intelligent systems on computers in which human language is embedded.

In order to develop a natural-language-based computing system the project needed to use and possibly adapt a model of language which considers contextual as well as linguistic features, and depicts the correlation between contextual environments and the language systems used within them. One such model, which tries to depict the nature of language in context, is SFL. Consequently, the project adopted SFL as the model of human language to be embedded in the computer systems.

SFL is regarded as a branch of functional linguistics. It is the linguistic theory which explains the structure of a given text in terms of the 'function' rather than the 'form' of language. According to SFL, the sentence 'The hunter shot the bear' consists of the functions 'Actor', 'Process' and 'Goal' ideationally. The functions 'Actor' and 'Goal' are realised by nominal groups 'the hunter' and 'the bear' respectively, and the function 'Process' by a verb 'shot'. However, SFL never explains the structure of this sentence in terms of the 'form'. So it never says that this sentence consists of two nominal groups and one verb without relating these forms to the functions borne by them. This is because the forms must be associated with the functions and forms, in themselves, can not play any role without the associated functions.[1]

In SFL, a text is stratified into four levels: context, meaning, wording and expression. The sub-frameworks of SFL-based study are thus context (of culture and of situation), semantics, lexicogrammar and phonology/graphology, respectively. The contextual stratum deals with the contextual features within the framework of SFL. This stratum explains the environment in which the linguistic systems work. The linguistic system is divided into three strata: meaning, wording and expression. The meaning stratum is depicted by the semantics. The wording stratum is explained by the lexicogrammar. That is, the lexicogrammar stratum depicts the syntactical and lexical features of the given language. In SFL syntax and lexis are not divided and lexis is regarded as the

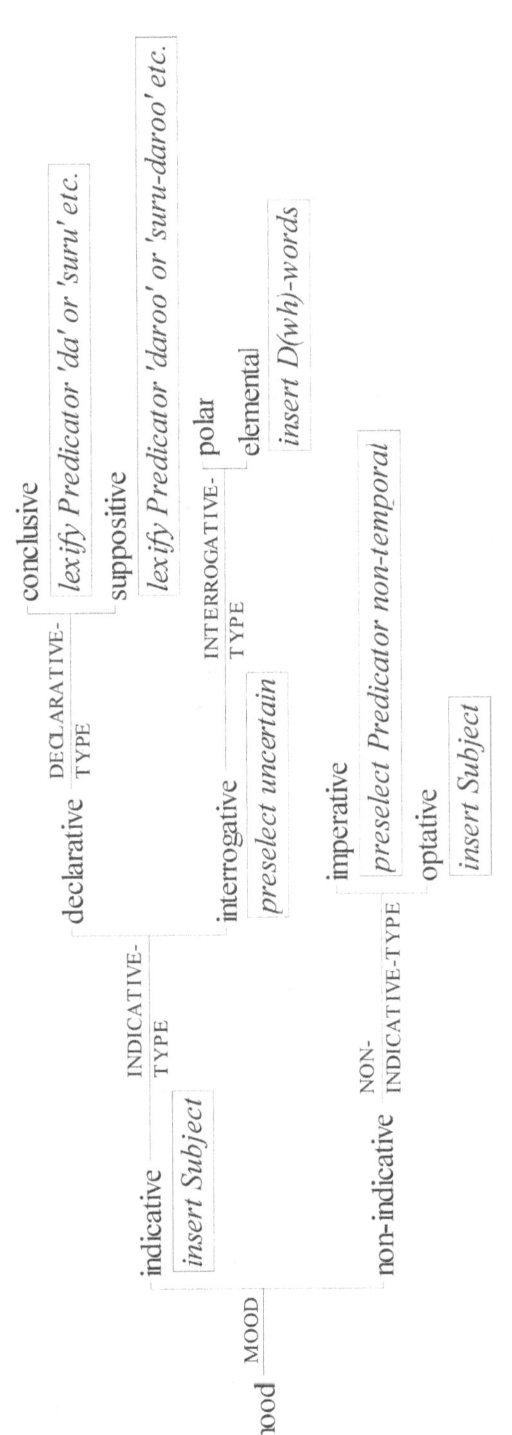

Figure 1: System network

delicate part of syntax, thus the term, lexicogrammar. The expression stratum is divided into sounding/writing and described with phonology/graphology.

Each stratum, except for the expression stratum, is classified into three metafunctions: ideational, interpersonal and textual[2]. The ideational metafunction corresponds to the group of functions used to constitute events and their logical relation to other events and happenings expressed through language. The interpersonal metafunction corresponds to the group of functions used to show the relationship between the interactants. The textual metafunction corresponds to the group of functions used to make the text coherent and appropriate for the context in which it is produced.

Each metafunction of every stratum consists of a set of system networks: a set of options for making meaning. According to SFL, meaning occurs by paradigmatically selecting one or more elements, or features, among the alternatives. For example, in the system network shown in Figure 1[3], 'indicative' mood involves a choice of 'declarative' or 'interrogative', and 'interrogative' mood is a choice between 'polar' and 'elemental'. A set of these alternatives is called a *system* and a resource for making meaning is regarded as a complex of these systems. This complex of systems is called a system network. One or more realisation statements are attached to a feature in a system network. It indicates syntagmatic realisations within a text, and also relationships with (or specifications of) other features within or outside the given stratum as a result of choosing the corresponding feature.

The Semiotic Base

Based on the theoretical architecture of SFL, the team built a text processing system known as the Semiotic Base. It consists of the four databases based on the conception of stratification: the Context Base, the Meaning Base, the Wording Base and the Expression Base. Each database contains system networks according to metafunctions. In addition, the Semiotic Base contains such extras as machine-readable dictionaries, a corpus and the Verbalised Knowledge as subsidiary resources[4].

Content of the Context Base

This section is about the content of the Context Base. The Context Base is a part of the Semiotic Base and deals with contextual features.

After introducing a text example, this chapter first explains what is addressed at the contextual stratum in SFL terms. Then, the content of the Context Base is explained. Last, this chapter shows the data structures of a situation type and generic structure.

Text example

Hereafter, by way of example[5], we will continue the discussion using the following dialogue. In this dialogue, a user is talking to a client secretary agent in his/her computer to produce a computer generated greeting card[6].

	Speaker	Utterance
1	Secretary	*konnichiwa, hisho no Natsume desu. Nani o shi mashoo ka?* hello secretary NO Natsume COP=FOR what O do-FOR=CIT Q (Hello, I am the client secretary, Natsume. Can I help you?)
2	User	*shochuumimai o kaki tai* summer-greeting-card O write-OPT=INF (I'd like to write a summer greeting card.)
3	Secretary	*shochuumimai o donata ni okuri masu ka?* summer-greeting-card O who NI send-FOR Q (Who would you like to send the summer greeting-card to?)
4	User	*yuujin to kaisha no dooryoo desu.* friend and company NO colleague COP=FOR (To friends and colleagues in my company.)
5	Secretary	*shochuumimai no bunmen o kae masu ka?* summer-greeting-card NO content O change-FOR Q (Would you like to change the content of the summer greetings?)
6	User	*hai, onegai shi masu.* yes ask-FOR (Yes, please.)
7	Secretary	*wakari mashi ta. waapuro o kidoo shi masu.* Understand-FOR-PST word-processor O boot do-FOR (OK, I will open the word processor.)

* The key for the inter-linear gloss can be found in Chapter 9, p.320.

The concept of context of situation in SFL theory

According to SFL theory, context is realised in text[7], with SFL dividing the context into two parts: context of culture and context of situation[8]. The context of culture is regarded as the total contextual potential within a society and the context of situation as an instantiation of this context of culture. In other words, a context of culture can be regarded as the total sum of contexts of situation within a society. Furthermore similar contexts of situation accumulate into a situation type, which can also be regarded as a subpart of the culture in a given society. The Semiotic Base deals with the context of situation according to this view of context[9]. A context of situation is represented as a combination of the variables of Field, Tenor and Mode. Field implies the social activity done in the interaction. Tenor implies the social relationship between the interactants. Mode implies the nature of the media (language, in this case) used in the interaction. The variables of Field, Tenor and Mode respectively correspond to ideational, interpersonal and textual metafunctions of the linguistic (i.e. semantic, lexico-grammatical and phonological/graphological) strata. The combination of these variables is called a contextual configuration (Hasan, 1996).

In this view, a situation type can be regarded as a set of contexts of situation with the same contextual configuration. A contextual configuration can be regarded as the 'paradigmatic'[10] characterisation of a situation type.

From the perspective of SFL, a set of texts with similar contextual configuration, that is, those within similar contexts of situation, have similar features. In other words, the texts within the same contexts share the same structure. We call this a generic structure which can be regarded as a 'syntagmatic' realisation of a situation type. A generic structure consists of necessary and/or optional stages, which illustrate the development of an interaction.

Networks of Field, Tenor and Mode

As mentioned earlier, the Context Base is incorporated as a component of the Semiotic Base. Figure 2 illustrates the overall content and structure of the Context Base.

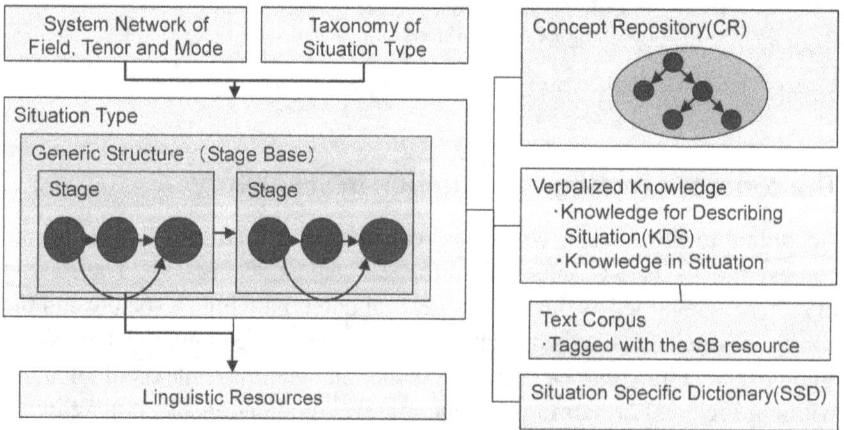

Figure 2: Overview of the Context Base

In the first instance, the Context Base incorporates the system networks of Field, Tenor and Mode[11]. The system network of Field describes the social activity in a given interaction. This system network consists of sub-system networks of sphere of action (topic of an interaction), material action, verbal action and goal orientation. With this system network, we can analyse the topic of the interaction, the action done in the interaction with regard to this topic and the goal of the interaction. Figure 3 shows part of a Field network[12].

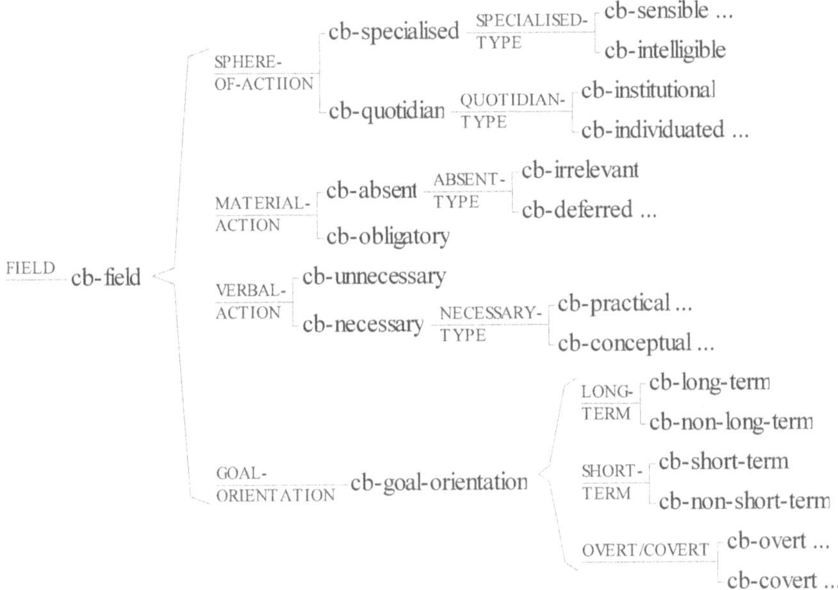

Figure 3: Part of Field network

The system network of Tenor describes the social relationships with the interactants in a given interaction. It consists of the sub-system networks of i) the agentive role (social position of the interactants in relation to each other), ii) social hierarchy, iii) social distance and iv) type of interaction. With these system networks, we can analyse what societal role the interactants play (agentive role), whether or not they have a hierarchic relationship (social hierarchy), how distant they are and how many relationships they have (social distance), and whether the interaction develops dialogically or monologically and the manner of interactant contact, that is, visual, oral or both (type of interaction). Figure 4 shows part of a Tenor network.

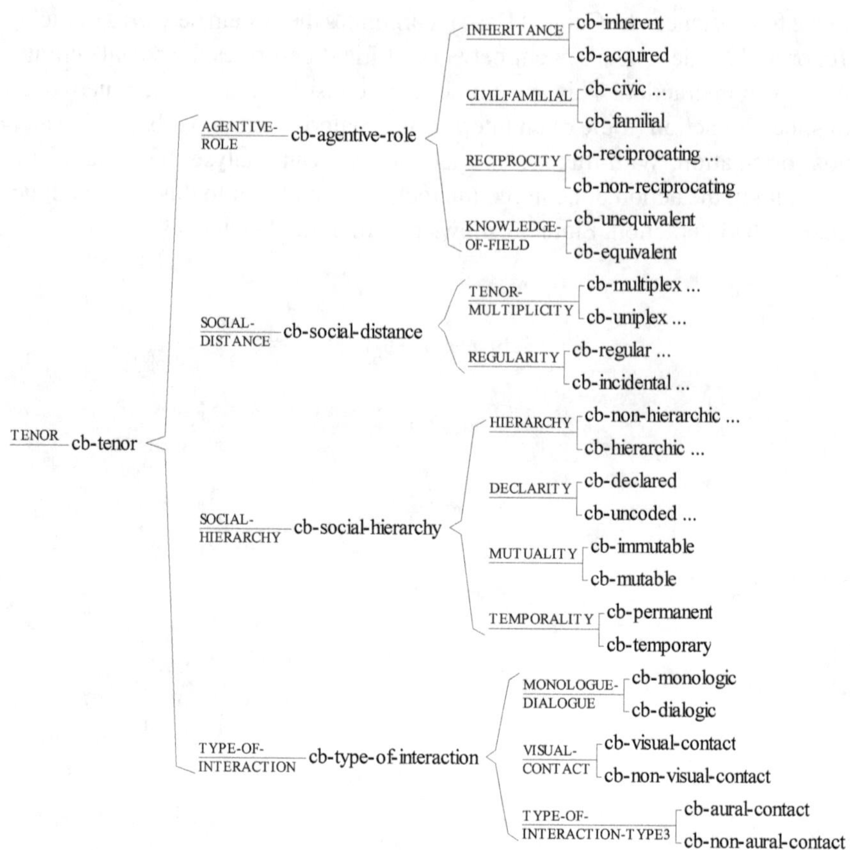

Figure 4: Part of Tenor network

The system network of Mode describes the medium used in the given interaction. It consists of sub-system networks of i) the role of language (whether the language is constitutive or ancillary to the interaction), ii) channel (in what way the language is displayed to the interactants: graphically, phonetically or both) and iii) medium (whether the language used is spoken-like or written-like). Figure 5 illustrates part of a Mode network.

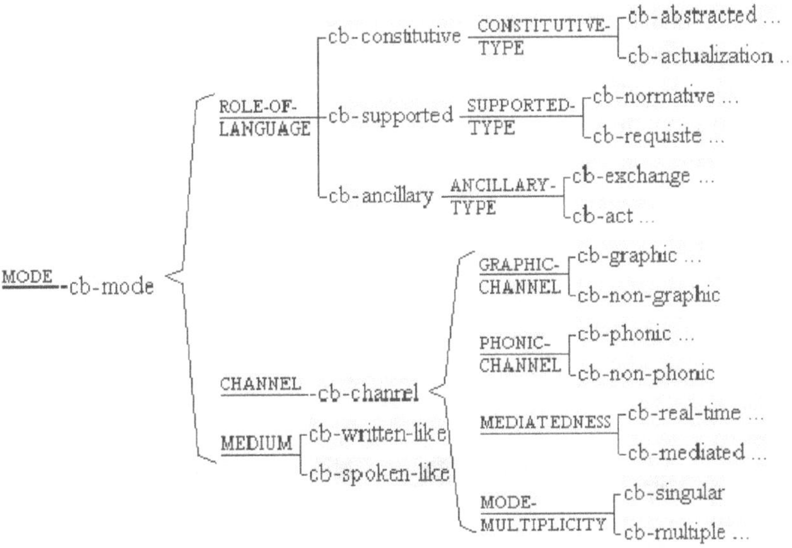

Figure 5: Part of Mode network

Situation type and stage base

The Context Base also incorporates a taxonomy of situation types. A situation type is characterised with the variables of Field, Tenor and Mode, as previously mentioned. These variables are given by the system networks of Field, Tenor and Mode, as explained above.

For the purposes of this discussion, two situation types are taken into account in relation to the dialogue shown above[13]. One is the situation in which the user and his/her secretary talk with each other in order to create a document using the word-processor. This is called the primary situation type. This situation type is realised within the dialogue between the user and the secretary. The other is the sub-situation type in which the user greets the addressee on the greeting card. This called the secondary situation type. This situation type is realised within the text of the greeting card being created by the user with the secretary. Both situation types are annotated with the same contextual system networks of Field, Tenor and Mode independently of each other.

Thirdly, the Stage Base in the Context Base describes the generic structure of the interaction in a given situation type. Just as a situation type is divided into primary and secondary types, a generic structure is divided into primary and secondary generic structures. So, there are the stages 'greetings,' 'task-identification,' 'task-performance' and so on as components of the primary generic structure, and 'receiver-identification,' 'content-editing,' 'picture-inserting' and so on as components of the secondary generic structure.

The secondary generic structure is embedded in the primary generic structure in implementation as shown in Figure 6. This is because it is convenient for us to adopt the viewpoint that a document is created through the interaction between the user and the client secretary for implementation purposes.

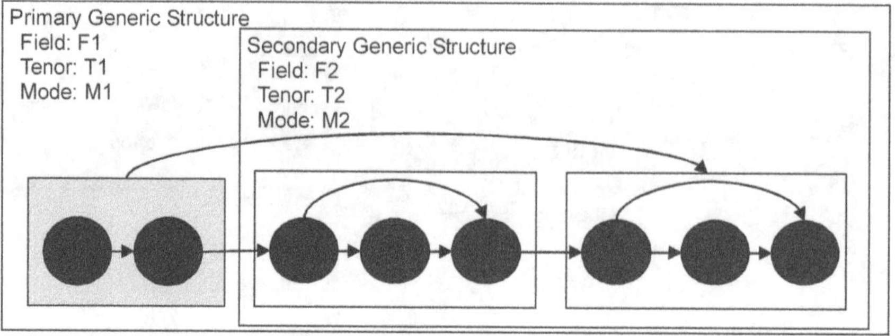

Figure 6: Stage Base with moves

Subsidiary Components: Concept Repository, Text Corpus, Verbalised Knowledge and Situation Specific Dictionary

The Context Base is also supplemented with the following components: the Concept Repository (CR), the Text Corpus, The Verbalised Knowledge and the Situation Specific Dictionary (SSD).

The CR contains all concepts used in a situation type. Figure 7 shows an example of an item of the CR. Each item of the CR describes the linguistic features for realisation into language and the relationships among other concepts within a given situation type, as well as the corresponding concepts of the existing machine readable dictionary used for actual implementation[14]. As shown in this table, each concept has its own slots, such as 'agent', 'object' and so on, and relates itself to other concepts based on these slots[15]. In addition, concepts make hierarchical relationships within the same context of situation through the slots of upper concept name and lower concept name. As for the concept 'changing' shown in Table 1, the upper concept 'operating' is a more general concept of 'changing' and the lower concepts 'bolding', 'magnifying' and 'emphasizing' are more specific concepts of 'changing'. In other words, concepts registered in a given CR constitute a domain ontology[16] of the given situation through the slots and hierarchical relationships.

<table>
<tr><td colspan="2">Head concept identifier</td><td colspan="2">changing</td></tr>
<tr><td colspan="2">Concept type</td><td colspan="2">class</td></tr>
<tr><td colspan="2">EDR concept identifier</td><td colspan="2">0e87a2 3ceec7 3cf4fc 3cf90d</td></tr>
<tr><td colspan="2">MB features</td><td colspan="2">fg-alteration</td></tr>
<tr><td colspan="2">WB features</td><td colspan="2">mat-alteration</td></tr>
<tr><td colspan="2">Upper Concept name</td><td colspan="2">operating</td></tr>
<tr><td colspan="2">Lower Concept name</td><td colspan="2">bolding magnifying emphasizing</td></tr>
<tr><td></td><td>Slot name</td><td>Slot value</td><td>SFL role</td></tr>
<tr><td>1</td><td>agent</td><td>agent</td><td>Actor</td></tr>
<tr><td>2</td><td>object</td><td>domain-concept</td><td>Goal</td></tr>
</table>

Figure 7: An item of CR

The concepts in the CR can be divided into three kinds: speech-acts, domain-propositions and domain-concepts. The combination of these three kinds of concepts constitutes a conceptual frame and becomes a conceptual expression of an utterance for processing. A speech-act concept implies the interpersonal meaning the speaker intends to convey to the hearer. It has the slots of 'speaker', 'hearer' and 'content'. The ideational meaning of a conceptual frame is expressed as the 'content' value of the 'speech-act' concept. The top of the 'content' value is usually a 'domain-proposition' concept. It implies the action of the given conceptual frame and has the slots of 'agent' and 'object'. These slots are correspondent to the Participant/Circumstance roles such as 'Actor', 'Goal' within the framework of SFL. A 'domain-concept' implies a nominal concept in the given conceptual frame and plays the role of an 'element' of the action shown in the conceptual frame. Furthermore, there are two types of concepts: concept class and concept instance. A concept instance is generated from its corresponding concept class. Furthermore a system within the Semiotic Base deals directly with the concept instances. In other words, a concept class plays the role of a matrix for its corresponding concept instance.

The Text Corpus stores the annotated texts which are analysed contextually and linguistically in terms of SFL. The Verbalised Knowledge component is the knowledge with which natural language is deployed in a given situation type and is divided into two subtypes: Knowledge for Describing a Situation (KDS) and Knowledge in Situation (KIS). KDS explains the context of situation with natural language, that is, KDS is the explanation of the material social settings (Hasan, 1996). For example, conventional knowledge such as 'a young person respects older people in a Japanese context' can be an instance of KDS. Knowledge in Situation (KIS) describes the knowledge to be shared between the interactants in the given situation, such as a problem-solving method for a task given to a computer user. The format of analysis of texts in the Text Corpus and the Verbalised Knowledge is essentially the same. The difference between them is that a linguistic expression deployed as a part of the Verbalized Knowledge has standard forms such as '<size> of <font> is <16pts>' whilst linguistic expressions stored in the Text Corpus do not have such standard forms and various linguistic expressions meaning the same thing can be stored there.

The Situation Specific Dictionary (SSD) contains the lexical items deployed in each situation type. As mentioned earlier, all concepts used in a given situation type are registered in the CR. This means that the SSD explains the linguistic features of the concepts registered in each of the CRs. Figure 8 presents an example of an item in the SSD.

Index	*kaeru*
Situation Type	ServiceEncounter
Frequency	0.4
Field	cb-creating-document
Tenor	---
Mode	---
Concept	changing
MB-feature	fg-alteration
WB-feature	mat-alteration&lg-concrete&spatial-cir

Figure 8: An item of SSD

Data Structure of the Situation Type and the Generic Structure

The computational data of a situation type is formatted in a manner similar to the example below. It consists of the following: the identity (ID) of the situation, which in this case is a service encounter; the selection path of the system networks of Field, Tenor and Mode; the upper situation type; lists of the KDSs, KISs and the concepts of the given situation type; and finally, the generic structure.

The upper situation type describes the situation type data, showing the position of the given situation type among the interaction to be enacted in the given culture. The embedded situation type shows what situation type is embedded in the given situation type. This implies that the embedded situation type is the secondary situation type (such as creating a document) whereas the embedding situation type is the primary situation type (such as service encounter).

The list of KDSs shows what kind of knowledge is deployed in the given situation type. Each KDS is given its unique ID and used by calling the ID when needed.

```
SituationType
# Hereafter, descriptions after '#' of each line are skipped when a
computational system works with the data (sample) written here; they
merely explain the content of the data described.
# Hereafter, elements in { } can be treated as members of a 'list'
except for the expression 'id_list of ...', which explains the nature of
the components to fill relevant part with.
id ServiceEncounter
field                                specialized sensible quasi virtual
                                     absent deferred
                                     necessary practical instruct create
                                     non-long-term short-term
                                     explicit-at-outset
tenor                                acquired civic by-office
                                     reciprocating complementary
                                     unequivalent uniplex business
                                     regular  recurrent hierarchic
                                     declared mutable  permanent  dialogic
                                       visual-contact
                                     aural-contact
mode                                 supported graphic mixed scripted by-
                                     letters eidetic pictured
                                     phonic machine speech-like humanoid
                                     real-time face-to-face
                                     multiple overlaid spoken-like
upperSitType                         {id_list of SituationType}
embeddedSitType                      {Computing CreatingText
                                     CreatingDocument Official
                                     Business Greetings}
                                     # id_list of embedded situation
                                     types
knowledgeForDescribinSituation       {id_list of KDS}
conceptRepository                    # corresponding CR
ConceptRepository
situationSpecificDic                 # corresponding items of SSD
SituationSpecificDic
knowledgeInSituation                 {id_list of KIS}
genreStructure_id GenreStructure     # corresponding generic structure
```

The generic structure consists of the ID of the generic structure, that is, the name of the genre and a list of possible stages. A stage consists of its ID, that is the name of the stage, and a list of possible stages. A move consists of the ID of itself, polarity, its structure, and a list of possible moves of transition[17].

A move is represented as a conceptual frame which consists of speech-function and speech-content. As previously mentioned, a speech function implies the interpersonal meaning the speaker conveys to the hearer. Its concept comprises the slots of speaker, hearer and content. A concept of speech-content is the slot value of content of the speech-function concept. It implies the ideational meaning of the given move. Furthermore, we have as a piece of the data structure not only the information of the present move but also the list of possible next moves.

A sample of the data of generic structure, stage and move is shown below.

```
GenreStructure
id WriteDocument
stage_list_id       {ReceiverIdentification, TemplateSelection,
                    DeclarationOfStart, ... }
                    #list of all possible stages
Stage
id                  ReceiverIdentification
move_list           {S3, U3, S4, S4'} #list of possible move in the stage
Move
id                  U3
move_polarity       1 # whether or not the user is to speak (1 or 0).
speech_function     giving-information
move_concept        givingInformation(speaker=user, hearer=secretary,
                    content=addressee(addressee=human))
move_candidates     {S4, S4'}
```

The relationship between other databases

As previously outlined, the Semiotic Base consists of more than just the Context Base. There is the Meaning Base and the Wording Base. The Context Base has a relationship with the Meaning Base and Wording Base via the subsidiary components in the Context Base. The CR registers all of the concepts used and specifies their semantic and lexicogrammatical features in the given context as previously mentioned. In addition, the corresponding part of SSD explains the lexicogrammatical features of the concepts registered in the corresponding CR. In this way the Context Base specifies the register of the context and is linked into the meaning and wording bases.

Algorithm for text generation

This section shows how the Semiotic Base containing the Context Base works in the text generation process. In general, the process of text generation is divided into two phases. One is the phase of content specification. The other phase involves linguistic representation of the specified content. In the first phase the generator determines the content to be generated using the database. We call this phase the text planning phase. After the content to be generated is determined, the generator converts the content into text strings through several steps. We call this phase the string generation phase. We shall first show the process of string planning and subsequently string generation using system networks. This process of text generation is based on the following example, which is a part of the dialogue previously shown:

S2 *shochuumimai o donata ni okuri masu ka?*
summer-greeting-card O who NI send-FOR Q
Who would you like to send the summer greeting-card to?

U2 *yuujin to kaisha no dooryoo desu.*
friend and company NO colleague COP=FOR
To friends and colleagues in my company.

S3 *shochuumimai no bunmen o kae masu ka?*
summer-greeting-card NO content O change-FOR Q
Would you like to change the content of the summer greetings?

In this example, the secretary asks the user about the addressee of the greeting card in order to obtain the addressee information from him/her at S2. In response to the user's utterance U2, the secretary asks if s/he will change the content of the greeting card according to the characteristics of the addressee. In order for the client secretary to generate utterance S3, the secretary must consider the social relationship between the user and the addressee of the greeting card and know that the more casual greetings can be sent to friends whereas more formal greetings must be sent to colleagues of the user's company. If the user makes a different response at U2, the secretary must be able to respond in a different way:

U2' *yuujin to saakuru no nakama desu*
Friend and circle NO colleagues COP=FOR
To friends and colleagues in my circle.

S3' *bunmen wa onaji de ii desu ka?*
Content WA same DE ok COP=FOR Q
Is it OK if the content is the same?

Text planning

The content to be generated is given by an instance conceptual frame selected in the Stage Base. The overall process is shown in Figure 9.

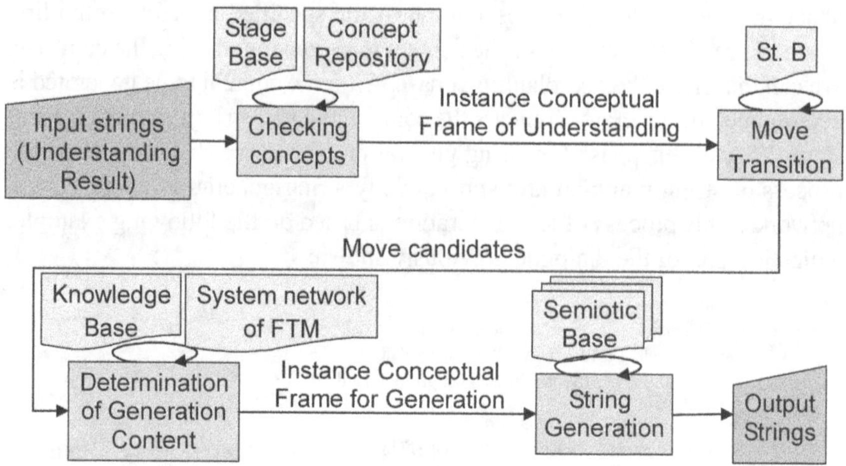

Figure 9: Overall process of text planning

In the example previously shown, moves S2 S3 (or S3') belong to the stage 'receiver-identification': between these moves the user specifies the addressee of the document. The structure of the stage is shown in Figure 10.

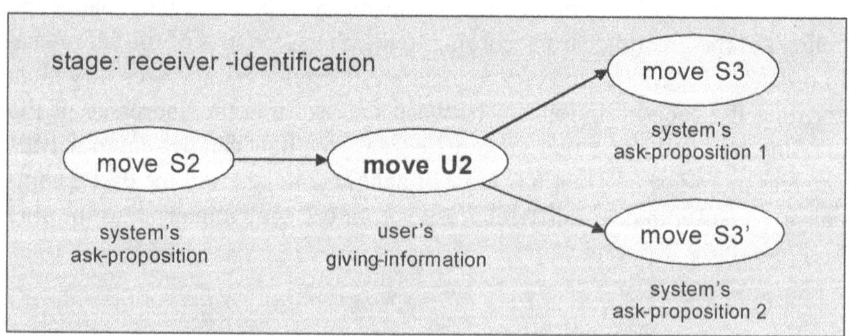

Figure 10: Moves in stage: receiver identification

At the first step of text planning, we check the conceptual analysis of the understanding result[18]. At this time, we compare the understanding result with the conceptual information of the prototype move in the Stage Base. If the conceptual feature of the understanding result is appropriate as a move, the process proceeds to the next step. An utterance is regarded as appropriate if all concepts and slots of the understanding result are the same as, or a subclass of, the corresponding concept or slots of the prototype in the Stage Base.

In the case of the example dialogue, after understanding U2, we first check the conceptual analysis of U2 and match it with the move U2. A stage in the Stage Base has the information of each move in the form of a conceptual frame. We match this frame with the conceptual analysis of the move U2. Figure 11 shows the conceptual analysis of U2 and its corresponding conceptual frame in the Stage Base.

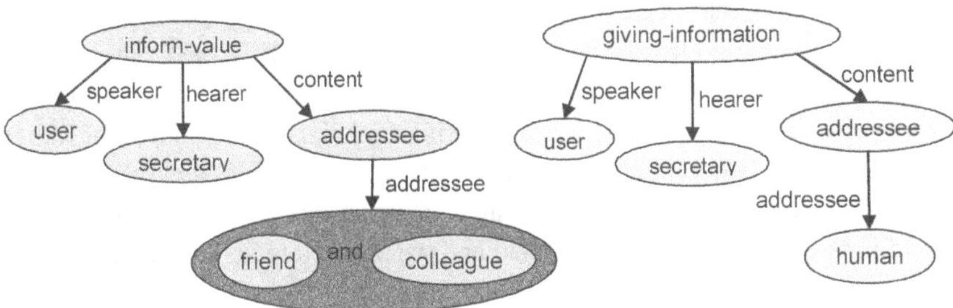

Figure 11: Conceptual analysis of understanding result of move U3 (left) and corresponding conceptual frame in the Stage Base (right)

If each concept or slot of the conceptual analysis result is the same as a subcategory of the corresponding concept or slot, then we regard the understanding result as appropriate for move U2 and proceed to the next step. The criterion of the conceptual hierarchy is indicated in the CR. In this case, we can find from the corresponding CR that 'inform-value' is a lower concept of 'giving-information' and both 'friend' and 'colleague' are lower concepts of 'human' and so on.

Second, we proceed to the next move according to the transition information described in the Stage Base. However, if we have more than two candidates in the Stage Base, we select the most appropriate move according to the constraints written in the Context Base.

In this case we must proceed from U2 to the next move. However there are two move candidates: move S3 and move S3', which have the respective meanings 'Would you like to change the content of the greeting card?' and 'Is it OK if the content is the same?' The conceptual frames of the move candidates are shown in Figure 12.

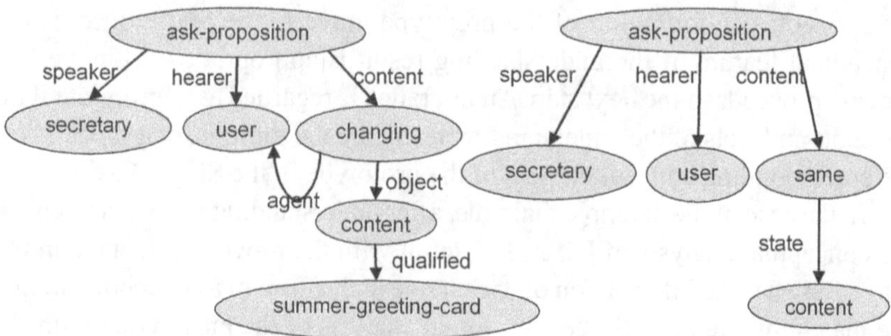

Figure 12: Conceptual frames of move S4 (left) and S4′ (right)

Third, we choose the most appropriate move among the candidates according to the constraints. The constraints are written in the Context Base. In this case, we use the contextual features concerning Tenor and KDS in the Context Base. According to the conceptual frame of utterance U2, there are two Tenors for addressees: friends and colleagues, and their social distance is found to be rather large. The KDS concerning the content or style of a card says that the content may differ according to the social distance of addressees. As a result, move U3 is selected as the content to be generated and we proceed to U3 as the next move.

String generation

The process of string generation is divided into four steps: 1) relating concepts to SFL roles 2) identification of case markers and word order 3) specification of the group structure and 4) lexical selection. The overall process is illustrated in Figure 13.

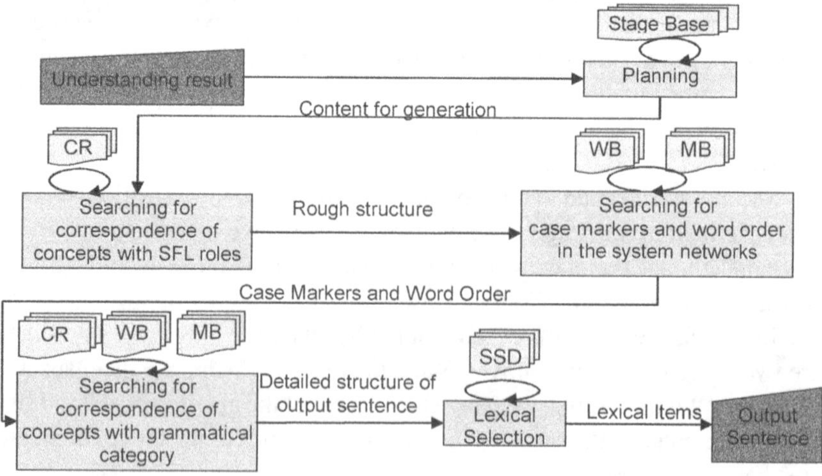

Figure 13: Overall process of string generation

First, we search the CR for the semantic features and the Participants and Circumstances which are needed. The CR describes the semantic features of the given concept and the relationship of its slots to the SFL-roles. We can determine the rough semantic structure of the text string by referring to the information written in the CR.

In this example, we first look up the CR for the semantic feature of the slot-value of 'content,' that is, 'changing,' which has been already illustrated in Figure 8. We can also find from the CR the Participant roles corresponding to the slot values of 'changing.' This process is illustrated as shown in Figure 14.

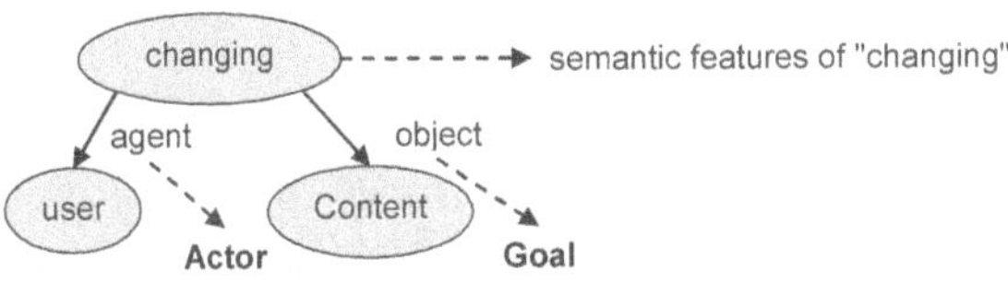

Figure 14: Relating concepts to SFL roles

Second, we find the lexicogrammatical features corresponding to the semantic features obtained at the last step, as well as case markers and word order, using the realisation statements attached to the system networks of the Meaning Base and the Wording Base. At this step, we obtain the lexicogrammatical features of the Process from the realisation statements in the Meaning Base. We also obtain case markers and the word order from the realisation statements in the Wording Base[19].

In this example, we can find the lexicogrammatical features of 'changing' from the realisation statement attached to the corresponding semantic features in the Meaning Base and the correspondences between Participant roles and the appropriate word order from the realisation statements in the Wording Base. This process can be illustrated as shown in Figure 15.

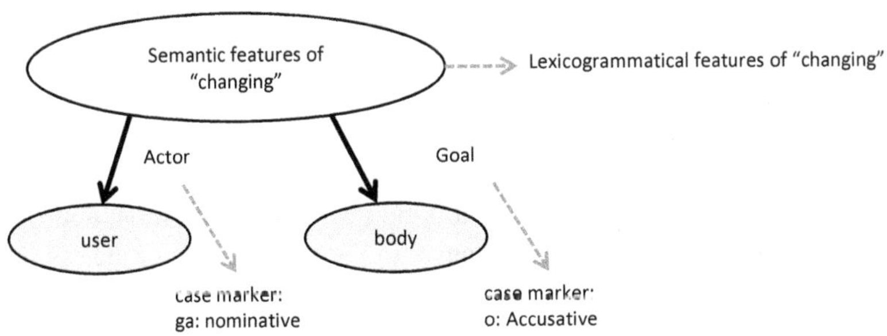

Figure 15: Case markers and word order

Third, after specifying the rough clause structure of the text strings to be generated, we determine the detailed internal structure of each group. At this step we relate the grammatical categories and concepts within functions used in SFL such as Participant, Circumstance and Process. At this step, the structure of the text string is also determined.

In this example, the 'object' slot and its slot value 'body' are related to the 'Head + Modifier' part of the internal structure of the 'Goal' group. Further, the 'qualified' slot and its slot value 'summer-greeting-card' are related to the 'Head + Binder' group. In both cases the slot values are related to the 'Head' part of the grammatical category unit. Figure 16 illustrated this process and Figure 17 shows the structure of the text strings.

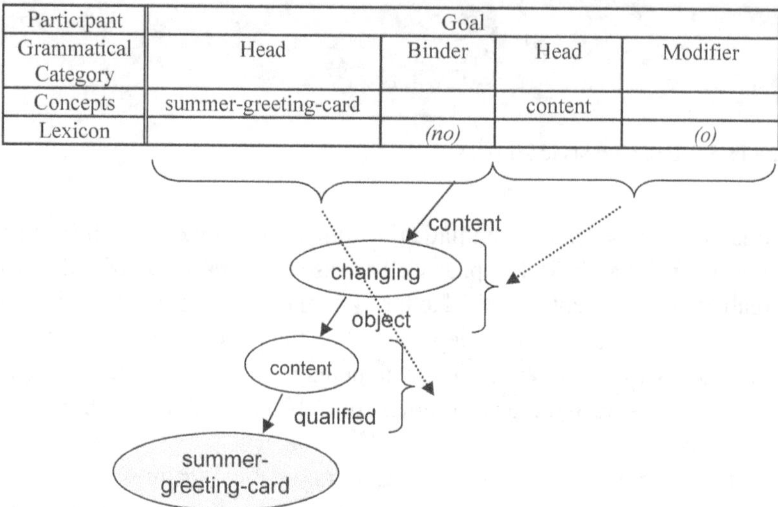

Participant	Goal			
Grammatical Category	Head	Binder	Head	Modifier
Concepts	summer-greeting-card		content	
Lexicon		*(no)*		*(o)*

Figure 16: Relation of Participant 'Goal' with the grammatical categories

Part.	Goal				Process	
Gr. Cat.	Head	Binder	Head	Modifier	Head	Negotiator
Concepts	summer-greeting-card		content		changing	ask-proposition
Lexicon		*(no)*		*(o)*		*(ka)*

Figure 17: Grammatical structure of output string

The last step is lexical selection. At this step we look up the most appropriate lexical expression of the concept instances in SSD. We search for the candidates of the lexical items while referring to the concept labels and situation types described in SSD. Then, we select the most frequent item as the most appropriate candidate by referring to the frequency information of the candidates chosen.

In this case, when specifying the (set of) lexical items for 'changing,' we first identify candidate lexical items on the basis of the concept label 'changing' and situation type 'service-encounter.' Then, we select the most frequent set of lexical items as the most appropriate candidate. According to Figure 18, we can specify 'kae-masu' from the candidates.

Index	Conceptual label	frequency
aratame-masu	changing	0.2
henkoo-simasu	changing	0.3
kae-masu	changing	0.5

Figure 18: Lexical candidates for 'changing'

The same procedure is followed to find the lexical items for 'content' and 'summer-greeting-card' as 'bunmen' and 'shochuumimai' respectively. The final text string and its structure are shown in Figure 19.

Part.	Goal				Process	
Gr. Cat.	Head	Binder	Head	Mod	Head	Negotiator
Concepts	s-g-c		content		changing	ask-proposition
Lexicon	*shochuumimai*	*no*	*bunmen*	*o*	*kae-masu*	*ka*

Figure 19: Result of text generation

In brief, this section has described the contents of the Context Base and illustrated how the Semiotic Base processes text planning and text generation using the Context Base. The main characteristics of the Semiotic Base as a database for text processing can be summarised as follows: The Semiotic Base contains contextual information in the Context Base presented in terms of SFL, and can be used in text processing, especially in generating text strings. The Context Base includes contextual configuration information, the situation type and generic structure based on a SFL conception as well as other supplementary components such as the CR and SSD, which explain linguistic usage in a situation specified by the Context Base.

Comparison with previous research

By way of further elaborating on the nature of the Semiotic Base, it is useful to consider how it differs from other SFL based text generation projects, some of which deploy information related to contextual features. For example, COMMUNAL (Fawcett, Tucker and Lin, 1993) and Multex (Matthiessen, Zeng, Cross, Kobayashi, Teruya and Wu, 1998) consider contextual features. However neither of them makes full use of the entire spectrum of contextual information in the manner that the Semiotic Base does. The text generator in the COMMUNAL system, GENESYS, comprises the system networks of 'situation,' which consist of TENOR, MODE and CONGRUENCE_SIT networks and is described as follows:

> The MODE system presents options which reflect the medium through which the sentence will be generated, and the TENOR system reflects the performer's assessment of the interpersonal relationship between herself and the addressee. [......] It is the third system, CONGRUENCE_SIT, that leads on to the main [lexicogrammatical] network. A 'congruent situation' is realised as a clause (not a nominalisation). (Fawcett et al. 1993:138)

In our terminology, however, the MODE system of GENESYS provides only the nature of the medium and does not provide any information on the role of language nor on the channel. The TENOR system provides information on how to 'speak', for example, formally, casually or consultatively. This is different from our Tenor system in that we accommodate the nature of the social relationship itself (social hierarchy or social distance and so on) as part of the Tenor system whilst COMMUNAL provides the nature of the text as a result of the social relationship between the interactants. Also, the CONGRUENCE_SIT(UATION) system indicates the grammatical structure of the given text. For example, it includes 'TRANSITIVITY,' 'SUBORDINATION_TYPE,' 'MOOD,' 'POLARITY' and so on. These analyses are considered within meaning and wording in our framework and are not considered as a component of context as is the case in the GENESYS system.

Another text generator, Multex also considers the contextual content in terms of SFL. It has as the resource for text generation, the Meaning base (different from our Meaning Base; roughly corresponding to our overall Semiotic Base), which contains 'multiple linguistic systems (eg. the lexico-grammar and semantics of English, Chinese, Japanese and so on), semiotic modalities (the resources for creating charts and maps), multiple domain models (eg. the knowledge about tourism and about communicable resources)' (Matthiessen et al. 1998:230). Among these components, the domain models correspond to our situation type and Verbalised Knowledge. The difference between Multex and our generator is that our system further characterises situation types with a contextual configuration using the system network of Field, Tenor and Mode and attaches generic structures to corresponding situation types.

Future work

The system described in the paper was demonstrated at the 18th conference of JSAI (Japan Society of Artificial Intelligence) in 2004 and this demonstration was closely associated with a session for the ELC project held at the conferences of JSAI from 2001 to 2005. This session was held as a part of special sessions called 'Challenge for Realizing Early Profits (CREP)' organised by JSAI. The CREP consists of survival sessions evaluated by the participants and if a session is survived it gets the right to have a session as a part of CREP next year. Furthermore, a session survived for five times is regarded to 'graduate' from the CREP session. Our studies were so highly evaluated every year that our session succeeded in surviving for full five years.

In addition, the study described in this paper, as a part of the ELC project, was reviewed by leading SFL researchers (Butt et al., 2005). According to this review, the Semiotic Base, including the Context Base, 'covers all strata defined by the hierarchy of stratification, modeling these within the overall semiotic base as the Context Base, the Meaning Base, the Wording Base and the Expression Base'(p.113) and 'is unique in its theoretical consistency' (p.113).

As a result of trialling the Semiotic Base we have identified seven areas which need further consideration. These are i) the structure of the Stage Base; ii) the links between the contextual and the linguistics resources; iii) the methods used for describing and using Verbalised Knowledge; iv) the nature of the input specification; v) the number of concept classes; vi) the need for a shortcut model of string generation and vii) a method of handling grammatical metaphor. Each of these considerations is briefly discussed below.

The need to reconsider the structure of the Stage Base is due to the fact that the move or turn structure in the current implementation is largely predetermined. This prevents us from processing content dynamically. For the most part we can only generate predetermined content. Originally we had intended to construct a Stage Base in which the speech content changes dynamically according to the user's utterances as the results of the understanding process. However this was not achievable given the time constraints on the project.

We must also consider how to link the contextual resources directly to the linguistic resources. In our present Context Base the subsidiary components play the role of specifying the register of a given context as previously mentioned. The contextual features are linked to linguistic resources via the concepts and linguistic features specified in CR and SSD. However, it might be theoretically more transparent to link the contextual to the linguistic stratum by the same formalism as intra-linguistic resources, that is, using the realisation statements from the Meaning Base to the Wording Base and so on.

We also must give more consideration to the method in which we describe and use Verbalised Knowledge. In our system the social settings or 'material social settings' (Hasan, 1996) are described with the Verbalised Knowledge as KDS. We describe all relevant social settings with natural language. However, we need to give more consideration to the criteria and the amount of Verbalised Knowledge for describing the social settings in language and to the coverage of such descriptions. In this context we must consider the appropriateness for describing the social setting in terms of the contextual configuration. For example, what is appropriate for describing the social setting and what is inappropriate and how many elements and relationships can or should we accommodate for a sufficient description of the social setting of a situation type?

As for the method of text generation, the problem of input specification is also significant. Our generation model starts from the conceptual frame as the content for generation, to which linguistic features are attached. However we need to consider what triggers the selection process and how the content for generation should be formed and expressed. To this end we would probably need the *intention* of the input specified so that the appropriate meaning features to be verbalised can be selected.

Furthermore, the number of concept classes registered in CR predicts the amount of Verbalised Knowledge needed because the Verbalised Knowledge is constructed using the concepts registered in the CR. We have constructed about 200 concept classes simply for executing the task of creating a document with a computer, for which a simple dialogue was presented. It is evident that we need to develop more concepts and the number is still expanding.

Also, we are constructing a shortcut model of string generation in addition to the general string generation algorithm using the system networks as described above. With this shortcut algorithm, we will be able to generate text strings from previously analysed text in the corpus instead of traversing the system networks in the Semiotic Base every time. With the general algorithm, on the one hand, we can determine the rough clause structure of the output string (case markers and word order) using the Meaning Base and the Wording Base. On the other hand, if we had a short cut model in which the corpus is pre-analysed with correspondences, we could obtain the appropriate case markers and word order pattern of the text string to be generated. We could also obtain the detailed group structures from the previously analysed text strings stored in the corpus instead of compiling the rules for determining group structure by searching the Semiotic Base every time.

Finally, we need a process for dealing with grammatical metaphor. *Grammatical metaphor* refers to the phenomenon that a semantic category is realised by a non-standard grammatical category. For example, the nominal group, 'Smoking by children ...' is a grammatical metaphor instead of the more congruent form, 'If children smoke ....' We need to enable the Semiotic Base to deal with grammatical metaphor in our framework[20].

Concluding remarks

In this chapter, after providing a rough sketch of our project, 'Everyday Language Computing' in which we developed the Semiotic Base and after describing how we have applied the systemic functional model of language to Natural Language Processing, we took a brief look at the contextual stratum in the SF model and illustrated the components and structure of the Context Base as a component of the Semiotic Base. As described, the Context Base consists of the system networks of Field, Tenor and Mode, the system network of situation types and the Stage Base as a resource of generic structures. Further, the subsidiary components of the Context Base, the Concept Repository, the Text Corpus, the Verbalised Knowledge and the Situation Specific Dictionary were described. We also showed the data structures of the situation type, of the generic structures and of the move.

The second part of this chapter presented a method of using the resources in the Semiotic Base for text generation. Text generation is divided into two phases: text planning and string generation. The former concerns 'what to say' and the latter 'how to say it.' Text planning is executed through the steps of concept check, move transition and content determination. String Generation is executed through the steps of relating concepts to SF roles, identification of case markers and word order, specification of the group structure and lexical selection.

Further, we showed that we have made more use of contextual features than other SFL-based systems and we concluded by listing some tasks we intend to accomplish in the near future.

Acknowledgements

We deeply appreciate Dr. Elizabeth A. Thomson of the University of New South Wales, Canberra and Dr. William S. Armour of the University of New South Wales for giving us the opportunity to publish this paper and for making many useful comments to the earlier versions of this paper. This gratitude is of course also directed to Equinox Publishing. Professor Michio Sugeno (presently Doshisha University) supervised and gave a lot of precious advice on our study, and the other members of Laboratory for Language-Based Intelligent Systems of Brain Science Institute,

RIKEN gave us a lot of useful comments. Emeritus Professor Michael Halliday of the University of Sydney, Professor Christian Matthiessen, Associate Professor David Butt, Dr. Wu Canzhong of Macquarie University and Dr. Kazuhiro Teruya of the University of New South Wales strongly supported our study by having a lot of fruitful discussions throughout the ELC project. This paper owes much to their support. Of course, however, we take full responsibility for our study.

The work which resulted in this paper was done when the authors were members of the Laboratory for Language-Based Intelligent Systems, Brain Science Institute, RIKEN, Japan (The project was held from 2000 to 2005). The original version of this paper was made in November 2004 based on Takahashi et al (2004). After the completion, two of the authors gave further presentations on text generation using the Semiotic Base (Kobayashi and Takahashi, 2005 and Takahashi and Kobayashi, 2005). However, those papers merely showed our ideas and simulations, which have not yet been implemented on the computer. On the other hand, the method presented in this paper was actually implemented based on the research results of the project.

Notes

* Sadly Dr. Takahashi passed away unexpectedly in February 2009 and is greatly missed by his colleagues. As the project linguist, he played a key role in the Everyday Language Computing project. This chapter was primarily written by him. We dedicate it to his wife, Michiko

1 As said later, the functions in SFL are divided into three metafunctions; the sentence exemplified here has the functions of 'Subject' and 'Predicator' interpersonally and 'Theme' and 'Rheme' textually.

2 The contextual stratum, which is not a linguistic system but the environment of linguistic systems, has the variables of Field, Tenor and Mode instead of the metafunctions of ideational, interpersonal and textual respectively.

3 This figure shows a part of the Wording Base which the RIKEN team has actually implemented. See Ito and Sugimoto (2006) for details of the Wording Base.

4 See Ito and Sugimoto (2006) for a comprehensive description of the Semiotic Base.

5 In the example dialogue, S1 means Secretary's 1st utterance and U2 means User's 2nd utterance.

6 We have made a prototype system equipped with the Semiotic Base which incorporates the Context Base based on the dialogue exemplified here. This system is made in order for ordinary people to operate a computer using everyday language. They can talk to a client secretary in the computer and create a document such as an invitation card, for example, by asking the secretary to make the card. See Iwazume et al. (2004) for details.

7 See Matthiessen (1995).

8 Henceforth we use the term 'text' and 'interaction' almost synonymously. We think that, in general, an 'interaction' as a social process results in a 'text' as a production thereof. However, the difference does not matter within the limit of this paper.

9 This view of context is based on the concept of instantiation. We are seeing the relationship between culture and situation as a cline of instantiation in context (Matthiessen, 1995). However, there is another view of this relationship in SFL whereby the context of culture and the context of situation are divided into different strata and the former is realised in the latter. See Martin (1992) for details.

10 At the contextual stratum, as the expansion of the notion of the syntagm/paradigm distinction of language, we recognise that syntagm refers to the structure of text which realises context and paradigm refers to contextual features which configure context. In other words we recognise that generic structure is the syntagmatic realisation of a given context and a contextual configuration is the paradigmatic expression of the context.

11 Our contextual system networks largely depend upon Butt (2004) with several minor revisions.

12 The features of the system networks in the Context Base begin with 'cb' (which stands for 'Context Base') in order to indicate that they belong to the contextual stratum. There are four kinds of system networks in the Semiotic Base as previously mentioned and the total number of the features in the system networks amounts to more than 2000. In building such a huge construction we had to avoid giving the same name to features in the different strata.

13 Some Systemic Functional linguists insist that a context can be divided into first-order and second-order contexts (Matthiessen, 1995, for example). This conception seems similar to ours at a glance. However, it must be noted that this conception is quite different to ours. The notion of first-order and second-order contexts depicts different aspects of the same context and realised into the same text. In contrast, our notion of primary and secondary situation types says there are two different contexts to be considered in the domain we deal with. These two are realised into different texts. The primary is realised into the dialogue between the user and the secretary and the secondary into the document itself created through the interaction.

14 We deployed EDR (Japan Electronic Dictionary Research Institute Limited 2001) as the machine readable dictionary for convenience.

15 It must be noted that the conception of 'slot' used here is quite different from 'grammatical category' in traditional grammar, although they seem to be similar at a glance and even if they might explain the same things as a result. The notion of 'concepts' with 'slots', which originates from information science, is deployed mainly for knowledge representation and procedure in a given information space whilst grammatical categories are for explaining linguistic phenomena in (a) given language(s).

16 A domain ontology means the expression of the configuration of the concepts used in a given (information) space.

17 This paper deals with a dialogue, each turn of which consists of only single move. As a result, 'move(s)' can be regarded as 'turn(s)' linguistically within the scope of this paper.

18 See Ito and Sugimoto (2006; in this volume) for details regarding the process of text understanding with the Semiotic Base.

19 In actual implementation, we previously extracted the realisation rules on case markers and word-order (respectively called 'LinkUnit' and 'OrderUnit') from realisation statements in the Semiotic Base and compiled them within the Semiotic Base.

20 Bateman (1990) considers ways of dealing with grammatical metaphor in his text processing system using an 'Upper Model', which roughly corresponds to our Meaning Base and Concept Repository.

References

Bateman, J. A. (1990) Finding translation equivalents: an application of grammatical metaphor *COLING 1990 Volume 1: Papers presented to the 13th International Conference on Computational Linguistics* 13–18. Helsinki.

Butt, D. G. (2004) Parameters of context: on establishing the similarities and differences between social processes, paper presented at The 31st International Systemic Functional Congress, Kyoto.

Butt, D. G., Halliday, M. A. K., Matthiessen, C. M. I. M., Teruya, K. and Wu, C. (2005) Review Report on the Research Results of the Lab. For Language-Based Intelligent Systems, BSI, RIKEN. In *Research Report* 112–125. Laboratory for Language-Based Intelligent Systems, Brain Science Institute, RIKEN, Wako, Saitama, Japan.

Fawcett, R. P. Tucker, G. H. and Lin, Y. Q. (1993) How a systemic functional grammar works: the roles of realization in realization. In H. Horacek and M. Zock (eds) *New Concepts in Natural Language Generation: Planning, Realization and Systems* 114–186. London and New York: Pinters.

Halliday, M. A. K. and Matthiessen, C. M. I. M. (1999) *Construing Experience through Meaning: A Language-based Approach to Cognition.* London and New York: Cassell.

Halliday, M. A. K. and Matthiessen, C. M. I. M. (2004) *An Introduction to Functional Grammar*. 3rd edition. London: Edward Arnold Publishers.

Hasan, R. (1996) *Ways of Saying, Ways of Meaning. Selected Papers of Ruquiya Hasan.* In C. Cloran, D. Butt, and G. Williams (eds) London and New York: Cassell.

Iwazume, M., Kobayashi, I., Sugimoto, T. Iwashita, S. Takahashi, Y. Ito, N. and Sugeno, M. (2003) Everyday Language Computing – toward language-based computational environment. *Transactions of the Japanese Society for Artificial Intelligence* 18(1): 45–56 (in Japanese).

Iwazume, M., Kobayashi, I. and Sugeno, M. (2004) Natural language mediated software control *Proceedings of International Conference on Systems, Man and Cybernetics 2004*. The Hague.

Ito, N. and Sugimoto, T. (2006) A computational model of language in context and its application to the understanding of Japanese text. In this volume.

Japan Electronic Dictionary Research Institute Limited (2001) *EDR Dictionary*, Japan Electronic Dictionary Research Institute Limited Tokyo, Japan.

Kobayashi, I. and Sugeno, M. (1997) Toward Everyday Language Computing: computing from a viewpoint of linguistic theory. *Journal of Advanced Computational Intelligence* 1(1): 1 – 8.

Kobayashi, I. and Takahashi, Y. (2005) Text Generation Based on the Constraints of the Systemic Resource. In J. Patrick and T. Hawker (eds) *Proceedings of the First Computational Systemic Functional Grammar Conference (CSFG05)* 56–64. Sydney: The University of Sydney, Australia.

Martin, J. R. (1992) *English Text: System and Structur*e. Amsterdam and Philadelphia: John Benjamins Publishing.

Matthiessen, C. M. I. M (1995) *Lexicogrammatical Cartography: English Systems* Tokyo: International Language Sciences Publishers.

Matthiessen, C. M. I. M., Zeng, L., Cross, M., Kobayashi, I., Teruya, K. and Wu, C. (1998) The Multex generator and its environment: application and development. *Proceedings of the 9th International Workshop on Natural Language Generation* 228–237. (INLG-98) Niagara-on-the-Lake.

Takahashi, Y., Kobayashi, I., Iwazume, M., Ito, N. and Sugeno, M. (2004) The Contents and Structure of the Context Base, and Its Application. In J. L. Vicedo, P. Martínez-Barco, R. Muñoz and M. Saiz Noeda (eds) *Advances in Natural Language Processing. 4th International Conference, EsTAL 2004, Alicante, Spain, October 20–22, 2004, Proceedings* 103–114. Lecture Notes in Artificial Intelligence 3230, Springer-Verlag, Berlin and Heidelberg.

Takahashi, Y. and Kobayashi, I. (2005) Text Generation Using Contextual Information. In *Proceedings of the Conference Pacific Association for Computational Linguistics (PACLING 2005)* 301–310. Hino-shi, Tokyo, Japan.

Index

References to illustrations, figures and notes are entered as, for example, 258ill., 333f, 351n.

adjectival group predicate 70, 71–2
Akerejola, E. 3
algorithms 287, 293, 300–11, 312, 313, 317–18, 339–45, 348
Ali Bardi, M. 3
Apposition 30f, 31–2, 42t
appraisal 179, 207n
Argument element 25–6, 49, 50–1, 52t, 53
argument (exposition) 8–9, 23–55
Armour, William S. 17, 238, 242n, 259, 280
artificial intelligence 318, 347. *see also* computational models
Asahi Shimbun 24, 25, 26, 109, 206n, 207n
attributive relational process 147, 148

back-channeling 221
Banno, E. 255
Barnard, Christopher 16
Bateman, J. A. 295, 298, 314, 316, 352n
Beckett, G. H. 213–14
Bernstein, Basil 213
beta clause types 116, 123, 125
bi-directionality, definition 281n
biographical recount genre 261–7, 258*ill.*
biology textbooks 137–69
Blair, Tony 174
Brain Science Institute (BSI). *see* Rikagaku Kenkyujo (RIKEN)
Butt, D. 8, 46, 295, 317–18, 347
Byrnes, H. 210

Cafferal, A. 3
Carroll. C. 256
causal-conditional relationships 30f, 37–9, 41, 42t, 47–8, 52–3
chaining 107, 134n
Challenge for Realizing Early Profits (competition) 318, 347
chart parsing 306–9
children's stories 68, 83, 109, 117–19
circumstance types 116, 119–20, 124
Clarification 32–4, 42t
classification (taxonomies) 137–69
Classifiers 151–5, 166–7
clauses 26–46
  chaining 107, 134n
  differentiation of relations between 27–8, 29f, 47–55, 143–8, 165–8
  ellipsis 105–7, 157–60, 264–5
  embedding 167–8
  MOOD elements 69–83
  and THEME 103–33
Cléirigh, C. 281n
clines 14, 16, 175–8, 193–4, 206n, 207n, 208n
closed systems, definition 13
clusters 27–8, 29f, 53–4, 55n
coding orientation 213, 237–9
collaborative dialogue 17, 211, 216, 217, 221–41
Colombi, M. C. 213
commands (imperative Mood) 66, 76–7, 79, 81–2
COMMUNAL (text generator) 346
computational models 13–14, 18–19, 285–318, 324–49, 351n–2n

computer-generated text 18–19
conceptual analysis (computational models) 311–12, 340–2
Concession element 25–6, 49, 50–1, 52t
conjunctions 35–6, 37, 38, 42t, 143–4
conjunctives 26–7, 31–40, 41, 42t, 55n
connectives 39–40
content plane, definition 9
context 8–9, 256–7, 259–60, 267–72, 281n
  computer models 287–300, 313, 325–6, 328–36, 347–8, 350n, 351n
contractions 264
corpus studies 24–8, 29f, 69, 108–12, 138–42, 175–8
Cross, M. 346
Crozet, C. 281n
culture 8–9, 46–9, 256–7, 259–60, 267–72, 281n, 329–30, 348
  children's stories 118–19
  interculturality 272, 281n

d-words 74–5, 79, 81, 86n
Daneš, F. 108, 133, 156
databases, and natural language processing 287–318, 324–49
declaratives 67, 73, 79, 81–3
deictics 150–1, 154
Democratic Party of Japan (DPJ). *see* DPJ (Democratic Party of Japan)
descriptive linguistics. *see* linguistic description
desu/~masu form 73, 86n
dialect, definition 212–13
dialogue 68, 80–3, 237–41
'dictionary' forms, definition 73, 86n
digital divide, definition 319n
discourse markers 10
domain ontology, definition 352n
DPJ (Democratic Party of Japan) 173–5, 183–7, 189–90

education 210, 213–15
  collaborative tasks 17, 211, 216, 217, 221–41
  cultural context 271–2
  writing skills 17–18, 214–15, 255, 267–81
educational language 137–69
Eggins, S. 65, 67, 69, 83, 85, 139–40
Elaboration 14, 30f, 31–4, 42t, 143
  definition 31
ellipsis 81, 105–7, 117–19, 134n, 157–60, 264–5
Ellis, R. 211, 239
Emele, M. 314
endophoric ellipsis 105–6, 119, 134n
English 14
  cultural context 8–9, 46, 260–1
  MOOD 6–7, 11, 12–13, 66–7, 69
  political discourse 190–3
  scientific discourse 139–41, 147, 148, 150
  subject 6–7
  THEME 101–3
  transitivity 169n
English For Specific Purposes School 268
Enhancement 14, 15, 24, 27–8, 30f, 36–40, 41, 42t, 47–55, 116, 123
  definition 36
error analysis 214–15, 217–41
Events 176–94
Everyday Language Computing Project 18–19, 285–318, 324–49
Exemplification 143
existential process 148, 164
Expansion 14, 29–40, 132
experiential metafunction, definition 9
expert interlocutors, and language development 17, 215–16, 217–18, 237–41, 242n
exposition 8–9, 23–55
  social purpose of 46–9
expression plane, definition 9
Extension 14, 30f, 34–6, 42t, 144
  definition 34

Fawcett, R. P. 314, 346
Feez, S. 255, 269, 270, 271
FIELD 259, 294, 330–1, 350n

Firbas, J. 135n
Firth, J. R. 3, 5–6
'focus on form' pedagogies 213–14
formal exophoric ellipsis 81, 107, 117, 264–5
Francis, G. 103
Fries, P. H. 103, 104, 133
Fukui, N. 7, 11, 15
functional tenor, definition 256–7
Furuya, Reiko 17, 280

general linguistic theory, definition 5–7
"Generation Y" 259–60, 266
generic skills 272, 281n
Generic Structure Potential 49–54, 55n
generic structures, definition 330, 333–4
GENESYS (text generator) 346
Genre Approach (teaching method) 268–81
genres 14, 15, 16, 108–10, 254–81
 biographical recount genre 261–7, 258*ill.*
 children's stories 68, 83, 109, 117–19
 and cultural context 259, 260–1, 271, 272
 definition 256–7, 281n
 dialogue 68, 80–3, 237–41
 expository texts 23–55, 129
 newspaper articles 104–5, 109, 119–20
 political discourse 173–94, 206n, 207n, 208n
 scientific discourse 137–69
geographical knowledge, construction of 139–41
Ghadessy, M. 135n
Givón, T. 134n
Gordon, T. H. 314
grammar, definition 13, 212–15
grammatical metaphor 349, 352n
grammaticalization 55n
graphology 9
Gregory, M. 256

Hagiwara, K. 255
Hajikao, A. 255
Hall, J. K. 211–12
Halliday, M. A. K. 3, 4–13, 17, 23, 26, 27, 31, 36, 40, 65, 66–7, 69, 84, 101, 102, 105, 111, 134n, 137, 140, 142, 146, 149, 164, 168, 169n, 173, 175, 211, 212–13, 215, 256, 259, 270, 281n, 288, 292–4, 296, 319n, 325
Hammond, J. 269–70
Hasan, R. 49, 55n, 81, 105, 107, 134n, 213, 239, 242n, 256, 264, 281n, 288, 293, 330, 335, 348
Hayakawa, Chie 11, 16
Hirano, Y. 289
Hjelmslev, L. 9, 206n
Hopper, P. J. 134n
Hori, M. 6–7, 67, 68
hyperthemes 156, 162, 167, 168–9
hypotactic structures 117, 121, 125, 132, 150
hypotaxis, definition 134n

IDEA relation 40–1, 42t
ideational metafunction 9, 15, 16, 296, 328. *see also* THEME
ideational Theme 115–19, 120–1, 122–3, 125–6
 definition 102, 135n
 markedness 127–33
Ikeda, Y. 255
Ikegami, Y. 8–9
imperatives 66, 76–7, 79, 81–2
implicit relations 27, 47–9, 187–90, 207n
implicit Theme 116–19, 125–6, 128–9, 132
informal writing styles 261–8
input, nature of (language development) 215–16
instantiation, definition 294–6, 319n, 351n
interculturality 272, 281n
interlocutors
 and power relationships 86n
 in second language

development 17, 215–16, 217–18, 237–41, 242n
interpersonal metafunction 10, 15, 296, 328
interpersonal Theme 102, 114–15, 120–1, 130
interrogatives 72, 74–5, 79, 80–1, 82–3
definition 66
intonation 10, 81, 82–3, 85
irregular verbs 86n
Ito, Noriko 14, 18, 19, 286, 350n, 352n
Iwashita, S. 286
Iwazume, Michiaki 18–19, 285, 319n

Japan Association of Systemic Functional Linguistics (JASFL) 4, 19
Japan Society for Artificial Intelligence 318, 347
Jimin-too. *see* LDP (Liberal Democratic Party)
Johns, A. M. 268, 269

Kaitei Seibutsu (Revised Biology) 138–9, 158–60
Kan, Naoto 174
Kanai, T. 190, 208n
Kano, C. 255
Kasper, R. T. 314, 315
Kataoka, S. 255
Kawahara, T. 286
Kawai, H. 25, 26, 31, 33–4, 35–6, 38, 39, 50
Kim, M. 3
Kimura, G. 174
Kinoshita, K. 167
Kitauchi, A. 289
knowledge, classification of 137–69
Kobayashi, Ichiro 18–19, 285, 319n, 346
Koizumi, Junichiro 174
Kokugo Gakkai 214
Kootoogakkoo Kaitei Seibutsu IB (High School Revised Biology IB) 138–9
koto 146–7, 167
Kramsch, C. 281n
kudasaru 76, 86n
Kudo, T. 289
Kyooiku kihonhoo - risoo moteasobu hima wa nai 24, 25, 26, 32, 33, 36, 37–8, 45, 50

L2 development. *see* second language development
Labour Party (Great Britain) 174, 175, 190–3, 208n
language, definition 212–13
Lantolf, J. P. 211
Larsen-Freeman, D. 242n
Lavid, J. 3
LDP (Liberal Democratic Party) 173–5, 179–82, 186–9, 208n
learner language 17–18, 210–41, 254–81
learning cycles 269–70, 273–9
learning objectives 272–3
Lee, A. 286
left accumulative pattern 43–4, 45
Lemke, J. 117
lexicogrammar 9, 10–11, 12–13, 15–16
comparison with English 139–41
computer models 288–318, 324–49, 351n, 352n
definition 7–8, 326–8
informal styles 261–8
and scientific classification 138–69
lexis, definition 13
Li, C. N. 6
Li, E. 3
Liberal Democratic Party (LDP). *see* LDP (Liberal Democratic Party)
Liddicoat, A. 281n
Lin, Y. Q. 314, 346
linguistic analysis, purpose of 5–6
linguistic description 3–16
principles 5–14
top-down vs. bottom-up analysis 140–1
literacy. *see* writing

Lo Bianco, J. 281n
Locution 40, 42t
logical metafunction, definition 9
logico-semantic relations 14, 15–16, 23–55
  classification and description 26–46
  clusters 27–8, 29f, 53–4, 55n
  implicit relations 27, 47–9, 187–90, 207n
  in political discourse 176–94, 206n, 207n, 208n
  progression patterns 43–6, 50t, 51
  in scientific discourse 142–55
Longacre, R. E. 105–7
longitudinal studies 211
Lukin, A. 212

Macken, M. 257
macro-scale lexicogrammatical resources 142, 155–68. *see also* THEME
manifestos, political parties 173–94
Mann, W. C. 288, 314
markedness 117, 126–30
Martin, J. R. 3, 9, 27, 103, 137, 138, 139–41, 160, 207n, 256–7, 268
Masaaki, Tatsuki 4
Matsuda, P. K. 267–8
Matsumoto, Y. 289
Matthiessen, C. M. I. M. 6, 7, 8, 10, 12, 55n, 65, 69, 102, 103, 105, 146, 169n, 175, 257, 288, 292–4, 296, 314, 316, 346, 351n
Maynard, S. 45, 53
McDonald, E. 3
meaning making 7–9
  in political discourse 187–94
  in second language development 17, 210–41, 270–2
metafunctions 9–10, 14, 15–16, 296, 328, 350n
metaphors 175, 349, 352n
methodology 5–14, 210–16
  appraisal 179, 207n
  cline construction 175–8
  computational models 13–14, 18–19, 285–318, 324–49
  computer-based analysis 27–8
  corpus studies 24–8, 29f, 69, 108–12, 138–42, 175–8
  error analysis 214–15, 217–18, 240–1
  formal models 9–11, 12–14, 29–46, 139–41, 272
  GSP notation 49
  limitations of 242n
  longitudinal studies 211
  paradigmatic relations 12–14
  role playing 217–18, 240–1
  textual analysis 261–8
  'Theme scrambling' exercise 104–5
  transcription annotation 56, 69, 86–7, 169n, 194, 319n
micro-scale lexicogrammatical resources 141–55
Minshu-too. *see* DPJ (Democratic Party of Japan)
Miyakoshi, M. 48–9
modal deixis 79
MODE 259, 260, 294, 330, 332–3f, 346, 350n
Mohan, B. 213–14
Momma, S. 314
Momotaroo 68, 74, 83, 116, 117–19, 123, 134n
MOOD 15, 65–85
  comparison with English 6–7, 11, 66–7, 69, 84
  incongruent realisation of 80–3
  types 66–7, 73–85
morphology
  informal styles 263–4
  and MOOD 73, 75, 76–7, 78–80
MULTEX (text generator) 346–7
multivariate Themes 120–1, 132

N-Rhemes 265
natural language processing 13–14, 18–19, 285–318
negation 206n–7n
negotiability 176–8, 187–90

Negotiatory Markers 72, 74, 79, 81, 82–3, 85
Nesbitt, C. 7, 256
nesting pattern 44–5
networks. *see* system networks
New Rhetoric School 268
newspaper articles 104–5, 109, 119–20
Nihongo Gakkai 214
Noboru, Yamaguchi 4
nominal adjectives, definition 169n
nominal groups 71–2
    in political discourse 179–94
    in scientific discourse 149–55, 167
nominalisation 16, 146–7, 167–8, 173–94, 206n, 207n, 208n
    comparison with English 190–3
    definition 173, 175
'noticing' 216, 239
nouniness 175–94, 206n, 207n, 208n
nuclear participants, definition 134n

oblatives 66, 77, 78, 79f, 83
O'Donnell, M. 27, 298, 299, 304
O'Donoghue, T. F. 314
offers (oblative Mood) 66, 77, 78, 79f, 83
Ohno, Y. 255
Okuma, T. 45, 53
~oo (volitional suffix) 77, 78
Orientation element 25–6, 49–50, 51, 52–3

Painter, C. 137, 215
Paltridge, B. 271
paradigmatic relations 11–14
paragraph boundaries 24, 45, 46f, 53–4, 55n
parsing 289, 306–9, 314–16
partial-structures 304–9
participant types 115, 117–18, 122–4, 127–9, 134n
Patpong, P. 3
Perrett, G. 210, 211, 217
persuasion 8–9, 15
phonology 9, 10–11

Plum, G. 256
polar interrogatives 74, 79
polarity 79
Polio, C. 267
politeness 77, 81–2, 232, 236, 263–4
political discourse 173–94, 206n, 207n, 208n
populations of texts 256, 281n. *see also* genres
postpositions 35, 36, 37, 38–9, 40, 42t
Prakasam, V. 3
predicates 69–72
process types, classification of 143–8
Projection 14, 30f, 40–6, 116, 123, 132
pronouns 150–1
prosody 10

Qualifiers 152
questions (interrogative Mood) 66, 72, 74–5, 79, 80–1, 82–3. *see also* research questions

Rampton, B. 242n
Ramsey, S. R. 214
Ramzan, Yuko 17–18
rank-shifting 187–90, 302
    definition 146–7, 169n
Real World Computing Partnership 68
realisation, definition 293–4
redundancy 117–19. *see also* ellipsis
register 86n, 215–16
    computer models 294–5, 319n, 329–30, 335–6, 337, 346
    informal styles 261–8
reification 145–7, 149, 168
research questions 19, 68, 85, 102–3, 133, 141, 175, 187, 216, 237–41, 255
RESIDUE 85
Rheme 101, 164, 265
right accumulative pattern 43, 45
Rikagaku Kenkyujo (RIKEN) 18, 285, 326
role playing 217–18, 237–41
Rose, D. 3, 137, 138, 207n

Ross, J. R. 176–7, 206n–7n, 212
ryakusuto 34, 55n

Sano, Motoki 8, 14, 15
Sasaki, M. 25, 26, 35, 37, 39, 40–1, 47, 51
Sato, Kinuko 16, 207n
scaffolding 211, 217, 231, 236, 237, 239–41, 242n, 269
Schleppegrall, M. J. 213, 214–15
Schmidt, R. 239
scientific discourse 137–69
  comparison with English 139–41, 147, 148, 150, 152
second language development 17–18, 210–41, 254–81
  teaching methods 210, 211, 213–15, 216, 221–41, 255, 267–81
  textbooks 236, 238, 255
semantic stratum 9–10, 11, 288, 309–11
Semiotic Base (*Everyday Language Computing Project)* 287–300, 313, 314, 316–17, 319n, 324–5, 328–36, 347, 348–9, 350n
semiotic mediation 222, 231, 237, 241, 242n
Shibatani, M. 134n
Shikano, K. 286
Slade, D. 69, 257
Smith, C. A. 175
Smith, K. B. 175
social relationships 7–9, 46–9, 81–2, 85, 86n, 256–7
  computer models 294–5, 319n, 329–30, 335–6, 337, 346, 348, 351n
  in second language development 17, 215–16, 217–18, 237–41, 242n, 259–60, 267–72, 281n
socio-cultural methodology 211
socio-historical methodology 211–12
sociolinguistic methodology 211
software tools 297–300, 319n
spatio-temporal relationships 39–40, 42t
specificity 176–8, 187–90
speech functions, definition 66
speech recognition 286
statements (declarative Mood) 66, 73, 78, 79, 81–3
Steiner, E. 3
stem accumulative pattern 44, 45, 50t, 51
stratal architecture (SF models) 9–11, 293–4, 326–8, 351n
string generation (text generation) 342–5, 348, 352n
structure (syntagmatic order) 292–3
sub-classification 143–55, 164–8
subject 6–7, 67
Sugeno, Michio 285–6
Sugimoto, Toru 18, 19, 286, 350n, 352n
superordination 148
Suto, Kinuko. *see* Sato, Kinuko
Suzuki, R. 255
Swain, M. 216, 240
Sydney School 268–72
system networks 12–14, 29–46, 289–90, 293, 294f, 327f, 328, 330–3f
  Mood types 78–83
  THEME 130–2
Systemic Functional theory 3–19, 206n, 210–16
  applications of 16–19, 210–12, 237–41, 268–81, 285–7, 316–18, 325–49
  principles of 5–14

Takahashi, Yusuke 18–19, 319n, 350n
taxonomies 137–69
teaching methods 210, 213–15
  collaborative dialogue 17, 211, 216, 217, 221–41
  cultural context 271–2
  writing skills 17–18, 214–15, 255, 267–81
Teich, E. 3, 314
TENOR 259–60, 264, 294, 330, 331–2f, 346, 350n
Teruya, K. 3, 7, 23–4, 75, 85, 86n, 105, 111, 146, 289, 295, 346

text generation systems 18–19, 324–49, 351n–2n
text processing systems 13–14, 18–19, 285–318
textual metafunction 10, 15, 16, 134n, 296, 328
textual Theme 113–14, 120–1, 129–30, 132
  definition 102
Thai, M. D. 3
Thematic Progression 156–69
THEME 15, 101–33, 155–69
  definition 101–3, 107–8, 135n, 155–6
  hyperthemes 156, 162, 167, 168–9
  markedness 117, 126–30
  multiple themes 119–21, 155–6
  system network 130–2
  and topic 134n–5n
  types 111–19
Theme unit, definition 156–7
Thesis element 25–6, 49, 50–1, 52t, 53
thingisation 187–90
Thompson, S. A. 6, 288
Thomson, Elizabeth A. 8–9, 11, 15, 16, 17–18, 23, 26, 108, 149–50, 156–7, 169n, 264
TIME 39–40, 42t
Tohsaku, Y. 255
topic, definition 134n–5n
Tosu, N. 118
transformational rules 206n–7n
transitivity 168, 169n, 176–8, 188–9
Traugott, E. C. 134n
'trinocular' view of grammar 11
Tucker, G. H. 346

univariate Themes 119–20
usuality 256

variation 212–14, 215–16
  computer models 294–5, 319n, 329–30, 335–6, 337, 346
Veel, R. 137
verbal groups 38, 39, 40, 42t, 69–70, 72, 75, 76–7
  informal morphology 263–4
volitional suffix 77, 78
Vygotsky, L. S. 211, 269

WAG systemic parser 304, 314–16, 320n
Wells, G. 239
wh-interrogatives 74–5, 79, 81
White, P. R. R. 207n
Wignell, P. 139–40, 142, 147
Williams, Geoff 242n
Winograd, T. 314
word classes 71–2, 75
word order 149–50, 152–4
  and THEME 103–5, 134n
Write it Right Project (Australia) 268
writing 23–55
  paragraph boundaries 24, 45, 46f, 53–4, 55n
  second language development 213, 214–15
  social context 46–9, 213, 214–15, 256–7, 259–60, 263–8, 281n
  teaching methods 17–18, 214–15, 255, 267–81
  thematic development 155–69
Wu, C. 295, 346

Yamashita, T. 289
Young, R. 211

Zeng, L. 346
Zone of Proximal Development 211

www.ingramcontent.com/pod-product-compliance
Lightning Source LLC
LaVergne TN
LVHW021127110826
R19582500001B/R195825PG844660LVX00013B/23
9781845530532